MANUFACTURING PHOBIAS

The Political Production of Fear in Theory and Practice

Edited by Hisham Ramadan and Jeff Shantz

Manufacturing Phobias explores how economic and political elites mobilize people's fears of terrorism, crime, migration, invasion, and infection to influence political and social policy and to advance their own agendas.

The contributors to the collection, experts in criminology, law, sociology, and politics, examine the role that politicians, pundits, and the media in general play in the creation of social phobias, and how they target the most vulnerable in our society. Tracing how social phobias can further the interests of those with political, economic, and cultural power, this work challenges the idea that such anxieties are merely expressions of individual psychology. Through numerous examples and in-depth analysis, *Manufacturing Phobias* offers a detailed exposition on the widespread consequences of our culture of fear.

HISHAM RAMADAN is a professor in the Department of Criminology at Kwantlen Polytechnic University.

JEFF SHANTZ is a professor in the Department of Criminology at Kwantlen Polytechnic University.

EDITED BY HISHAM RAMADAN
AND JEFF SHANTZ

Manufacturing Phobias

The Political Production of Fear in Theory and Practice

UNIVERSITY OF TORONTO PRESS
Toronto Buffalo London

© University of Toronto Press 2016
Toronto Buffalo London
www.utppublishing.com
Printed in the U.S.A.

ISBN 978-1-4426-3727-6 (cloth)   ISBN 978-1-4426-2884-7 (paper)

♾ Printed on acid-free, 100% post-consumer recycled paper with vegetable-based inks.

Library and Archives Canada Cataloguing in Publication

Manufacturing phobias : the political production of fear in theory and practice / edited by Hisham Ramadan and Jeff Shantz.

Includes bibliographical references and index.
ISBN 978-1-4426-3727-6 (cloth).–ISBN 978-1-4426-2884-7 (paper)

1. Fear–Political aspects. 2. Fear--Social aspects. 3. Social phobia.
I. Ramadan, Hisham M., author, editor II. Shantz, Jeff, author, editor

JA74.5.M35   2016   320.01'9   C2015-908524-1

University of Toronto Press acknowledges the financial assistance to its publishing program of the Canada Council for the Arts and the Ontario Arts Council, an agency of the Government of Ontario.

Canada Council
for the Arts
Conseil des Arts
du Canada

ONTARIO ARTS COUNCIL
CONSEIL DES ARTS DE L'ONTARIO
an Ontario government agency
un organisme du gouvernement de l'Ontario

Funded by the   Financé par le
Government   gouvernement
of Canada   du Canada

Canadä

For those Brave Hearts who are never silent about evil
Give me justice and I will give you peace and prosperity

Contents

Acknowledgment

We extend very special thanks to P.J. Lilley for her unlimited support in putting this volume together.

MANUFACTURING PHOBIAS

The Political Production of Fear in Theory and Practice

Phobic Constructions: An Introduction

HISHAM RAMADAN AND JEFF SHANTZ

The twenty-first century is a fear culture. As a number of commentators have observed, we increasingly engage in a range of social and political issues – whether economic, cultural, or environmental – predominantly through narratives of fear (see Engelhardt 2011; Gardner 2008; Glassner 2010; Linke and Smith 2009; Napoleoni 2008). While this trend developed in the twentieth century, in recent years "it has become more and better defined, as specific fears have been cultivated" (Furedi 2007, n.p.). Various analysts, from Ulrich Beck to Frank Furedi, have noted this peculiar condition of contemporary social life. According to Beck, for instance, populations within advanced capitalist liberal democracies, and growing sectors elsewhere, experience the world through frameworks of fear associated with risk. We live in a risk society. Such a society is marked by broad and relatively rapid changes in culture, technology, economics, politics, and even ecology. This is coupled with global movements of people, capital, and symbols. For Beck, traditional or established institutions, on which people have depended, can no longer maintain even the appearance of a capacity to meet crucial needs (material or ideational, social or personal) in the shifting context. The result is a sense of fearfulness and anxiety associated with risk. Economic and political entrepreneurs mobilize these fears according to their own aims (Arnstein and Arnstein 2007; Flynn 2007).

These fears have been articulated – condensed – in the specific forms of social phobias (from the ancient Greek for "fear"). The notion of articulation refers to the process by which the fluidity and multiplicity of discourses are fixed temporarily. These fixings form nodal points around which meanings coalesce (Althusser 1971; Hall 1985; Laclau and Mouffe 1985). In the current context social phobias provide nodal points in the articulation of generalized fears in a risk society, within specific forms. Fear is normalized in the particular articulations of politicized social phobias (especially against migrants, the terrorist, and the "other"). Phobias become means by which the social world is ordered and in which responses are formulated. Social phobias have come to play key roles in the expression of twenty-first-century consciousness (see Alexseev 2005). They become part of policy making, as each chapter in this work illustrates in distinct ways. Yet the social character of phobias and the articulation of fear within them have been under-analysed.

The manufacture of phobic discourses and practices has become a noteworthy feature of twenty-first-century social relations, perhaps particularly since the events of 9/11, 2001. These phobias (of terror, crime, migration, invasion or infection, cultural decay), often involving a targeted "other," a physical representative of the phobic object, provide frames by which people make sense of changing socio-political environments (of economic crisis, political austerity, ecological disaster, and so on). While much has been made of privatized fears (of crime, unsafe food, household threats), phobias provide the means for expression of collective insecurity. Contemporary phobias provide the twenty-first-century equivalents of historic fears such as of famine or the "dangerous classes" within advanced capitalist, industrially developed, and diverse, societies. And they serve to mobilize collective responses, even beyond the tangible harm posed by the phobic object or threat (Napoleoni 2008; Virilio 2010).

The chapters that follow consider the intersecting themes and targets in contemporary social phobias, documenting and analysing the discursive practices, political, economic, and cultural forces, and social policy outcomes that relate to phobic constructions in the current context. As well, contributors offer compelling and insightful examinations of the manufacture of phobias and of phobic reactions.

Constructs

Phobias, rather than being a straightforward outcome of lived experience (how many Canadians, for example, have been victims of a terrorist attack?), are nurtured in and through social institutions such as political parties, government agencies, corporations, or mass media (which are typically multinational corporations themselves). They are narrative, abstract. Yet as Michel Foucault has suggested, narratives also express modes of power, of inclusion and exclusion.

The fear of terror or migration, or the "other," is not directly associated with a clearly formulated actual material threat. As journalist Dan Gardner asserts, terrorism poses "an infinitesimal risk" to the lives of residents in Western countries (2008, 300). Similarly, Napoleoni (2008) notes that the likelihood of someone in the West being killed in a terrorist event was higher in the 1970s than today (and the number of terror killings was higher in the 1980s than any decade since). It is not the same as the fear of an enemy state (in war) or famine or natural disaster. These latter examples pose a real, identifiable, even imminent threat. Yet, as Furedi notes, since 9/11 the fear of terrorism "has continually expanded to cover almost all aspects of modern life" (2007, n.p.). This is partly explained by the activities of phobic entrepreneurs who work to articulate phobic expressions socially in ways that are outlined throughout the current collection.

Furthermore, the fixing of meanings in nodal points articulates fear discourses, melding them together. And this intersecting of discourses transforms the perception of danger. Since 9/11, for example, "what were previously seen as fairly normal hazards have been turned into exceptional threats by their association with the actions of terrorists" (Furedi 2007, n.p.). Associations across phobias – terror and the migrant (extremism and difference), for example – amplify the effects of both.

And the phobic constructions have real, tangible outcomes, politically, economically, and culturally. There are, indeed, real policy implications that flow from developing our understanding of social phobias. Phobias, as articulating public discourses, can be politically and economically profitable, as the chapters in this work make clear. Public social phobias provide a strong currency for politicians seeking tougher laws and the extension of law-and-order policies. They reinforce cultures of insecurity and justify the expansion of regulatory surveillance and control apparatuses, as several of the following chapters illustrate.

Beyond Therapy: Towards Social Analysis

Furedi argues that a proper sociological understanding of fear today requires further research and analysis of cultural frameworks for expressing fears. These public frameworks are the socio-political manifestations or articulations of phobias.

Despite the significant place of phobic constructions in everyday life in the twenty-first century, phobias have received too little attention, both empirically and theoretically, in social sciences such as sociology and criminology. Elemér Hankiss (2001) suggests that such articulated fears have received some attention within philosophy and psychology but have received only minimal attention in sociology and anthropology. We suggest that the situation is even worse within criminology, despite the significance of concepts like moral panic that address local aspects of fear management. There is a need to develop analyses beyond the psychological to reveal political, economic, social, and cultural factors and processes.

Most discussion of phobias has been viewed through a therapeutic lens focused on the individual and its personal anxieties, stresses, or neuroses. This collection takes an alternative approach to social phobias and the broad construction of fear in stratified capitalist societies. Rather than investigate phobias as a psychological disorder, it focuses on how, why, and by what means social phobias, as an industry, are created by special interest groups (such as political lobbies, corporations, politicians, psychological industries, and agenda-driven media) to target the most vulnerable in our society to achieve what is, indeed, impossible to achieve by ethical means. As Furedi (2007) suggests, social phobias typically involve – indeed, require – the intervention of what we might term "phobic entrepreneurs" who work to fix meanings in ways that resonate economically or politically with their own concerns.

Phobias Examined: Notes on the Chapters

Each chapter in this collection sheds light on various, often intersecting aspects of contemporary social phobias at the same time as it examines a specific characteristic or feature of phobic production. Heidi Rimke examines the connections between neoliberal policy making and psychological discourses in the construction of social fear/security. Hisham Ramadan theorizes the employment of law to create and/or endorse social phobia. Melissa Ames shows that while 9/11 created unprecedented social phobia, ordinary fictional TV programs have tended to remediate the 9/11 effects. Jeff Shantz examines political phobias and the construction of terror discourses in the context of anti-globalization movements and protests that have been interpreted within a developing fear of radicalism. Johann Pautz's research focuses on conspiracy theories and millennial movements in particular as relating to domestic terrorism in the United States. Dmitry Shlapentokh explores the current trends of phobia against non-European-looking people in Russia. Amir

Mirfakhraie examines the use of phobia in school narratives to construct the ideal citizen in Iran. Davina Bhandar and Michael C.K. Ma discuss phobic construction of migrants and the use of terror discourses in Canadian regimes of border control and restrictions on labour mobility. Penny Koutrolikou explores the processes of manufacturing the ghetto by analysing the "construction" of poverty, the ghetto, and the *avaton* in two inner-city neighbourhoods of Athens, Greece.

Manufacturing Phobias is divided into three parts. The chapters in the first part examine some of the explanatory frameworks – psychological, legal, sociological, political, criminological – used in analysing and discussing social phobias. Chapters in the second part explore issues associated with phobic productions and concerns over national identity, migration, and borders. The third part examines explicit political frameworks underpinning phobic productions, discussing issues of political ideology, political mobilization, and policy in relation to specific social phobias.

Heidi Rimke in chapter 1 provides a critical theoretical framework for analysing the image of the monster as a political technology of neoliberalism by focusing on two contemporary social forces: (1) psychopolitics, or the entrenched psychocentrism characteristic of a culture dominated by "psy" discourses that simultaneously depoliticize the political while capitalizing on the emotional, especially fear, paranoia, and anger; and (2) the post-9/11 explosion of the security industry/apparatus. Within that context, the chapter examines several related themes: the politics of emotions and the emotions of politics, the politics of security and insecurity, and the politics of dangerization, victimization, and dehumanization. Rather than normalizing psychocentrism, Rimke provides a socio-political analysis of emotional practices of power productive of neoliberal subjectivities. The chapter offers a genealogical approach to the psychopolitics of emotional governance of the insecure society as a means to critically interrogate the social production and consumption of fear and terror intrinsic to dominant and dominating rationalities that govern through insecurities.

In chapter 2, Hisham Ramadan explores the relationship between law and social phobias. He proposes that their relationship proceeds through two stages. In stage one, law – including fundamental human rights, albeit inadvertently – can be employed to advance phobia against the most vulnerable groups in the society. In stage two, once social phobia is vindicated under the law, further legal provisions can be moulded either legislatively or through court interpretations to oppress the group subject to social phobia. The chapter concludes by raising a question for further discussion: What can be done to prevent use of the law as a tool of social phobia and oppression?

Jeff Shantz and Hisham Ramadan (chapter 3) explore contemporary psychological, sociological, and criminological framings of phobias. They note that while phobias are socially produced, most of the social scientific work on phobias has focused on individuals through the lens of psychology. They then present varying theoretical approaches to understanding social phobias and the social factors underpinning phobic constructions, discussing notions of articulation, the bringing together of different themes within phobic discursive practices, and the relations of phobic expressions and identity.

The second part of this work addresses issues of nationalism, borders, migration, and identity. In chapter 4 Amir Mirfakhraie analyses how present/non-present discursive/textual phobias about women, ethnic minorities, non-Muslims, and non-Iranians are configured into school textbooks in manufacturing knowledge about Iran and the Iranian national identity in phobic productions. He outlines how the narration of nation represents certain local and global groups, such as Euro-Westerners, women, Arabs, the state of Israel, tribal pastoral nomads, and the global Muslim community, as friendly insiders and outsiders or external and internal enemies that need to be controlled, helped, led, and feared or distrusted. These groups are essentialized and narrated through discourses that end up othering the other within a deterministic definition of the ideal citizen. Consequently, fractured selves have different loyalties and points of identification that are in conflict with the essentialized characteristics of the ideal citizen or with the characteristics of internal and external selves and others and how they are differentially positioned against many forms of sameness and otherness.

In a different context, the United States, Melissa Ames (chapter 5) examines the role of another public sphere, television narratives, in phobic productions. Ames notes that television has long been associated with the catastrophic and the affect of fear. News programming, for examples, exists both to instil fear in viewers and then to quickly quell that fear. Television's manipulation of fear is not limited to non-fictional programming. In fact, the affect of fear is predominant in the majority of fictional texts in the new millennium, as is the theme of a nation in crisis or in need of "saving." Ames' chapter analyses three recent fictional narratives that constantly remediate the tragedy of 9/11:

ABC's *Lost*, NBC's *Heroes*, and Fox's *Fringe*. For Ames, these programs suggest that the fear American citizens feel as a nation post-attack unconsciously resurfaces and seeks resolution in narrative spaces through repetition. Therefore, the consumption of these narratives is a means by which viewers "work through" the lingering emotional trauma caused by the attacks.

Dmitry Shlapentokh (chapter 6) offers an analysis of phobic productions through conflicting views of the nation in the ideas and practices of Russian fascist mobilizations. His analysis uncovers several important social/political and ideological layers. First, it reveals that the conditions leading to outbreaks of violence are implicitly connected with the global demographic and geopolitical shift that is occurring. Russia, in this case, is possibly just one of the proverbial "weakest links." Second, the ideology of the extremists illustrates the peculiarities of the process in Russia. It reveals the idiosyncratic features of present-day Russian capitalism, which is marked not only by increasing social polarization but also by a strong regional polarization, where the social-ethnic animus is directed not just against the elite and the minorities but against the capital – in fact, against the Russian state itself. An analysis of the views of Russian extremists also points out the peculiarities of the vision of social/ethnic mobilization. Some of these extremists are full of a twisted form of historical optimism. They believe that Russians will finally rise and smash the regime of the minorities and the rich; for them the two groups are actually the same. For others, Russia and Russians have no hope and will disappear as had happened with other nations.

The final chapter in part 1, by Davina Bhandar and Michael Ma, examines the international migration regime and current ministerial reactions to new migrants in Canada and Australia. It argues that in their attempt to create a regional response to refugees seeking asylum, Canadian and Australian governments – who *ratified* the UN convention on refugees – are embarking on the creation of phobic and schizophrenic institutional responses to global migration. Bhandar and Ma consider the current Canadian/Australian reaction to boat arrivals of Tamil refugees, and ask: "In a post migrant-rights geopolitical world, is it possible, or even rhetorically feasible, to ensure that the rights to safety, mobility, and protection are afforded to refugee claimants?" They examine the discourse of refugee claimants as "human cargo" and the rhetoric of human smuggling currently circulated through institutions who are reorganizing their structure and mandate to better enforce restrictive interpretations of lawful/unlawful migration – in so doing, denying unwanted migrants their refugee status.

The third part of *Manufacturing Phobias* examines political mobilizations of social phobias, phobias as politics by other means. Johann Pautz (chapter 8) points out that the far-right rhetoric associated with the Tea Parties and New Right has its origins in conspiratorial and apocalyptic discourses that have characterized socially and politically regressive movements throughout the history of the United States. American traditions of millenarian religious prophecy and xenophobic conspiracism have converged into a single, highly fungible apocalyptic conspiracy trope referred to as the New World Order (NWO) conspiracy. While formerly occupying the fringe and surfacing from cultural latency during time of cultural stress and social change, the NWO conspiracy has become a simulacrum of the contemporary world as articulated by far-right political, media, and religious figures. Positing a hidden and nefarious agenda behind mundane policies and progressive social reforms, leaders of the American far-right increasingly use signifiers associated with the NWO conspiracy to mobilize their political bases by invoking fears of loss of national sovereignty and the oppression and extermination of "traditional Americans."

Jeff Shantz (chapter 9) looks at the political underpinnings of social phobias in relation to anti-terror discourses and the military-industrial complex within the context of the Canadian state. He outlines the role of conservative phobic entrepreneurs who work to construct phobias, particularly through manufactured concerns over so-called extremism. Of particular focus in the conservative narratives of terror and extremism are ethnic and religious minorities. Shantz notes that panics have spread through high-profile cases involving imagined threats and the activities of state agents who help to create the situation they in turn respond to. Social phobias have played a part in the rise of conservative politics in Canada in the twenty-first century.

In the final chapter Penny Koutrolikou analyses issues of class and spatial configurations of the city in relation to social phobic constructions. Phobias and fears influence how we perceive and behave towards others, particularly the "others." Phobias also become elements of governance tactics by invoking "public" sentiments and (re) actions. These cultural, psychological and political aspects of phobias often entail spatial associations. One point of intersection of political, cultural, and spatial phobias is the "construction" of the ghetto, which simultaneously embodies phobias of crime and insecurity, of decline, of "others," and tactics of control and real estate. Koutrolikou explores the processes of manufacturing the ghetto by analysing the "construction" of the ghetto and the *avaton* in two inner-city neighbourhoods of Athens. Exarcheia, the *avaton*, in "public" perceptions is associated with anarchists and riots, while Agios Panteleimonas is increasingly stigmatized as "ghetto" by media and policy makers. Examining these cases allows us to explore how phobias concerning these neighbourhoods are manufactured, mobilized, and manipulated by the media, governments and political groups, and real estate interests.

There are recurring themes or points of focus in contemporary phobias. The chapters that follow reveal certain themes or targets within phobic productions across national contexts. Among these are fears of the alien "other" – the outsider, the migrant, the culturally different. Associated with this fear is the fear of contagion and anxieties over proper inoculation. As Bhandar and Ma, Pautz, Shlapentokh, and Shantz show, the phobic construction of migrants plays an evolving role in the development of national discourses in countries as diverse as Canada, Russia, and the United States. Related to this, and expressing fears of contagion or invasion, is a concern with borders and their perceived permeability – even as borders tighten under regimes of securitization, surveillance, and militarization. Another repeated theme is the phobic construction of religion, particularly Islam. In various contexts Islam is positioned as not only different but deviant – as posing a threat of violence.

Violence is a key factor in current phobic constructions, a point reflected in various ways in each of the chapters. The threat of invasion or infiltration that plays a role in phobic articulations is typically violent in intent and in character. As Koutrolikou shows, even the internal threat of the poor, the more classical "dangerous classes," is a threat of violent disorder. Yet this violence is often mythic in character. Terror, rather than a plausible, real, material threat, plays an ideological role or legitimation function in the proliferation and maintenance of many contemporary phobias, as the chapters by Ames, Pautz, Rimke, and Shantz show.

The contributors also find that phobias play an important, even crucial, part in the construction of national identities. As Mirfahkraie, Pautz, Ramadan, and Koutrolikou show, phobias, in addition to targeting the external "other," provide discourses for expressing norms, values, and beliefs promoted by national states. They construct the civilizing narratives by which the nation is understood. They also frame policy developments, allowing for shifts in long-held values (as in due process or civil liberties, for example).

A Peculiar Place: The Canadian Context

Although phobia, in various guises, is a universal phenomenon, Canada is in a peculiar position. On one hand, the country shares numerous aspects with its southern neighbour, the United States, including history, language, and legal system origins. These similarities greatly influence Canadian society. Phobia created by the US media crosses the border and almost immediately affects Canadian thinking. The Canadian Parliament and judiciary are significantly influenced by US laws and court decisions although such influence fails to reflect Canadian basic morals. For instance, shortly after the September 11 attacks on the United States, the Canadian Parliament hastily enacted the Anti-terrorism Act, which contains controversial provisions that undermine fundamental rights, including Charter rights. The Supreme Court of Canada surprisingly in R. v. Khawaja upheld the Anti-terrorism Act, maintaining that violent acts are not protected under the Charter of Rights and Freedoms. Here, what had started as an act on foreign soil developed into a massive social phobia that resulted in a redefining of the limits of fundamental Canadian rights and freedoms.

On the other hand, ties to Europe, especially to France and the United Kingdom, along with colonial relations within indigenous communities, forged the historical origins of the Canadian state. These commonalities prompted the Supreme Court of Canada to cite the decisions of the European Court of Human Rights as an influential authority. The problem is that phobia against the "other" in Europe is more commonplace and widely justified by the European Court of Human Rights, as Ramadan explains in chapter 2. Mere citing of human rights decisions that address the issue of phobia against the "other," absent its social context, merits scrutiny. Koutrolikou (chapter 10) sheds light on a number of these social factors that shape phobia in Europe.

Ultimately the Canadian state is not a solitary player in the international arena; rather, it is part of the international state system that has crafted various international instruments to deal with groups deemed to be less desired or desirable within a given society, including victims of social phobia. In this context, when Canada deals with social phobia and measures its impact on fundamental rights, it should give proper weight to social phobia as an international phenomena that affects the less desired "other." Numerous chapters in this volume, including those by Shlapentokh, Pautz, and Ma and Bhandar, help us to understand how, why, and by what means social phobias emerge and affect many people's lives in diverse contexts, including within Western liberal democracies.

Furedi recalls FDR's invocation that "the only thing we have to fear is fear itself." While Roosevelt sought to reassure a public anxious and restless in a period of crisis (and threatened revolt), there is now a need to re-examine the socio-political content of fear, and the manufacture of fear, in a new century. As Furedi suggests, "Today, politicians are far more likely to advise the public to fear everything, including fear itself" (2007, n.p.). This is amply demonstrated in the various contexts analysed within these pages.

To our knowledge, there is no other work that analyses the construction of fear and xenophobia in the current context through the socio-political framework of social phobia. As noted above, those studies that do discuss social phobia take a strictly psychological approach emphasizing individual personality characteristics, whereas this work emphasizes the social, political, and cultural relations of power that construct phobias as processes of power. This collection also moves beyond notions of moral panic that emphasize media practices in the limited construction of fear associated with specific "folk devils."

Social commentator Ryszard Kapuśiński (2008) suggests that the encounter with the "other" is *the* challenge of the twenty-first century. It is our hope that this contribution to understanding phobic social constructions, their processes and discourses, will also contribute to understandings of these encounters with the "other" and the political struggles over meaning associated with social fear. Perhaps it will also contribute to an environment in which, as Kapuśiński suggests, we are less fearful and more friendly towards one another.

Analysing and understanding social phobias as aspects of broad social processes can perhaps help us to address the harms inflicted on phobic subjects – those who are the focal points of phobias. It is hoped that these analyses will contribute to positive social change – to a move towards some liberation from the structures of fear and associated policies and practices. At the very least, they should serve to situate phobic productions within relations of struggle in contemporary contexts. This may serve to lessen some of the intensity, the panic, the anxiety around which, and through which, phobias circulate and re/produce. Yet we recognize that phobias can be persistent, for reasons outlined in the chapters that follow, and the need to develop our understanding of their manufacture and circulation remains, for the foreseeable future, pressing.

REFERENCES

Alexseev, Mikhail A. 2005. *Immigration Phobia and the Security Dilemma: Russia, Europe, and the United States*. Cambridge: Cambridge University Press. http://dx.doi.org/10.1017/CBO9780511528064.

Althusser, Louis. 1971. *Lenin and Philosophy and Other Essays*. London: New Left.

Arnstein, Zack, and Larry Arnstein. 2007. *The Ultimate Counterterrorist Home Companion*. Santa Monica: Santa Monica Press.

Engelhardt, Tom. 2011. *The United States of Fear*. Chicago: Haymarket.

Furedi, Frank. 2007. "The Only Thing We Have to Fear Is the 'Culture of Fear' Itself." *Spiked*, 4 April. http://www.spiked-online.com/newsite/article/3053#.VkYgW9KrRiw.

Fierke, K.M. 2007. *Critical Approaches to International Security*. London: Polity.

Flynn, Stephen. 2007. *The Edge of Disaster*. New York: Random House.

Gardner, Dan. 2008. *Risk: The Science and Politics of Fear*. Toronto: McClelland and Stewart.

Glassner, Barry. 2010. *The Culture of Fear: Why Americans Are Afraid of the Wrong Things*. New York: Basic.

Hall, Stuart. 1985. "Signification, Representation, Ideology: Althusser and the Post-Structuralist Debates." *Critical Studies in Mass Communication* 2 (2): 91–114. http://dx.doi.org/10.1080/15295038509360070.

Hankiss, Elemér. 2001. *Fears and Symbols: An Introduction the History of Western Civilization*. Budapest: Central European Press.

Kapuściński, Ryszard. 2008. *The Other*. London: Verso.

Laclau, Ernesto, and Chantal Mouffe. 1985. *Hegemony and Socialist Strategy*. London: Verso.

Linke, Uli, and Danielle Taana Smith. 2009. *Cultures of Fear: A Critical Reader*. London: Pluto.

Napoleoni, Loretta. 2008. *Rogue Economics*. New York: Seven Stories.

Regina v Khawaja. 2012 SCC 69, [2012] 3 S.C.R. 555.

Virilio, Paul. 2010. *The Administration of Fear*. New York: Semiotext(e).

PART 1

Endless Facades: Rethinking Social Phobias

The challenge of explaining social phobias in modern societies is oner-ous for several reasons. The dual task of exposing as a tool of social con-trol what are labelled as socially accepted norms and policies that serve to mask phobic practices and mapping the construction of social phobia is perhaps too large to achieve in one volume. To further complicate matters, there are numerous overlapping and intertwining factors that shape the façade of phobias and contribute to their development. These factors include competing religions, social classes, economic theories, and political ideologies. All this should not be examined in isolation, but rather in the context of the historical, social, political, and economic life of a particular setting at a particular moment.

Part 1 of this volume attempts to shed light on a few of the factors that contribute to the making of social phobias. It challenges the cur-rent perception of the "true" nature of phobia through unveiling dis-criminatory practices often employed by academicians, politicians, law makers, and social scientists alike to achieve a particular goal, in violating principles of fairness and disregarding the impact on vulner-able social groups (Rimke, Ramadan). It also questions the success of social phobia as a social control measure to contain the "other" (Rimke, Ramadan). This part of the volume discusses examples of these unfair practices, including religious phobia, which is designed to demonize the "other" in order to ensure supremacy of the dominant group, jus-tifying reprehensible actions towards the "other" or simply serving as a tool against competitors (Ramadan). The courts, law makers, and politicians have historically been, and remain, guilty of such practices, notwithstanding the commonly celebrated notion of religious freedom in modern societies. Labels such as "Canadian social morality," "shared values of the Canadian society," or "public morality" have been used generously to justify questionable actions. Similarly, scientific inquiries, media including movies and news articles, and academic scholarship have been employed to create taxonomies to degrade the "other" (Ramadan).

In this contested social environment, a trend in critical scholarship has emerged not only to voice the vulnerable "other's" distress but also to blow the whistle on common phobic practices that harm society at large, including the dominant group (Rimke, Shantz and Ramadan). According to Rimke, the real success of phobia's mighty machine in generating any true social benefits is highly questionable; only a balanced approach solves social problems (Rimke). For example, in the fight against "terrorism," social science has historically defined terrorism as an "individual's disorder," which has never helped advance understanding of this phenomenon (Rimke). Only when a number of public actors conclude that today's "terrorists" are average citizens, not psychopaths, can harm be avoided. A grasp of the issues outlined in critical scholarship offers hope of a brighter future, free from unfounded assumptions and rhetoric about crucial social problems (Rimke). Activists can play a positive role in defending the vulnerable "other," society's right to live in harmony, and the equal right of all individuals to live with dignity (Rimke, Ramadan). Again, this benefits not only the vulnerable "other" but the entire society, including the dominant group.

Canada is in a peculiar situation as regards the history of social phobias, due to its diverse demographic and competing political and economic interest groups. This complex situation calls for examining the phenomenon in a local context as well as in the international arena to discern the causes and profiles of, and reactions to, social phobia (Shantz and Ramadan), a task taken up in the subsequent parts of this volume.

1 Pathologizing Resistance and Promoting Anthropophobia: The Violent Extremism Risk Assessment (VERA) as Case Study

HEIDI RIMKE

Persons convicted of crime are commonly viewed as "sick" and "abnormal" in North American culture. The notion that crime is a result of biology rather than social structure is regularly expressed in everyday discourses, mainstream academic writings, government propaganda, the entertainment fields, and mass media alike. As an effect of the Western culture of therapy, those persons classified as criminals are commonly represented as inherently defective individuals suffering from some form of pathology, or abnormal condition, rooted in the mind and/or body (Rimke 2010b, 2011a). While this view dates back to at least the nineteenth century (Foucault 1978), its current popularity can now be seen as a taken-for-granted "natural" human-type in modern culture. As such, it hardly comes as a surprise that in the post-9/11 climate of government-sponsored anthropophobia, expert security discourses have shaped and promote a new category of pathological criminality rooted in the growing popularization and scientization of the "terrorist" identity: "the violent extremist."

I discuss the emergence of the newly constructed category of "violent extremism" and challenge its place within the hegemony of security discourses as it relates to both the criminalizing and pathologizing of resistance. Specifically, I examine the sociopolitical construction of anti-capitalist activism as a criminal pathology or psychocriminalization in the context of the post-9/11 so-called war on terror. In this case study,

The author thanks the Anti-Security Collective, Daniel Church and Shayna Gersher for their research assistance, the University of Winnipeg Research Committee for supporting this scholarship with a Major Research Grant, and the editor for his helpful suggestions.

I treat the classification of violent extremism recently constructed by traditional security experts as the primary data to be examined through a critical discourse analysis. While popular conceptions of the criminal as "ill" or in some other way psychologically and/or biologically constituted have become taken for granted in everyday discourses, radical and critical criminological and sociological approaches have long rejected this hypothesis on theoretical, empirical, and ethical grounds (Taylor, Walton, and Young 1973).

To provide a bit of context, the ongoing and in-progress research presented here is the culmination of my other studies on, for example, the pathological approach to crime (Rimke 2010a, 2011a), the criminalization of organized resistance or radical activism (Rimke 2011b), the colonization of "psy" discourses in everyday life, or what I call psychocentrism (Rimke 2000, 2003, 2010b; Rimke and Brock 2012), and earlier research on the doctrine of moral insanity used by Western legal and medical experts to identify, diagnose, and prosecute socially ungovernable or otherwise difficult subjects throughout the nineteenth and early twentieth centuries (Rimke 2003, 2010b, 2011a; Rimke and Hunt 2002). As I have argued elsewhere (Rimke 2010c, 2011b), security discourses can be understood as dominant governing modes of thought; here I discuss the role of the human sciences in replicating the fetishization of security in capitalist society. However, the task of critical criminology is to provide an alternative understanding of the dominant discourses and practices that reproduce the current social organization and configuration of power relations. The analysis provided in this essay thus seeks to disrupt the relations of ruling intrinsic to the conceptual practices of power that fetishize and reify political resistance as deviant, criminal, and pathological, rather than viewing it as the result of social organization, social injustice, or social relations.

Pathologizing Radicalization as Violent Extremism

Through their academic fields and court-sanctioned diagnostic process, assessing psy – increasingly referred to as "forensic" – experts influence not just the long-term consequences for the accused and convicted; they also have a potentially wide-ranging effect on juridical decisions. As a "regime of truth" (Foucault 2002, 131), the dominant security doxa can be conceived as a heterogeneous network of agents, sites, practices, discourses, and techniques for the production, dissemination, legitimation, and utilization of truths. Thus the ways of speaking about subjects, events, and experiences and the particular language deployed are central to the inextricable relationship between the exercise of power and the constitution of truth. The construction of the concept of "violent extremism" as seen in the contemporary psy discourse of the violent extremism risk assessment provides an example of how expert discourses go about constituting a particular "story" and world view based on both terminology and positivist epistemological conventions employed to create, bolster, and legitimate a particular version of reality as truth.

The violent extremism risk assessment (VERA) was designed to act as a social scientific measurement and tool to assess the risk of what traditional security experts increasingly refer to as "violent political extremism." Focus is placed on the factors perceived to be relevant to the process of "radicalization" (i.e., the means by which and the reasons that a person becomes "radical"), which the dominant view naturally represents as a process of leading to violent extremism as seen in security rhetoric that refers to radical or militant activists as "political terrorists."[1]

Pressman (2009, 30) argues that violent extremism differs from ordinary crime in that the latter is motivated by financial gain, aggressive narcissism, or other personal motivation. Terrorism/violent extremism/radicalism are theorized to be driven by loftier ideological goals and issues. And while violent extremist acts are violations of criminal law, the underlying motivation renders these acts significantly different from other types of ordinary crime. Although over one hundred definitions of terrorism have been identified in the literature, there is a general consensus in the dominant security literature that terrorism is more than a criminal act and must include the intention of instilling fear in a social group or population (Pressman 2009; Record 2003).

According to the FBI, the category of "domestic terrorism" refers to "left-wing groups, [who] generally profess a revolutionary socialist doctrine and view themselves as protectors of the people against the 'dehumanizing effects' of capitalism and imperialism. They aim to bring about change ... through revolution rather than through the established political process" (FBI website, 2001). By "established political process" we know exactly what is meant: conformity to the highly controlled and restrictive processes of parliamentary democracy as the preferred form of political engagement and expression. Thus alternative forms of politics and political action such as radical and militant activism – historical movements one could argue are at the base of, and key to, social change and progress – are represented through the dominant security doxa as irrelevant, absurd, pathological, or even criminal. Militant and effective activism should thus be understood as posing a threat to the reproduction of the dominant social, political, and economic order, which relies upon the neoliberal parliamentary democratic electoral process to maintain the capitalist structures, systems, discourses, and practices, a point neatly summed up by the popular anarchist statement that "if voting changed anything, it would be illegal."

Deconstructing the Politics of In/Security: An Anti-Security Approach

The concept of anti-security can be understood as a means of addressing, challenging, and moving beyond the hegemony of security. Since the concept of security depends upon the concept of insecurity as a relational construct, the notion of anti-security moves beyond the dominant dualism central to the pacification efforts underpinning official narratives of crime and danger. The emphasis on security, understood as the most powerfully productive and repressive political trope of contemporary social and political life (Neocleous and Rigakos 2011), means that at some fundamental level the order of capital is an order of insecurity (Rimke 2011b). It is through this politics of in/security that the current wave of state repression against anti-capitalist activists is organized, structured, rationalized, legitimated, and celebrated. The critical concepts of pacification and anti-security help to make sense of the processes and practices through which civility as obedience is constituted, maintained, reproduced, and resisted.

The deployment of security resources against subversive groups can be described as the effect of the ongoing class war against any and all disobedient and defiant citizen-subjects. Only the state, through its rhetoric of asserting its ability to act for the common good, is capable of sustaining, maintaining, and increasing class conflict and class domination in attempts to not only absorb but profit from the inevitabilities of resistance capitalism has produced. Thus, to demand security – and therefore increased policing – is inevitably a demand for greater state repression. By reproducing the very divisions and categories of the criminal sciences, the state appears to objectively resolve the problematic of crime, when in fact such constructions can be said to be the most powerful exercise of state power of all – the power to define, delineate, and control resistance and to re-present it as crime and criminality (Rimke 2011b).

Psychocriminalization: The Criminal and Psychocentric Hybrid

Psychocentrism, or the reduction of human life to "psy" discourses (Rimke 2000, 2010b, 2010c, 2011a), can be understood as the cultural corollary of neoliberalism that attempts to govern what becomes viewed as dangerous and disorderly populations. Psychocentrism recuperates or nullifies all forms of human resistance as disorderly, and as such provides a means for discussing and analyzing the ways in which different forms of human resistance have been, and continue to be, pathologized in Western legal (increasingly referred to as "forensic") and medical texts. Psychocentricity thrives on the human deficit model while obscuring societal deficits and social relations of power that frame, underlie, and create human struggles, difficulties, and resistance. Rather than challenging social deficiencies and economic corruption, the human deficit model incites modern subjects to focus on personal or inner deficiencies of the self and others. This Western mode of understanding ourselves has not only normalized and naturalized the discourses of normalcy/abnormality; it has also had the effect of rendering its own power invisible. Psychocentric attitudes, perceptions, and interpretations thus dominate the social world. Thinking of all human life in terms of "the normal" and "the pathological" is a major modern development based on the potency of socially derived rules, or what Foucault refers to as "normation" (Foucault 2007, 57) – the emergence of scientifically established norms. Social scientific discourses reproduce norms that work as regulatory mechanisms for the official classification and naturalization of subversive groups as high risk or dangerous, thus highlighting the political and cultural functions of psy discourses. The pathological regime of truth is witnessed in the dominant Western tendency to reduce everything about human life to psy discourses, neatly summed up by what Marsh refers to as "the compulsory ontology of pathology" (Marsh 2010, 12).

The construction of "violent political extremism" provides a scientific category and rationalized explanations to account for those persons who resist dominant sociopolitical prescriptions by intentionally rejecting commonly accepted social and political codes of conduct and subjectivities of desire. The VERA experts have provided a theoretical corpus of knowledge, which advances its relevance in categorizing resistance as individual pathology without ever seriously examining the social conditions that produce resistance, problems, and struggles. Yet, those in positions of authority who engage in disorderly conduct – especially police and security agents, not to mention bosses and state executives – are rarely if ever pathologized, and never does official corruption appear as an example of anti-social conduct or violent extremism in the guides and handbooks. This peculiar misrepresentation operates primarily through psychocentrism. It produces selves, individuals, and citizen-subjects committed to a personal identity, where the individual is made to be overly responsible and authorities assume no responsibility over the lives they negatively affect. Resistance and outcries become (mis)represented as "violent" and official violence becomes legitimated and rationalized in multiple ways. This provides a stark example of the contemporary trend to incite modern subjects to evade social and political structural critique and engagement in favour of individualistic or self-critique (Rimke 2000, 2010c). Resistance and political critique thus become "symptoms" or "signs" of abnormality whereas conformism and submission are taken as indications of normalcy.

The VERA experts have reconfigured resistance in a novel positivistic way. The politically motivated extremist or radical is not (or is no longer) viewed as suffering from an anti-social personality disorder, or sociopathy/psychopathy. Instead, the new human scientific discourses marshalled by criminal and terrorist experts such as Mitchell D. Silber and Arvin Bhatt of the New York Police Department's so-called Intelligence Division, for example, claim that terrorists have been rather "unremarkable individuals, who have led unremarkable lives, have held unremarkable jobs," and have had little or no previous criminal record (Silber and Bhatt 2007). Such an unremarkable observation, of course, not only widens the police's scope considerably, but also problematizes unproblematic subjects as valid objects of police monitoring and harassment.

According to Sageman's (2004) study, political extremists were not found to be poor or angry. Pressman (2009) cites Sageman's research results that indicated that

> many of the social explanations previously assumed with regard to terrorists were incorrect. Terrorists were not found to be poor, angry or fanatically religious. Instead, the terrorists analyzed were found to be largely middle-class, educated men from caring, stable and religious families. They grew up with strong positive values of religion and community concern. Sageman found that the terrorists did not display any psychiatric pathology nor patterns of emotional trauma in their past. No evidence of pathological hatred or paranoia was observed in the sample studied. In terms of past

experience or historical factors, terrorists did not suffer long-term relative deprivation nor did they suffer from pathological prejudice. (7)

One security expert went so far as to claim that a non-violent past increases the probability of radicalism, now nebulously referred to as terrorism in post-9/11 society. Characteristic attributes of radicalism include: uncompromising and rigid ideology; deeply held convictions; high worth attached to ideology; acceptance of responsibility for action; a moral justification by a higher authority; selective empathy (i.e., empathy does not extend to the "enemy" target); study, training, and focus on goals; no prior criminality; belief in ideological (unrealistic) long-term goals; the person is responsible/employed; and stable family history showing no early problems.

Pressman (2009) concludes that the violent extremist or, following the security logic presented by mainstream academics, what may be referred to as the political criminal is significantly set apart from the common or ordinary criminal in all regards. For example, she closes by stating that among contemporary experts there is

> consensus that terrorists do not act out of mental imbalance, psychopathology or psychopathy. They are not typically unemployed, under-employed, undereducated or poor. They are not generally irresponsible, or impulsive. They may have a well-developed moral code but this code may not include empathy for those whom they consider the enemy. Their acts are planned, coordinated, morally justifiable within their value system and high in social conscience. Their background and historical factors, situational factors and attitude factors differ from [those of] ordinary criminals. (30).

The claim that the so-called terrorist or radical or politically motivated extremist is unremarkable or "normal" is especially significant socially because, in essence, the claim being made is that the terrorist could be anybody – the unsuspecting and average subject, and not the spectacular psychopath as previously thought and promulgated. The list of attributes still constructs a psychopathological subject, but one that is simultaneously – and paradoxically – both normal and abnormal.

Conclusion

If the psy sciences and forensic experts are vested with the role of determining the appropriate way of being human or "normal," they can be said to wield significant social power, especially in our crises-riddled era, providing a proliferation of medico-moral discourses centering on the ethical flaws of individuals rather than the epic failures of capitalist practices, structures, and institutions. Cultural domination enables psy authorities to contribute to pacification by nullifying subversive or transgressive subjects in rendering them pathological and dangerous to the public. The psy complex's moralizing engagement with diverse populations both generates and ministers to anxieties about the disorder consequent upon both individual and collective resistance. The dominant (and dominating) human sciences thus provide a form of social policing that recuperates social and political struggle as dangerous and pathological. Concern for economic and political resistance translates into "individual disorder" that is really about "social disorder" and the consequent threat to the economic and cultural privileges of those who benefit from current social and economic arrangements. Threatening subjects thus become the legitimate objects of social control via scientific inquiry and taxonomies.

Whether viewed historically or in the light of growing (and global) opposition to the crisis that is capitalism, it is becoming increasingly clear that pacification through psychocriminalization is class war exercised by other means. The psychocriminalization of anti-capitalist resistance, operating under the guise of "national security," contains opposition, penalizes, criminalizes, and pathologizes dissent, and represses or erases meaningful political debate. Critical or radical criminological scholarship from an anti-security perspective questions the current assumptions and rhetoric about terrorism. Such an approach understands that activists who engage in symbolic and direct action to fight in solidarity with communities under attack and to ensure the survival of the planet face ongoing state repression not only in the form of individualized and collective criminalization but, equally significantly, as pathologized subjects, subject to the power and knowledge of human scientific experts.

NOTE

1 Some of the main agents involved in the design of measures and tools used to assess the risk of so-called terrorism include D. Elaine Pressman, PhD, Senior Research Fellow at the Canadian Centre for Security and Intelligence Studies, Norman Paterson School of International Affairs,

Carleton University, Ottawa (the main architect of VERA, which was funded by Public Safety Canada [http://www.publicsafety.gc.ca/res/cor/rep/2009-02-rdv-eng.aspx]); John Flockton, a so-called expert in "radicalization" who is clinical director, Corrective Services, New South Wales High-Risk Management Correctional Centre, Goulburn, Australia; Sean Norton at Defence Research and Development Canada (DRDC); and Wayne L. Hanniman of the National Security and Criminal Investigations Division of the Royal Canadian Mounted Police.

REFERENCES

Foucault, Michel. 1978. "About the Concept of the 'Dangerous Individual' in Nineteenth-Century Legal Psychiatry." Trans. Alain Baudot and Jane Couchman. *International Journal of Law and Psychiatry* 1 (1): 1–18. http://dx.doi.org/10.1016/0160-2527(78)90020-1.
– 2002. *Power.* Vol. 3 of *The Essential Works of Foucault.* Ed. J.D. Faubion. London: Penguin.
– 2007. *Security, Territory, Population: Lectures at the College de France 1977–1978.* New York: Palgrave. http://dx.doi.org/10.1057/9780230245075.
Marsh, Ian. 2010. *Suicide: Foucault, History and Truth.* Cambridge: Cambridge University Press.
Neocleous, Mark, and George Rigakos, eds. 2011. *Anti-Security: A Declaration.* Ottawa: Red Quill.
Pressman, Elaine D. 2009. "Risk Assessment Decisions for Violent Political Extremism 2009-02." Public Safety Canada: Reports and Manuals.
Record, J. 2003. *Bounding the Global War on Terrorism.* Carlisle, PA: US Army War College.
Rimke, Heidi. 2000. "Governing Citizens through Self-Help Literature." *Cultural Studies* 14 (1): 61–78. http://dx.doi.org/10.1080/095023800334986.
– 2003. "Constituting Transgressive Interiorities: C19th Psychiatric Readings of Morally Mad Bodies." In *Violence and the Body: Race, Gender and the State,* ed. A. Arturo, 403–28. Indiana: Indiana University Press.
– 2010a. "Beheading aboard a Greyhound Bus: Security Politics, Bloodlust Justice, and the Mass Consumption of Criminalized Cannibalism." *Annual Review of Interdisciplinary Justice Research* 1 (Fall): 172–92.
– 2010b. "Consuming Fears: Neoliberal In/Securities, Cannibalization, and Psychopolitics." In *Racism and Borders: Representation, Repression, Resistance,* ed. Jeff Shantz, 95–113. New York: Algora.

– 2010c. "Remembering the Sociological Imagination: Transdisciplinarity, the Genealogical Method, and Epistemological Politics." *International Journal of Interdisciplinary Social Sciences* 5 (1): 239–54.

– 2011a. "The Pathological Approach to Crime: Individually Based Theories." In *Criminology: Critical Canadian Perspectives*, ed. Kristen Kramer, 78–92. Toronto: Pearson Education Canada.

– 2011b. "Security: Resistance." In *Anti-Security: A Declaration*, ed. Mark Neocleous and George Rigakos, 191–215. Ottawa: Red Quill.

Rimke, Heidi, and Deborah Brock. 2012. "The Culture of Therapy: Psychocentrism in Everyday Life." In *Power and Everyday Practices*, ed. M. Thomas, R. Raby, and D. Brock, 182–202. Toronto: Nelson.

Rimke, Heidi, and Alan Hunt. 2002. "From Sinners to Degenerates: The Medicalization of Morality in the 19th Century." *History of the Human Sciences* 15 (1): 59–88. http://dx.doi.org/10.1177/0952695102015001073.

Sageman, M. 2004. *Understanding Terrorist Networks*. Philadelphia: University of Pennsylvania Press. http://dx.doi.org/10.9783/9780812206791.

Silber, Mitchell D., and Arvin Bhatt. 2007. Radicalization in the West: The Homegrown Threat. New York: The New York Police Department. http://www.nypdshield.org/public/SiteFiles/documents/NYPD_Report-Radicalization_in_ the_West.pdf (accessed 22 April 2012).

Taylor, Ian, Paul Walton, and Jock Young. 1973. *The New Criminology*. London: Routledge & Kegan Paul. http://dx.doi.org/10.4324/9780203405284.

United States Federal Bureau of Investigation. 2001. http://www.fbi.gov/congress/congress01/ freeh051001.htm (accessed 5 October 2001). Reproduced in testimony provided to the Senate Select Committee on Intelligence by Dale L. Watson, Executive Assistant Director, Counterterrorism/Counterintelligence Division of the Federal Bureau of Investigation, 6 February 2002. http://www.fbi.gov/news/testimony/the-terrorist-threat-confronting-the-united-states (accessed 11 October 2012).

2 Conflicts of Rights: Free Speech, Freedom to Practise a Religion, and the Social Phobia Mighty Machine

HISHAM RAMADAN

Scepticism is a common human trait manifested when dealing with the unknown or different "other." The "other" can be different from the majority in any number of distinguishing traits, including culture, religion, or race. With respect to religion, opinions on "other" religions vary, from concluding that they are a great threat to the current civilization to calling for a sweeping change in the "other" to comply with the majority's beliefs. Unfortunately, it is not uncommon that in the competition between religions, followers of the majority religion defame "other" religions. Likewise, it is not uncommon to find followers of a particular political view or social theory employing religion to demoralize the "other" race or religion for socio-economic or political reasons. History bears witness that what we now consider abhorrent acts, such as slavery, have been defended vigorously. Professor Thomas Dew, thirteenth President of the College of William and Mary, in 1832 used the Bible to justify slavery. Yet the problem becomes much greater when anti-"other" propaganda exerts influence on many levels, including influencing top government officials and their actions. This manifestation of scepticism is not surprising given that much of the public's knowledge of the "other" is marked by intentional and unintentional misrepresentation, misunderstanding, or even wilful blindness regarding basic facts. When anti-"other" propaganda becomes widespread it forms a phobia towards the "other." Groups that create phobia because of religious competition, political conflict, or the struggle for cultural superiority may use all possible tools, including legal ones, to demonize the "other." Typically these groups shield themselves from liability by invoking a great fundamental human right, the right to free speech, notwithstanding the harm to the weakest, voiceless "other." What is usually overlooked is that the limits of freedom of speech allow free exercise of a religion free from harassment, branding, or denial of fundamental government services.

This chapter highlights the problem of religious phobia from various perspectives, including government officials' explicit and implicit inequitable treatment of religious minorities and the courts' response to phobia towards the religious "other." Examples from academic writings and think tanks that incite phobia will be given. This chapter is comparative in nature: it compares and contrasts perspectives in the United States, Canada, and the European Union. The American model is the closest to Canada's both in heritage and in law. Legal analysis of the American approach will not be comprehensive due to the large number of cases decided by the US Supreme Court. However, it will be extensive enough to indicate the general American approach to freedom to practise religion. Because the Supreme Court of Canada on numerous occasions referenced EU human rights cases, without examining their socio-political background, it is important to closely examine these cases to disclose the inherent religious biases in Europe.[1] The purpose of this chapter is to reveal the current state of affairs and to raise critical questions: If phobia truly exists and harms the weakest elements of our society, what is the best course of action to erode its prejudicial impact? Should we expand the scope of anti-hate-speech legislation to prevent social phobia? Should the government introduce new measures to fight phobia and to salvage human dignity?

Approach to Religious Freedom as Fundamental Human Right

The renowned philosopher Ronald Dworkin, in voicing the modern philosophical approach to the enforcement of human rights, has suggested that it is wrong for the government to deny an individual his or her rights, albeit such denial generates greater social interest (Dworkin 1978). Writing specifically of freedom of worship, Dworkin realizes that that freedom, as a moral right, is vulnerable to restriction if it depends on the utilitarian computation of the collective interest or on the majority vote. The same line of analysis was followed in a number of Supreme Court of Canada decisions. Dickson C.J. in *R v. Morgentaler* concluded that "liberty in a free and democratic society does not require the state to approve the personal decisions made by its citizens; it does, however, require the state to respect them."[2] This philosophical approach, which has been re-emphasized in several court decisions, advocates for freedom to practise religion regardless of the majority views of such practice. Thus, at least in theory, the majority is not allowed to use their overwhelming voting power or to exercise other fundamental rights, such as the right to free speech, to erode the minority's right to practise their religion.

In the international community sphere, there has been a collective affirmation of individual freedoms and the importance of tolerance of others. For instance, article 4 of UNESCO's Universal Declaration on Cultural Diversity (2001) affirms that the defence of cultural diversity is an ethical imperative, inseparable from respect for human dignity. It implies a commitment to human rights and fundamental freedoms, and in particular the rights of persons belonging to minorities and those of indigenous peoples.

Implementation of these international moral standards, particularly with respect to freedom to practise religion, necessitates their inclusion in states' laws and constitutions. This actually occurs almost universally. However, states' constitutions address these essential human rights doctrines in broad terms, leaving its interpretation and application to court and government executives. For instance, the First Amendment of the US Constitution reads: "Congress shall make no law respecting an establishment of religion, or prohibiting the free exercise thereof; or abridging the freedom of speech, or of the press; or the right of the people peaceably to assemble, and to petition the Government for a redress of grievances." Article 9 of the European Convention for the Protection of Human Rights and Fundamental Freedoms reads: "'ECHR' guarantees everyone, whose country is a member of the convention, the right to freedom of thought, conscience and religion subject to limitations that are prescribed by law and are necessary in a democratic society in the interests of public safety, for the protection of public order, health or morals, or for the protection of the rights and freedoms of others." Similarly, section 2 of the Canadian Charter of Rights and Freedoms reads: "Everyone has the following fundamental freedoms: (a) freedom of conscience and religion; (b) freedom of thought, belief, opinion and expression, including freedom of the press and other media of communication."

The application by courts and governments of the freedom to exercise a religion has been rather interesting. Courts, on numerous occasions, have used their unreviewable power to interpret and apply this fundamental right to advance preferential treatment to majority religious beliefs. Similarly, governments, in many aspects, have manifested a great deal of intolerance to minorities.

The following sections illustrate the majority authoritarianism that creates religious phobia concerning the "other" in the United States, Canada, and the European Union, and shows its impact on court and governmental official decisions.

The "Other" Phobia Influence in Canada

In 2009, the widely distributed magazine *Maclean's* conducted a poll that found "many Canadians harbour deeply troubling biases" (Geddes 2009, 28). The poll surveyed more than one thousand Canadians. The finding was that 72 per cent said they have a generally favourable opinion of Christianity. Only 28 per cent had a favourable opinion of Islam. Sikhism scored 30 per cent, Hinduism 41 per cent, Buddhism 57 per cent, and Judaism 53 per cent. These findings were not a surprise to religious minorities in Canada. In 2010, Quebec Justice Minister Kathleen Weil, a Quebec Liberal Party member, tabled bill 94, which barred women wearing a niqab, a veil worn by some Muslims, from essential public services. The Parti Québécois opposed bill 94, *suggesting that the bill should go even further*. This legislation has not yet passed.

A few years ago, a Muslim community in Ontario proposed forming an arbitration tribunal that would utilize Islamic law to settle family matters among Muslims in their community ("McGuinty Rules Out Use of Sharia Law in Ontario," 2005). This was not a radical proposal, given that other permitted religious family arbitration had flourished all over Ontario for years. The Ontario provincial government rejected the proposal under a crushing campaign organized by numerous NGOs, including Amnesty International Canada. Numerous Canadian Muslims were puzzled by the Ontario provincial government's quick rejection of an Islamic law tribunal. Naturally, the proposed tribunal must comply with equality rights under the provisional human rights codes and the Canadian Charter. If so, why was it rejected? One should keep in mind that the UK, the mother of common law jurisprudence and a member state in the European community with its constitutional safeguards, had shortly thereafter approved an Islamic law tribunal. Indeed, Canadian Muslims may believe that that there are widespread religious biases against them created by the majority's unfavourable views towards other religions, including Islam. This is exactly what was delineated by the *Maclean's* poll.

A majority unfavourable view of certain social behaviours is neither a fairy tale told by a magazine nor a creation of elected government executives attempting to satisfy the majority of voters. Various signs lead to the conclusion that it might have taken root in the Canadian system of governance, including the judiciary. In *R. v. Labaye*, the Supreme Court of Canada concluded that contemporary Canadian social morality regards acts such as child pornography, incest, and polygamy as unacceptable regardless of whether or not they cause social harm.[3] Furthermore, the court concluded that Parliament enforces social morality by enacting statutory norms in legislation such as the Criminal Code.[4] As much as this approach seems innocent of discrimination, it does pose a major threat to fundamental rights because the court has created irrefutable presumptions of immorality/deviance regarding certain kinds of conduct. The problem with these presumptions is not the appropriateness of such acts, but rather the lack of a tangible, objective standard rendering an act illegal. Furthermore, the ruling carries the risk of grouping certain practices such as polygamy, which is acceptable and common in many regions of the world, such as Africa, as well as tolerated by several religions, with such practices as incest and child pornography, which are neither accepted neither within any religion nor, as a norm, in any region worldwide. To further muddy the waters, the court gave Parliament, a representative of the majority, unlimited power to enforce so-called social morality notwithstanding the constitutional safeguards that protect the minority from the tyranny of the majority.

Certainly, there is no reliable evidence to support the conclusion that certain behaviours, in the diverse Canadian society, are regarded as morally unacceptable. Even if such evidence were obtainable, the majority opinion might be tainted by religious biases. Parliament, at best, represents the majority, including their negative views of minority religions. Accordingly, Parliament may enact majority preferential legislation that undermines citizens' rights to be treated with equal concern and respect as mandated under section 15 of the Charter. The Supreme Court of Canada, the last resort for the weak and outcast, was rather quick to brand acts, such as polygamy, as immoral and therefore illegal, to vindicate the majority authoritarianism.

Majority authoritarianism classically masks humankind's infirmities, such as racism, religious intolerance, and culture supremacy. For instance, a recent incident in Quebec reveals the unspoken feelings of some law makers. Parti Québécois candidate Djemila Benhabib had refused to support the Catholic crucifix at the National Assembly, something her party wants to maintain at the same time as it wishes to ban other religious symbols in public life. Saguenay mayor Jean Tremblay, in response to Benhabib's position, has stated in a radio interview, "What shocks me is to see us, the gentle French-Canadians, being told how to behave by someone from Algeria whose name we can't even pronounce."[5] Tremblay's viewpoint might be shared by other politicians and law makers but remain unspoken because politically incorrect, leading to suppression of the "other's" freedom to practise a religion by masking the majority authoritarianism with correct-sounding, widely appealing statements such as "shared values of the Canadian society" or "public morality." The worst scenario for the weak and voiceless "other" is the judicial rubber-stamping of majority authoritarianism.

The prohibition of polygamy is a classic example of the negative influence of the majority, who hold Christian views, towards other religions, including Mormons. While there are no scientifically reliable evidence affirming that polygamy is considered morally wrong by the majority of Canadians or that it causes harm to children or spouses, Parliament has nevertheless prohibited polygamy.[6] It is a moral paradox that a man can legally cohabit and engage in sexual intercourse with as many men or women as he likes, but he cannot engage in an official, ceremonial relationship with more than one man or woman. In addition, the state's intrusion into the zone of freedom to practise religion, in prohibiting polygamy, may deprive spouses and children of the socio-economic benefits of an official marriage. It is again difficult to understand the Supreme Court of Canada's objection, given that a man can simultaneously have multiple sexual partners with the full blessing of the law, but a marriage ceremony that guarantees spousal and children's rights renders his acts immoral and illegal.

To be sure, intolerance to the "other" and the forcible assimilation into majority norms is noticeable in numerous court decisions. In *Jack and Charlie v. The Queen*, the defendants, native Canadians, were convicted on the charge of hunting outside the hunting season on land that their tribe historically hunted.[7] The Supreme Court of Canada affirmed the conviction, concluding that "if Indians wish to exercise their historic religious practices there are ways within the bounds of the provincial statute in which to exercise those religious practices."[8] In other words, it is the duty of natives to adapt to majority norms, notwithstanding their historical, unalienable, undeniable land rights. This same line of analysis was reintroduced in *Alberta v. Hutterian Brethren of Wilson Colony*.[9] In this case, Alberta had introduced photo driver's licences in 1974. Members of Wilson Colony were granted exemption from the photo requirement until 2003, when new regulations were introduced requiring all licences, with no discretionary exemption, to have a photo. Members of the Wilson Colony had the option either of complying with the regulation and abandoning the part of their faith that prohibits photography or of doing without a driver's license, which was necessary for work. The Supreme Court of Canada approved the government regulation, concluding that certain enactments impose burdens, and these burdens might be justifiable limits on the freedom to practise religion. Members of the Wilson Colony must accept these burdens; they can hire a driver or find alternative transportation to avoid a conflict with their religious beliefs.

Most recently, in *R. v. N.(S.)* an Ontario Superior Court Justice refused to grant a request that the alleged victim of a sexual assault be permitted to testify while wearing her veil.[10] The court acknowledged the fact that common law does not recognize the right of face-to-face confrontation with one's accuser; otherwise, blind barristers could not perform basic duties at court.[11] Nevertheless the court concluded that "we cannot have accommodations which, for a minority of Canadians, increase the number of identity markers and lead to a self-selected segregation."[12] In other words, the court refused to accommodate the alleged victim's request because such an accommodation would distinguish minority Canadians as different from the majority. The decision also means that any departure from the majority's norms may not be tolerated, and definitely will not be supported, in Canada. Interestingly, section 714 of the Criminal Code allows the court to accept witness testimony and cross-examination inside and outside Canada by means of technology (e.g., telephone). Given this fact, what is the government's objective in forcing a woman to disclose her face? The Ontario Court of Appeals affirmed the Superior Court's decision, and the case is now awaiting hearing before the Supreme Court of Canada. Given that court's decision in *Alberta v. Hutterian Brethren of the Wilson Colony*, it is difficult to imagine it will change its mind and uphold N.(S.)'s fundamental right to free exercise of religion.

Remarkably, Canada has made many accommodations in response to requests of minorities that are more vocal, and better represented in Parliament and the government. Sikh police officers, for example, are allowed to wear their turban instead of the police uniform hat. The contrast between the government's tolerance towards Sikhs and its earlier allowance of Jewish and Catholic family law tribunals, on the one hand, and the above cases of intolerance to the weak and voiceless "other" minorities raises a question: do minorities need a powerful lobby in the government to defend their rights? Will a social phobia directed against the unknown or weak minority "other" achieve its target if there is no powerful lobby defending the minority's civil liberties? If so, the core idea of the Canadian Charter has failed to achieve its objective: protecting the minority from majority tyranny. Any legal paradigm justifying this failure is only for lawyers to entertain. What a member of a minority really needs is respect for her or his human dignity exemplified in the freedom to exercise fundamental rights, especially if such exercise produces no real, as opposed to speculative, harm to society. Forcing assimilation by eroding the identity markers of a minority group is nothing less than majority tyranny.

Religious Phobia Successes in Europe

A close look at Europe's current state of affairs reveals unprecedented phobia towards minority religions, especially Islam, concurrent with promoting the state's official Christian sect at the expense of other minority religious and non-religious groups. In 2010, Belgium enacted a ban on wearing the burka, a face veil worn by some Muslims, in public notwithstanding human rights groups' (including Amnesty International) criticism of the legislation as an attack on religious freedom. The Swiss People's Party (SPP), the largest party in the Swiss Parliament, proposed a referendum on banning the building of minarets or "mosque cupolas" in Switzerland because minarets are a sign of "Islamization" ("Switzerland Votes on Muslim Minaret Ban" 2009). The referendum passed with a clear majority of 57.5 per cent of voters (Cumming-Bruce and Erlanger 2009). In July 2003, former French president Jacques Chirac established an investigative committee to examine the application of the principle of laïcité (the separation of state and religion) in the educational system (Fournier and Yurdakul 2006, 168). The committee published a report recommending that the wearing of religious clothing in schools be prohibited. The prohibition would forbid Muslim female students to wear headscarves, Jewish boys yarmulkes, Sikh boys turbans, and Christians large Christian crosses. However, small crosses and the Star of David would be allowed. The French government adopted the recommendations shortly thereafter. The unavoidable observation is that France did not disallow religious symbols altogether; it allowed Catholic nuns to wear habits, Christians to wear average-size crosses, and Jews to wear the Star of David, and the rationale presented for this stance was *separation of state and religion*. Subsequently, former French president Nicolas Sarkozy made it clear that French citizenship requires full integration or assimilation into the French lifestyle. Consequently, the French government refused to grant a Muslim woman French citizenship because she insisted on wearing a veil ("A Veil Closes France's Door to Citizenship" 2008). And in Germany, current chancellor Angela Merkel, in addressing a congress of her conservative Christian Democrats (the ruling party), emphasized that "mosque cupolas" should not be higher than "church steeples" (Crossland 2008).

These vocal governmental actions are not isolated acts. Rather, they are a product of a massive phobia towards the "other" that runs deeply in European systems of governance, including the judicial system. Article 9, Freedom of Thought, Conscience and Religion, of the European Convention for the Protection of Human Rights and Fundamental Freedoms (ECHR) guarantees everyone whose country is a signatory of the convention the right to freedom of thought, conscience, and religion subject to limitations that are prescribed by law and are necessary in a democratic society in the interests of public safety, for the protection of public order, health, or morals, or for the protection of the rights and freedoms of others.[13] The ECHR mandates a protection system to examine alleged violations and to ensure that states comply with their obligations under the convention. Disputes arising from alleged violations of the conviction are subject to review by the European Court of Human Rights after the applicant has exhausted the remedies available in the country in which the alleged violation was committed. The court initially mediates the dispute; if resolution is not possible, it rules on the case. The ruling is binding on the states found to have violated the convention.

So far, the European community's governance of laws of human rights and dispute resolution mechanism seems neutral and fair. However, its application by the court is interesting. In *Dahlab v. Switzerland*, a Swiss Muslim primary school teacher was prohibited from wearing a headscarf while teaching.[14] Initially, the European Court of Human Rights recognized that forbidding teachers to wear religious symbols, such as headscarves, constitutes a violation of the freedom to manifest religion. However, the court concluded that the prohibition is a justifiable limitation, citing two rationales: religious peace at schools and the unknown influence on students of merely wearing a headscarf. The court, in upholding the principle of *laïcité*, concluded that that principle requires the neutrality of the state educational system. Interestingly, the court's reasoning for the decision equated Islamic religious norms, such as wearing a headscarf, with gender oppression, concluding that voluntary wearing of headscarves by adults violates the principle of gender equality.[15] In this the court ignored the arguable similarity between Muslim women wearing headscarves and Catholic nuns wearing habits. It is quite common in Switzerland to see Catholic nuns teach while wearing habits; the doctrine of separation of state and religion seems not to come into a play here, yet it is invoked in the case of Muslim headscarves to prevent the "other" from manifesting their religion publicly. It seems that this legal doctrine of *laïcité* is in play to impose a mandatory assimilation policy. The message sent to the "other" is: If you want to live in a European country you must look and act like the majority. Notions of diversity and individuality do not seem to exist within the legal framework. Phobia, especially religious phobia, created by the majority not only justifies government actions but also influences European Court of Human Rights decisions.

The following cases reveal that all minority religious groups must confine themselves to the majority standard. In *Pichon and Sajous v. France*, the applicant refused to sell prescribed contraceptives to three women for religious reasons.[16] On the same day that the women complained, the applicant was convicted for violating the French Consumer Code and other statutes. He claimed freedom to practise a religion as the motive for his refusal to sell contraceptives. His claim was denied in the European Court of Human Rights, which adopted a narrow perspective on the freedom to practise religion. The court pointed out that article 9 protects personal convictions and associated acts such as worshiping, teaching, practising, and observance, but does not always guarantee the right to behave in public in a manner governed by that belief.

In *Bruno v. Sweden*, the applicant objected to paying taxes that implicitly support a certain faith.[17] The Swedish tax authorities levied municipal taxes on the applicant that included a church tax to support the Lutheran Church of Sweden. Because the applicant is not a member of that church, he was entitled to a reduction of the church tax under the Swedish Dissenter Tax Act, to be paid to parishes, by 25 per cent of the amount he would have had to pay had he been a member of the Church of Sweden. The government of Sweden emphasized that the dissenter tax is levied to allow the parishes to perform civil services. However, the court "agree[d] with the Government that the administration of burials, the care and maintenance of church property and buildings of historic value and the care of old population records can reasonably be considered as tasks of a non-religious nature which are performed in the interest of society as a whole."[18] In other words, both members and non-members of the Church of Sweden are legally obligated to maintain Church of Sweden buildings and support Christian burial.

In *Alujer Fernandez and Caballero Garcia v. Spain*, the applicants were unable to allocate part of their income tax directly to the financial support of their own church, the Evangelical Baptist Church, on their tax returns.[19] Under Spanish law, taxpayers are given a choice between allocating part of their income tax to financial support for the Catholic Church or to other charitable causes. Other churches do not enjoy the advantage of automatic financial support by their followers, via tax return, unless they strike an agreement with the government of Spain, which the Evangelical Baptist Church had not done. And because they had not done so, the European Court of Human Rights did not find any violation of article 9. In other words, if your church fails to make an arrangement with the government, or you are member of a no-faith group, or you simply do not want to support a charitable purpose, you are compelled to support the majority religion.

Alujer Fernandez and Caballero Garcia v. Spain and *Bruno v. Sweden* invite two conclusions. First, the European Court of Human Rights sees the fundamental rights, including the freedom to exercise religion, as the collective right of a group rather than an individual's right that ought to be protected if unjustifiably undermined. Second, that court emphasized the supremacy of ordinary laws over the fundamental rights. In *Alujer Fernandez and Caballero Garcia v. Spain*, the court upheld legislation that gives an advantage to a particular religion notwithstanding the impact of that legislation on other religions or non-religions. Again, in *Bruno v. Sweden*, the court emphasized the supremacy of ordinary laws over the fundamental rights by upholding a statute that benefits the Lutheran Church of Sweden, which receives municipal financial support to maintain churches buildings, although a portion of those municipalities' budgets is paid by non-members of the church.

In *Leyla ahin v. Turkey*, the applicant, a student at the University of Istanbul, was denied access to courses and examinations because she was wearing an Islamic headscarf.[20] She alleged that the university violated her right to express her religious convictions guaranteed under article 9 of the ECHR. The European Court of Human Rights recognized that the ban on wearing the Islamic headscarf in teaching institutions violates the applicant's right to express her religious beliefs. However, the court observed that such a violation is permissible because the Turkish law banning headscarves pursues the legitimate aims of protection of the rights and freedoms of others and protection of public order. The court accepted the government's view that upholding the principle of secularism and ensuring the neutrality of universities mandates dress restrictions in Turkey, concluding that the protection of secularism and pluralism in a university may be seen as meeting a *pressing social need* given the fact that the majority of the population adheres to the Islamic faith and the existence of extremist political movements using religious symbols for political purposes.

Leyla Şahin v. Turkey is a classical model of judicial activism against manifestation of Islamic belief, the minority religion in Christian Europe. Two years prior to the Leyla Şahin decision, an Islamic party won the Turkish election and expressed a desire to lift the ban ("Turkey's old guard routed in elections" 2002). The European Court of Human Rights in a Grand Chamber judgment reached a decision, sixteen votes to one, that the Islamic extremist political movement uses religious symbols for political purposes.

The contrast between *Otto-Preminger-Institute v. Austria* and *Choudhury v. United Kingdom* shows that the European Court of Human Rights is willing to interpret the law in a manner that empowers majority religious beliefs at the expense of the "other" or minority, thereby vindicating phobia against the "other."[21] In *Otto-Preminger-Institute v. Austria* the applicant complained that the confiscation of a film offending the Catholic religion was in violation of freedom of speech under the ECHR. The court concluded that freedom of expression was prescribed by law but the seizure and forfeiture of the film were aimed at the protection of the rights of others, namely the right to respect for one's religious feelings, and at ensuring religious peace. The court noted: "The Court cannot disregard the fact that the Roman Catholic religion is the religion of the overwhelming majority of Tyroleans. In seizing the film, the Austrian authorities acted to ensure religious peace in that region and to prevent that some people should feel the object of attacks on their religious beliefs in an unwarranted and offensive manner."[22] In contrast, in *Choudhury v. United Kingdom* the applicant complained that the authorities in the UK failed to grant him equal protection of law by refusing to prosecute Salman Rushdie, author of the book *Satanic Verses*, and the publisher of the book on the grounds that author and publisher unlawfully published a book that is blasphemous and libels the religion of Islam. The application was dismissed on the basis that the offence of blasphemy relates only to Christian beliefs as held by the Church of England.

The Battle of Religious Phobia in the United States: Law versus Special Interest Groups

Perhaps because the United States is a superpower with a mighty armed forces and gigantic economy, the attempt to demonize the weak "other" has never been greater, for a variety of religious and political reasons. The prime example of the weak "other" is Muslims and the Islamic religion itself. Numerous Muslims believe that demonization of Muslims and Islam is in full force in the media, in academic writing, and in political speeches aimed at creating Islamophobia. Yet there is clear resistance to Islamophobia by patriotic Americans in positions of power, those who give priority to American interests and examine the information they received objectively. As well, federal courts, and especially the US Supreme Court, seem to distance themselves from the mighty phobia machine and have decided cases on individual merit. The following are only a few examples of the current state of affairs in the United States.

With respect to academic writing distributed in the United States, both American and non-American authors rely on readers' ignorance of Islam in text that is marked by a negative view of Islam and Muslims. These negative views, found in numerous books and scholarly articles, contribute to the common phobia and have created a new social bias: Islamophobia.

Rudolph Peters' 2005 book *Crime and Punishment in Islamic Law*, published by the prestigious Cambridge University Press, is an exemplar of an Islamophobic publication. It manifests to a high degree two common features of Islamophobia: the unjustified claim that some ill practices of governments of Muslim states are acceptable within Islam, and inadequate and erroneous descriptions of Islamic law. In an example of confusion, the author employs a description al-Mawardi, a medieval judge and scholar, gives of eleventh-century practices in a Muslim state to emphasize that beating an accused during interrogation is allowed (9). Similarly, the author concludes that "simple suspicion was sufficient for establishing guilt" (10). Undeniably, such practices are never sanctioned by the authentic sources of Islamic law, Qur'an and Sunna. A famous *hadith* (saying of the Prophet of Islam, Muhammad) explicitly states that any suspicion of innocence precludes the application of punishment in *hudud* (a class of serious offences) crimes. Nevertheless, the author portrays ill treatment of an accused as an application of Islamic law.

The book is also rife with erroneous descriptions of Islamic law. Peters mangles the concept of compensatory damages (*diya*), which is closely tied to the victim's capability of earning money and is awarded to the victim's family in cases of homicide, with the application of capital punishment. This intermingling of concepts leads to the view that Islamic law is unfair and primitive. He states, "the yardstick for determining equivalence is a person's status, to which a monetary value is attached. This status, as we shall see, is determined by sex, religion, and by whether a person is a slave or free. The principle of equivalence prescribes that a person may not be sentenced to death for killing a person of lower monetary value" (39–40). Accordingly a man cannot be killed for killing a woman or a child.

The confusion of basic concepts continues throughout the publication. While initially the author correctly classifies both theft and *zina* (unlawful sexual intercourse) as criminal acts (*hudud* offences) with mandatory fixed punishments (7), he later incorrectly describes these acts as torts, not crimes (55, 59). Any novice student of Islamic studies would affirm that both theft and *zina* are *hudud* offences.

The bias of the author becomes clearer as one progresses through the book. On pages 103–4, he attempts to justify religious intolerance of Islam and Muslims by the imperialist powers of the nineteenth century. Their abolition of Islamic law, he concludes, was justifiable because the law must be enforced impartially; all subjects should be treated with equal footing before the law.

This ignores the fact that when Europeans arrived in the colonies, especially the Middle East, they gave themselves preferential treatment in the courts, in the sense that they were literally above the law. For instance, the establishment of the mixed courts in 1874 in Egypt under British colonial rule mandated that the majority of sitting judges be non-Egyptians. Although the jurisdiction of the courts was limited to conflicts arising either between Egyptians and foreigners or between foreigners, it became notorious not only for usurping the Egyptian national judiciary's original powers, but also because it was nearly impossible for an Egyptian national to prevail in any case involving a European. Similarly, in the "consular courts" in Egypt, with civil and criminal law jurisdiction, the judges were the counsellors for the

European states, without any prior legal education whatsoever. These courts applied European laws, the law of the European counsellor, instead of Egyptian law. They originally had limited jurisdiction in matters arising between Europeans, but under colonial rule their jurisdiction expanded to deal with conflicts between Egyptians and Europeans. Here again, it was virtually impossible for Egyptians to prevail in any litigation because of the counsellor "judge's" bias. Can this undisputed fact be squared with Peters' statement that abolishing Islamic law was intended to allow that all subjects should be treated with equal footing before the law? Such contextual facts are typically missing within Peters' monograph. Unfortunately, his book is only one example of the majority of publications on Islam published in the West that contribute greatly to the creation of Islamophobia.

The production of most US think tanks is not much different from academic writing as regards the creation of Islamophobia. For instance, the Washington Institute for Near East Policy in its mission statement gives its aim as "to advance a balanced and realistic understanding of American interests in the Middle East and to promote the policies that secure them."[23] However, its practical approach has been neither balanced nor realistic Here a careful examination of the institute's publications is enlightening. Recently, in response to the American movie *The Innocence of Muslims*, which depicted the Prophet Muhammad as a womanizer, murderer, and homosexual, a group of Egyptians violated Islamic, Egyptian, and international law in scaling the outer walls of the American embassy in Cairo and mounting a black flag displaying the phrase "No God but Allah and Muhammad is the messenger of Allah." This flag is one of the early Islamic State's flags, of the Abbasid Caliphate era in particular, and is usually referred to as one of the Muslim identity flags. The institute, in an article entitled "How to Send Egypt a Message," portrayed the incident as follows: "The image of a black Al Qaeda flag flying above the United States Embassy in Cairo on Sept. 11 shocked Americans."[24] In fact, neither Egyptian nor American authorities found any link between Al Qaeda and the incident of the flag; the actors were a group of individuals acting in the heat of passion. Equating Al Qaeda with the general Muslim population brands all Muslims as terrorists. Again, this is only one example of how think tanks erroneously portray Muslims. The question again arises, is this the institute's political agenda? Given that the vast majority of think tanks in the United States adopt the same misrepresentative approach when portraying Muslims, one should question their intentions.

Islamophobia's influence is quite successful in the United States at the state level and in everyday practice by numerous average Americans. On 28 September 2007, the Egyptian ambassador to the United Nations, Majed Abed Al-Fatah, was walking on First Avenue in New York City when he was stopped by a police officer and told that Muslims and Arabs were not allowed to walk on First Avenue. The Egyptian government officially protested such discriminatory treatment to the US government. But an average Muslim or US citizen of Arab descent would have difficulty in addressing such issues, given the cost of litigation in the United States and the sheer number of such incidents. The Council on American Islamic Relations (CAIR), an American Muslim civil rights organization, reports thousands of hate crimes against Muslim Americans, including murder, violence, discrimination, and harassment, over the past ten years.[25] About twenty state legislatures have considered prohibiting state court and government agencies from using Islamic law when making decisions, and some of these bills have been successful, such as a recent Kansas anti-sharia bill, while others were defeated after widespread criticism by American Muslims.[26] Those who promote anti- sharia bills, including Kansas governor Sam Brownback, allege that Islamic law is discriminatory. American Muslims have raised the same question over and over: is it not true that the United States' laws and constitution prevails over all legislation, and therefore any application of foreign laws, including Islamic law, cannot have any discriminatory effect?

At the federal level it seems that US jurisprudence, at least, has so far avoided being unduly influenced by religious phobia, as can be seen in the following summary of the development of free exercise of religion in the United States and its impact on Islamophobic legislation.

The First Amendment of the United States Constitution offers two types of protection to freedom of religion: the establishment clause, which prohibits the government from establishing an official church or religion, and the free exercise clause, which protects individuals from governmental interference with the practice, act, or holding of religious beliefs. Since there is no establishment clause in Canadian constitutional law, that country falls outside the scope of this paper and will not be discussed.[27]

The free exercise clause offers two means of protection: protection from unjustified discrimination against the practice of some or all religious beliefs; and protection from unjustified burdening of the practice of religion.

Unjustified discriminatory practices may occur by the state's enacting non-neutral laws.[28] Facial neutrality is not determinative, for the free exercise clause protects from "covert suppression of particular religious beliefs."[29] The law is not neutral if its objective is to infringe upon or restrict practices because of religious motivation.[30] If the law is not neutral, it can be justified only if the government successfully proves a compelling governmental interest and shows that the law is narrowly tailored to advance that interest.[31] A non-neutral law that targets religious conduct for distinctive treatment or advances legitimate governmental interests only against conduct with religious motivation will survive only in rare cases.[32]

Unjustified burdening of the practice of religion can take various forms, such as prohibiting conduct mandated by a particular religion, compelling an individual to do something against his or her religion, or simply imposing a general burden on the practice of a religion.[33] Perhaps the most important question is this: What makes burdening the practice of religion unjustified? Does general compliance with the law, although it burdens the practice of religion, constitute an unjustifiable burden? The US Supreme Court has visited this question several times. In *Reynolds v. United States* (1878), the Supreme Court refused to grant Mormons an exemption from a congressional statute that made it a crime for a person to have more than one spouse.[34] The Supreme Court adopted "belief-action" or, in other words, a distinction between "freedom to believe and freedom to act."[35] It concluded that freedom of belief deserves greater protection than do religiously motivated acts.[36] It reasserted the same approach in *Cantwell v. Connecticut* (1940).[37] Later the court in *Sherbert v. Verner* (1963) and *Wisconsin v. Yoder* (1972) made historic changes to the interpretation of the free exercise clause, concluding that imposing a burden, although it is a by-product of a generally applicable law, can be justified only if there are "compelling state interests."[38] In this context, when Mr Yoder, a member of the Amish religion, requested an exemption from the state school system for his children because of religious beliefs, the court did not find a compelling state interest and granted him an exemption. However, in *Goldman v. Weinberger* (1986), the court refused to grant an exemption to an Orthodox Jew who wished to wear a yarmulke contrary to the Air Force dress code, finding that uniformity in the military is a compelling state interest.[39] In a landmark case, *Employment Div. v. Smith* (1990), the court overrode the *Yoder* and *Sherbert* approach, concluding that the free exercise clause does not offer exemptions from a neutral and generally applicable law even if the general application of such law imposes a substantial burden on the practice of a religion.[40] In response to the Smith decision, the US Congress enacted the Religious Freedom Restoration Act of 1993 (RFRA).[41] Under RFRA, the federal government may not, as a statutory matter, substantially burden a person's exercise of religion "even if the burden results from a rule of general applicability."[42] The RFRA restored the rationale adopted in *Yoder* and *Sherbert* that any burden on the practice of religion is unjustified unless there is a compelling government interest, and added the requirement that any such law in the service of a compelling government interest constitute the least restrictive means of furthering that interest.[43] The Supreme Court in *Gonzales v. UDV* (2006) affirmed the applicability of RFRA to federal statutes. In this case, the government confiscated a sacramental tea used in communion by a religious sect with origins in the Amazon rainforest. The tea, brewed from plants unique to that region, contains a hallucinogen regulated under the US Controlled Substances Act. The court concluded that the federal government failed to show compelling government interests, which in turn permitted the religious sect to import and use the hallucinogenic sacramental tea.

In November 2010 in Oklahoma a legislatively-referred voter referendum amendment to the state constitution passed by a 70 per cent majority. The amendment banned any reference to sharia or international law in arriving at judicial decisions. Following the same line of analysis as US Supreme Court jurisprudence, the 10th Circuit Court of Appeals in *Awad v. Ziriax* ruled that Oklahoma's anti-sharia law was unconstitutional for a number of reasons, including lack of evidence of any concrete problem, or of any harm, that the anti-sharia law is supposed to remedy.[44] The court also concluded that the proposed amendment was speculative at best and could not support a compelling state's interest.

In the light of *Awad v. Ziriax*, it is more likely that Kansas' new anti-sharia law, mentioned above, will be found unconstitutional. However, it is difficult to speculate whether the federal courts and the federal legislature will continue on the same path given that Islamophobia continues to grow.

Conclusion

Judges, academics, Law makers, media workers, and government executives are only human, with all the meritorious characteristics and infirmities that are deeply rooted in humankind. All, with the exception of a few, see the world through the lenses of the collective moral standard, which at best represents majority views. In everyday practice, they advance their perspective, the collective moral standard, mechanically through their legitimate powers. Given that human rights are intended to protect minorities from the tyranny of the majority and to ensure equal human dignity, the last resort of the "other," the undesirable, weak, and voiceless, is the court. But courts' decisions vary.

In Europe, courts have become a prime tool to influence general public opinion and to enforce the collective moral standard of the majority. Vulnerable minorities have no option but to obey or suffer the painful consequences. The European Court of Human Rights has not only failed to protect the "other" from governmental executive decisions and discriminatory legislation, but has vindicated the majority's authoritarianism.

In other instances, we have seen a very positive outcome. The US Supreme Court in *Yoder, Sherbert, Gonzales v. UDV*, and *Awad v. Ziriax* tipped the balance of interests – the state interest that manifests the collective moral standard of the majority versus individual freedom of the "other" – in favour of individual freedom. Freedom to practice religion can be burdened only if there is a compelling state interest. When the court reversed its position in *Smith*, Congress responded by enacting RFRA, which restored the *Yoder* and *Sherbert* rationales as well as requiring that any burden placed on the practice of religion in the service of compelling government interests must be the least restrictive means of furthering that interest. Unmistakably, the US Supreme Court, in contrast to the European Court of Human Rights, upheld constitutional supremacy over parliamentary supremacy. It was a great success for American jurisprudence, at the federal level, to insulate itself from the negative influence of Islamophobia. The case is not same at the state level, where phobia is alive and well and gaining influence daily.

In Canada, where the vast majority of Canadians unfavourably view non-Christian religions, one expects the nation's highest court to scrutinize government actions given that government officials, the decision makers, are simply Canadians who are likely to share the same sceptic view of other religions. These officials are capable of creating laws that, though legally founded, restrict the free exercise of other religions. The possibility of bias on the part of governmental officials is simply undeniable. The Supreme Court of Canada has followed the path of the European Court of Human Rights, vindicating the government's actions, as we have seen in *Alberta v. Hutterian Brethren of Wilson Colony*. However, the court still has a very good chance in *R. v. N.(S.)* to correct past mistakes. As Dworkin realizes, freedom to worship, as a moral right, is unduly restricted if it depends on the utilitarian computation of the collective interest or the majority vote (Dworkin 1978). In this context, when the vast majority of Canadians – including government officials and decision makers, as Maclean's research suggests – hold negative view of other religions, their collective vote would unduly restrict the practice of other religions. Additionally, if we allow the collective vote to hold sway, citizens' rights to be treated with equal concern and respect mandated under section 15 of the Canadian Charter of Rights and Freedoms might be undermined.[45]

As for the phobia makers and beneficiaries, including academicians, media workers, and special interest groups who do not scruple to advance their cause at the expense of the weak "other," there is not much that can be done to instil greater humanity. They are shielded from all legal liability by the freedom of speech doctrine. However, every murder, assault, or vandalism committed by an offender under the influence of their views renders all of them collectively morally liable.

Perhaps it is time to revisit the two questions I raised in the introduction. Should we expand the scope of anti-hate-speech legislation to prevent social phobia? Should the government introduce new measures to fight phobia and to defend human dignity? In fact, the government of Canada and the Supreme Court are going in the opposite direction. Recently a conservative member of the federal Parliament introduced Bill C 304, which is intended to repeal section 13 of the federal Human Rights Act. Section 13 gives the Canadian Human Rights Commission the power to hear complaints about public hate speech over the telephone or on the Internet. So far, Bill 304 has received applause from the government, and it is expected to pass. On the other hand, the Supreme Court of Canada has not yet overruled the *Alberta v. Hutterian Brethren of Wilson Colony* decision. We may have to wait for a new generation of Canadians that values the Canadian liberal spirit and aims to defend the "other's" human dignity.

NOTES

1 See the court conclusion in *R. v. N.S.* [2009] O.J. No. 1766, 95 O.R. (3d) 735 (Ontario Superior Court of Justice).

2 *R. v. Morgentaler*. [1988] 1 S.C.R. 30.

3 *R. v. Labaye*, [2005] 3 S.C.R. 728, 2005 SCC 80, para. 109.

4 *R. v. Labaye*, [2005] 3 S.C.R. 728, 2005 SCC 80, para. 109.

5 "Pauline Marois Struggling with 'Hijab' Backlash," *Montreal Gazette*, 14 August 2012.

6 Section 293 of the Criminal Code of Canada.

7 *Jack and Charlie v. The Queen*, [1985] 2 S.C.R. 332.

8 *Jack and Charlie v. The Queen*, [1985] 2 S.C.R. 332, para 18.

9 [2009] 2 S.C.R. 567.

10 *R. v. N.(S.)*, [2006] 95 O.R. (3d) 735.

11 See *R. v. N.(S.)*, [2006] 95 O.R. (3d) 735, para. 109.

12 See *R. v. N.(S.)*, [2006] 95 O.R. (3d) 735, at para. 141. Most interestingly, the court accepted a New Zealand view expressed in *Police v. Razamjoo*, [2005] DCR 408 (N.Z. Dist. Ct.) that "to authorize the giving of evidence from beneath a covering would be such a major departure from accepted process and the values of a free and democratic society that it would seriously risk bringing the District Court into disrepute" (at para. 133). It seems that the court s in *Police v. Razamjoo* and in *R. v. N.(S.)* attempt to inject the notion of face-to-face confrontation into the right to confront the accuser and provide full answer and defence, including the right to cross-examination. If this is true, then blind individuals should not be admitted into law societies. In fact, current practices prove otherwise.

13 Article 9 states: "1.Everyone has the right to freedom of thought, conscience and religion; this right includes freedom to change his religion or belief and freedom, either alone or in community with others and in public or private, to manifest his religion or belief, in worship, teaching, practice and observance. 2. Freedom to manifest one's religion or beliefs shall be subject only to such limitations as are prescribed by law and are necessary in a democratic society in the interests of public safety, for the protection of public order, health or morals, or for the protection of the rights and freedoms of others."

14 *Dahlab v. Switzerland*, App. No. 42393/98, 2001-V Eur. Ct. H.R. 447 (2001).

15 *Dahlab* v. *Switzerland*, App. No. 42393/98, 2001-V Eur. Ct. H.R. 447 (2001). The court held: "It must also be acknowledged that it is difficult to reconcile the wearing of a headscarf with the principle of gender equality." The court never explained why only the Islamic norm is a sample of oppression while other dress norms, such as the skullcap worn by Jewish people, the turbans worn by Sikhs, or the habit worn by Catholic nuns, are not.

16 *Pichon and Sajous v. France*, Application no. 49853/99, (2001).

17 *Bruno v. Sweden*, Application no. 32196/96, (2001). See also Lundberg v. Sweden, Application no. 36846/97, (2001).

18 *Bruno v. Sweden*, Application no. 32196/96, (2001) at 7.

19 *Alujer Fernandez and Caballero Garcia v. Spain*, Application no. 53072/99(2001).

20 *Leyla Şahin v. Turkey*, Application no. 44774/98 (2004).

21 *Otto-Preminger-Institute v. Austria*, (13470/87) (1994) and *Choudhury v. United Kingdom*, Application 17439/90.

22 *Otto-Preminger-Institute v. Austria*, (13470/87) (1994) at 17.

23 https://www.washingtoninstitute.org/about/mission-and-history.

24 http://www.washingtoninstitute.org/policy-analysis/view/how-to-send-egypt-a-message.

25 For example, *Same Hate, New Target: Islamophobia and Its Impact in the United States*, January 2009–December 2010, http://www.cair.com/images/pdf/2010-Islamophobia-Report.pdf.

26 http://www.msnbc.msn.com/id/47574780/ns/us_news-crime_and_Courts/t/kansas-governor-signs-shariah-bill-ban-islamic-law/.

27 See, e.g., Richard Moon, "Liberty, Neutrality, and Inclusion: Religious Freedom under the Canadian Charter of Rights and Freedoms," 41 *Brandeis L.J.* 563, 563 (2003). There are some challenges to the non-existence of a Canadian Establishment clause. See Jeremy Patrick, "Church, State, and Charter: Canada's Hidden Establishment Clause," 14 *Tulsa J. Comp. & Int. L.* 25 (2007).

28 Probably the clearest example is *Torcaso v. Watkins*, 367 U.S. 488 (1961), where the US Supreme Court held that the state could not make the right to public office conditional on whether the individual believes in God.

29 *Bowen v. Roy*, 476 U.S. 693, 703, 90 L. Ed. 2d 735, 106 S. Ct. 2147 (1986) (opinion of Burger, C. J.)

30 *Employment Div., Dept. of Human Resources of Ore. v. Smith*, 494 U.S. at 878–9.

31 *Church of the Lukumi Babalu aye v. City of Hialeah*, 508 U.S. 520, 533 (1993).

32 *Employment Div., Dept. of Human Resources of Ore. v. Smith*, 494 U.S. at 888.

33 With respect to prohibiting conduct mandated by particular religions, see *Gonzales v. O Centro Espirita Beneficente Uniao Do Vegetal.*, 546 U.S. 418; 126 S. Ct. 1211; 163 L. Ed. 2d 1017(2006). Compare the earlier decision *Employment Div., Dept. of Human Resources of Ore. v. Smith*, 494 U.S. 872, 110 S. Ct. 1595, 108 L. Ed. 2d 876 (1990), which was decided prior to the enactment of the Religious Freedom Restoration Act of 1993 (RFRA), 107 Stat. 1488, as amended, 42 U.S.C. § 2000bb et seq. With respect to compelling individuals to do something against their religion, see

Wisconsin v. Yoder, 406 U.S. 205; 92 S. Ct. 1526; 32 L. Ed. 2d 15 (1972). With respect to imposing a general burden on the practice of a religion, see *Thomas v. Review Board* (450 U.S. 707 (1981)) (U. S. Supreme Court held that the state could not deny unemployment benefits to an employee who quit his job rather than accept transfer to a section of the employer's factory that produced armaments when the employer had religious objections to that type of work). See also *Hobbie v. Unemployment Appeals Commission* (480 U.S. 136 (1987)) (the court held that a state could not deny unemployment benefits to an employee who was fired for refusing to work on her Saturday sabbath.)

34 *Reynolds v. United States*, 98 U.S. 145 (1878). It seems that the court was driven by fear that granting an exemption from the general applicable law might open the door to absolute lawlessness and disorder. The court noted that "laws are made for the government of actions, and while they cannot interfere with mere religious belief and opinions, they may with practices. Suppose one believed that human sacrifices were a necessary part of religious worship, would it be seriously contended that the civil government under which he lived could not interfere to prevent a sacrifice? Or if a wife religiously believed it was her duty to burn herself upon the funeral pile of her dead husband, would it be beyond the power of the civil government to prevent her carrying her belief into practice?" (166).

35 *Reynolds v. United States*, 98 U.S. 145, 166.

36 *Reynolds v. United States*, 98 U.S. 145, 162–6.

37 *Cantwell v. Connecticut*, 310 U.S. 296 (1940).

38 *Sherbert v. Verner*, 374 U.S. 398, 403(1963); Wisconsin v. Yoder, 406 U.S. 205, 214–6(1972).

39 *Goldman v. Weinberger*, 457 U.S. 503 (1986).

40 *Employment Div., Dept. of Human Resources of Ore. v. Smith*, 494 U.S. 872, 110 S. Ct. 1595, 108 L. Ed. 2d 876 (1990) (the court rejected a challenge to an Oregon statute that denied unemployment benefits to drug users, including Native Americans engaged in the sacramental use of peyote).

41 42 U.S.C. § 2000bb et seq. Notably, RFRA originally was applicable to state and federal governments. The US Supreme Court in *City of Boerne v. Flores*, 521 U.S. 507 (1997) limited the application of RFRA to the federal government only. See also *Gonzales v. O Centro Espirita Beneficente Uniao Do Vegetal.*, 546 U.S. 418; 126 S. Ct. 1211; 163 L. Ed. 2d 1017(2006), which affirms the same conclusion. Also note that in response to the Boerne ruling, the US Congress, relying on its constitutional power to regulate commerce, enacted the Religious Land Use and Institutionalized Persons Act (RLUIPA) (2000). While RLUIPA is more limited in scope than RFRA,

it applies to the states and restored some of the protection provided under RFRA.
42 42 U.S.C.§ 2000bb-1(a).
43 42 U.S.C. § 2000bb-1(b).
44 *AWAD v. ZIRIAX*, 754 F.Supp.2d 1298, 1308.
45 *Andrews v. Law Society of British Columbia*, [1989] 1 S.C.R. 143, 152; Law v. Canada (Minister of Employment and Immigration), [1999] 1 S.C.R. 497, para 78. See also Ronald Dworkin 1978, 272.

REFERENCES

BBC. 2002. "Turkey's Old Guard Routed in Elections." *BBC News*, 2 November. http://news.bbc.co.uk/2/hi/europe/2392717.stm
– 2009. "Switzerland Votes on Muslim Minaret Ban." *BBC News*, 29 November. http://news.bbc.co.uk/2/hi/8384835.stm
Bennhold, Katrin. 2008. "A Veil Closes France's Door to Citizenship." *New York Times*, 19 July. http://www.nytimes.com/2008/07/19/world/europe/19france.html
Crossland, David. 2008. "Germany's Homegrown Intolerance." *Spiegel Online*, 18 January. http://www.spiegel.de/international/germany/0,1518,529322,00.html.
Cumming-Bruce, Nick, and Steven Erlanger. 2009. "Swiss Ban Building of Minarets on Mosques." *New York Times*, 9 November. http://www.nytimes.com/ 2009/11/30/world/europe/30swiss.html.
Dworkin, Ronald. 1978. *Taking Rights Seriously*. Cambridge, MA.: Harvard University Press.
Fournier, Pascale, and Gökçe Yurdakul. 2006. "Unveiling Distribution: Muslim Women with Headscarves." In *France and Germany in Migration, Citizenship, Ethnos*, ed. Y. Michal Bodemann, and Gökçe Yurdakul. New York: Palgrave Macmillan.
Geddes, John. 2009. "What Canadians Think of Sikhs, Jews, Christians, Muslims." *Maclean's*, April, 28.
"McGuinty Rules Out Use of Sharia Law in Ontario." 2005. *CTV News*, 12 September 12. http://www.ctv.ca/ CTVNews/TopStories/20050912/mcguinty_shariah_050911/.
Montgomery, Sue, and Dougherty Kevin. 2012. "Pauline Marois Struggling with "Hijab" Backlash." *Montreal Gazette*, 15 August. http://www.montrealgazette.com/ news/Pauline+Marois+struggling+with+hijab+backlash/7094413/story.html#ixzz28Im9ouCD.

3 Phobic Constructions: Psychological, Sociological, Criminological Articulations

JEFF SHANTZ AND HISHAM RAMADAN

Fear and hope are among the greatest forces that move nations. Fear is generally a negative force that may trigger wars and force individuals to accept extraordinary measures, tolerate the unthinkable, and sacrifice their basic human rights. Hope, on the other hand, can build peace, justice, and prosperity. However, the nobility of hope does not reliably serve the purpose of some leaders, lobbies, and political forces, even as hope can provide political leaders some space for manoeuvre (as the case of Obama shows). At the same time fear can readily justify wrongs and create an erroneous perception of what is just and fair. When fear distorts the moral perception, victimization becomes the norm so long as it is publicly perceived as a necessity to avoid greater evil. The target of this directed fear can be domestic or foreign. When domestic, the target of public fear, naturally, is a minority group and perhaps the most vulnerable group. Such fear progresses into social phobia focusing on the most vulnerable, less desired "other."

The tone of phobic discourses, in the mass media and the vocalizations of political decision makers, intensifies commensurate with the need to demonize the "other" for economic, political, social, or cultural gain. In this context, if it is desired to deprive a religious group of their right to practice religion, phobia makers may initiate a campaign of lies and deliberate misrepresentation of the religious group, to demonize them as a threat to mainstream or dominant social or cultural values, practices, and institutions. If it is desired to cut social services to the poor and needy, a campaign might be launched to represent the poor as lazy and unworthy of support. But more, the phobic discourses portray the poor as a social contagion, an infection of the social body, with visible poverty being infectious. Such has been the case in public discourses in which politicians identify homeless people as a scourge (e.g., repeated association with vermin and plague carriers, as in various political discourses in Western liberal democracies; see Shantz). In denying equal employment opportunities to migrant newcomers to Canada, for example – the so-called lack-of-Canadian-experience factor – phobia is an effective tool.

Social phobias are constructed at macro and meso (mid-range) sociocultural levels as well as at the micro or personal level. Although personalistic explanations tend to dominate public discussions, often in terms of personal or individual bias, prejudice, or discrimination, the macro and meso levels are the most significant in structuring and framing phobic expression, and paradoxically are the least emphasized or studied.

While phobia receives overwhelming attention within psychology, it has received virtually no notice in sociology and none at all in criminology. Yet these social perspectives are perhaps best suited, and needed, for properly understanding the construction and mobilization of phobic discourses and practices in the current period.

Constructing Phobias: Sociological Approaches

In psychological terms, social phobia is discussed as an anxiety disorder characterized by intense fear of and in social situations. The psychological designation social anxiety disorder or social phobia is currently identified as the third largest mental health care problem in the world (Richards 2013). US government epidemiological data suggest social anxiety affects more than 7 per cent of the population at any given time. The lifetime prevalence rate, or the chances of developing social anxiety disorder at any time during one's lifespan, is said to stand at slightly more than 13 per cent (Richards 2013, n.p.). Related streams of research related to social anxiety examine the need for social acceptance or social standing, and the public emphasis on social standing within diverse societies. This is associated with media emphasis on "normal" or "appealing" personal characteristics, which is said to fuel feelings of inferiority or insecurity.

Yet despite the prominence of public discussions of phobias in the present period, almost no attention has been given to the production of phobias as political and social practice, particularly as these relate to what are predominantly social phobias or fears of others within contemporary society. The present collection takes a different approach to understanding phobias. From the perspectives of the various contributors to these pages, the manifestation of public fear must be understood in a social context. Phobic responses are outcomes of social, economic, political, and cultural mobilizations of power.

Ruth Simpson's is among the earliest work to examine the psychological concept of phobia as a sociological phenomenon. Simpson treats phobias not as irrational fears but as violations of the appropriate framework for contextualized fear or safety. A supposedly psychological concept is intersubjective – it is socially constructed. Significantly, not all in society have the same capacity to determine the appropriateness of frameworks in given situations, nor do they have equal opportunities to shift or disrupt frameworks.

As Simpson (1996) suggests, danger in modern societies is quite often, despite assumptions, neither clear nor present. She notes: "Warning labels, safety equipment, and other precautions assume danger exists as part of an objective environment to which we must adapt our behavior" (550). For her, "ironically, it is an objective quality of danger – that danger is often unobservable – that permits and encourages intersubjective perceptions of safety and danger. Still, despite the necessarily social nature of beliefs about safety and danger, the perception that these beliefs are objective strongly persists" (559). There is an assumption that fears have an objective basis in reality, and this assumption, rarely called into question, can assist phobia producers in constructing new targets or objects of fear where resources are deployed to create the impression that a threat exists (even where it may not).

This does not mean, as Simpson points out, that objective dangers do not exist (549). They of course do. Rather, "perceptions of safety and danger are 'intersubjective' – products of social construction, collective agreement, and socialization. While objective danger certainly exists, perceptions of danger do not derive directly from observation of the empirical world. The objective environment provides only inconsistent and ambiguous information, permitting ample room for socially constructed beliefs" (549). Fears are shared through socialization and communication (552).

Simpson notes that perceptions of danger and safety, threat and security, are intersubjective rather than straightforwardly personal or biographical. They are the products of socialization and collective definition – they are fundamentally *social* constructions.

As Shantz (2012) suggests, phobic constructions are even more the outcomes of social struggles – of contests over theory and practice, meaning and identity – over social resources and social standing. Disputes often arise over danger. Conflicts emerge over sources of identified harms or threats. Interpretation is, of course, shaped by structures and relations of power. As Simpson suggests: "symbolism, politics, profit, and other factors influence perceptions of danger, diverging from and sometimes contradicting observation" (1996, 552). They reflect shifting (im)balances of forces within stratified societies.

The social constructedness of phobias, and the central part played by organizations and institutions of power and authority, are beginning to attract attention in relation to psychological or physiological issues such as sexuality. As Baber and Murray suggest:

> Rather than seeing sexuality as a purely natural phenomenon characterized by fixed, inherent drives that are essentially different for men and women, sexuality is seen to be constructed in relation to, and in interaction with, historically and culturally variable social practices [that is, institutional structures] like religion, education, and medicine (J. Harding, 1998). Conceptualizations of sexuality are believed to reflect social relations regarding gender, ethnicity, and class and to be culturally managed through the ways we talk, think, and practice. (2001, 24)

Ince (2005) examines the specific forms of fear associated with sexual practices as representing the social construction of intolerant, anxious, and fearful environments. Philaretou (2006) suggests that these environments consist of prejudicial beliefs, discriminatory behaviours, and stereotypical attitudes, constructed and reinforced throughout lifetimes, that discourage people from developing a more liberal or expressive ethos.

With reference to the driving factors and forces behind erotophobic constructions, Ince (2005) suggests that "they are largely due to the existence of powerful political forces enacted by stakeholders with vested moral, power, and economic interests" (Philaretou 2006). In the case of erotophobia, there are stakeholders who benefit from the perpetuation and expansion of patriarchal institutional systems or profit from specific experiences and practices (typically within pornographic industries). Notably, these phobic interests and practices tend to downplay or denigrate practices or experiences that promote egalitarianism or highlight aspects of power within human relations (Philaretou 2006).

Sociocultural contradictions and ambivalences and the anonymous, often detached, character of social life in advanced capitalist societies provide the ground for phobic constructions. These in turn condition micro-phobic inclinations. Ince (2005), looking at erotophobia, or social fears of sexuality, suggests that phobic conditioning is brought to fruition through complex political systems. Anonymity reinforces a cautious or fearful framework in which people assume the worst about strangers and are predisposed to guard against them.

In the grim novel *Battle Royale*, a stark anti-authoritarian story in which a class of junior high students are selected by a totalitarian government and forced to partake in a survival game in which they are instructed to kill one another until only one remains, there is a harsh and telling moment in which two characters realize that they know very little about their fellow students. At first, hopeful that the students might band together to avoid hunting each other and thus beat the game, the two come to an awareness that they are all strangers despite being together regularly over the course of years. With this awareness, suspicions and fears mount.

> "I mean ... I just realized I don't know a thing about everyone else. I don't know what they're really like. I mean ... you can't see into someone's mind."
>
> *I don't know a thing about everyone else.*
>
> She was right, Shuya thought. *What do I know about this group that I spend the day with at school?* He suddenly felt like there was an enemy out there.
>
> Noriko continued, "So I – I'd be suspicious. Unless it was someone I really trusted, I'd be suspicious of them. I'd be afraid they might want to kill me."
>
> Shuya sighed. The game was horrible. But it also seemed flawless. In the end, it was a bad idea to invite everyone indiscriminately to form a group unless you were certain about them. (Takami 1999, 66–7)

This dystopian scenario exemplifies the impact of anonymity and the social separation and detachment that characterize conditions of advanced capitalism. Uncertainty about which framework to deploy – trust versus fear – leads to heightened anxiety or excitability. Phobia producers play upon, and with, this anxiety in various ways, as the chapters herein illustrate.

Fear exacerbates suspicions. Later in the novel, two other characters discuss the part fear plays in motivating their actions:

> Yumiko nodded. "Exactly. That's why I think no one here really wants to kill anyone. I think it's because we're so terrified we become deluded that

everyone else is out to kill us and so we resort to fighting. And in that state even if no one attacked, we might even end up attacking others on our own." She interrupted herself, unfolded her arms, and put her hands on the floor. "I think everyone's just terrified." (Takami 1999, 136–7)

Phobic constructions play key parts in the mobilization of fearful frameworks and regimes of security and punishment. These mobilizations and emergent frames have facilitated various mechanisms of power, exclusion, containment, and control. The deployment of psy discourses, and the construction of social processes as personal or psychological, as discussed by Heidi Rimke in this volume, underscore regimes of biopower (as in security certificates, detention, and deportation as well as in incarcerations and medicalization) in the current period. Mobile populations (especially precarious ones), constructed as outsiders, as different, as "others," are constructed as bearers of threat and danger who must be contained and regulated lest they infect or despoil host groups.

Simpson also makes the suggestion that societies can be phobic. In her view, stated before the events of 9/11, American society is crime phobic: there is an intense level of fear of crime, even though most Americans will not be victims of crime (certainly beyond low-level property crimes) and even as crime rates drop over the years. Indeed, it might be suggested that American society exhibits phobiphobia, or the fear of fear itself. American society is obsessed with not being afraid and securing conditions under which fear itself has been evacuated. The instrument for this is the enactment of laws and punitive criminal justice policies and practices.

Fear of …?: Criminology and Crises of Causality

Beyond the emotionality of fear and the responses to it, we must examine what Furedi (2007) calls the crisis of causality shaping fear. There is a mismatch between the presence of real-world threats and people's sense of fear, mediated by intervening constructs. The intensity of phobias is not directly related to the objective level of threat posed by the phobic target. The development of social phobias occurs at the same time as "the decline of tangible threats to corporeal existence that were brought about by war, for example, in earlier eras" (Furedi 2007, n.p.). Fear of terror, as for fear of crime, is a problem distinct from the real acts of terror, or crime, themselves in the current period (Furedi 2007;

O'Grady 2008). In the present period, managing phobias, and feelings about and responses to them, become the focus rather than addressing the source of the phobia.

In the current context, phobia develops a relative autonomy from its object or source. Furedi notes that "a distinguishing feature of contemporary fear is that it appears to have an independent existence" (2007, n.p.). Phobias, over terrorism for example, are more potent than the actual threat posed by the object of the phobia, which may be quite remote or unlikely. On the other hand, ecological threats, have lacked the urgency of terror or migration/border insecurity threats – despite being far more prevalent and devastating. The connection of states and corporations to ecologically destructive practices such as fracking or tar sands development (or wars) may say something about this discrepancy, and about the articulation of fears around ecological disaster (as "acts of god," for example).

The disjuncture between real threats, perceptions of threats, and associated fears – the crisis in causality – can be examined in the form of phobic constructions by which political, social, or economic concerns are given form. Further, the outcomes of phobias, in the form of public discussion, policy, public administration, or political practice, can be analysed.

One can look at the generalized fear of crime in contemporary advanced capitalist societies. Fear of crime is distinct from, detached from, actual occurrences of crime in the society, as is well documented to be the case in Canada and the United States, for example (O'Grady 2008). As Bannister and Fyfe suggest, fear of crime is "now recognized as a more widespread problem than crime itself" (2001, 808). Indeed, numerous studies (Altheide 2006; Barak 2012; Jewkes 2004; Marsh and Melville 2009; Pollak and Kubrin 2007; Surette 2011) show that fear of crime goes up, often dramatically, even as actual crime rates decline significantly. Reiner (2002) suggests that media accounts of crime occur at 1,400 times the actual rates of crime. Lowry, Nio, and Leitner (2003) note that public perceptions of crime as the "most important problem" in the United States jumped from 5 per cent in 1992 to 52 per cent in 1994. Representations of crime tend also to focus on violent crimes to the person rather than non-violent property crimes, which make up the bulk of real-world crimes. Reiner (2002) reports that while the proportion of violent to non-violent crime reported in the news is eight to two in the United States, the actual rates in crime data are nine to one for nonviolent and violent crimes respectively.

Many criminologists have pointed out that the disparity between actual rates of crime or violence and expressions of fear over crime and violence is partly a result of media emphasis and representation: "if it bleeds it leads." This is also true in the cases of contemporary social phobias. As Melissa Ames shows in this volume, phobias are both amplified by mass media presentations and serve to amplify media narratives of fear and insecurity. Similarly, media representations of crime are expressed through often highly racialized and class-based discourses that focus on specific ethnic and cultural targets, especially the poor (Bjornstrom, Kaufman, Peterson, and Slater 2010; Maneri and ter Wal 2005). This bears similarities with the targets of contemporary social phobias.

Yet despite the lack of tangible harm associated with phobic objects, these phobias have their own very real impacts. As criminologist David Garland has concluded in the case of crime: "Fear of crime has come to be regarded as a problem in and of itself, quite distinct from actual crime and victimization, and distinctive policies have been developed that aim to reduce fear levels rather than reduce crime" (2001, 10). Chris Hale goes even further to suggest that crime panics reflect not a fear of crime but rather "some other attribute, which might be better character-ized as 'insecurity with modern living,' 'quality of life,' 'perception of disorder' or 'urban unease'" (1996, 84). So too for phobic constructions.

Indeed, as Melissa Ames, Johann Pautz, Davina Bhandar and Michael Ma, and Jeff Shantz show in their respective chapters, the phobias gen-erated around terrorism mark other cultural concerns (around immi-gration or cultural and religious diversity, for example). Or, as Shantz shows, they offer opportunities for political transformations (including repressive mechanisms) that might otherwise generate visible dissent.

Social phobias always require the intervention of social actors, social forces, those who socially construct or manipulate anxiety – articulate it towards specific responses, for specific ends (policy changes, border practices, national identity, and so on), as the cases in the following chapters examine. In each case we see the roles played by what might be termed, following Furedi, phobic entrepreneurs.

Social phobias represent social conditions to be managed, and poten-tially manipulated. On the one hand they are managed by media cor-porations to capture audiences (and advertising revenues). On the other they are managed by states to mobilize publics for specific ends (war, border controls, criminalization of dissent, electoral success, etc.). At the same time, though, they render those same publics vulnerable to intrusions by the state, ostensibly to protect them from the phobic object or target.

Thus, any range of policies that might otherwise be opposed by the public – from increased security presence in and regulation of public space to limits on mobility to increased surveillance to detention – can become legitimized, or at least tolerated, by phobia-influenced publics. The recent revelations in the United States about the National Security Agency (NSA) spying on civilians and the widespread surveillance of communications, from computers to cell phones, provide telling examples. That the phobia around foreign terror was the immediate, reflexive excuse offered by politicians, including President Obama, reveals the potency of phobic discourses.

In the Canadian context one might refer to the case of security certificates. Security certificates are provisions drawn from Canadian state immigration policy that allow for the arrest and indefinite detention, without charge, of non-citizens. The security certificate regime has been expanded beyond the purview of immigration policy to cover any non-citizen that the government wishes to detain on grounds of some, usually unproven, connection with terrorism. The connection can be as vague as expressions of support and may be as minimal as simply wearing symbols of a terrorist group or possessing literature associated with a terrorist group. The security certificate process is a gross violation of civil rights and contravenes numerous principles of justice in a liberal democracy, including due process, rights of disclosure of evidence, access to legal representation, the right to a public trial, even *habeas corpus*. Yet, after 9/11 the Canadian government, behind cover of the social phobias around terrorism, has been able to hold several people under security certificates with limited public outcry over threats to civil liberties and social freedoms.

In most cases the national state is presented as the source of protection from the phobic object. Even as liberal democratic states contribute to the phobias, they present themselves as the antidote. The state not only diagnoses the threat but provides the therapy for its population.

Shifting Frames: Phobic Constructions

Ince (2005) and Philaretou (2006) argue that even personally held or seemingly unconscious phobic beliefs, values, or ideas are deeply rooted in surrounding historical, cultural, or social environments. This makes it very difficult to dig them out and expose them as inaccurate, invalid, or untrue. In the context of erotophobia, Philaretou notes: "Various institutions, such as education, religion, economy, media, and jurisprudence, are invisibly engaging in everyday 'brainwashing' and propaganda, imprinting irrational sexual fears and anxieties in billions of minds while remaining relatively unaware of it" (2006, n.p.). Such processes are at play in the construction of the range of social phobias at play in the late twentieth and early twenty-first centuries. Beliefs about danger can seem to follow from observation or experience. The role of the mass media can blur observation and experience and impel the rooted sense of danger as experienced even when it has, in reality, not been experienced directly.

Beliefs about danger always involve interpretation as well as observation. Simpson argues that "the objective environment provides only inconsistent and ambiguous clues about danger, leaving wide latitude for inference and interpretation. Given this ambiguity, beliefs about danger, and particularly safety, can arise with little or no reference to the objective world they describe" (1996, 550). This constructed aspect of fear and danger (and safety and security) leaves room for (re)interpretation, which facilitates the mobilization and manipulation of phobic constructions.

Most of everyday life is marked by neutral frameworks. The environment is assumed as neutral with dangerous and safe entities marked as exceptions. Thus the phobic perspectives themselves are typically exceptional or even deviant (Simpson 1996, 557). Yet social phobia producers attempt to mark their exceptionality (or deviance) as typical, customary, usual, practical, pragmatic, or visionary – as a dominant perspective. As Simpson suggests, "were there a consensus that dogs were dangerous, there would be a corresponding attempt to exile them from safety zones, as we do with rats, wolves, and other feared animals" (1996, 560).

Phobics suffer because others do not share their fear. Thus there is a push in constructing social phobias to secure broad recognition of the legitimacy of the fear (in social phobias, for example, of the poor, of refugees, of outsiders). Failure to secure such broad legitimacy can lead the phobic to be viewed as deviant (in maintaining an inappropriate frame on a particular entity).

Deviation from an appropriate framework forms the basis of phobias. The work of social phobic producers is to effect a shift in which entities are viewed within an inappropriate framework (or a framework that is appropriate for select economic and political powerholders but not in keeping with social evidence). For Simpson, "the same logic underlies the anti-gun control slogan 'Guns don't kill people. People kill people.' The slogan casts people as dangerous carriers of a neutral tool, locating the source of harm in the carrier rather than the weapon itself. (Gary Trudeau's satirical version of the same slogan, 'Guns don't kill kids. Kids kill kids,' strikes a chord because it relocates the danger from the gun to children" (1996, 552). The construction of safe entities (the poor, refugees, religious minorities) as threatening, as dangers, is particularly unsettling because it disrupts the sense of appropriate or secure frameworks.

Social phobias can place specific groups within a cautious or suspicious framework, classifying all members of a group as dangerous or posing a threat. This is not a paranoic perspective since it does not organize everything through a suspicious lens. Certain entities or areas are marked as threatening or dangerous. Simpson notes: "Phobics are less noticeable than paranoics and the pathologically overconfident because, in general, they use the socially appropriate framework. However, within that framework they mark as dangerous a specific item most would consider neutral or safe" (1996, 559).

In supposedly safe contexts there is always the risk that danger lurks undetected and unseen. This is a condition that terror, by nature underground and illicit, plays into and promotes. As Simpson notes: "Because danger is often unobservable, it is impossible to determine for certain when we are safe. As the absence of danger, safety is the absence of something that it is often unobservable in the first place. While it is sometimes possible to tell when danger is present, it is impossible to tell for certain that it is completely absent" (1996, 551). This is coupled with the uncertain and imprecise character of safety, as Simpson points out: "safety does not manifest itself in any observable way. There are no 'safety signs' to establish unequivocally when we are safe, as danger signs warn about harm" (1996, 551).

Treatment of phobia is about resocialization to dominant social norms, values, and beliefs. It encourages people to reject certain framings of entities while accepting those fears that others accept (of crime, for example)

What is perhaps truly astonishing is that the vast majority of the population, including victims of phobia, can be mobilized to buy into the established phobia as unquestionable fact and to accept its consequences. For example, in the phobia about homelessness, a hungry (and possibly ill) person is inhibited by a psychological barrier that prevents him or her from grabbing a loaf of bread from the local supermarket to satisfy hunger, instead eating from the trash bin. This then is deployed in public discourses to reinforce the social phobic responses. Phobias towards homelessness may also prevent people, in sub-freezing temperatures, from breaking and entering an abandoned property to keep warm rather than dying from exposure. The list of social phobias is long and the harm they cause is extensive, with the price paid largely by the most vulnerable in our society.

Identity and Articulation

Articulation (from Althusser 1971; Hall 1985; Laclau and Mouffe 1985) refers to the process by which meaning is created, from discursive expressions, and temporarily fixed. It is the putting together of discourses from the diversity of social utterances (Fierke 2007, 86). Even more, how these discourses are articulated, socially produced and reproduced, is a political struggle involving the legitimation of particular representations.

At the same time it cannot be assumed that publics will accept the forms of articulation. Thus Althusser also employs the notion of interpellation. *Interpellation* refers to the processes by which people come to recognize themselves, to identify with articulated discourses (1971, 174). Through interpellation, as Fierke suggests, "concrete individuals come to identify with these subject positions and the representations in which they appear. As subjects identify with them, the power relations and interests entailed in discourse are naturalized and these representations seem to reflect the world as it really is" (2007, 86). Thus, this also involves the constitution of social identities.

Identities and dangers are both produced in phobias. The task is not one of seeking objective, permanently and unproblematically fixed conditions. Phobias arise and develop in processes of production and change, and they in turn contribute to further change, further (counter)productions. Too much of the discussion of fear in contemporary societies, particularly neoliberal democracies, is unspecific, general, and connected with therapeutic approaches centred on the individual (Fierke 2007; Furedi 2007). Yet the individual, and its identity, is a social expression.

Identity is a relational concept defined through forms of difference (Fierke 2007). Furthermore, these differences are contested. Often, in phobias, the difference involves a "dangerous other" against which mainstream, preferred identity can be fixed. The construction of a dangerous "other" (migrant, poor, terrorist, extremist, fundamentalist, etc.) effectively constitutes conflict. It establishes clear insides and outsides and expresses a ranking or hierarchy of acceptable and unacceptable subjects. The acceptable and unacceptable are mutually constituted through what Fierke calls the "jostling of politics" (2007, 97).

From a Foucauldian perspective discourse is not only narrative; it generates modes of power, of inclusion and exclusion (Furedi 2007). Phobias certainly assert a logic of exclusion – inoculation against the phobic target. In phobic constructions this logic is accompanied by criteria for inclusion "by which populations have to show that they are fit for consideration" (Fierke 2007, 156). Phobias express a strategy of what Foucault terms biopolitics – governance through discursive practices of bodily shaping and marshalling populations. The phobic target can be located in specific bodies (racialized, for example) signifying the articulated "other." An examination of phobias offers insights into the relationships and processes by which identities are articulated and derive meanings.

Conclusion

For Ruth Simpson, mobilized frameworks organize perceptions of danger and safety. In this collection we explore the mobilization of frameworks, particularly related to terror and invasion or migration and border breaches, through the construction of phobic designations of the "other" in the twenty-first century. Various groups have recognized that hope and fear are very powerful driving forces capable of moving nations and shaping their actions. Nations have used both of these emotions to achieve their target, notwithstanding the negative impact on society as a whole.

Having established these facts, we must recognize that it is impossible to deal with phobia in a vacuum, absent of comparative prospective. Multinational analysis of judicial and legislative as well as cultural and media reactions to social phobia sheds much-needed light on the current state of affairs.

These phenomena are not necessarily new. However, the current trends require investigation in order to properly understand emergent practices within the social politics of contemporary social life, beyond individualizing constructions or naturalist discourses about terror or security. There is no book that analyses the construction of fear and xenophobia in the current context through the socio-political framework of social phobia. Those works that discuss social phobia take a strictly psychological approach emphasizing individual personality characteristics. The present work emphasizes instead the social, political, and cultural relations of power that construct phobias as processes of power. This collection also moves beyond notions of moral panic that emphasize media practices in the limited construction of fear associated with specific "folk devils."

For John Ince, overcoming phobias, even something as seemingly micro-phobic and personal as sexuality, is a crucial step in developing and promoting democracy and social equality (2005; see also Philaretou 2006). Doing so requires increased awareness regarding the rights of minorities and the marginalized (or phobic targets) and the assertion of personal and social freedoms and liberties.

REFERENCES

Altheide, David L. 2006. "The Mass Media, Crime, and Terrorism." *Journal of International Criminal Justice* 4 (5): 982–97. http://dx.doi.org/10.1093/jicj/mql061. Althusser, Louis. 1971.
Lenin and Philosophy and Other Essays. London: New Left.
Baber, K.M., and C.I. Murray. 2001. "A Postmodern Feminist Approach to Teaching Human Sexuality." *Family Relations* 50 (1): 23–33. http://dx.doi.org/10.1111/j.1741-3729.2001.00023.x.
Barak, Gregg. 2012. "Media and Crime." In *The Routledge Handbook of Critical Criminology*, ed. Walter DeKeseredy and Molly Dragiewicz, 373–85. London: Routledge.
Bjornstrom, Eileen E.S., Robert L. Kaufman, Ruth D. Peterson, and Michael D. Slater. 2010. "Race and Ethnic Representations of Lawbreakers and Victims in Crime News: A National Study of Television Coverage." *Social Problems* 57 (2): 269–93. http://dx.doi.org/10.1525/sp.2010.57.2.269.
Fierke, K.M. 2007. *Critical Approaches to International Security*. London: Polity.
Furedi, Frank. 2007. "The Only Thing We Have to Fear Is the 'Culture of Fear' Itself." Spiked, 4 April. http:// http://www.spiked-online.com/newsite/article/3053#.VkYgW9KrRiw.
Hall, Stuart. 1985. "Signification, Representation, Ideology: Althusser and the Post-Structuralist Debates." *Critical Studies in Mass Communication* 2 (2): 91–114. http://dx.doi.org/10.1080/15295038509360070.
Ince, John. 2005. *The Politics of Lust*. Amherst, NY: Prometheus.

Jewkes, Yvonne. 2004. *Media and Crime*. London: Sage.

Laclau, Ernesto, and Chantal Mouffe. 1985. *Hegemony and Socialist Strategy*. London: Verso

Lowry, Dennis T., Tarn Ching Josephine Nio, and Dennis W. Leitner. 2003. "Setting the Public Fear Agenda: A Longitudinal Analysis of Network TV Crime Reporting, Public Perceptions of Crime, and FBI Crime Statistics." *Journal of Communication* 53 (1): 61–73. http://dx.doi. org/10.1111/j.1460-2466.2003.tb03005.x.

Maneri, Marcello, and Jessika ter Wal. 2005. "The Criminalisation of Ethnic Groups: An Issue for Media Analysis." *Forum: Qualitative Social Research*. http://www.qualitative-research.net/index.php/fqs/article/view/29/61.

Marsh, Ian, and Gaynor Melville. 2009. *Crime, Justice and the Media*. London: Routledge.

O'Grady, William. 2008. *Crime in Candian Context*. Toronto: Oxford University Press.

Philaretou, Andreas G. 2006. "The Social Construction of Erotophobia." *Journal of Sex Research* 43 (3): 292–5.

Pollak, Jessica M., and Charis E. Kubrin. 2007. "Crime in the News: How Crimes, Offenders, and Victims Are Portrayed in the Media." *Journal of Criminal Justice and Popular Culture* 14 (1): 59–83.

Reiner, Robert. 2002. "Media Made Criminality: The Representation of Crime in the Mass Media." In *The Oxford Handbook of Criminology*, ed. Robert Reiner, Mike Maguire, and Rod Morgan, 302–40. Oxford: Oxford University Press.

Richards, Thomas A. 2013. "Social Anxiety Fact Sheet: What Is Social Anxiety Disorder? Symptoms, Treatment, Prevalence, Medications, Insight, Prognosis." Social Anxiety Association. http://http://www.socialphobia. org/social-anxiety-fact-sheetsocialphobia.org/social-anxiety-fact-sheet.

Simpson, Ruth. 1996. "Neither Clear nor Present: The Social Construction of Safety and Danger." *Sociological Forum* 11 (3): 549–62. http://dx.doi. org/10.1007/BF02408392.

Surette, Ray. 2011. *Media, Crime, and Criminal Justice: Images, Realities, and Policies*. Belmont: Wadsworth.

Takami, Kōshun. 2009. *Battle Royale*. San Francisco: Haikasoru.

PART 2

Bordering on Fear: Phobias, National Identities, Citizenship

This section explores various causes for social phobias in modern societies. The discussion in this part is especially enriched by a comparative outlook that examines phobias from several sources: those manufactured by the government to achieve governmental objectives, those propagated by special interest groups to incite fear of the "other" in order to justify or promote policies against the "other," those incidental to social changes with or without governmental blessing, and those generated by self-infusing fear of the "other's" failure to meet the majority rules of conduct, regardless of any inconsistency with basic humanitarian standards.

Mirfakhraie (chapter 4) presents a case involving the deliberate manufacturing of social phobia to create the ideological state. The state, in this case Iranian, promotes a model of the ideal citizen who possesses a certain religious and ethnic background along with favoured characteristics. The state also demonizes the "other" that would challenge the state's norms and ideologies, utilizing as a means to this goal the educational curriculum in the public school system. The curriculum drives citizens psychologically to fit into the image of the ideal citizen by encouraging the comparison of oneself to the ideal citizen who lives in conformity with the state's promoted values. Any citizen who challenges the governmental "norm" might be subject to stigma and to being branded as, for example, "unpatriotic" or "anti-popular."

Focusing on another institution, Ames (chapter 5) shows that the media, which is owned and controlled by special interest groups, can also promote or defy social phobia and heal or hurt society. She notes that the media can play a positive role in healing society from the psychological trauma of terrorism, fuel national debate on important issues such as torture, and make individuals rethink the "other" by portraying them as average citizens instead of monsters or animals. Alternatively, it can play a negative role by capitalizing on fear to promote social phobia. Thus, individuals can fall victim to a media-promoted agenda, for better or worse, without realizing that that agenda functions as a tool of social control to reinforce a notion or justify horrendous actions towards the "other."

On the other hand, social phobias can promote social changes in cases where the state fails to understand or address the causes for them. Shlapentokh (chapter 6) notes that the majority might fear the "other" who fails or refuses to accept the norms of that majority, posing an apparent threat to that majority's lifestyle, identity, or national values. When the majority, especially youth, express their dissatisfaction with the current states of affairs, they are branded as fascist, racist, or the like. Notions of assimilation may not work at all. The chapter offers an insightful analysis of social phobias in several respects, including that the point that that fear of the "other" is not limited to one side but can be bilateral. The chapter also explains that numerous factors may contribute to social phobia, such as language, race, or religion.

A similar type of phobia is explained in the essay by Ma and Bhandar (chapter 7), with one fundamental difference: the majority fear of the "other" is government driven. The government creates rules of conduct towards the "other," notwithstanding its obligation to comply with humanitarian standards or international law. This may occur because the government, controlled by the dominant group, is afraid that enacting and enforcing "imported" rules of conduct will loosen the governmental grip on the "other." Or the government may fear that non-compliance with its rules is an invitation to lawlessness or disorder. Or it may simply want to limit the number of "others," especially if they are immigrants with religions, cultures, or customs that the majority feel threatened by. Whatever the basis underlying the fear, it is undeniable that creating laws designated primarily to control the minority "other" is a contravention of basic human rights.

4 Constructions of Phobias, Fractured and Stigmatized Selves, and the Ideal Citizen in Iranian School Textbooks

AMIR MIRFAKHRAIE

In this chapter, I analyse how the Iranian school curriculum[1] produces positioned readers, and problematize those privileged present and non-present discourses that frame the ways students come to understand themselves in relation to various forms of otherness, locally, nationally, and globally. I examine the ways through which students are discursively positioned in hierarchical relations to other dominant and oppressed groups around the world, resulting in the production of various forms of *fractured selves*. Fractured selves reflect the contradictory textual positioning of racialized, patriarchal, nationalistic, and religious selves and forms of otherness in the official knowledge that situates students to imagine themselves in discriminatory ways in relation to internal and external otherness and to the ideal Iranian citizen. I explore how present/non-present discursive/textual phobias about women, ethnic "minorities," non-Muslims, and non-Iranians are configured in school textbooks.

I argue that, in narrating the official knowledge about the Iranian national identity, the authors of school textbooks construct certain groups and bodies as outsiders who must be feared and controlled. Phobia plays an important foundational/structural role in imagining what and who Iran and Iranians are. School knowledge represents the ideal self and the nation based on manufactured fears and phobias that define and relate Iranian students to the world around them in contradictory and fragmentary ways. The types of phobias that are promoted in Iranian school textbooks are multiple and interrelated: political and economic dependency, disorder, *bī-ḥijāb* (uncovered women), *bī-īmān* (non-believer), anti-God, non-white, lack of cooperation, underdevelopment, non-modern, Baha'ism, women's agencies, agents of colonialism, and Western imperialism. The ideal Iranian citizen is produced through a narration of nation that draws upon Islamized, Orientalist, ethnocentric, nationalistic, and racialized discourses in depicting who is considered an outsider or alien.

I examine the ways in which this dominant non-Western self is constructed as a double-edged raced-group. That term refers to the ways in which a non-dominant and marginalized group, in the context of post-colonial relations, defines others from a racialized perspective at the same time as it is also defined by other powerful non-group members at local and global levels through highly racialized epistemologies. Racialization is an important element and process in the construction of phobia that functions as both present and non-present "traces"[2] in othering groups. Racialization refers to how social relations are affected by the "signification of human biological" and socio-cultural characteristics in informing the construction of "social collectivities," resulting in the categorization, fracturing, and stigmatization of racial-ethnic groups and the construction of them in unequal and differential ways (Dei 1996, 21; Henry and Tator 2006, 351–2). Racialization and ethnicism intersect other factors such as gender, religion, and geography, and hierarchically position school-aged readers in relation to the national self and to internal and external others, who may be constructed as both friendly insider/outsiders or enemy insiders/outsiders.

Historically, during the process of nation building in countries such as Iran that were influenced by nationalism, and restructured through the introduction of modernization projects, "citizenship education" and national identity were constructed based on a conception of the ideal citizen that emphasized similarity in order to establish categories of insiders based on universal shared values (Sadiq 1931). The project of nation building assumed that the solution to traditionalism in Iran was to re-socialize students and citizens of the country based on new conceptions of the self in modernity and on the culture of the Persian "race"[3] from highly racialized, ethnocentric, and nationalistic discourses despite the multi-ethnic-religious characteristics of Iranian society (Atabaki 2000; Banani 1961; Shaffer 2002). The most evident aspect of the Persianization process remains the usage of Persian as the official language of instruction, which was accompanied with the proliferation of racist and chauvinistic myths that assumed all Iranians are part of the "pure or genuine Aryan race," resulting in "genocide, ethnocide and linguicide" (Mojab & Hassanpour 1995, 231–2). Although these policies were opposed by "minority" groups in Iran as hegemonic ways of erasing diversity and Persianizing the population, Persian hegemony has resulted in ethnic inequalities, such as mass poverty, a high level of illiteracy, and underdevelopment in various non-Persian provinces (Mojab & Hassanpour 1995, 234).

Following the Islamic Revolution of 1978–79, Islamic principles and ideology became influential factors and considerations in devising educational policies (Mohsenpour 1988, 83). The Islamization of Iran is considered as a modern "reaction" to the process of Westernization, conceptualized as *gharbzadegi* ("West-toxication" or "West-struckness"). It was initiated through the implementation of the "Cultural Revolution" that aimed at cleansing and purging the educational system (especially the universities) in terms of pedagogical goals, curriculum content, and staff that were considered to be *gharbzadeh* ("West-struck"), pro-Shah, non-Muslim, and tyrannical (Menashri 1992; Mohsenpour 1988; Rastegar 1995, 220; Sanasarian 2000; Shorish 1988). However, as Spivak reminded us:

> No perspective critical of imperialism can turn the "other" into an insider [i.e., the national self and the ideal citizen and a member of the "us" category] because the project of imperialism has always already historically refracted what might have been the absolutely Other into a domesticated Other that consolidates the imperialist self. (as quoted in Parry 2004, 20–1)

Furthermore, as Mazzini (as quoted in Bowden (2003, 355)) maintained, revolutionary movements often "seek to make the centre of the movement their own country or their own city. They do not destroy nationality; they only confiscate all other nationalities for the benefit of their own. [Their conception of] a chosen people" often homogenizes the past and limits reflections of diversity in the construction of who belongs to the nation and who does not (Abrahamian 1993, 60–110). Said (1994, 270–1, 298–9) also pointed out that being critical of imperialism needs to be read in the context of being critical of anti-imperialist movements and their hegemonic policies towards the Western "other," internal and external "minorities," and their constructions of insiders and outsiders across the world. That is, it is as important to note that the images of the self produced by non-Western "others," such as Iranians, also include constructions of other marginalized groups that may not reflect their voices and historical memories (Rahnema and Behdad 1995, 9).

I argue that despite the revolutionary propaganda of the Iranian state, the Islamic Republic does not represent the oppressed groups across the globe through balanced and emancipatory discourses that are sensitive to their struggles and histories. Despite the fact that the Iranian curriculum is very critical of the effects of colonialism in various parts of the world, especially in Asia and Africa, such representations of colonialism, I maintain, are discursive tools to demonize the West as the dangerous "other" without truly reflecting on how other marginalized groups have resisted colonialism and post-colonial structures. The positionality of the subaltern "others" within the context of global political economy, as narrated in Iranian school textbooks, points to the situational and dynamic position of the "other" as both oppressed and oppressor. The self-other image is no longer constructed based on (nonlinear) unlinear and dichotomous relations, but is based on multiple relations that are contradictory and segmented. The images of the self are perpetually inflicted by the images of the "other" that are no longer produced by the "other." Iranian national identity is constructed as a fixed and stable identity in relation to multiple shifting forms of otherness (collectivities). The self is compared to a set of shifting otherness and entities that are diametrically different from the self. These forms of otherness objectify for students what the self is not. The self is constructed in light of conceptions of others that represent them as abnormal and with stigmas that must be avoided.

Representations of the ideal Iranian citizen resemble what Baudrillard refers to as "simulacrum" (Seidman 1994, 210). Iranian school textbooks "no longer refer to any reality; they create the idea of a reality which simultaneously claim to represent it" (Seidman 1994, 210). The ideal citizen is constructed based on (re)representations of representations and images of various Oriental and non-Oriental "others" that are produced by other non-Orientals and Orientals for different purposes. Iranian school textbooks function as hegemonic tools of domination that identify the ideal Iranian citizen as the leader in anti-colonial and anti-imperialist movements without questioning the role of the Iranian self in promoting discrimination against various forms of internal and external self-other-other. It is through a patriarchal, religious-centric, and racialized conceptualization of Iran that Iranian elite groups' positions are legitimized through the normalization of conflicting binary oppositions in light of various socio-political and cultural discourses that continue to depict a homogenized, essentialized, and polarized world as official knowledge about Iran and other continents (countries). They divide the world's population into multiple groupings that are conceptualized according to a narrow understanding of the forces

of "good" and "evil" from both highly critical and ideological and dog-
matic perspectives. Despite the recent revisions of textbooks introduced
in 2001 based on the discourse of global education, the constructions
of otherness in Iranian school textbooks are racialized, nationalist, and
Islamic-centric narrations that problematize and highlight oppression
and diversity only as textual tools to dominate various forms of otherness. These forms of otherness are constructed in light of diametrically
opposite categories of exploiters and exploited that are positioned discursively in relation to Muslim revolutionary Iranians as the symbol of
an independent and free non-Western nation.

Iranian school textbooks are not simply based on a self-other dichotomy but invoke self-other-other constructions that are discussed/con-
structed in light of the discourses of whiteness, $b\bar{\imath}$-$\bar{\imath}m\bar{a}n^4$ (non-believer),
anti-God, $b\bar{\imath}$-$h\bar{\imath}j\bar{a}b$ (without ĥijāb), disorderliness, lack of cooperation,
and anti-leadership to distinguish between Iranians proper and others.
Yet school textbooks also distinguish between different forms of whiteness based on factors such as nationality, geographical location, religion, gender, ability, and levels of social, cultural, moral, and economic
development. Multiple racialized images in light of other political and
apolitical categories are presented through the invocations of these
diverse discourses that, in their dialectical and discursive relations to
one another, represent essentialized politicized relations between the
West and the East. The result of such discursive practices is "a particular kind of nation state ... organized increasingly as a fortress, with rigid
boundaries," rules, and regulations that determine who belongs in the
nation and who should be denied their civil rights (Razack 2008, 6).

The images of the oppressive and oppressed "others" that are incorporated into the construction of the ideal Iranian citizen are stigmatized
constructions that situate these "others" as the opposite of the normal
self that has freed itself from colonial and post-colonial forms of domination through faith in Islamic and revolutionary ideology. Stigmas
are bodily signs, historical characteristics, economic relations, moral
attributes, and religious and cultural practices that "expose" something
or someone (its bearers) as a "menace" and as something that should
be avoided due to the moral status of the signifier (Goffman 1963, 1).
Stigmatization occurs when an undesired differentness is attributed to
members of a group that results in their being excluded from inclusion
within the category "normal" (Goffman 1963, 5). They are feared.

The phobia of the "other" is based on constructing the "other" as
either unjust, unfair, or dominated. They are the ones who have been

exploitive and/or exploited. The "us" category is constructed in light of the discourses of liberty and freedom. The ideal citizen is depicted as male, Pars, White, Aryan, Shi'a, progressive, rational, and revolutionary through several contradictory discourses of Islamic leadership, Zionism, martyrdom, sacrifice, the family, 'ashayir (nomadic tribes), Ummat-i Islamī (Islamic nation/community), Īrān-dūstī (loving Iran), velayat-e-faqih (the most powerful religious-political office in Iran), colonialism, the Palestinian "other", and the Arab "other", all of which function as tools of domination, discipline, and normalization. If the self is a believer, then the "other" is a non-believer. If the self is modern, then the "other" is living in traditional and pre-modern conditions. If the self is peaceful, then the other is "warlike." If the self is also "warlike," it is only because "it" must defend "its fatherland" and "its" family due to the aggressive behaviours of the foreign invaders or their agents in the region. The self is differentiated from the "other" socially, politically, culturally, and geographically. The "other" is encapsulated and is identified as those who must be feared because they undermine the sovereignty of the nation and the state. The ways in which the ideal citizen is constructed and represented make that status unattainable for Iranian students whose identities are not reflected in school textbooks, and for some their ethnic, gendered, classed, racialized, and religious identities are depicted as (dangerous) "other"s who must be gazed at, controlled, and monitored. As Kelly (1998, 19) maintains, the process of gazing enables the dominant group to "control the social spaces and social interaction of" marginalized groups. Through the process of gazing, subordinated groups are simultaneously made visible and invisible.

Iranian school textbooks are informed by what I call *stigma-theorizing discourses* that are ideologically oriented to explain the inferiority of "others" in relation to the ideal citizen. They highlight the danger that the stigmatized "others" represent, and rationalize the animosity expressed towards the individuals or groups that are constructed as the "other" based on some differences that set them apart from the ideal citizen (Goffman 1963, 5). Goffman speaks of three different types of stigma, which can also be found in Iranian school textbooks. The first stigma that he highlights is the deformities of the body. The ideal citizen is an able-body individual who has full control of all his faculties and bodily functions. "Next there are blemishes of individual character perceived as weak will, domineering or unnatural passions, treacherous and rigid beliefs, and dishonesty, these being inferred from a known record of, for example, mental disorder, imprisonment addiction, alcoholism, homosexuality, and unemployment" (Goffman 1963, 4). There are several blemishes highlighted as stigmas that differentiate between the Iranian ideal citizen and the other. They are characteristics such as lack of cooperation, underdevelopment, *bī-ḥijāb*, *bī-īmān*, disorder, anti-leadership, disunity, anti-God, and non-modern. The final forms of stigma are the stigmas of "race," gender, ethnicity, nation, and religion, such as pagan religions, ethnic clothing, racialized facial characteristics, gender roles, nationality, and the "man-made" religions of the Baha'i faith. The stigmas of "race," gender, and ethnicity become important signifiers to differentiate within and between Iranians and non-Iranians that are given moral significance in light of the discourses of underdevelopment, *bī-ḥijāb*, and *bī-īmān*.

One of the most prominent forms of phobia that permeate the curriculum is the fear of being dominated by outsiders and non-Iranians, non-Muslim, non-Shi'a, and non-Aryans. This fear of being dominated correlates with the fear of being "duped" by foreign powers and their agents into submission. Yet the fear of being dominated does not coincide with a fear of losing cultural identity. As is clearly argued in the textbooks, despite being dominated by various world powers throughout its history, Iranian culture has always assimilated the foreign invading cultures rather than being absorbed by them. This myth of cultural survival is manufactured in light of another myth that constructs defence of the nation and country as a sacred historical practice, which requires excluding others from membership in the category of the ideal citizen. The fear directed towards the internal forms of otherness is presented in the language of development and modernization that highlights the role of the ideal citizen in assisting these forms of otherness to "enter the age of modernity." Equality and higher standards of life are the outcomes of programs and policies for rural, marginalized, and non-dominant populations that are identified as non-Persian and traditional. The role of the Islamic state is to help these groups to improve their social, economic, cultural, and economic conditions, not as ethnic "minorities" but as "noble savages" whose clothing, ethnicity, racial identities, religions, and cultural practices mark them as abnormal.

The end result of producing curriculum based on stigma-theorizing discourses and various discourses of phobia is what Pinar calls a *fractured self* (Pinar 1995, 23). This fractured self is also a *repressed self* (Pinar 1995, 23). It is a self that must hide its many internal selves-others and police them. The Iranian identity as a fractured self can never form a complete, unified, and firm self because its many forms of selves are denied and relegated to the status of "minority" and outsiders. Iranian school textbooks reproduce several notions of repressed selves that function discursively as political tools and as "ideological state apparatus" due to the segmentalized characteristics of identity politics. They are given specific meanings within school textbooks that function as both Orientalist and Occidentalist texts. This is the characteristic of the post-colonial self that is not aware of how the West and Western epistemologies remain important defining elements of itself. The Iranian self, then, is "instructed" to emulate the West not based on anti-oppressive Western and non-Western discourses, but according to imperialist agenda that uses religion to highlight the role of the Aryan-Pars group as the saviour of marginalized populations around the world, especially in the Islamic world. However, due to its Orientalist characteristics and Shi'a-centric views, it ends up separating the Iranian self from the collectivities that it attempts to free from the grip of Western imperialist domination.

The Phobias of Anti-God and Anti-leadership

Two of the most important phobias presented in Iranian school textbooks are the discourses of anti-God and anti-Islamic leadership. They are drawn upon to differentiate between the ideal Iranian citizen and non-Persians and non-Iranians and to exclude these other forms of self from membership within the category of the ideal citizen. Those who question the position of the Supreme Leader and the Islamic leadership must be feared, since they undermine the basic principles of the Islamic Republic, which is constructed as the highest evolution and form of Islamic governance since the proliferation of Islam in the seventh century. The discourse of leadership is based on the invocation of the idea of "Iran," symbolized as one's home, which needs to be protected from the influences of foreigners (i.e., the discourse of the enemy outsider) and their attempts to plunder its wealth and resources. The Islamic revolutionary period and the establishment of the Islamic Republic signify the Iranian nation's control over the administration of the country. The role of Iranians is to secure their revolution and independence by avoiding waste (the discourse of *isrāf* [wasting]) and by becoming prudent, parsimonious, and economical consumers (the discourse of *ŝarfa-jūī* [conservation]).

The category of leadership is conceptualized and depicted from a religious and nationalist perspective and within a hierarchal framework. The curriculum asserts that the leader is the legitimate heir of the Prophet. The role of the leadership within the Islamic Republic is equated to the role of the Prophet, who must be obeyed without dissent. Those who question this position are labelled as anti-God and anti-Islam. The textbooks emphasize that belief in God is the most important characteristics of the Islamic Republic government and its citizens (*Social Studies 5*, Ministry of Education 2004h, 135). God is identified as the supreme leader whose teachings and decrees all citizens must submit to. Students read that

> God is the creator of all creatures [*majūdāt*] and humans must obey [God] [*az ū itā'at kunand*]. God's commands [decrees] [*dastūr*] and laws [are communicated to] humans through the Prophets. The Prophet is the leader of society and obedience [*itā'at*] to [the Prophet] is obedience to God. After the Prophet, the leadership of the Islamic society is the responsibility of religious leaders [those who know religion] [*Pīshvā yan-i dīnī*]. In our time, the leader of the Islamic society has this responsibility. A government [*hukūmat*] in which Islamic laws are observed and its leadership is in the hands of a person who is [knowledgeable about] Islam is called the government [*hukūmat*] of the Islamic Republic. (*Social Studies 5*, Ministry of Education 2004h, 135)

Students are informed that there is a general consensus among the population that Islamic laws must inform private/public relations. The idea of freedom is conceptualized within the limits and confinements of Islamic laws, which is both a non-present and present trace informing the conceptualization of the ideal citizen. Freedom is contingent on the interpretation of the Quran and the Iranian Constitution by the Supreme Leader of Iran, who, by definition, is male and religiously learned. The Islamic Republic is reincarnated as the protector of Islam and Iranians in light of the discursive representations of the roles of Muslim clergies as major players in implementing modernization policies and resisting Westernization since the Qajar period (see below). The celebration of the clergy as the main and true followers of Islam and as leaders of the nation of Iran is epitomized in the status of the *vali-e faqih*, held by *Hazarat-i* (Excellency) Ayatollah Khamenei.

In a lesson entitled "Leadership," moreover, the Islamic Revolution of 1978–79 is depicted as a victorious social movement due to three main factors: its base belief (*īmān*) in God, the leadership of Imam Khomeini, and the unity of the people. Leadership of the Islamic

Republic is portrayed as the result of the will of the people and as the consequence of their agencies. In *Social Studies 3* (Ministry of Education 2004f), the transition of power after the death (*riħlat*) of Ayatollah Khomeini is narrated as the sign of continuity within the revolutionary leadership. After his death in 1989, in another lesson, the text states that *Ħazarat-i* Ayatollah Khamenei was chosen as the leader of the Iranian Islamic Revolution and took over the leadership of the Islamic country of Iran (*Social Studies 5*, Ministry of Education 2004h, 140–1). The leadership of Ayatollah Khamenei is depicted as the manifestation of the Ayatollah Khomeini's ideals and goals for Iran, which are identified as anti-colonial, anti-Zionist, and Islamo-centric (*Social Studies 3*, Ministry of Education 2004f, 33). The Iranian constitution is portrayed as a blueprint that assists the Iranian nation to achieve its goals and ideals based on Islamic laws and principles (*Social Studies 5*, Ministry of Education 2004h, 140). The leader of such an Islamic society is depicted as a pious man (*sic*). Students are informed that the leader must be a well-deserving and qualified (*shāyistah*) individual (*Social Studies 5*, Ministry of Education 2004h, 140). He must be knowledgeable (*'alam*) and fair (*'ādil*); must follow the commands of Islam in all matters; and must be aware of the state of affairs of society in order to lead and direct it in the most effective way (*Social Studies 5*, Ministry of Education 2004h, 140). The leader is identified as the ideal Moslem/citizen. The ideal citizen is supposed not only to love the nation, but also to express his/her love for both supreme leaders of Iran, and thus the state. This is an essential characteristic of the ideal citizen. Lack of such a love identifies one as an outsider who should be feared and controlled. Such individuals are *bī-īmān*, lack faith and, by definition, function as agents of colonialism and imperialism.

An important non-present trace in the above lessons is the discourse of *velayat-e-faqih* (religious jurist or jurist guardianship), as the "theoretical" base for the institutionalization of the *ulama*'s (clergy's) power over the state through the creation of the Office of the Supreme Leader, as the highest political position within Iran. *Velayat-e-faqih* is a narrative framework through which the textbooks celebrate the ascendency of Shi'a political Islam to the position of formal power in modernity without accounting for the fact that it is also based on a repressive ideology. It is a discourse that defines who should lead the nation and who should be led; who should listen; and whose voices must remain silent. The state, under the leadership of the *marja'-i taqlīd* (source of emulation), is seen as the symbolic representation of God's rule in contemporary

Iranian society. The state is viewed as the "reality of ethical life in the present" in accordance with the interpretations of the Islamic laws and customs, a task that only a *mujtaed* (senior cleric) is capable of achieving (Abrahamian 1993, 9). The rhetorical message of the Iranian Revolution is that Islam and an Islamic state are the solutions to poverty and that revolutionary Islam promotes a "class-less" society (Abrahamian 1993). But as the massacre of political dissidents during the 1980s and demonstrators in south Tehran during the 1990s attests, this modern Islamizing state has not hesitated to use force against oppositional political parties, unions, and poor and disinherited citizens, whom Ayatollah Khomeini in his speeches referred to as the *mustāżafin* (the oppressed) (Abrahamian 1993).

The discourse of *velayat-e-faqih* is a monologue rather than a dialogue that informs the narration of nation. The textbooks lack any discussion of the diversity of ideas about and controversies surrounding the role and legitimacy of that discourse. Many powerful religio-politicians who were involved in the administration of the revolutionary government argued that religious competence and knowledge were not the only necessary criteria for becoming the Supreme Leader (*Vali Faqih*). It was also assumed that such an individual must be knowledgeable as a *faqih* (jurist) about the political and economic issues that face the nation. However, a number of the *ulama*, who were qualified as *faqih*, argued that religio-politicians, who were mainly lower ranking clerics, did not meet these requirements. As Menashri (2001, 17) pointed out, after 1989 several amendments were made to the constitution that separated the positions of *marja'iyya* and *velayat*, thus allowing any *faqih* with "scholastic qualifications for issuing religious decrees" to assume the position of the Supreme Leader (articles 5 and 109). The 1979 stipulation (article 5) that the Supreme Leader be "recognized and accepted" by "the majority of people" (a requirement for the *marja'iyya*) was also dropped. At the same time, the new constitution stressed that preference must be given to those better versed in "political and social issues" (article 107).

As a result of these constitutional amendments, not only were the religious requirements for leadership lowered, but greater weight was placed on political experience as a criterion in selecting the male leader (Menashri 2001, 17). The concept of *velayat-e-faqih* and its principles in the post-revolutionary period have not simply been accepted as an unproblematic approach to leadership in the Islamic Republic. As Menashri (2001, 24–6) pointed out, there is division among the clerical leadership in terms of the position of *vali-faqih* under the Islamic Republic. Ganji referred to this religious government as a state that attempts "to impose governmental religion" on clerics who are critical of the state and its leadership and who advocate a separation between religion and state (as cited in Menashri 2001, 31). Many Iranians and young clerics have also been critical of the role of *velayat-e-faqih*. They argue that the *ulama*'s "political involvement is 'compromising their historic spiritual role' and that it would be better for Iran and Islam if the clergy 'returned to the mosques and left the task of government to professional politicians'" (Menashri 2001, 34). In this light, Soroush, who was one of the supporters of the Islamic Revolution, distinguished between religion and ideology (Menashri 2001, 33). As Tavakoli-Targhi (2000, 570) maintained, Soroush, who was involved in the process of the Islamization of the universities, questioned the "homogenization and totalization of the West" and considered the West, pre-Islamic Iran, and Islam "as constitutive components of modern Iranian culture." He maintained that religious ideas and modern views regarding human nature, natural history, and epistemology are closely related and "constitute[ed] 'parts of [the] circle'" (Vahdat 2002, 201). At the same time, Soroush argued that the "ideologization of religion" is a reflection of its "vulgarization and [has led] to its deterioration" (Menashri 2001, 33). He asserted that the contemporary understanding of the *Shari'a* is not reflective of the essence of the *Shari'a* in itself, but that one's understanding of the *Shari'a* is "historically situated" and is mediated through "the extra-Quranic cultural capital that informs juristic exposition" (Tavakoli-Targhi 2000, 571).

Lack of discussions and knowledge about controversies surrounding *velayat-e-faqih* reflect the view of dissention as dangerous and to be avoided. The fear of dissention is Islamized through the discourse of anti-leadership, which is depicted as a sign of opposition to the sovereignty of the Iranian state and the democratic choices of all Iranians who overwhelmingly voted for the establishment of the Islamic Republic soon after the revolution. This discourse finds meaning in light of an interrelated and important but non-present (trace) discourse of anti-God, which functions as a symbolic tool of phobia that elevates the leadership of the Islamic Republic, as the sole representative of God, who should be emulated and followed without question. This is not because the individual leadership should not be questioned per se, but because the rule of God and his wisdom and fairness must not be subverted under any circumstances. One who questions the leader is depicted as a dangerous *bī-īmān* outsider who must be gazed at and destroyed. This fear of the other who undermines the power of God, reflected in the establishment of the Islamic Republic and the idea of *velayat-e-faqih*, is a textual tool to justify violence and oppression by the ruling elite. As such, the self ends up fearing itself, since the only persons who can really be considered as ideal citizens and true leaders of Iran are those who possess the criteria espoused by the discourse of *velayat-e-faqih* and the ruling *ulama*. The phobia of dissention expressed in the discourse of anti-God highlights the inadequacies of Iranians, their unworthiness to be considered as full members of the society, as ideal citizens, as subjects with agencies. This fear of the self tears the self away from itself and creates a fractured self that is in the perpetual condition of incompleteness. It becomes an object of the gaze. It can never achieve a complete sense of normalness, and it is relegated to the category of abnormal.

It is important to note that although the self is torn away from achieving the status of the ideal citizen, it can still achieve membership in the categories of nation and Iranian. It is for this reason that, despite the prevalence of the discourses of anti-God and anti-leadership, school textbooks are not hegemonic tools that successfully legitimize the status of the leadership. Yet the curriculum reproduces the nation and the country as entities that must be respected, reproduced, and protected from enemies within in hegemonic religious ways based on the assumed characteristics of the ideal citizen, who is a pious Muslim and supports the leadership. The construction of knowledge about the nation, as an objective entity, relies on the invocations of phobias about anti-Muslims and anti-Islamic values and ideas. Any dissention is construed as undermining the will and efforts of the nation, the leader, and thus the commands of God.

Fearing the "Other": The Discursive Formations of Phobia

The discourse of leadership is an important aspect of the narration of nation that relates the ideal citizen to national and regional identities. It defines the limits of the discourse of "people," a term that is used to refer to all Iranians, regardless of religious, ethnic, gender, class, ideological, and political differences. Although one does not have to be a Shi'a Muslim to be included in the category "people," non-Muslims are textually excluded from membership in the categories of "leadership" and "ideal citizen." This is due to the fact that the constitution of the

Islamic Republic is depicted as a reflection of *Shari'a* laws and the will of God. Despite the fact that the ideal Iranian is defined as Muslim, non-Muslims are included in the category "Iranian" as *outsiders within*. As a member of the category "people," nevertheless, one is assumed to support the Islamic leadership and to be a believer in God. The construction of the leadership is also based on paternalistic discourses that exclude women from the role of leading the nation and the Islamic government. Women are not permitted to ever imagine themselves the leaders of the Iranian state, regardless of their levels of knowledge about Islam and Islamic jurisprudence.

An important non-present trace in the discourse of *velayat-e-faqih*, as a central component of the construction of the Islamic Republic and the discourse of leadership, is the discourse of the Baha'i "other" as the agent of the West and colonialism. As Tavakoli-Targhi argued,

> anti-Baha'ism and anti-communism provided the mechanisms for the transformation of religious piety into dissident political subjectivity. The discourse that is widely misrecognized as "Islamic Fundamentalism" [see also Abrahamian, 1993] was a product of an intricate and protracted process of de-familiarization of borrowed concepts and their re-circulation as Islamic and Qur'anic terminology. *Vilayat-i faqih* [*velayat-e-faqih*] is such a de-familiarized concept that it conceals its dialogic relationship to the Baha'i concept of *Vali-i Amr*. (2000, 569)

The textbooks identify the Baha'i people and religion and their impacts on Iranian political and intellectual history as the *internal enemy others*. They are portrayed as anti-Iranian and anti-Islam individuals who must be feared because they are also depicted as the agents of imperialism. In describing how the policies of previous governments during intense political and social changes – from the 1850s to the Constitutional Revolution of 1905–11 and culminating in the Islamic Revolution of 1978–79 – were detrimental to the country, and the extent to which such policies were resisted through the efforts of the *ulama* such as Ayatollah Nouri and Ayatollah Khomeini, the Baha'i religion is depicted as a manifestation of British colonialism. Baha'ism is constructed as a Western form of ideology influenced by Western modernist epistemology that undermined the sovereignty of Islam and Iran. In *History 8* (Ministry of Education 2004k), the Babi movement and the Baha'is are identified as perpetuators of socio-cultural change based on values and norms that promoted the interests of foreign powers. In a subsection of a lesson entitled, "Colonial Denomination/Sect Building" ("*Firqah Sazī Isti'mārī*"), the facts that Ali Mohammad called himself *Bāb* (gate), a person who is considered as the communicator between the people and the hidden Shi'a imam; declared himself the Messiah; and, finally, claimed to be a prophet are portrayed as blasphemous anti-Islamic acts. The rise of Baha'i religion is depicted as a sacrilegious social movement. Baha'ism is portrayed as a colonial conspiracy, resulting in chaos and disunity. Students read that the Russian and British governments were fearful of a unified Iranian nation and attempted to create divisions and to cause disunion (*tafragha*) among the population through their support of "man-made," false, and untrue (*durūgh-gū'ī*) religions such as Baha'ism and the Babi movement (*History 8*, Ministry of Education 2004k, 37). The murder of Sayyid Ali Mohammad, the leader of the Babi movement, who was executed by the order of Amir Kabir, is celebrated (*History 8*, Ministry of Education 2004k), and Baha'i Iranians are seen as enemies within who have been historically resisted and disliked by the Iranian "people" and its "pious" religious and liberal leaders. They are constructed as the "other" of the self who must be feared since their colonial and Westernized thoughts and actions have undermined Islam and the Iranian nation. They are the source and cause of disunity.

The silent "other" in these depictions is the Baha'i category despite the fact that they are mentioned and named in the text. They are othered in the sense that the Baha'i faith is depicted as a blasphemous religious-moral deviation from the true teaching of God and Islamic tradition. The movement is not considered an important social movement or a reflection of the wider diversity among the Shi'a majority of Iran (see Abrahamian 1982, 15). The reference to the Babi movement, as a manifestation of colonial policy, ignores internal divisions within Islam in modernity and the genocidal aspects of the nationalist discourse that have manufactured a homogenized and peaceful image of the ideal Iranian citizen. In fact, the other non-present trace is the silence of the textbooks about the massacre of Babi Iranians in Zanjan in 1851 by the order of Amir Kabir in "the name of Shi'a Islam" (Mackay 1996, 132). Such exclusions of historical facts result in "historical amnesia" that offer students a narrow, hegemonic, and homogenized understanding of their varied and contradictory national selves. In the same light, the textbooks do not discuss the violence experienced by the Baha'i people during the Pahlavi era and after the revolution (see Rejali 1994). This exclusion is a form and the result of what I call *textual genocide*, or the discursive exclusion of discussions about genocide and mass killing and representations of these issues in demonizing depictions of those massacred that take for granted the effects of prejudice on human relations.

This depiction of Baha'ism and lack of information about its adherents is especially problematic since it goes against the pedagogical message that students are introduced to in their *Persian 2* (Ministry of Education 2004b, 4, 49) textbook about peace and friendship among all people of the world. In the Persian textbooks, students are encouraged to talk about their ideals, norms, values, and understanding of various issues as part of the "class activities" sections. Inadvertently, in such assignments and homework, the identities of Baha'i students are placed under the gaze since their religious identities are intertexually categorized as anti-God. The term "people," thus, is not inclusive of the experiences of the Baha'i people and the extent to which they have experienced social injustice. It is a category that highlights only the experiences and views of those who support the ideology of the revolutionary leaders of Iran. The Baha'is can belong to the category "people" only when they hide their true sense of selves and identities.

The West, Baha'ism, and the Shah's government are not the only forms of enemy others that are highlighted in the textbooks. Students are also textually positioned against those internal groups who argued for the rights of women and "minority" individuals to be enshrined in the constitution during the 1960s and the Constitutional Revolution of 1905–1909. In *History 8* (Ministry of Education 2004k), the opposition of Ayatollah Khomeini to the reforms of the Shah's government is not only portrayed as anti-imperialist, but is also constructed in relation to his opposition to policies aimed at increasing the visibility of women and "minority" groups within Iran. The Shah's "White Revolution" is constructed and referred to as an imperialist ploy intended to subdue local social movements, undermining American attempts to establish a market for their industrial goods in the region (*History 8*, Ministry of Education 2004k, 72). Those who promoted these policies are portrayed as enemy "others" and agents of the West. They are blamed for altering the laws of Iran in October 1962 that enabled women to vote in the election of local councils. Students, then, are textually positioned to view these laws as undermining the legitimacy of Islam and the rights of the ideal citizen (*History 8*, Ministry of Education 2004k, 72), since this law and its consequences are portrayed from a paternalistic perspective as attacks on Islam and Iran. In reference to voting rights, students read: "It is obvious that in Iranian society of the time, even men did not have the real right to vote, in fact, the Shah wanted to deceive [*fārīb*] women and the public" (*History 8,* Ministry of Education 2004k, 72).

The non-present trace in this depiction of events is the views of Ayatollah Khomeini about this issue at the time:

> We do not object to women's progress. We are against this prostitution. We object to such wrongdoing. Do men in this country have freedom, that women should have it?
>
> Is progress achieved by sending four women to the *Majlis* [the National Assembly]? (as quoted in Esfandiari 2004, 138)

Ayatollah Khomeini's sexist construction of these events legitimizes the textbook authors' critique of "granting freedom to women" at the same time as it requires it. Women's issues are relegated to the margins of societal concerns in a religious nationalistic discourse that portrays the right to vote as a form of prostitution and an element of *gharbzadegi* (Westtoxication), and thus foreign to Iran and not supported by the majority of the population (see Esfandiari 2004, 138). Here, the rights and bodies of women become symbolic spaces through which the West and the East engage in imperialist and anti-imperialist relations. Women's bodies are depoliticized and women's voices are silenced as their concerns and political voices are depicted in light of the discourse of prostitution (which is also a non-present trace of this lesson). This prostitution undermines the moral reproduction of the Islamic nation and is not viewed as promoting progress. Progress, then, is understood in the context of the discourse of patriarchy that relegates women's issues to their sexuality as the source of their modesty. The role of women in demanding more freedom and improved legal protection against Islamic, traditional, and androcentric customs and mores is also overlooked and silenced. In fact, social studies and history textbooks do not mention any positive contributions by women to Iranian political economy. In a sense, women should be feared because they are easily manipulated and deceived by non-Muslims, agents of the West, and Western imperialist ideals. They are viewed as permanent internal otherness: women's involvements in political affairs are represented as sources of fear.

One of the few instances in which a woman is included in discussions about contemporary or historical socio-political events is presented in *History 8* (Ministry of Education 2004k, 38). This lesson introduces Amir Kabir, the prime minster of Iran during the late Qajar period (a Turkish dynasty), as a reform-minded Iranian who was concerned about the political stability of Iran and attempted to improve the economic, political, and social position of the country in the region. Students also read about the involvement of Naser al-Din Shah's[5] mother's (known as *Mahd-iUlya*) in Iranian political affairs. *Mahd-iUlya*'s politics are conceptualized as "interference" since she and members of the royal court conspired against Amir Kabir by influencing the Shah to replace him and order his assassination (*History 8*, Ministry of Education 2004k, 38). The textbook states that the colonial (*isti'mārī*) governments of Russia and Britain took advantage of the assassination of Amir Kabir and seized parts of Iran in the province of Khorasan and the city of Harat (*Social Studies 5*, Ministry of Education 2004h, 118). This loss of territory and undermining of Iranian sovereignty is blamed on such unpatriotic actions. The death of Amir Kabir also marks the point after which Iran granted major concessions in banking, natural resources, and customs (*gumruk*) to the British and Russian governments. This depiction of concessions to foreigners coincides with the representation of a female political figure as a mother and an internal enemy, whose ethnic and racial identity also categorizes her as non-Aryan. Her Turkish identity, as a descendant of the early Turkish tribal "immigrants" and an outsider within, inadvertently positions her against the ideal citizen, who is considered to be of Aryan/Pars and male origin (see below). As such, gender, religion, "race," and ethnicity are configured in depicting non-Iranian and non-Aryan reformers and rulers of Iran as undesirable. Such a representation is also based on the non-present trace that assumes, despite women's lack of direct political control at the societal level, they still manage to influence men within the context of private spaces with significant economic and political consequences.

Such a construction of historical events ignores the fact that, as Nashat (2004, 14) argued, conflict and tension between *Mahd-iUlya* and Amir Kabir might have been due to her relative power and influence within the court, which, in the opinion of Amir Kabir, was undermining patriarchal relations. She played an influential role in the ascension of her son to power. In fact, she was able to preside "over the state council and [to] maintain calm in the capital and nearby provinces," which enabled her son to arrive in Tehran from Tabriz and claim the title of king (Nashat 2004, 14). Amir Kabir interpreted *Mahd-iUlya*'s relative influence in political affairs as an "intrusion into the male world" (Nashat 2004, 14). Such a construction legitimizes the Irano-Islamic values of the time that viewed women's participation in public affairs and politics "with suspicion" (Nashat 2004, 13). Women's political involvement and the Babi social movement are depicted as sources of disunity and divisions: they are constructed as sacrilegious and anti-nationalistic.

The paternalistic depiction of women's issues in the narration of nation also finds expression in a discussion of Reza Shah's law banning women from wearing *ḥijāb* (Islamic dress) in public places, in a lesson entitled "The Dictatorship of Reza Khan" (*Social Studies 5*, Ministry of Education 1993b, p. 176). The authors explore how the regime used violence to deal with those who opposed his unveiling proclamation, especially the killing of those who demonstrated against this decree in the Goharshad Mosque in Mashhad (*Social Studies 5*, Ministry of Education 2000, 131). Reza Shah is described as an authoritarian leader and an agent of colonialism "who insisted that people emulate the outsiders (the West), even in the ways they dressed" (*Social Studies 5*, Ministry of Education 1993b, 176). The authors maintain that women were forced by the army, the police, and other coercive forces to unveil and dress in foreign and modern Western clothing. Women's modesty and self are constructed in light of adhering to and accepting covering their bodies, which are depicted as patriarchal public space that must be protected from Western elements and the influence of Western agents.

In addition to women as internal forms of otherness, religious "minorities" are also constructed as outsiders within. For example, the textbook authors emphasize that the decrees that attempted to extend voting to women during the early 1960s also allowed individuals of non-Muslim backgrounds to take oaths (*saugand*) on any holy book and not solely on the Quran (*History 8*, Ministry of Education 2004k, 72). Ayatollah Khomeini is identified as the first *marja'-i taqlīd* (the source of emulation) who opposed these measures, which, the authors claim, reflected the animosity of the Pahlavi state and the elite towards Islam (*History 8* Ministry of Education 2004k, 72). In this sense, it is also the West and its agents who are identified as fearing Islam, which is reflected in the policies that were implemented during the Pahlavi era. However, as Esfandiari (1997, 27) pointed out, the clergy's opposition to this law also stemmed from their resistance to any law that distinguished between Moslems and non-Moslems, especially the Baha'i people. In these lessons, rather than viewing such laws as ways of affirming diversity and dealing with gendered and religious inequalities, women and "minority" groups are treated as non-present enemy "others." As such, women and "minority" peoples, as internal forms of otherness, are important components of constructing the Islamic leadership as pious and the epitome of the ideal citizen.

Furthermore, in *History 8* (Ministry of Education 2004k, 46), in exploring the political events during the late Qajar era leading to the Constitutional Revolution of 1905–19011, the authors emphasize that the Iranian constitution was based on the ideals and values reflected in the constitutions of European countries. Such a negative Western influence, it is stated, resulted in the deviation (*inhirāf*) of the Constitutional Revolution of 1905–1911 (*History 8*, Ministry of Education 2004k, 51). The deviation of the constitutionalists is also reflected in their decision to execute Ayatollah Nouri, who is constructed as one of the most important leaders of the Constitutional Revolution. His Islamic leadership qualities are portrayed as guiding the nation in its struggles against colonial and *istibdādī* ("system of absolute and arbitrary rule") relations that are depicted as oppressive structures and as responsible for the plundering of Iranian wealth (*History 8*, 2004k, 51). The authors conclude that "This great martyr's analysis and understanding of the events were accurate and correct" since the people of Iran witnessed that the *Majlis* never passed Islamic laws (*History 8*, Ministry of Education 2002b, 51). The lesson ends with Ayatollah Nouri's response to a suggestion that he seek asylum in the Russian embassy: "After seventy years of serving Islam, is it now that I should seek protection under the flag of infidels [and non-believers] (*kufr*)?" (*History 8*, Ministry of Education 2004k, 51). Here, the love for one's flag is historicized in the context of the discourse of martyrdom and Islamic leadership. The non-present trace in this lesson is the discourse of "*Īrān-dūstī*" (loving Iran), which is implied by the reference to seeking refuge under the enemy "other's" flag, that constructs all those Iranians who have sought refugee status in various parts of the world since the establishment of the Islamic Republic of Iran as enemy others. Those who love Iran are willing to die for the country, as did Ayatollah Nouri. Those who seek refuge under the flag of other countries are traitors, deviants, and non-believers (*bī-īmān*). In addition, the constructions of these events become meaningful only in light of the discourse of the Western "other" as dangerous. However, the important element of this lesson is not the othering of the West, but the emphasis on Ayatollah Nouri's opposition to the constitutionalists, as West-toxicated elements. His actions are discussed in terms of the constitutionalist's deviation (*inhirāf*) from Islam and from God (*History 8*, Ministry of Education 2004k, 51). Fear of the national and global otherness is Islamized within the limits of the discourse of nationalism and patriarchal relations.

Family, Gender Roles, the Israeli and Palestinian "Others," and Phobias: Discourses of Disorder and Cooperation

Gendered phobia is reflected in how women's bodies are considered and treated as the source of contestation between male-centric forces of "good" (the Islamic Republic and its leadership) and "evil" (the West and their internal agents). It is also manifested in how fear of disorder informs the construction of gender relations within the family. The curriculum emphasizes the importance of order and its significance in an Islamic society. Disorder is considered as dysfunctional and a social condition that must be avoided and fought against. Through the discourse of family, Islamic society is characterized as an organized system in which stability, hard work, harmony, conformity to authority, and shared values and norms are highly prized: the family is considered as the backbone of an Islamic society. It is within the family setting and within the context of an Islamic vision of rights and responsibilities that children become familiar with their future roles as they are socialized about religion and good deeds. In such an Islamic setting, the ideal society consists of individuals who have a strong sense of their social responsibilities towards other family members and society at large. The ideal family is characterized as a caring and cooperative institution.

Family relations are viewed from a heterosexist, patriarchal, and religiously conservative perspective that excludes non-Muslim families as contributors to the nation-building process. Family life is constructed as the marriage between a man and a woman. Marriage between same-sex individuals is, thus, considered a form of disorder. The fear of homosexuality is the non-present trace in the construction of the ideal family (*Social Studies 3*, Ministry of Education 2004f; *Social Studies 5*, Ministry of Education 2004h). The construction of family also invokes the discourses of hegemonic masculinity and emphasized femininity. Men and women are imbued with specific characteristics and functions within the family that also reflect their natural positions within the wider society. The basis of the Islamic household is conceptualized on the assumption that society is made of different parts: each part is connected to various other segments that have specific functions and roles for the survival of the whole. The whole is represented in light of man's natural leadership position in society. The centre and core of the institution of family is defined as Islamic and patriarchal: the female body, power, and histories are placed outside the centre of power. Men are supposed to provide the basic material needs of family members.

Women are conceptualized as dependents and as the wards of patriarchal structures. The independence of women is a source of fear, thought to result in disunity and lack of cooperation in the family and nation (*Social Studies 3*, Ministry of Education 2004f; *Persian 5*, Ministry of Education 2004d, 182–4). An independent woman, like the West, undermines the assumed political, social, and cultural independence of the Islamic Republic. She, then, is conceptualized as a source of deviance that subverts the normalcy of male social order (read: hegemony).

The patriarchal ideology that informs the curriculum conceptualizes the presence of the father as necessary and essential and a gift from God. This hegemonic construction of masculinity is omnipresent. The division of labour is based on a private/public (*andarūnī/bīrūnī*) dichotomy that reflects the state's views regarding gender/sex differences. The father is the leader and controls the family's external affairs (*Persian 2*, Ministry of Education 2004b, 53). Iranian school textbooks explicitly state that children must perform their tasks and responsibilities without resistance to the leader of the family, who is represented as a fair and likeable individual. In a lesson entitled "How Do Members of the Family Consult with One Another?" (*Social Studies 6*, Ministry of Education 2004i, 34), the authors explain that fathers often ask for the opinions of their family members in making important decisions, such as renting or buying a house and when purchasing household items (*Social Studies 6*, Ministry of Education 2004i, 34). Fathers also transfer (give) some of the responsibilities of the household to mothers and respect their opinions (*Social Studies 6*, Ministry of Education 2004i, 34). The responsibility of the father in regard to household chores is "to prepare the tea; the brother is responsible to buy the bread; and the sister to set the table" (*Social Studies 6*, Ministry of Education 2004i, 26). The mother's role is to act as the manager of the internal affairs of the household (*Persian 5*, Ministry of Education 1993a, 211–212; *Social Studies 3*, Ministry of Education 2004f; *Social Studies 6*, Ministry of Education 2004i, 47). The discourse of motherhood is the framework within which a woman's worth is measured, and women's unpaid labour in the household is viewed in light of the discourses of unselfishness (see below).

Such constructions of gender relations promote a limited understanding of female citizenship that is anchored in private spheres of the family but within a discourse of social responsibility that cultivates a singular image of national citizenry: females as sources of morality due to their practice of *ħijāb*. Such conceptions of gender are also reflected in the legal codes of the country. As the current Supreme Leader of Iran maintained, "Islam authorizes women to work outside the household. Their work might even be necessary but it should not interfere with their main responsibility that is childrearing" (as quoted in Kian-Thiebaut 2005, 55). Men are given excessive privileges according to the civil codes on the "ground[s] that the economic function is the main attribute of men" (Kian-Thiebaut 2005, 55). The hegemonic aspects of the construction of leadership in light of paternalistic views within the family are also reinforced by how women are constructed in the textbook pictures and texts (Mirfakhraie 2011).

An important element of the discourse of order in the family is the act of cooperation. Cooperation in the family is one of the most important ideological messages that informs the construction of the Iranian self. A well-functioning family unit is one whose members cooperate with one another and adhere to strict forms of gender roles. Lack of cooperation is considered a sign of disorder that is reflected in aversion towards traditional gender roles. In a lesson entitled "Why Should We Cooperate in the Family?" a mother's daily tasks in the household include "the responsibility of washing the dishes and putting the breakfast items in their specific place" (*Social Studies 6*, Ministry of Education 2004i, 24–8). To avoid being stigmatized, students are told they should adhere to their essentialized roles that support a well-functioning society in which order is desired and required by God. The discourse of cooperation assumes that conflicts should be avoided and members of the family (read: nation) should follow the direction of the leader. In a lesson entitled "Unselfishness in the Family" (*Social Studies 6*, Ministry of Education 2004i, 53–56), students read that families face problems and family members should not only be concerned with their individual desires – they also must take into account and provide for the needs of other members of the family. The authors state that the roles and responsibilities of mothers are "to consider her children's success as her own success; if able, to help her children with school work and attempt to ensure her children's success in school" (*Social Studies 6*, Ministry of Education 2004i, 54). Mothers are constructed as caring individuals who are willing to sacrifice their own needs and dreams so that their children can achieve theirs. Mothers are also constructed as emotional individuals who are able to share the pain of their loved ones' defeats and lack of success in life. Cooperation and caring for one another imply accepting the status quo as something that is natural and normal. The non-present aspect (trace) of the discourse of cooperation is the discourse of *velayat-e-faqih* and androcentricity. Cooperation is another way of institutionalizing acceptance of male authority and the dictates of the leaders of the family and nation. Students read that the leader is an important person who acts in the best interests of the group and is concerned with the needs of group members. The members of the group, in return, must obey his commands (*Social Studies 6*, Ministry of Education 2004i, 45). Lack of obedience is viewed as an element of disorder that undermines the power of the leader and the goals of the Islamic state.

The supposed and mystical order and equilibrium within the family and within the country and Islamic community is viewed as natural and in accordance with God's will. Men are considered as the leaders of families, protectors of households, and representations of God. Anything that undermines this equilibrium is discursively considered as abnormal. Those who disrupt or cross the borderlines of such rigid constructions are feared. In a lesson entitled "What is the Role of Family in Our Lives?" (*Social Studies 6*, Ministry of Education 2004i, 17), the authors talk about those families that have lost their fathers in the Iran-Iraq War, to natural causes or, like the Palestinians, due to the barbaric actions of the oppressive regime of Israel. In this lesson, fatherhood is conceptualized as a blessing (*na'mat*) (*Social Studies 6*, Ministry of Education 2004i, 47). In reference to the Palestinians whose fathers have been martyred, students are instructed that "All Moslems will assist these Moslem Palestinians to revenge the deaths of their loved ones" (*Social Studies 6*, Ministry of Education 2004i, 47). That is, the responsibility of family members includes seeking revenge for injustices against their leaders, which in this case is defined from a nationalistic perspective in light of global relations and the idea of *Ummat-i Islamī* (Islamic nation/community). "Revenge" is partly a reflection of cooperation and caring among Muslims and the act of loving the "Nation of Islam."

"Revenging" the murder of Palestinian Muslim "brothers" assumes that they are a homogenous group. As well, the non-present trace in this reference is the assumption that the Jewish people are now confronted with the hegemonic presence of Zionism. Zionism is considered to be the global symbol of Jewish politics. The Israeli "other" must be feared not because they are Jewish but because of Zionist politics and Israel's invasion of Palestine. The textbooks rely on the discourse of "us" and "them" that bifurcates the Semite people into two objectively distinct categories. They are not viewed as two interrelated groups with shared historical and cultural sentiments. Fearing the Israeli "other" also results in denying voice to the progressive elements of Israeli society and "minority" Jewish communities, which eliminates any possibility of bridging cultural and political gaps and attempts to create solidarity with factions within the Israeli society that want to promote democracy in Israel. The fear of the "other" due to his/her aggressive and dehumanizing practices towards Palestinians since the 1920s also ignores how the Zionist "other" discriminates against internal "other" Jewish communities based on factors such as "race," immigrant status, and religious factions.

The Zionist "other" plays an important role in situating the Iranian ideal citizen as a leader in the Middle East and anti-oppressive movements, enabling Iranian leadership to construct themselves as the leader of the transnational Muslim family unit via another "other," the Palestinian self. The Zionist "other" is presented as a fixed point, an ideology, and as claiming a historical landmass that has been unjustly occupied due to colonial and imperialist policies. It is not constructed as an entity that should be engaged, deconstructed, or defragmented, but as a unified object of gaze that must be challenged due to its hegemonic policies towards the Palestinian self-other as an example of the global/Muslim oppressed who need the assistance of Iranians to be freed from the shackles of domination. This phobia of the state of Israel is not due to that entity's inherent characteristics, but to Israeli practices that deny the achievement of stability, order, freedom, and democracy for the family/nation of Islam.

Racialization, Phobia, and Stigmatization: Non-Whites, Ethnic "Minorities," and the Narration of Nation

The emphasis on order and continuity in narrating the history of nation is related to how racialized stigmas and phobias inform the construction of the ideal citizen. The discourse of Iran as "the land of Aryans" is both a present and non-present trace in the narration of nation and all the lessons about Iran and Iranians. "Iran" is explicitly defined as "the land of Aryans" in *History 6* (Ministry of Education 2004j, 34) and *Social Studies 4* (Ministry of Education 2004g, 79). In reading about the founding nation of Iran, students are informed that

About four thousand years ago, tribes that called themselves Aryan came to our land from the Northern parts of the Caspian Sea. They settled in the green and fertile pleasant [*khurram*] plains [*dasht*] and mountainous pastures.

Since then, our land was [is] called Iran. The Aryans were [consisted of] three groups: Medes, Parthian and Pars. These groups settled in different regions of Iran. (*Social Studies 4*, Ministry of Education 2004g, 86)

After strengthening their [control over the governance of the country], the Medes kings began to oppress people and [to engage] in pleasure seeking [activities]. Consequently [and as a result of the exploitation of the people by the kings of the Medes tribe and their excessive lifestyles], [the Medes] government became weak and the people also stopped cooperating with [their kings]. During this time, the leader of the [Pars tribe] whose name was Cyrus [Achaemenians dynasty, 550–331 BCE] took advantage of this weakness and went to war with the Medes. Ultimately, he defeated them and became the King of Iran. (*Social Studies 4*, Ministry of Education 2004g, 88)

The construction of Iranian heritage in light of the history of Aryan migration achieves two objectives. First, Iranians and European imperial powers are conceptualized as originating from the same ethno-racial backgrounds. Second, the Iranian branch of the Aryan is distinguished from other Aryan backgrounds due to the Pars heritage of Iranians and their ability to establish the first world empire. The Persian ethnic group is identified as the rightful founding nation of Iran, and the category "Iranian" as the dominant ethnic group. In differentiating between various groups of Aryans, the Pars category is depicted as the centre of the Aryan segmented identity, which is composed of several competing selves: the Iranian self, the Indo-European self (occupying northern India), the European/Western self, the Parthian self, the Medas self, and the Pars self. The main message of the textbooks is that despite being dominated by a number of ethno-racialized groups (i.e., Turkish "immigrants," Arab and Greek rulers, and non-Shi'a dynasties) Iranians, due to their Pars Aryan civilization, have continued to dominate the invader "others," culturally and politically. As mentioned, the category "Pars" is the trace in all the discussions about the category "Iran." Another important non-present trace in these depictions of the birth of Iran is the argument that the name "Iran," denoting a nation state in modernity, also refers to the same geo-political boundary some thirty-five hundred years ago. According to Vaziri (1993), this misconception is based on the incorporation of Orientalist knowledge about the national identity.

The discourse of Aryan migration is Persianized from a nationalist perspective that also invokes the discourse of whiteness as the most important characteristic of the ideal citizen. That is, the discourse of the Aryan ancestry is a framework that legitimizes the whiteness of Iranians. It functions as a racialized trace that distinguishes between insiders and friendly outsiders without directly discussing "race." It is through this construction of Iranians as white and as the same "stock" as the Europeans, but at the same time different from them due to cultural and religious factors, that Iran is situated in relation to the world's civilizations. The ideal citizen is constructed as descending from the likes of Cyrus the Great, who allowed for the coexistence of various local cultures, such as "the Hebrews whom the Persians encountered in Babylon" (Tragert 2003, 41). The Achaemenians empire is characterized as a liberating political system due to the importance of equality, honour, and freedom among the "Aryans" (*History 6*, Ministry of Education 2002a, 40; *Iranian and World History 1*, Ministry of Education 2005, 58, 59). This discourse helps to convert the identity ambivalence of Iranians into an objective and knowable form that provides Iranians a framework and some measure of control about who they are and where they come from in the context of modernity (see Ward 2001, 64). The construction of the Aryan birth also reifies "race" as an objective category of human grouping. It reproduces Orientalist discourse about the self that ends up othering the Iranian self as the "other" in the discourse of Orientalism. As such, it mimics the stigmas that Europeans associated with non-Westerners (i.e., despotic, irrational, and traditional). The Aryan discourse is used to distinguish Iranians from other invaders, at times despite their supposed shared Aryan ancestry (i.e., the Greeks). This racialized knowledge about the self historicizes the desire to defend one's country by emphasizing the role of the Pars tribe in preserving Iran from the influences of historical and contemporary foreign elements (*Social Studies 4*, Ministry of Education 2004g; *History 6*, Ministry of Education 2004j).

The emphasis on Orientalist knowledge as the basis of Iranian national identity is a reflection of phobia of the "other." It is a manifestation of the fear of being categorized as non-white and thus as "uncivilized" and non-modern. Whiteness is a discourse employed to deal with the negative connotations of being labelled as the "other" in the imperialist discourses of domination. It is based in the anxiety associated with being placed outside history. Textually, it subverts the Iranian "other" and renders it equal or superior to the European self because of its Persian and Muslim characteristics. Whiteness also separates the Iranian self from various forms of otherness that are also talked about and imagined in the discourse of Orientalism. As such, the emphasis on whiteness reflects the fear of being associated with characteristics such as disorder, "simplicity," "ignorance," and "savagery." The non-white other, thus, is also excluded from having inherent rights to the nation and national space. For example, despite the fact that non-Iranian Arabs (external Arabs) are depicted as white-skinned people, Arab Iranians are represented as having darker skin (see below). Skin colour is employed to exclude Arab-Iranians from the founding nation of Iran due to their non-Aryan origin. They are placed outside of power. To construct the ideal Iranian as white but never critically problematize this construction is a racist discourse and a central aspect of phobia. Fear of the "other" finds manifestations in racially charged views that distinguish between the self and the other and legitimize these differences as historical truths about Iranians and otherness. The birth of the nation is glorified in light of whiteness as both a present and non-present trace that excludes critical discussions on how various forms of historical non-Persian ethnic identities have been shaped and affected due to the policies of the Pars group (read: Persian majority). The cultural, political, and social supremacy of Iran and Iranians is maintained through a racialized narration that normalizes the whiteness of Iranians as a historical fact and categorizes other groups as different. Persians are depicted as simply humans. Iran is portrayed as more "civilized," an important geographical space, and the most influential centre of Islamic and scientific explorations/knowledge (*History 6*, Ministry of Education 2004j, 51; *Social Studies 4*, Ministry of Education 2004g; Mirfakhraie 2011).

Iranian school textbooks also offer racialized images of Asia and the rest of the world (*Social Studies 5*, Ministry of Education 1993b, 64–9; 2001, 47–52). Asians, for example, are divided into identifiable categories of difference. Each raced group[6] is associated with specific geographical areas:

> More than half of the world's population lives in Asia. [They are mostly yellow skins than white skins]. A number of black skins are also seen [i.e., live] in Asia. In some parts of Asia, white skins have mixed with yellow skins and blacks ... The people belonging to each [*tīrah*, racial group] speak their specific language. (66–7)

The discourse of whiteness intersects other discourses in positioning the Iranian self in relation to other peoples. Contemporary Asians are constructed by reference to four criteria of difference/sameness: "race" (*nizhād*), religion, civilization, and culture (*Social Studies 5*, Ministry of Education 1993b, 64–9; 2001, 47–52). In fact, the three categories of "race," language, and colour of skin are intersectionally used in the depiction of diversity in Asia in such a way as to demonstrate how similar (i.e., sharing anti-colonial attitudes with a strong base in religious beliefs) and different (due to colour of skin, racial composition, and religious diversity) Iranians are from other Asians (*Social Studies 5*, Ministry of Education 1993b, 69). However, the two most important criteria considered in categorizing the population in Asia are "race" and religion. The textbooks portray the majority of Muslims as "white skin," Brahmans as "black skin" or hybrid (black and white), and Buddhists as mainly "yellow skin." The reification of "race" and its association with specific geographical locations and religions functions as a hegemonic tool since the most important Muslim white group is intertextually defined and objectified as the Pars-Aryan-Shi'a category. Also, these categories of sameness are depicted without any reference to internal divisions, diversities, and conflicts and their effects on "white" Muslims groups or "yellow-skin" Buddhist groups. In these representations, Iranians are intertextually distinguished from other groups due to their Indo-European characteristic. At the same time, Indo-Europeans in northern India are portrayed as different from Black Dravidians in the south and mixed "white and black" and "black and yellow" Indians. The racial "purity" of the Pars group is assumed through such constructions.

The division of Asia's population into discrete religious and skin-colour categories is also reinforced through textbook pictures of these various groupings. These pictures are not simply apolitical representations of "diversity." They essentialize facial characteristics of non-Iranian and non-Aryan Asians and portray them as objective representations of diverse groups of people that are specific to a time/space without critically accounting for facial, skin colour, linguistic, class, cultural, religious, and political diversities within each group. Diversity and difference are turned into homogenized constructed images of sameness that have political consequences. The representation of Iranians as white and Muslim inadvertently views them as superior to other Asians such as the Dravidian category, which is presented as non-white, non-Aryan, non-Indo-European, non-Muslim, slim, partly clothed, rural, and traditional. The inclusion of pictures of most Asians in their traditional clothing reproduces stereotypical snapshot representations of the "authentic" others that are assumed to represent the "other" eternally and accurately in the late twentieth and early twenty-first centuries. These pictures reproduce Orientalist and imperialist attitudes that have historically depicted Asia as undeveloped, poor, non-industrialized, and traditional. Clothing, in this sense, symbolizes tradition, understood as lack of industrialization, within "non-Western modernity." In these depictions of Asia, the West is also represented as a homogenized dangerous imperialist "other" in relation to the segmented Asian selves, who are also depicted as homogenized groups. Exclusion of diversity within each oppressed and oppressor group constructs them as essentialized entities, which "reduc[es] the complex identity of a particular group to a series of simplified characteristics and den[ies] individual qualities" (Henry, Tator, Mattis, and Rees 2000, 408). Essentialism is "the [crude] reduction of an idea or process to biological or cultural characteristics," or, in this case, to rural/urban and modern/non-modern dichotomies (Henry et al. 2000, 408). Asia is thus constructed as a set of traditional societies that lack modernization due to the effects of colonialism. The discourse of modernization is an important non-present trace in these representations of Asia, a discourse that assumes and requires a certain degree of cultural change in order to consider a society as advanced and "modern." That is, the cultural values or religious beliefs of Asians are not celebrated, but their lack of forms of modernity that characterize technologically advanced (Western) societies are highlighted. This fear of being labelled as technologically "backward" is a central message of textbooks that informs the role of Iranian students: the aim of all Iranians must be to develop the country. The ideal student is one who studies hard and assists in developing and defending Iran (the discourse of martyrdom), by following rules and accepting his or her leader's commands (*Social Studies 3*, Ministry of Education 2004f, 38). Citizens who are not brave, are not chivalrous, and do not contribute to the economic independence of Iran are textually constructed as outsiders within. Emphasis on technological development and economic independence is based on the phobia of being dominated by outsiders, since efforts to foster independence have historically been undermined by foreign enemies and their internal agents, such as the kings of the Pahlavi dynasty (1924–79) and the Baha'is (*Social Studies 3*, Ministry of Education 2004f, 37–38). The fear of being dominated and attacked by foreigners is used as a tool to demand obedience to the Islamic leaders.

Related to the above issues is how space is represented and constructed for students. Geographical space is depicted as enclosed territories, not based on imagined national boundaries materialized as "lines" on various maps of the world. Geographical space is also represented through religious divisions that divide the population of various countries into discrete and identifiable categories with diverse belief systems without explaining the basis of their values and worldviews. These images of diversity are coded with racialized images that are based on biological distinctions of raced groups and portrayed in light of anti-colonial sentiments that profess economic and political independence without accounting for the multifaceted effects of such relations. The outcome is the "territorialization" of difference and its essentialization in terms of characteristics that are imposed on both Iranians and non-Iranians. According to Grossberg (1993) , "a territorializing machine distributes subject positions in space" (100) that in the context of Iranian school textbooks become objectified, knowable, and distinguishable based on real moral and ethical principles. Such a machine "diagrams lines of mobility and placement; it defines or maps the possibilities of where and how [students] can stop and place themselves" (100).

"Race," Ethnicity, Internal Otherness, and Stigma:
The Discourse of 'Ashayir

The inclusion of the tribal "other" as a topic of curriculum marks out another important defining element of the ideal citizen. Ethnic diversity is explored in the context of discussions of pastoral nomadism and animal husbandry (*Social Studies 5*, Ministry of Education 2004h, 15–16). Students learn that tribes are called '*ashayir* and live all over Iran (*Social Studies 3*, Ministry of Education 2004f, 12–14). Students are also informed that "Iran belongs to all of them" and, regardless of where they live in Iran, they are all Iranians and must "like [*dūst-dārīm*] Iran and Iranians" (*Persian 1*, Ministry of Education 2004a, 118). Loving the nation is central to constructing phobias about otherness. Colour-of-skin distinctions and rural/urban differences are also employed in portraying cultural and population diversity within Iran. In fact, ethnic diversity is often portrayed through traditional clothing and geographical locations/spaces (*Persian 1*, Ministry of Education 2004a, 48). Style of dress is used to depict ethnic "minorities" or non-Persians in rural settings (*Persian 3*, Ministry of Education 2004c, 24; *Persian Writing 3*, Ministry of Education 2004e, 106). In various lessons and textbooks, tribal boys and girls are represented as different through their traditional clothing, which identifies them as members of the '*ashayir*, yet similar because they are Iranian. They are not presented as city-dwellers. Such depictions imply that outside their rural regions and without their traditional clothing, non-Persian (read: non-Iranian) ethnicities do not exist. The clothing of the tribal people is a stigma symbol, implying that a group and its members are non-Pars (outsiders within), non-modern, and in need of assistance (*Social Studies 4*, Ministry of Education 2004g, 128–9).

The diversity of pastoral nomads is reduced to the term *'ashayir* (nomadic tribes) and its ethnic connotations are eradicated. The *'ashayir* is not composed of nations. Rather, the general term *mardum*, denoting all "people," is used, which does not refer to one's national/ethnic origin. The main ethno-national identity that is associated with the term *mardum* is the category "Iranian" (read: Pars-Aryan). The *'ashayir* are portrayed as brave (*shujā*) and heroic (*dalīr*) people, who "serve the country through animal husbandry and God forbid, if the enemy attacks Iran, these people [*mardum*] will defend the boundaries of our nation" (*Social Studies 3*, Ministry of Education 2004f, 12–14; *Social Studies 4*, Ministry of Education 1999, 137). In fact, students learn that "some of them participated in the tribal *Basīj* organization. Tribal *Basīj* plays an important role in protecting the boundaries of our Islamic country" (see *Social Studies 3*, Ministry of Education 2000, 14). The "roles" of the *'ashayir* and their economic and civic obligations to the state are not only to defend Iran's borders but also to produce agricultural goods and dairy products for the nation. However, their tribal and sub-tribal identities remain secondary to their constructions, as they are depicted as "Iranians" and not, for example, as specific national/cultural nations, such as Baluch or Kurd. The *'ashayir* is simply one apolitical group amongst many more that form the nation (see Beck 1991). Despite acknowledging that Iran is culturally diverse, the textbooks depict Iran as a country with a homogenized population (i.e., descendants of the Aryans).

The apolitical discourse of *'ashayir* is reinforced through representations of the Iranian nation as a household/family and of the Islamic constitution, as symbols of Islamic morality, cooperation, and justice that protect all Iranians as long as they obey the rule of God and the Islamic leadership (see *Social Studies 4*, Ministry of Education 2004g, 128–9; *Social Studies 5*, Ministry of Education 1993b, 214; *Farsi 3*, Ministry of Education 2004). Contemporary Iran is immortalized as a revolutionary state and depicted as "a Moslem nation that has a shared constitution, flag, national anthem, [language] and calendar"

(*Social Studies 4*, Ministry of Education 2004g, 129, 130, 131, 132,143; *Persian 1*, Ministry of Education 2004a, 116; *Persian 2*, Ministry of Education 2004b, 103–5). The authors inform students that regardless of their ethnicities, "race," gender, social classes, and religious differences, all Iranians are protected by the laws of the country: it is in the context of Iran as a stable Islamized nation state that the rights of the *'ashayir* are protected. In other words, the authors imply that the *'ashayir* have chosen to join the Islamic and revolutionary nation of Iran due to the rights and privileges afforded to them since the Islamic revolution. The Islamic Republic is constructed as the ideal society with unified citizens who have common goals. Ethnic differences are normalized and viewed as reflections of cultural differences rather than as manifestations of deep political divisions within the nation. Ethnicity is constructed as non-pathological only when it is perceived to be local, peaceful, and nationalized.

Ethnicity, as a stigma symbol, is also imbued with "previous knowledge about it," such as the fact that these groups have never legitimately ruled Iran and are not its founding nations. These attributes are highly discrediting of the groups' authentic selves: they have no historical right to Iran and its resources. For example, as mentioned, the depiction of the Arab "other" in his traditional clothing and by references to skin colour differentiates him or her as an outsider within in relation to the modern Aryan/Muslim who is, by definition, white (*Persian Writing 3*, Ministry of Education 2004e, 106). This is a racist construction that reduces the internal Arab "other" to blackness, which is often depicted in light of the discourses of slavery, poverty, colonialism, and hunger in other lessons about Africa and the United States (Mirfakhraie 2011). The Arab "other" is feared. This is especially the case since Arab incursions into Iran (excluding the introduction of Islam to Iran by Arabs) are viewed in a negative light by depicting the invaders as villains who were resisted and disliked. Iranian students are not presented with positive images of Arabs before the introduction of Islam to Arabia. The Arab "other" is constructed as the enemy outsider whose religion was paganism: they had already been separated from the real teachings of God. The only time the Arab "other" is positively depicted is when the authors of history and social studies textbooks discuss the period when Islam was introduced to both Iran and Arabia. The term *Arab* is de-emphasized only when depicting Muslim "attacks" on Iran. Rather, the text states that the Muslims attacked the Sassanids government and not the Iranian nation (*millat*).

There are several main images of the Arab "other" that are constructed in relation to Iran and Iranians: the pagan and ignorant Arab, the "dangerous" tribal Arab, the friendly wise Arab, and the "ruthless" Muslim-Sunni Arab. These constructions relate to the following statements: Iran (the land of Aryans) was "raped" (*tajāvuz*) by dangerous pre-Islamic Arabs; Iranians had consensually protected the wise Pre-Islamic Arab groups; the Muslim Arabs saved Iran since Iranians in Arabia belonged to the first "army" of the community (nation) of Islam; and the Arab Sunni Muslim leadership exploited Iran. Arabs are different from Iranians not due to Sunni and Shi'a differences alone, but also to the apparent Indo-European (non-Semite) heritage of Iranians (*Social Studies 4*, Ministry of Education 2004g, 104–5; *History 6*, Ministry of Education 2004j, 67; *Social Studies 5*, Ministry of Education 2004h, 95–7). In fact, Iranian students are informed that Arabs and other invaders have historically relied on Iranians for cultural, scientific, and economic knowledge (*Social Studies 5*, Ministry of Education 2004h, 98).

In representations of Iran, ethnicity, religion, Aryan ancestry, and rural and urban diversity/differences are intertwined in depictions of the ideal citizen and of who has historical and political legitimacy to rule Iran. Such depictions are not inclusive of diversity, but rather homogenize diversity based on a romanticized conception of the "other" and his or her relationship with the land and nature, without accounting for how this relationship has been mitigated by the state's economic and modernization policies and the Iran-Iraq War, resulting in the migration of many ethnic groups into major urban centres. These representations of ethnic diversity are based on a non-political worldview that sanitizes the conflicts experienced by ethnic/tribal groups. Even in discussing the reforms of the Pahlavi governments that had devastating effects on tribal groups in Iran, the authors focus on the effects of other elements of the Westernization programs of the two Pahlavi kings. In *Social Studies 5* (Ministry of Education 1993b, 176; 2004h, 124–5), for example, Reza Shah is portrayed as anti-Islamic, ruthless, illiterate, and as an agent of the West. Reza Shah's banning of the *ḥijāb* from public places is discussed. The non-present trace in this lesson is the reaction of the *'ashayir* to Reza Shah's "dress reforms ... [that] reflected his Europeanizing policies. All Iranians including Persians were forced to wear versions of European dress" (Beck 1990, 206). The text ignores the Persian-centric aspects of this policy. In fact, this royal decree regarding clothing reinforced and exacerbated the division between the modernized/Westernized and "the rest of the society, which resented the intrusion in their lives" (Chehabi, as quoted in Keddie 2003, 100). "Minorities", in particular, viewed the decree as a way for the state to enforce its policy of Persianizing the ethnic population by stripping from them their traditional forms of clothing as indicators of cultural/ethnic membership and identity. In the textbooks, traditional clothing is used as a marker to distinguish between Iranians without accounting for the consequences and effects of the Shah's dress policy, which was a racist policy, based on cultural assimilation assumptions about diversity. The anti-hegemonic histories of ethnic groups do not find expressions in the narration of nation, out of fear of acknowledging the politics of ethnic nationalism. The Islamic Republic disregards their political aspirations through invocation of a nationalist Islamized discourse that assumes the Persian culture and majority define the limits of the dreams of the nation.

The authors of the textbooks do not completely ignore ethnic uprisings. In *History 8* (Ministry of Education 2004k, 88), in a subsection entitled "Plots/Conspiracies [*tauti'ah*] and Problems/Difficulties [*mushkilāt*]" that covers events from the establishment of the Islamic Republic to 1988, ethnic and political unrests are mentioned. These topics are discussed in light of the discourse of "problems initiated by small groups of thugs." The history of ethnic resistance against present and past governments is sanitized by depicting these uprisings as the outcome of the small-scale activities of pockets of *guruhak* (groups), influenced by outside forces. Ethnic resistance is equated with destruction: the members of these *guruhak* "burn[ed] villagers' agricultural products ... [and] also martyred a number of great *ulama* such as Ayatollah Motahari and Dr. Beheshti amongst many more" (*History 8*, Ministry of Education 2004k, 93). These two "martyrs" were assassinated by the Mujāhidīn Khalq-i Iran, a political group that supposedly took responsibility for killing more than seventy members of the government and the Majlis (the parliament). By equating ethnic uprising with the actions of the Mujāhidīn-i Khalq, the authors equate ethnic nationalism with the "terrorist" actions committed by a political group. From this perspective, all past, present, and future ethnic uprisings are considered as acts of "terror" against the nation of Iran and Islam by enemy insiders/outsiders. In other words, any ethnic uprising is viewed as undermining the sanctity of the nation of Iran, and as such is categorized as un-Islamic, anti-God, and anti-leadership. Ethnicity is indirectly pathologized and the members of a given group depicted as *bī-īmān* (unbeliever) individuals who do not possess a sense of loyalty and love for the nation of

Iran. They must then be avoided and destroyed: they are "disorderly" and in need of "discipline."

An interesting factor that keeps emerging is that internal and regional external others are often constructed by reference to their relations with the West, especially the United States (*Social Studies 5*, Ministry of Education 1993b, 192–3; 2001, 137–9). The authors state that, as a result of the victory of the Islamic Republic, the interests and imperialist position of Western powers were undermined in Iran and other parts of the world (*History 8*, Ministry of Education 2004k, 93). Anti-government activities are associated with the activities of those outsiders who want to interfere in the internal affairs of Iran. For example, America's attempt to rescue their hostages in the early 1980s and the Iran-Iraq War are conceptualized as a source of "conspiracies and problems" that Iranians have had to face since the Islamic Revolution of 1978–79 (*History 8*, Ministry of Education 2004k, 93). The political groups that oppose the central government are also labelled as agents of imperialist and foreign powers. As Spivak (as quoted in Dei, Karumanchery, and Karumachery-Luik 2005, 55) pointed out in reference to India, "It seems that [Iran] is often positioned as the other of the 'West,'" but in reality it is constructed against many other "things." It is also an internal 'us' [us among many others]" (Dei, Karumanchery, and Karumachery-Luik 2005, 55). Iranian identity is constructed in the context of historical elements that are "negotiated in relation to other [historical] identities that are [depicted as] inherently unequal" and are othered in the process (Dei, Karumanchery, and Karumachery-Luik 2005, 55). In these textbooks, "difference is not only constituted dialectically relative to the [imperialist] other [or various forms of anti-imperialist others], but also within the [ideal citizen and the] self" (Dei, Karumanchery, and Karumachery-Luik 2005, 57).

Conclusion

Narrations represent romanticized images of the ideal citizen that discursively reproduce official stories about the dominant culture (Hall 1996, 613). Narrations consider certain events, individuals, and cultural artefacts as important; they elevate the dominant society "to the status of legend" (Francis 1997, 11); and they idealize the founding nation(s) by demonizing otherness. The narration of Iranian nation represents certain local and global groups, such as Euro-Westerners, women, Arabs, the state of Israel, tribal pastoral nomads, and the global Muslim community, as friendly insiders and outsiders or external and internal enemies that need to be controlled, helped, and led or feared or distrusted. These groups are essentialized and narrated through discourses that end up othering not only the various forms of otherness, but also the self and its components. They hierarchically situate the Iranian national self via constructions of difference and sameness as morally and culturally superior to these forms of otherness, thus perpetuating the construction of fractured selves. The depictions of the ideal citizen as pious, male, religious, Shi'a, Aryan-Pars, and knowledgeable person about politics and world affairs, who is also a leader in fighting imperialism, results in the manufacturing and manifestation of various fractured selves due to the partial inclusions of the fragmented nature of identity politics.

These fractured selves are incomplete selves. A fractured self is a self whose essence is denied due to exclusion of any meaningful national and global collective histories of the diversity of life. Fractured selves are the outcomes of nationalistic, heterosexual, Aryanist, revolutionary Shi'aist, and androcentric discourses. A fractured self is represented through Manichean, modernist, and essentialist definitions of the self-other-other that in isolation from one another divide students into camps of insider/outsider and exclude them from membership in the category of ideal citizen. A fractured self is simultaneously a member of various insider and outsider categories who must be both loved and feared. These dislocations are produced due to the ways in which various discourses are used in narrating the story of the nation. A fractured self is a dissected and marginalized self. It is fragmented not due to the agency of students, but to the ideological biases of the discourses that are employed in depicting Iranians and non-Iranians. The incorporation of the fragmented nature of identity politics functions as a tool of domination and surveillance and a platform through which students are encouraged to think through their own constructions of the selves within the discursive limits of how otherness is incorporated as part of the definition of the self (Thompson 1996, 570). As such, school textbooks reproduce limitations that are imposed on the range of meanings that are available to students in understanding themselves as citizens of Iran in relation to other nationalities and nations. Consequently, fractured selves have different loyalties and points of identification that are in conflict with the essentialized characteristics of the ideal citizen or with the characteristics of internal and external selves and others and how they are differentially positioned against many forms of sameness and otherness. The discourse of the *'ashayir*, the *basīj*, martyrdom, the Islamic Revolution, and binary oppositions, such as enemy/friend and *bā-īman/bī-īmān* (belief/unbeliever), are employed to situate the reader in respect to his/her future responsibilities as a citizen of Iran. Due to the characteristics of the discourses used, the reader finds him/herself in an oppositional reader-position that distinguishes between groups based on highly charged political and religious terms.

The ideal citizen is also constructed as a stigmatized self. In school textbooks, students are faced with a historical "problem": confronting their national stigma. The term *stigmatized self* refers to those representations of manifold selves in relation to the national self, based on multiple, dual, and contradictory perceptions of the ideal citizen. This stigmatized self is at once proud of his or her past and at the same time "feels unsure of how normals [the Western and Iranian elite] will identify him [or her] and receive him [or her]" (Goffman 1986, 13). Stigmatized Iranians and other non-Western societies, and technologically advanced Westerners and pious leaders of Iran, meet one another and enter into "social situations" that are pre- and re-presented to reflect the manufactured "truth" (see Goffman 1986, 12). By constructing the ideal citizen through differences and similarities and binary categories, Iranian students are advised to "correct [their] condition[s] indirectly by devoting much private effort to the mastery of areas of activity [often associated with modern Western others and religious and economic leaders of Iran]" (Goffman 1986, 10). This constructed sense of self ends up in "proving [Iranian] is what [Iranian] is not" and how representations of the self aim "at proving [Iranian] is not what [Iranian] is" (Goffman 1986, 63). The textbooks end up constructing stigmatized images of the ideal citizen that elevate the West and the Persian/Aryan/Muslim male as the idealized normals. However, in gazing at the East through an Orientalist lens, the gaze is not directed towards the present (i.e., Iranian leadership), but at the historical Easterners, the internal enemy others, and the external enemy others. Viewed in this light, school textbooks consist of stigmatizing discourses and become stigmatizing texts that construct images of normal and stigmatized that lead to an "awareness of inferiority [that would] mean [the Iranian student] is unable to keep out of consciousness the formulation of some chronic feeling of the worst sort of insecurity" (Sullivan, as quoted in Goffman 1986, 13). This insecurity is best conceptualized as and is the manifestation of, among other discourses, Orientalism and "Orientalism in reverse," which are employed as tools of representation and domination. Students are overexposed to conceptions of the national self and the ideal citizen that do not truly reflect who they are, but these stigmatizing discourses serve political and economic purposes that, nevertheless, reproduce the East and West dichotomy. By exposure to this emphasis on patriotic and Islamic sentiments, students are socialized according to a textual-space in which they are always reminded (or better put, questioned) about their loyalty to the nation and to Islam. In this sense, the state has two criteria for stigmatizing its citizens: unpatriotic sentiments and those values that undermine Islam. This construction presents two types of selves that students should avoid: those who are not willing to die for their country and nation and those who do not participate in developing Iran. Both of these qualities are also constructed as counter to the efforts of the state and the nation of Iran to modernize and protect Iran from its enemies.

The phobia associated with the "other" is reconciled with the discourse of loving Iran. Fear also implies caring for the nation and external and internal forms of otherness. Yet, this love for otherness and the self is the outcome of first defining the so-called abnormals in the midst of the self. It is in this sense that the ideal citizen is distinguished from the Iranian self. Fearing otherness is a racialized discourse that distinguishes between the insider and outsider within an economic discourse that, on one hand, requires Iranians to develop their country and, on the other hand, to protect it against imperialist encroachment and from internal forces (i.e., Baha'ism or the human rights discourse of the Carter era) that undermine the rule of God and "its" representatives on earth and attempt to reform Iran based on West-toxicated principles. Phobia of the "other" is presented in light of non-present discourses of primordial religious and cultural superiority of Iranians that link culture and geography, making them inseparable entities that reinforce one another in hegemonic and repetitive cycles of historical events. The "other" is always non-Pars and non-Shi'a who exploits Iran and Iranians. He is also often a king who does not account for the needs of the nation and is corrupt and whose rule is not supported by the people. The "other" is also a male who should not be trusted. But that does not mean that the other could not be a female; in fact, the fear of women and their unwanted involvement in politics is an important discourse in constructing the ideal citizen.

Iranian textbooks de-culturate "minorities" and marginalize the worldviews of these groups that lie outside the centre of power. Iranian school textbooks are based on "non-violent" forms of cultural genocide (Pinar 1995 refers to similar views through his term "fractured self"). I call this *textual genocide*. The exclusions of violence committed by the dominant groups in its historical and contemporary forms cannot be merely considered as "null curriculum." Such exclusions are forms of genocide since they often normalize violence by idealizing the past and sanitizing history from all wrong-doings and acts of ferocity. Violence is only portrayed as a characteristic of outsiders when they attack Iranians or other Muslims. This erasure of violence is also related to omissions of discussion about "race": racialized constructions of the ideal citizen are not interrogated for their economic and social consequences.

Politically, moreover, Iranian school textbooks explain and dictate the role of Iran in the liberation of all oppressed Muslims and peoples of the world. As Welch pointed out, in reference to imperialist Christianity,

> The cultural genocide of … [revolutionary, modernizing, and Islamizing] is not accidental, but is grounded in such an arrogant approach to liberation. It is oppressive to "free" people if [critical reflections on] their own histor[ies] and culture[s] do not serve as the primary sources of the definition of their freedom. (as quoted in Giroux 1988, 211)

The dominant discourse in Iranian school textbooks is based on a problematic ideology of "imperialism of anti-imperialism" where Islamic liberty stands for "empire" (see Dabashi 2011, 35). Iranian school textbooks, then, are a form of comprador texts that are produced by a group of writers who have been trained in Western-style thinking and revolutionary ideology and who end up mediating "the trade in cultural commodities of world capitalism at the periphery" (as quoted in Dabashi 2011, 39). This "trade" is the construction of otherness in modern societies through problematic discourses of nationalism, racialization, and economic development. The result is the facilitation of cultural domination and political pacification of a population about its understanding of otherness that is not inclusive of varied voices and their cultural and social upheavals (Dabashi 2011, 40). In this sense, school textbooks become *nativized informers*. They betray their selves and the history of otherness and their struggles for ideological positioning of the ruling elite in a non-Western part of the world that attempts to situate itself as a leader in anti-hegemonic endeavours. Yet the outcome of their discursive production of texts about history, society, geography, and the nation is the projection of a dislike onto the collective identities of non-Western otherness despite the construction of the West as the nemesis of the Iranian self. This is due to the fact that the hidden and anonymous self of the Iranian self is the Western "other", which is simultaneously both celebrated and despised. The textbooks as nativized informers highlight their role in promoting Western capitalist relations and nationalism in a language that is Islamized, but has not been purged of its imperialist, sexist, and racist underpinnings. The textbooks "serve to convey [to students] the master's [economic prowess]" and are involved in a "white civilizing mission" (Dabashi 2011, 27). School textbooks "speak for the white-identified, transnational bourgeoisie" that is nativized through the discourse of Orientalism. The language of the dominator is used to portray Iranians as of the same stock as other Europeans and Indo-Aryans, but at the same time different from the rest due to their ethnic/tribal characteristics and religious beliefs. Iranian school textbooks produce colonized minds that rely on a Western-centric language of exclusion that alienates otherness and eliminates "others" from participation in the construction of self and the ideal citizen. In an ironic way, the ideal citizen is a native informer who desperately wants to look and act like his or her master "other": the Western self (Dabashi 2011, 27).

In conclusion, Iranian school textbooks are "border-patrolling" (Dalmage 2006, 153) texts that highlight a historical separation between groups and "races" of the world in relation to the culture and civilization of Iran. Iranian culture and civilization are presented in a way that suggests Iranian culture has mainly been influenced by three central elements: Pars culture, Islam, and Shi'ism. Those who cross these boundaries are viewed as dangerous outsiders. Borderism, Dalmage (2006) explains, is "a unique form of discrimination faced by those who cross the color line, do not stick with their own, or attempt to claim membership ... in more than one ... group" (151). As a result, the textbooks highlight a border that is racialized, ethnicized, and Islamized for students. This knowledge is then used in self-assessments and self-reflections in the form of textbook assignments and questions. Individual students may resist these images and the official constructions of the ideal citizen. However, due to its national and universal reach, school knowledge also "locates" and "labels" criminal and pathological personalities by singling out certain characteristics in values, ethnicities, and geographical places as important criteria in the construction of the ideal citizen.

NOTES

1 In this chapter, I analyse a number of the 2004 and pre-2004 editions of Persian, social studies, history, and geography elementary school (five years) and guidance level (three years) textbooks. I refer to the three years of junior high as years 6, 7 and 8. However, in Iran, they are referred to as junior high years 1, 2 and 3.

2 Traces are the absent others and knowledge about them. Traces are those elements and discourses that are non-present but necessary for constructing the insider and the self. However, their non-presence should not be understood as "not being present" (Royle 2000, 7). The trace changes in light of external changes but retains its basic principles. It is a form of "unseen non-presence" (Royle 2000, 7–8). It does not have to be actually present at the moment, but is discursively related to many other forms of otherness, sameness, and knowledge about the nation.

3 Although in popular discourse in the West, *Iranian* and *Persian* are used interchangeably (Shaffer 2002, 1), I will use *Persian* to refer to the dominant ethnic group and *Iranian* to refer to the national identity.

4 Since there is no universal system for transliteration from Persian to English, I have followed the transliteration style adopted by Steingrass in *A Comprehensive Persian-English Dictionary* (fifth impression, published 1963 in London by Routledge & Kegan Paul) with the following modifications: z is used for ض; ż is used for ظ; s is used for ث; ŝ is used for ص; h is used for ه; ĥ is used for ح; y is used for ی; kh is used for خ; v is used for و; t is used for ط; aw, au, and ay are used to represent combined vowels and dipthongs; only the three elementary vowels a, i, u are used; and the silent و (v) following خ (kh) is retained.

5 Naser al-Din Shah, a Qajar king of Turkish background, is depicted in the textbooks as an incompetent ruler who was more concerned with satisfying his excessive needs for European consumer goods.

6 By *raced group* I mean the ways in which a non-dominant and marginalized group is defined by non-group members who have the power to depict the former in light of a racial epistemology.

REFERENCES

Abrahamian, Ervand. 1982. *Iran between Two Revolutions: Essays on the Republic Islamic*. Princeton: Princeton University Press.

– 1993. *Khomeinism: Essays on the Islamic Republic*. Berkeley: University of California Press.

Atabaki, Touraj. 2000. *Azerbaijan: Ethnicity and the Struggle for Power in Iran*. London: I.B. Tauris.

Banani, Amin. 1961. *The Modernization of Iran, 1921–1941*. Stanford: Stanford University Press.

Beck, Lois. 1990. "Tribes and the State in Nineteenth- and Twentieth-Century Iran." In *Tribes and States Formation in the Middle East*, ed. P.S. Khoury and J. Kostiner, 185–225. Berkeley: University of California Press.

– 1991. *Nomad: A Year in the Life of a Qashaq'i Tribesman in Iran*. Berkeley: University of California Press.

Bowden, Brett. 2003. "The Perils of Global Citizenship." *Citizenship Studies* 7 (3): 349–62.

Dabashi, Hamid. 2011. *Brown Skin, White Masks*. Halifax: Fernwood.

Dalmage, Heather. 2006. "Tripping on the Color Line." In *Race and Ethnicity in Society: The Changing Landscape*, ed. E. Higginbotham and M.L. Anderson, 151–5. Belmont: Thomson Wadsworth.

Dei, George J. Sefa. 1996. *Antiracism Education: Theory and Practice*. Halifax: Fernwood.

Dei, George J. Sefa, Leeno Karumanchery, and Nisha Karumanchery-Luik. 2005. *Playing the Race Card: Exposing White Power and Privilege*. New York: Peter Lang.

Esfandiari, Haleh. 1997. *Reconstructed Lives: Women & Iran's Islamic Revolution*. Washington: Woodrow Wilson Center Press.

– 2004. "The Role of Women Members of Parliament, 1963–88." In *Women in Iran: From 1800 to the Islamic Republic*, ed. L. Beck and G. Nashat, 136–62. Urbana: University of Illinois Press.

Francis, Daniel. 1997. *National Dreams: Myth, Memory, and Canadian History*. Vancouver: Arsenal Pulp Press.

Giroux, Henry A. 1988. *Schooling and the Struggle for Public Life: Critical Pedagogy in the Modern Age*. Minneapolis: University of Minnesota Press.

Goffman, Erving. 1986 [1963]. *Stigma: Notes on the Management of Spoiled Identity*. New York: Simon & Schuster.

Goffman, Erving. 1963. *Stigma: Notes on the Management of Spoiled Identity*. New York: Simon & Schuster.

Grossberg, Lawrence. 1993. "Cultural Studies and/in New Worlds." In *Race, Identity and Representation in Education*, ed. C. McCarthy and W. Crichlow, 89–105. New York: Routledge.

Hall, Stuart. 1996. "The Question of Cultural Identity." In *Modernity: An Introduction to Modern Societies*, ed. S. Hall, D. Held, D. Hubert, and K. Thompson, 596–634. Oxford: Blackwell.

Henry, Frances, and Carol Tator. 2006. *The Colour of Democracy: Racism in Canadian Society*. 3rd ed. Toronto: Thomson Nelson.

Henry, Frances, Carol Tator, Winston Mattis, and Tim Rees. 2000. *The Colour of Democracy: Racism in Canadian Society*. 2nd ed. Toronto: Harcourt Canada.

Keddie, Nikki R. 2003. *Modern Iran: Roots and Results of Revolution*. New Haven: Yale University Press.

Kelly, Jennifer. 1998. *Under the Gaze: Learning to Be Black in White Society*. Halifax: Fernwood.

Kian-Thiebaut, Azadeh. 2005. "From Motherhood to Equal Rights Advocates: The Weakening of Patriarchal Order." *Iranian Studies* 38 (1): 45–66.

Mackay, Sandra. 1996. *The Iranians: Persia, Islam and the Soul of a Nation*. New York: Plume.

Menashri, David. 1992. *Education and the Making of Modern Iran*. London: Cornell University Press.

– 2001. *Iran: Religion, Society and Power*. London: Frank Cass.

Ministry of Education, Islamic Republic of Iran. 1993a. *Farsī Sāl-i Panjum-i Dabistān* (Persian, Year 5, Elementary School). Tehran: Shirkat-i Chāb va Nashr-i Kitāb-hayī Darsī Īrān (The Iranian Textbook Publishing and Writing Company).

– 1993b. *Ta'limat-i Ijtimā'ī Sāl-i Panjum-i Dabistān* (Social Studies, Year 5, Elementary School). Tehran: Shirkat-i Chāb va Nashr-i Kitāb-hayī Darsī Īrān (The Iranian Textbook Publishing and Writing Company).

– 1999. *Ta'limat-i Ijtimā'ī Sāl-i Chahārum-i Dabistān* (Social Studies, Year 4, Elementary School). Tehran: Shirkat-i Chāb va Nashr-i Kitāb-hayī Darsī Īrān (The Iranian Textbook Publishing and Writing Company).

– 2000. *Ta'limat-i Ijtimā'ī Sāl-i Sivum-i Dabistān* (Social Studies, Year 3, Elementary School). Tehran: Shirkat-i Chāb va Nashr-i Kitāb-hayī Darsī Īrān (The Iranian Textbook Publishing and Writing Company).

– 2001. *Ta'limat-i Ijtimā'ī Sāl-i Panjum-i Dabistān* (Social Studies, Year 5, Elementary School). Tehran: Shirkat-i Chāb va Nashr-i Kitāb-hayī Darsī Īrān (The Iranian Textbook Publishing and Writing Company).

– 2002a. *Ta'rikh Sāl-i Aval-i Daurah-i Rāhnamā' ī Tahsīlī* (History Year 1 Guidance Cycle, Junior High). Tehran: Shirkat-i Chāb va Nashr-i Kitāb-hayī Darsī Īrān (The Iranian Textbook Publishing and Writing Company).

– 2002b. *Ta'rikh Sāl-i Sivum-i Daurah-i Rāhnamā' ī Tahsīlī* (History, Year 3 Guidance Cycle, Junior High). Tehran: Shirkat-i Chāb va Nashr-i Kitāb-hayī Darsī Īrān (The Iranian Textbook Publishing and Writing Company).

– 2004a. *Farsī Aval-i Dabistān Bikhanīm* (Persian, Year 1 Reading, Elementary School). Tehran: Shirkat-i Chāb va Nashr-i Kitāb-hayī Darsī Īrān (The Iranian Textbook Publishing and Writing Company).

– 2004b. *Farsī Duvum-i Dabistān Bikhanīm* (Persian, Year 2 Reading, Elementary School). Tehran: Shirkat-i Chāb va Nashr-i Kitāb-hayī Darsī Īrān (The Iranian Textbook Publishing and Writing Company).

– 2004c. *Farsī Sivum-i Dabistān Bikhanīm* (Persian, Year 3 Reading, Elementary School). Tehran: Shirkat-i Chāb va Nashr-i Kitāb-hayī Darsī Īrān (The Iranian Textbook Publishing and Writing Company).

– 2004d. *Farsī Panjum-i Dabistān* (Persian, Year 5, Elementary School). Tehran: Shirkat-i Chāb va Nashr-i Kitāb-hayī Darsī Īrān (The Iranian Textbook Publishing and Writing Company).

– 2004e. *Farsī Sivum-i Dabistān Binivīsīm* (Persian, Year 3 Writing, Elementary School). Tehran: Shirkat-i Chāb va Nashr-i Kitāb-hayī Darsī Īrān (The Iranian Textbook Publishing and Writing Company.

– 2004f. *Ta'limat-i Ijtimā'ī Sāl-i Sivum-i Dabistān* (Social Studies, Year 3, Elementary School). Tehran: Shirkat-i Chāb va Nashr-i Kitāb-hayī Darsī Īrān (The Iranian Textbook Publishing and Writing Company).

– 2004g. *Ta'limat-i Ijtimā'ī Sāl-i Chahārum-i Dabistān* (Social Studies, Year 4, Elementary School). Tehran: Shirkat-i Chāb va Nashr-i Kitāb-hayī Darsī Īrān (The Iranian Textbook Publishing and Writing Company).

– 2004h. *Ta'limat-i Ijtimā'ī Sāl-i Panjum-i Dabistān* (Social Studies, Year 5, Elementary School). Tehran: Shirkat-i Chāb va Nashr-i Kitāb-hayī Darsī Īrān (The Iranian Textbook Publishing and Writing Company).

– 2004i. *Ta'limat-i Ijtimā'ī Sāl-i Aval-i Daurah-i Rāhnamā' ī Tahsīlī* (Social Studies, Year 1 Guidance Cycle, Junior High). Tehran: Shirkat-i Chāb va Nashr-i Kitāb-hayī Darsī Īrān (The Iranian Textbook Publishing and Writing Company).

– 2004j. *Ta'rikh Sāl-i Aval-i Daurah-i Rāhnamā' ī Tahsīlī* (History, Year 1 Guidance Cycle, Junior High). Tehran: Shirkat-i Chāb va Nashr-i Kitāb-hayī Darsī Īrān (The Iranian Textbook Publishing and Writing Company).

– 2004k. *Ta'rikh Sāl-i Sivum-i Daurah-i Rāhnamā' ī Tahsīlī* (History, Year 3 Guidance Cycle, Junior High). Tehran: Shirkat-i Chāb va Nashr-i Kitāb-hayī Darsī Īrān (The Iranian Textbook Publishing and Writing Company).

– 2005. *Iranian and World History 1* (First Year, High School). Tehran: Shirkat-i Chāb va Nashr-i Kitāb-hayī Darsī Īrān (The Iranian Textbook Publishing and Writing Company).

Mirfakhraie, Amir. 2011. "Racialization of Asia, Africa and Americas and the Construction of the Ideal Iranian Citizen: Local and Global Representations of Colonialism, Geography, Culture, and Religious Diversity in Iranian School Textbooks." In *From Colonization to Globalization: The Intellectual and Political Legacies of Kwame Nkrumah and Africa's Future*, ed. Charles Quist-Adade and Frances Chiang. Surrey, BC: Daysprings.

Mohsenpour, Bahram. 1988. "Philosophy of Education in Postrevolutionary Iran." *Comparative Education Review* 32 (1): 76–86.

Mojab, Shahrzad, and Amir Hassanpour. 1995. "The Politics of Nationality and Ethnic Diversity." In *Iran after the Revolution: Crisis of an Islamic State*, ed. S. Rahnema and S. Behdad, 229–50. London: I.B. Tauris.

Nashat, Guity. 2004. "Introduction." In *Women in Iran: From 1800 to the Islamic Republic*, ed. L. Beck and G. Nashat, 1–36. Urbana: University of Illinois Press.

Parry, Benita. 2004. *Postcolonial Studies: A Materialist Critique*. New York: Routledge.

Pinar, William F. 1995. "The Curriculum: What Are the Basics and Are We Teaching Them?" In *Thirteen Questions: Reframing Education's Conversation*, 2nd ed., ed. J.L. Kincheloe and S.R. Steinberg, 25–30. New York: Peter Lang.

Rahnema, Saeed, and Sohrab Behdad. 1995. "Introduction: Crisis of an Islamic State." In *Iran after the Revolution: Crisis of an Islamic State*, ed. S. Rahnema and S. Behdad, 1–18. London: I.B. Tauris.

Rastegar, Asghar. 1995. "Health Policy and Medical Education." In *Iran after the Revolution: Crisis of an Islamic State*, ed. S. Rahnema and S. Behdad, 218–28. London: I.B. Tauris.

Razack, Sherene. 2008. *Casting Out: The Eviction of Muslims from Western Law & Politics*. Toronto: University of Toronto Press.

Rejali, Darius M. 1994. *Torture and Modernity: Self, Society, and State in Modern Iran*. Boulder: Westview.

Royle, Nicholas. 2000. "What is Deconstruction?" In *Deconstruction: A User's Guide*, ed. N. Royle, 1–13. New York: Palgrave.

Sadiq, I. 1931. *Modern Persia and Her Educational System*. New York: Bureau of Publications, Teachers College, Columbia University.

Said, Edward W. 1994. *Culture and Imperialism*. New York: Vintage.

Sanasarian, Eliz. 2000. *Religious Minorities in Iran*. Cambridge: Cambridge University Press. http://dx.doi.org/10.1017/CBO9780511492259.

Seidman, Steven. 1994. *Contested Knowledge: Social Theory in the Postmodern Era*. Oxford: Blackwell.

Shaffer, Brenda. 2002. *Borders and Brethren: Iran and the Challenge of Azerbaijani Identity*. Cambridge, MA: MIT Press.

Shorish, M. Mobin. 1988. "The Islamic Revolution and Education in Iran." *Comparative Education Review* 32 (1): 58–75. http://dx.doi.org/10.1086/446737.

Tavakoli-Targhi, Mohamad. 11 2000. "Mehrzad Boroujerdi, Iranian Intellectuals and the West: The Tormented Triumph of Nativism." Book review. *International Journal of Middle East Studies* 32 (4): 565–71.

Thompson, Kenneth. 1996. "Social Pluralism and Post-Modernity." In *Modernity: An Introduction to Modern Societies*, ed. Stuart Hall, D. Held, D. Hubert, and K. Thompson, 565–94. Cambridge, MA: Blackwell.

Tragert, Joseph. 2003. *The Complete Idiot's Guide to Understanding Iran*. Indianapolis: Alpha.

Vahdat, Farzin. 2002. *God and Juggernaut: Iran's Intellectual Encounter with Modernity*. Syracuse: Syracuse University Press.

Vaziri, Mostafa. 1993. *Iran as Imagined Nation: The Construction of National Identity*. New York: Paragon.

Ward, Ivan. 2001. *Phobia: Ideas in Psychoanalysis*. London: Icon.

5 How to Save ... A Nation?: Televisual Fiction Post-9/11

MELISSA AMES

To claim that the national tragedy of 9/11 is a defining moment in the first decade of the twenty-first century for the United States is not profound, nor is the statement that it directly and indirectly influenced the cultural production within American society throughout these years. Regardless of the obviousness of these claims, it is exactly upon these assumptions that this chapter rests. In the years following the attacks on the World Trade Center and Pentagon, cultural products have been sites for interrogating and remediating the trauma that 9/11 caused for the citizens of a country that believed itself to be untouchable. Although these cultural concerns were played out in both non-fictional and fictional spaces across media, this essay argues that televisual narratives in particular provide great insight into societal concerns during the start of this century. They do this in a unique space that repackages these concerns from "reality" and displaces them into the safe comforts of "fiction" where they can be addressed time and again with more favourable results.

In terms of rapidity of response to 9/11, there was no contest: in general, television was quicker to respond to the tragedy than any other medium (e.g., film, print novel), both as it was happening and in the months after. Obviously, there was the real-time news broadcasting the day of the events, but also special programs and documentaries in the weeks that followed. However, the events of 9/11 also seeped into the fictional worlds found in television sitcoms and dramas within only a few weeks' time. The speed of this response is attributed more to television's production processes and freedoms and less to its actual desire to be the pioneers of post-9/11 narrative. But what is more interesting, and not as theorized, is how television responded to 9/11 (and continues to respond) to it years later. Although, to be fair, there were some early televisual attempts at understanding the tragedy. CNN re-aired its documentary *Beneath the Veil* and its sequel *Unholy War* – both focused on the plight of Afghani women under the Taliban regime – in the weeks following 9/11, and to commemorate the six-month anniversary of the attacks CBS aired Jules and Gedeon Naudet's documentary *9/11* on 10 March 2002.

However, as might be expected (and partially planned to await audiences ready to consume such narratives), Hollywood did not begin producing films inspired by or based on 9/11 until 2006 with the release of both Paul Greengrass's *United 93* and Oliver Stone's *World Trade Center*. It is this specific year, one marking the five-year anniversary of the attack, that grounds my analysis of televisual narratives as well. However, when compared to the films being released at this time, the stories delivered through television separate themselves from the documentary-style narratives of 9/11-related film and enter into the deep recesses of fiction – into the realms of science fiction even, where it is once again acceptable to be playful and perverse while trying to work out cultural concerns lingering from a half decade prior. But before getting to that year of 2006 – the year that broadcasted loud and clear that the United States was a nation waiting to be saved – one must start at the beginning: TV post-9/11 and TV's history of being a cultural tool for coping with the catastrophic.

The Televisual Landscape in the Wake of 9/11

Television did not immediately begin spawning fictional narratives loosely related to the attacks. In fact, right after 9/11 television executives were quite concerned about the content of their programming, and specifically any fictional narratives that might be considered disturbing, violent, or traumatic in the aftermath of the national crisis. Lynn Spigel (2004, 235) recounts how films like *Collateral Damage, The Siege, Lethal Weapon, Carrie*, and even *Superman* and *King Kong* were pulled from television line-ups. However, inadvertent censorship and coverage changes also occurred during this time. For example, Spigel (2004, 236) notes that "humorists Dave Letterman, Jay Leno, Craig Kilborn, Conan O'Brien, and Jon Stewart met (their) late-night audience(s) with dead seriousness" on the nights following 9/11, causing some critics to declare "that the attacks on the Pentagon and World Trade Center had brought about the 'end of irony.'" Although the industry heads were altruistically attempting to save viewers from their pre-packaged violent imagery, during this time period the public was actually eager to consume such depictions of trauma. Video retailers reported an increase in customer check-outs of films like those pulled from the network's line-ups, suggesting that the consumption of explosions, toppling buildings, and apocalyptic scenarios – at least when situated in fictionalized backdrops – was just what the doctor ordered in terms of coping strategies and escapism (Spigel 2004, 236). So it is not really a surprise that televisual narratives would pick up on these motifs in a relatively short period of time in the crafting of new programs and episodes.

Although much was going on in the fictional programming found on television, for the most part media scholarship on 9/11, the US attacks in Afghanistan, and the early stages of the "war on terror" focused on print and television news coverage (Spigel 2004, 238). This work from the academy often attended to "the narrative and mythic 'framing' of the events; the nationalistic jingoism …; [the] competing global news outlets, particularly Al Jazeera; and the institutional and commercial pressure that has led to 'infotainment'" (Spigel 2004, 238). But as Spigel states, despite its important achievements, "the scholarly focus on news underestimates (indeed, it barely considers) the way the 'reality' of 9/11 was communicated across the flow of television's genres, including its so-called entertainment genres" (238). In order to investigate this lacuna, her essay "Entertainment Wars: Television Culture after 9/11" analyses Comedy Central's 7 November 2001 episode of *South Park* and NBC's 3 October 2001 episode of *West Wing* to showcase the various ways that television genres responded to the attacks through their narratives. Similarly, this essay aims to address this academic void by analysing various thematic motifs that appeared (or are amplified) in televisual fiction post-9/11 in order to show that these are important sites where the "'reality' of 9/11" is being worked out.

Although one might have expected television programming to "step up" and grow more serious in the wake of September 11th, the opposite ultimately occurred. Some reporters, such as Louis Chunovic of *Television Week*, were hopeful that the face of television would change following the attacks:

In the wake of the terrorist attack on the United States, it's hard to believe Americans once cared who would win Big Brother 2 or whether Anne

Heche is crazy. And it's hard to believe that as recently as two weeks ago, that's exactly the kind of pabulum, along with the latest celebrity/ politician sex/murder/kidnapping scandal, that dominated television news ... We cannot afford to return to the way things were. (2001, 15)

But as Spigel notes, ironically, "the industry's post 9/11 upgrade to quality genres – especially historical documentaries – actually facilitated the return to the way things were" (2004, 241).

Susan Douglas (2006) suggests it was not that television was incapable of a shift into a more permanent state of serious programming. In fact, she returns to Marshall McLuhan's infamous (and idealistic) notion of technology uniting everyone within a global village to prove that, although it is quite possible in the era of around-the-clock coverage and international media collaboration to have this sort of worldly programming, it was not at all what Americans wanted. No: they wanted escape. She writes:

After 9/11, when one would have expected the nightly news programs to provide a greater focus on international news, attention to the rest of the world was fleeting, with the exception of the war in Iraq. After a precipitous decline in celebrity and lifestyle news in the immediate aftermath of the 9/11 catastrophe, a year later the percentages of these stories in the nightly news were back to where they had been pre-9/11. In 2004, despite the war, the percentage of stories about foreign affairs on the commercial nightly news broadcasts was lower than it had been in 1997. (619)

Rather than 9/11 bringing about an era of entertainment Enlightenment, American society returned quickly to a state of global/foreign affairs ignorance. In the United States, Douglas claims, "new communication technologies have not created a global village but have, ironically, led to a fusion of ethnocentrism and narcissism, best cast as a 'turn within'" (619). Enter in escapism. Analysing the popularity of reality television in the early years of the twenty-first century, Douglas argues that if television news, in particular, bears especial responsibility for squandering its ability to enhance a global awareness despite its ever-augmented capabilities to do so, reality TV, colonizing television as it did between 2001 and 2005, insisted that the most productive way to use communications technologies was to focus them on individual Americans in confined and controlled spaces hermetically sealed from foreign peoples and culture. (621)

Studying this exploding genre was, indeed, important, as "by January 2003, one-seventh of all programming on ABC was reality based" (632). This televisual trend continues to date, with entire networks devoted to the genre. Arguably, at least in the early years, these shows provided emotional comfort and quelled the negative affect from which they derived. Although Douglas discusses primarily the escapism provided by the format of reality TV, I argue that the escapism provided by televisual fiction during this time period is even more fascinating and operates in a slightly different way.

Watching Trauma Unfold (on the Small Screen)

In order to understand how the consumption of television narratives could work this affectual wonder, one must first attend to exactly how 9/11 was framed as a trauma *to be seen* (in order to be felt) and how television has long been the medium in charge of controlling feelings through the art of "seeing" specifically constructed imagery. First of all, to many Americans, 9/11 unfolded in front of their eyes much like a Hollywood blockbuster film – almost too spectacular to believe. Slavoj Žižek writes: "when we watched the oft-repeated shot of frightened people running toward the camera ahead of the giant cloud of dust from the collapsing tower, was not the framing of the shot itself reminiscent of spectacular shots in a catastrophe movie, a special effect that outdid all others?" (2002, 11). Indeed, many survivors used the simile that it felt "like a movie" to explain the experience (Redfield 2007, 68). As Susan Sontag argues, "'it felt like a movie' seems to have displaced the way survivors of a catastrophe used to express the short-term unassimilability of what they had gone through: 'It felt like a dream'" (2003, 22). So is it really a surprise that the American public turned to the realm of visual culture/media to "replay" the event dominating their own memories? Marc Redfield argues that the phrase "'it was like a movie' conjures up not just an excess of event over believability, but a sense that this event *is to be mediated*, that it would have no sense, perhaps would not even have occurred, if it were not being recorded and transmitted" (2007, 69). In this explanation it would seem that the media was needed; it was the only way that people could move from disbelief (that which they could not comprehend and some could not physically see) to belief (that which they could only comprehend through repeated seeing).

This "hard to believe" tragedy of 9/11 is often classified as a cultural trauma, but it actually differs quite a bit from other national catastrophes. Redfield points out:

> That the attacks inflicted a shock of historical scale seems clear, but the shape and scope of this wound is not ... If we try to conceive of trauma on a cultural level things become more ambiguous ... [The attacks] were not of a society-threatening scale (as warfare, genocide, famine, or natural cataclysm have been for so many human societies) and the literal damage they did to the military and commercial orders symbolized by the Pentagon and the World Trade Center was minuscule; it is of course as symbolic acts of violence that they claim culturally traumatic status. (2007, 56)

He continues to analyse the common affects of trauma and the coping process that individuals usually go through: "trauma involves blockage: an inability to mourn, to move from repetition to working-through. It is certainly plausible that hyperbolic commemorative efforts such as those on display in '9/11 discourse' ... are in fact testimonials to blockage" (56). He argues that "wherever one looks in 9/11 discourse, trauma and the warding-off of trauma blur into each other, as the event disappears into its own mediation" (56). I propose that a very similar process is at work in the televisual narratives that proliferate after 9/11; through their mediation of fictionalized scenarios they present trauma in order to do away with it, hence becoming a sort of emotional security blanket for viewers existing in an unstable post-9/11 world.

Douglas posits that communications technologies "have some inherent capabilities that privilege some senses – and thus some cognitive and behavioral processes – over others" (2006, 635). I agree, and claim that these cognitive and behavioural processes relate to certain affects – the most prevalent being the affect of fear.[1] To claim that television has this emotional power is not new, nor is the association of television with fear. However, in determining how television portrays 9/11 (and post-9/11 concerns) the association seems important. Television scholar Louise Spence observed that her students a year after 9/11 "still understood the events of 9/11 in affective and emotional terms" (2004, 101). It could be argued that over a decade later most Americans still do. Part of this emotional understanding, and emotionally charged memory, of the events is due to the way it was presented through the medium of television.[2]

Television and the Catastrophic: A Brief Overview
of Affect Theory

A short overview of affect theory is useful here. In his work on affect, Silvan Tomkins states that "affective responses are of course 'caused'" and that "there are specific conditions which activate, maintain them, and reduce them" (Sedgwick and Frank 1995, 37). I suggest that the viewing of television programming can be one of these "specific conditions." Tomkins comes up with the notion of a weak affect theory, which, despite what its name might imply, is one that works efficiently to produce (or not produce) certain affects. So a weak affect theory relating to negative affect (such as fear) would work to prevent an individual from feeling the negative affect. In other essays I have argued that the viewing of certain television programming, like the nightly news, might operate like a weak negative affect theory, helping viewers to *not* experience negative affect as a result of the habitual exposure to certain content (i.e., violent imagery) they receive from the programming's staple imagery (Ames 2009, 2012, 2013, 2014).

How the news is able to operate in this fashion is worthy of note. Mary Ann Doane builds on Roland Barthes's discussion of photography, in particular its *noeme* (the essence of "that-has-been" or its "past-ness") to argue that television offers quite a different visual experience, that of "this-is-going-on" or a sense of "present-ness" (1990, 222). Likewise, Jay Bolter and Richard Grusin (2000) explore the connected concept of immediacy in regard to new media. They argue not only that immediacy is a sense of transparency in which the media gives off the illusion that it is *not* a mediation or a representation, and hence indicates an absence or erasure of mediation, but also that immediacy can be tied to "the viewer's feelings that the medium has disappeared and the objects are present to him, a feeling that his experience is therefore authentic" (70). News broadcasts obviously capitalize on television's claim to immediacy. The capitalized word "LIVE" in the lower corner of the TV screen and the anchor's quip of "this just in" help transport the viewers to the event, giving them the illusion that they are there, that they are witnessing this event unfolding before their eyes (and allow them to ignore the fact that it is being delivered to them across distance and through tainted technology).

It is important to note that networks do exploit their power as a "live" supplier of coverage and do systematically manipulate the viewer's affective responses. The news attempts to deliver anxiety (or the illusion of said affect) in order to have its role of relieving it. In fact, Patricia Mellencamp argues that "anxiety *is* television's affect" (1990b, 243, emphasis added) and suggests that when studying this media we should shift "our analysis from theories of pleasure to include theories of unpleasure." She states, "TV envelops the shock, delivering *and* cushioning us from stimuli which it regulates in acceptable levels ... turning news or shocks into story and tragic drama" (254). The reporter is there to inject viewers with anxiety, fear, and anger (or try to do so) but also to quickly administer the antidote, the assurance that everything will be just fine, and that he or she will be there to present that final happy diagnosis just as soon as it occurs. Richard Grusin argues that this media practice is increasingly common post-9/11 and is a crucial component of what he terms "premediation" (2004, 21). He explains the logic of premediation as insisting "that the future itself is ... already mediated, and that with the right technologies ... the future can be remediated before it happens" (19). Grusin argues that a new media environment has arisen in post-9/11 United States, one that "is preoccupied with the mediation not of the present or the immediate past but of the future." As a result, "news media have begun to give up on – or perhaps more accurately to subordinate – their historical role in favor of a prophetic or predictive role of reporting on what might happen" (23). However, "unlike prediction, premediation is not chiefly about getting the future right ... In fact, it is precisely the proliferation of future scenarios that enables premediation to generate and maintain a low level of anxiety in order to prevent the possibility of a traumatic future" (28–9). This line of analysis might very well be aligned loosely with the argument that repeated television news consumption functions like a personalized form of a weak negative affect theory. Grusin writes: "because of the repetitive structure of the everyday built into televisual programming, the repeated premediation of future disasters or catastrophes works to guard against the recurrence of a trauma like 9/11 by maintaining ... an almost constant low level of fear" (26). Brian Massumi (2005) would likely agree with this. In his essay "Fear (The Spectrum Said)," which deals with the government of the United States' use of the colour-coded terrorist alert system put into place by the Homeland Security Office, he argues that the terrorist alert system is a dangerous political tool that allows the government post-9/11 to conduct a sort of "affective modulation of the populace" and create a climate of controlled "affective attunement" (primarily grounded in fear) (1).

The everyday news does this on a small scale, but in attending to large-scale catastrophes this practice, which indeed predates 9/11, is all the more noticeable. The affect manipulation in this notice-able practice is often quite evident. Mary Ann Doane discusses these moments of impact that disrupt "ordinary routine" (1990, 228). TV from its onset has had the capacity to capture these moments and deliver them right to the viewer in his or her living room: Kennedy's assassination, the Challenger's explosion, Chernobyl, the rescue of Baby Jessica, the massacre at Columbine, 9/11, the 2005 tsunami, Hurricane Katrina, the earthquake in Haiti, and countless other natural disasters, acts of violence (bombings, wars), or unexpected death (plane crashes, fires) (Doane 1990, 229; Mellencamp 1990b, 249). These mediated moments not only disrupt our routine, drawing us to the screen to consume them in endless (even painful) repetition, but they end up acting as time markers for those who witness them, epochal reference points, and they most likely play a large role in a generation's structure of feeling. Doane claims that "catastrophic time stands still" (1990, 231). The lyrics of a popular country song by Alan Jackson, written in the aftermath of 9/11, echo this sentiment: "Where were you when the world stopped turning on that September day?" Hence the event, the frozen moment in time, becomes one shared with an entire generation, so that every member of the current generation can answer the question "Where were you when the twin towers were attacked," just as the previous one can quickly supply their whereabouts when they heard that Kennedy had been shot, and probably how the generation before that could remember where they were when they heard of the atomic bombs being dropped on Japan or the attack on Pearl Harbor – shared moments, shared affect that make a generation.

The reason people are able to "feel" these events so strongly, other than their out-of-the-ordinary nature and the tragedy they encapsulate, is largely due to how they are packaged and distributed by the networks thriving during their height. The non-stop news coverage of such dis-asters brings about a "condensation of temporality," in which "the cri-sis compresses time" (Doane 1990, 223). When something abnormal is unfolding, television has the capacity to make its audience spellbound, watching the same image flash across the screen, listening to the same reports recapped hour after hour. It also has the power to reinforce cer-tain beliefs and emotional states. In the aftermath of 9/11, two motifs seemed to receive this constant reinforcement in both fictional and non-fictional television programming: the rejuvenated theme of national patriotism and the fear of the "other."

Post-9/11 Thematics

In the news broadcasting world these two areas of focus seem quite interrelated. Scholars have compared this current trend of a patriotism grounded in fear to the post–World War II cold war era. Dennis Broe argues:

> The reading of the so-called war on terrorism as similar in scope and aim to the anticommunism of the former cold war is, of course, denied by media outlets such as the Fox News Channel, which operate in a perpetual present or in a historical moment that began on September 11, 2001. The promotion of an external enemy for the purposes of global domination and of quelling domestic dissent, coupled with the revival of a faltering economy through military spending, are characteristics in common with the Cold War. The current endless war is a global civil war fought by an apparently triumphant capitalist system against both a new, more ethnically diverse and predominantly female working class and a global anticorporate movement. At the center, this war takes the form of attacks on wages and curbs civil rights, while at the periphery, war is more openly declared against states with natural resources (oil, natural gas, water). (2004, 98)

In this sense the media can be seen as acting the part of the man behind the curtain shouting: "Look over here, look over here. Focus on those dark, dangerous 'others' around the globe – don't think about the dark, dangerous downfalls happening right here in your own country" (e.g., the economic crisis plaguing the United States at the end of the first decade of the twenty-first century).

But regardless of the selfish motives that sparked the rhetoric for this move to national unity, waves of patriotism did flow across the country post-9/11 and flood the cultural narratives of the time. Spigel notes, "given the political divisions that have resurfaced since 2001, it seems likely that the grand narratives of national unity that sprang up after 9/11 were for many people more performative than sincere. In other words, it is likely that many viewers really did know that all the newfound patriotism was really just a public performance staged by cameras" (2004, 255). But as she notes, what is problematic is the fact that after 9/11 "many people found it important to 'perform' the role of citizen, which included the performance of belief in national myths of unity. And if you didn't perform this role, then somehow you were a bad American" (255).

With all of this going on in supposedly non-fictional television programming, it is not surprising that these same thematic messages and cultural concerns seeped into fictional programming as well. In television shows airing in the years following the attacks, there was a sudden preoccupation with this notion of unity at both the national level and on a larger scale (themes of interconnectedness, fate, and destiny). There was also a common thematic obsession with the necessity of being "saved." In the following pages I turn to the analysis of fictional narratives on television, focusing on an overview of the programming popular in the years immediately following the September 11th attacks, the specific television season of 2006–2007, which marked the five-year anniversary of the attacks (concentrating on two breakout shows, NBC's *Heroes* and ABC's *Lost*), and the continuation of these televisual trends at present (proving that both the narratives and viewers remain haunted by the national crisis even as it approaches the decade's close).

Some would claim that "Americans have yearned to see current geopolitical realities portrayed in popular culture ever since the terrorist attacks of Sept. 11, 2001" (Stillwell 2007, 1). I would argue that Americans want to see a *version* of those realities on television. Of course, ideally this version would be one that can be brought to a neat and tidy, Hollywood-style dénouement by the end of the season and/or series. The show that best showcases this desire is Fox's *24*, which debuted on the heels of 9/11 on 6 November 2001. Broe (2004) critiques Rupert Murdoch's news corporation, the parent entity of the Fox network, arguing that it is no surprise that *24* found a comfortable (and long) run-time with this conglomerate. In fact, Broe states that the show "was seen as a prestige item in the Murdoch canon" (100) and argues:

> In *24*, the sensationalism that marks Murdoch entertainment is employed in the service of promoting and rationalizing the endless war. The emphasis on the clock, on racing against time during both the hour of the show and the show's six-month running time, keeps the audience afraid of terrorists, nuclear bombs, and viruses. Meanwhile the sympathetic vigilante ignores the legal rights and speeds rapidly ahead in his battle to save humanity (with humanity reduced to the United States only), while, as Adorno would say, fear and anxiety replace contemplation. (101)

Most definitely, the show is a hyped-up version of current events, a compressed hyperbole of many of the viewer/citizen's concerns. For example, as Stillwell argues, "the political and moral dilemmas raised by the show could be ripped straight out of the headlines. References to the Patriot Act, NSA surveillance and Guantanamo Bay figure in the show's plot. Probably the most controversial topic is Jack Bauer's (Keifer Sutherland) propensity for torturing prisoners, particularly in cases where a 'ticking time bomb' terrorist plot is involved" (2007, 3). Although 24 might be the most blatantly obvious show broadcasting this motif of needing to be saved (specifically from an "other" in the form of a terrorist), a motif that reinforces the beliefs of the non-fictional programming surrounding it, it is not alone in exploring this televisual theme.

ABC's *Alias* actually aired over a month before 24 on 30 September 2001. Like 24, this show focuses on a world (read: country) in crisis needing to be saved. While Jack Bauer is part of the government's CTU (Counter Terrorist Unit), *Alias*'s main character, Sydney Bristow (Jennifer Garner), is an undercover CIA agent working to bring down SD-6, a component of the Alliance of Twelve, an international crime group wreaking havoc on the world. Some of this fictional organization's goals consist of black market weapon trading and the assembling of ancient relics that might help form a weapon of mass destruction like none existing in current times. While 24 finds Bauer fighting to prevent one major national crisis per season/day, *Alias* exists as a more traditional drama with plot arcs that both exist within an episode and stretch through episodes and seasons. Therefore, Bristow often has to defuse more bombs (so to speak) in one season's time. (And she is more likely to be the one tortured than the one doing the torturing.) Shows such as these continued to be made even years after 9/11. In March 2006 another network decided to create its own drama centred on a governmental protection group: CBS released *The Unit*, which focuses on a top-secret military unit modelled after the real-life Delta Force.

While these dramas were maintaining popularity, another format was having varied success: dramas that focused on saving the country from the top down. From 1999 to 2006 NBC's *The West Wing* found popularity as a television drama focused on the behind-the-scenes happenings of a fictional president, his family, and his staff as they navigated through particular legislative or political issues. In the seasons following 9/11, not surprisingly, plots often turned to the spectre of both foreign and domestic terrorism. In 2005, ABC attempted a short-lived series, *Commander in Chief*, focusing on the presidency and familial life of the first female president of the United States, President Mackenzie

Allen (Geena Davis). This show, like the others, attended to the global tension and domestic insecurity present at the start of the twenty-first century.

Although the theme of needing to be saved has been prevalent throughout all time (and throughout all narrative forms), the abundance (and popularity) of this motif on television is quite interesting in the wake of 9/11. What can one make of viewers' attraction to watching fictional figures do this saving (be it in the field or from the oval office) time and time again? And what happens when this motif of needing to be saved shifts? By 2006 television was still obsessed with this motif but not necessarily in the same ways that it had been five years prior. Shows like *Alias* and *West Wing* reached their series close and other programming lined up to fill the void. Salvation was still the name of the game, but one would have to look closer to see the links to the tragedy of 9/11 lurking beneath this regurgitated theme. A snapshot of a year – the television season of 2006–2007 – reveals quite a bit about American society's preoccupation with this notion of being saved.

Five Years Later: An Analysis of 2006–2007 Television Programming

In fall 2006 one of ABC's hit dramas, *Grey's Anatomy*, launched its season with television promos and a special viewer initiation (or refresher) episode centred on The Fray's hit song, "How to Save a Life." This same fall NBC released its soon-to-be hit series, *Heroes*, with its tagline "Save the Cheerleader; Save the World." As mentioned, although the fictional landscape of American television had been dominated by the theme of needing to be saved for much of the new twenty-first century (especially post-9/11), never before had this motif been so clearly vocalized and marketed. Doled out alongside this theme was the aforementioned focus on unity/interconnectedness. Quite often in the televisual texts of this time these two themes worked together; in fictional spaces, a world connected, a group united, was one that would survive and/or be saved.

During this television season, twenty-nine shows ran on the four major networks of ABC, CBS, NBC, and FOX that could fit into these categories. While some fit loosely into this grouping, like the crime dramas (CBS's *CSI: Crime Scene Investigation, CSI: Miami, CSI: NY, NCIS, Criminal Minds;* NBC's *Crossing Jordan;* Fox's *Bones, Cops,* and *America's Most Wanted: America Strikes Back*), the law dramas (CBS's *Shark;* NBC's *Law & Order, Law & Order: Criminal Intent, Law & Order: Special Victims*

Unit; ABC's *Boston Legal;* Fox's *Justice*) and the medical dramas (NBC's *ER*; ABC's *Grey's Anatomy,* Fox's *House*), others more obviously earn this classification due to their central preoccupation with needing to be saved from personal predicaments or national crises. This category would include shows previously discussed like *24* and *The Unit,* but also similar shows like CBS's *Jericho* (concerned with the aftermath of nuclear attacks on twenty-three American cities), ABC's *Traveler* (focused on the road trip of three college graduates that results in a terrorist attack on a museum), and Fox's *Standoff* (about an FBI Crisis Negotiation Unit). This grouping also includes shows that discuss needing to be saved in different ways: ABC's *Lost* and NBC's *Heroes* (both of which will be analysed in greater depth below) as well as Fox's *Prison Break* (which focuses on a governmental conspiracy that sends a man to death row for a crime he did not commit) and ABC's *Day Break* (a *Groundhog Day*–type series replaying one day in the life of a detective accused of murdering the assistant district attorney). And still other programs fall into this grouping due to their focus on interconnectivity, shows like ABC's *The Nine* (which follows the lives of nine strangers who survive a hostage crisis) and *Six Degrees* (as evidenced in the title, this show plays on the theme that everyone is connected to one another in some way).

Although many of these shows did not enjoy a long run-time, the fact that these themes were so prevalent is telling. Even more intriguing is the central affect that each of these shows share: fear. Logically, it makes sense that each would foreground this human emotion. In situations where one needs rescuing or redemption, fear is often the affect that drives individuals. And, just as nonfiction television programming operates, these narratives exist to deliver this fear so that they can also be credited with having alleviated it. At first thought it might seem that consuming this constant array of fear-evoking, life-threatening situations might make viewers more fearful in their everyday lives. However, "the quotidian fare of violence, disaster, and death that TV audiences consume (actually) nourishes fantasies of invulnerability" and hence diminishes fear (Redfield 2007, 73). As in the regular consumption of serial news broadcasts, the habitual consumption of these fictional series operates like a weak negative affect theory – repressing societal fears through narratives of salvation.

Not surprisingly, many of these narratives grounded their installations of fear in a problematic "us" versus "them" binary. Although this opposition has long been used to stimulate dramatic conflict, its possible tie to the media rhetoric of 9/11 is hard to overlook. In discussing this common binary, Michael Bader explains that the "feelings of insecurity and disconnectedness that plague us in our personal and social lives" are often "blamed on the actions of some 'other' who is then demeaned and attacked" (2006, 584). Like in the case of the political powers-that-be post-9/11, "this process of projection is deliberately used by conservatives to solidify their base. By creating an imaginary 'us' and 'them,' they can then promise satisfaction of deep and legitimate longings for a community safe from both real and illusory threats posed from the outside" (584). This us-versus-them binary also exists to nurture a superiority complex common to citizens of the United States.

In analysing the responses of her students in the wake of the national disaster, Spence noted:

> The idea that the greatest power in the world might not also be the greatest country seemed to be too much for the students to handle. As a matter of fact, for some, the only way of explaining the "why" of the attacks was that "they" hated "us" because of our freedoms and affluence, because "we" are so great. They wanted so much to believe in our goodness and innocence that they ignored everything they had "learned" [previously] about the banality of evil. (2004, 102–3)

This sort of mindset, beyond solidifying this dangerous (and hierarchical) binary, also resulted in the "sentimentalizing of 9/11" – again showcasing how emotion is deeply intertwined in the (mediated) events of September 11th (Spence 2004, 104). In order to prove that this emotional fixation was not short-lived and played out in narratives long after the attacks, I turn to two specific hit shows of 2006: NBC's *Heroes* and ABC's *Lost*. Both of these successful narratives utilize fear amplification, the us-versus-them binary, and motifs of unity/fate/interconnectedness to subtly tease out this theme of a nation needing to be saved.

NBC's *Heroes* (2006–2010): Season 1

The main premise of *Heroes* revolves around a plot where seemingly ordinary individuals realize they have extraordinary (super) powers. Throughout the first season of this series these main characters begin a physical odyssey that forces their paths to cross with those of the other "heroes" and a spiritual odyssey that forces them to come to terms with the responsibility that accompanies their special abilities. The inner conflict these characters face symbolizes larger societal conflicts: when does one step up, when does one speak up, when does one strike back, when does one actively play the role of the hero, and when does one passively lie back and wait to be saved. In their analysis of the show, Lynette Porter, David Lavery, and Hillary Robson pick up on this cultural conflict: "If heroes can be (or are, according to the series) genetically enhanced, then the rest of us regular mortals are off the hook as far as trying to save humanity collectively or one person at a time. Not everyone can be a hero. Heroism becomes a genetic imperative of the few, who can then wield their power as they see fit" (2007, 6). But although the show's foundation does in part enable a mindset of passing the proverbial buck, its use of everyday individuals aligning themselves for a common altruistic goal does tap into the common longing to be part of the larger scheme of things, to make a difference, to be one of the good guys. *Heroes* encourages "viewers to think about what makes a modern hero and how each person might be called upon to do something extraordinary. Because *Heroes* deals with life-or-death events and presents so many characters facing crisis points in their lives it quite naturally provides a more philosophical framework for thinking – at least sometimes – about life's larger themes" (Porter, Lavery, and Robson 2007, 33). And some of these large themes become more important to viewers in the wake of a national tragedy.

This being so, one of the major themes of the show circulates around the previously theme of interconnectedness/fate/destiny. In fact, in the final episode of season 1, "How to Stop an Exploding Man," Mohinder's voice-over states this directly: "So much struggle for meaning and purpose, and in the end we find it only in each other, our shared experience of the fantastic and the mundane" (*Heroes* 2007c). Of course, it is the shared experience of the fantastic that dominates the show. In this final episode all of the characters' paths, their destinies, have crossed so that they are all at one shared point in time where they can prevent a national tragedy, one foreshadowed throughout the season's run.

Returning to the previous discussion of censorship post-9/11, this apocalyptic storyline actually changed quite a bit from its original creation to its eventual airing. Tim Kring, the creator of *Heroes*, recounts the revamping of the explosion storyline:

> The bomb that ultimately goes off or is prevented from going off in New York was actually attached to a terrorist story and at the heart of that

terrorist story was a very sympathetic character, a Middle Eastern engineer. A young, very brilliant engineer who had become disillusioned and disenfranchised and finds himself involved with a terrorist cell and is basically the architect of the bomb. That character could actually generate and emit a tremendous amount of radioactivity through his hands. That character became Ted on our show once we moved away from the terrorist story. The terrorist story was actually shot and beautifully finished, but it never saw the light of day. It didn't make it past the screening at the network. (Porter, Lavery, and Robson 2007, 59)

Changed or not, a terrorist-like disaster did end up bringing all of the characters together at the closure of season one. In analysing the tragedy that motivates them to join forces, we should not overlook the allusions to 9/11.

The first mention of this pending disaster within the show, and hence the first allusion to 9/11, comes in the form of Isaac's painting on the floor of his art studio – a vision of a New York cityscape in flames (*Heroes* 2006). This disaster finally becomes "reality" towards the end of the season when, "in 'Five Years Gone,' *Heroes* presents an alternative future vision not only of the characters' world but also of the series itself. In terms of the season's story line, the episode reveals a dystopia that is yet to come" (Porter, Lavery, and Robson 2007, 149). The echoes of 9/11 are not all that subtle, as Porter, Lavery, and Robson note: "Rather than opaquely addressed, references to terrorism are hammered home. After the introduction of the Linderman Act, Homeland Security is called upon to clamp down on attackers 'acting against America's interests'" (149). In this episode, as the president speaks to a sober crowd in the ruins of the city beneath a banner reading "America Remembers," the scene is reminiscent of memorials stationed at Ground Zero years after September 11th.

This episode highlights our fascination with the theme of the "do-over." Viewers are shown this post-explosion scene in order to hope (along with the main characters) that it can still be prevented. Television scholars suggest that "a deeper reason" behind our love of this theme

might be that since 9/11, we are perhaps collectively foreseeing a terrible future and shuddering at the view. Now the kaleidoscope turns into a mirror, and in "Five Years Gone" we are suddenly looking at a distorted image of ourselves, at what we could become in the aftermath of 9/11. Viewers experience a shock of recognition when President Nathan Petrelli (actually Sylar) appears in front of a devastated New York landscape to speak inspirational platitudes designed to unite Americans and prevent another disaster. The scene is a slightly twisted reflection of ceremonies upon the fifth anniversary of September 11, 2001. (Porter, Lavery, and Robson 2007, 162–3)

As Porter, Lavery, and Robson (2007) note, the timing of this episode is important. In it the characters have travelled to a time five years in the future – one that if they could go back in time *just five years*, they could change. If they could go back in time (and some do have this power) and alter events, an explosion would not hit New York and forever change the world. And when viewers are watching this episode full of longing to rewrite the past, it is not unimportantly *five years* after the attacks of September 11th, 2001.

These visual images of the fictionalized ground zero are quite stirring and interesting from an ideological standpoint. Marc Redfield analyses the term "Ground Zero" which "emerged quasi-spontaneously as a proper name in American mass media immediately after the attacks. As a proper name, uncontextualized and capitalized, it refers to the site formerly occupied by the World Trade Center towers" (2007, 63). He explains that "as an idiom in more general use, it refers to the impact point of a bomb or the exact locus of an explosion. The term was military jargon when it was used at the Trinity site during the development and testing of the atom bomb; after the bombing of Hiroshima and Nagasaki, it entered the American sociolect and is now commonly used to describe centers of devastation, natural or man-made" (62). The term "both calls up and wards off ghosts of Hiroshima, remembering that other scene of destruction while also distancing or demoting it by rendering it an *other* ground zero" (62). Redfield claims that

> just as "Ground Zero" appropriates and effaces the past, it appropriates and effaces the future. Invoking the nuclear threat, it imagines the future *as* past, and as imaginable. The hammer-blow has fallen: Ground Zero itself has appeared in the world – and yet we have survived. Thus "the worst," in Derrida's phrasing (or at least a version of the worst) is at once conjured up and conjured away. (63)

Therefore, I would argue that remediated fictionalized images of ground zero, like that seen in *Heroes*, reassure viewers that they can survive the worst – that humans can and will save themselves.

Although that analysis may suggest the scene is comforting, the viewer's first exposure to it is likely somewhat disturbing. However, it is not necessarily the images of this fictionalized ground zero that are so chilling, but rather the rationalization given within the narrative for allowing it to come to be. It is a rationale grounded in the affect of fear. In ".07%" Daniel Linderman, one of the key "villains," offers this justification to up-and-coming politician Nathan Petrelli for allowing the explosion to occur: "I said people needed hope but they trust fear. This tragedy will be a catalyst for good, for change. Out of the ashes, humans will find a common goal. A united sense of hope couched in a united sense of fear. And it is your destiny, Nathan, to be the leader who uses this event to rally a city, a nation, a world" (*Heroes* 2007a). When Nathan objects to the plan, stating that half of New York will be lost, Linderman states that it will amount to *only* a .07 per cent decrease in the total world population – an acceptable loss. The importance here is again the amplification, the manipulation, of fear.

This idea of capitalizing on fear surfaces one episode later when Claire speaks to Sylar, the principle bad guy of season 1, as he is disguised as Nathan: "You made everyone afraid of us" (*Heroes* 2007b). Sylar responds, "I made everyone aware of us, fear is just a natural response." Again fear is stressed, but this time the focus is the fear that arises out of a societal structure founded upon the binary of us versus them, as the characters are now living in a world where "normal" humans are terrified of the "heroes" because of their special powers.

ABC's *Lost* (2004–2010): Season 3

Another show that plays out these issues of us versus them, fate/ destiny, and fear in a fascinating way is *Lost*. In the fall of 2006 when *Heroes* was debuted, *Lost*, a show some credit as being an ancestor text for *Heroes*, was beginning its third season. This program, when read at the surface level, is about a group of passengers who survive on an unknown island after a plane crash. However, it is actually a show about much, much more, as its complicated thematic undertakings show.

There have been over one hundred references to fate/destiny or free will in the show to date.[3] Once of the most obvious scenes is when Charlie scribbles the letters *F-A-T-E* across his taped fingers at the start of the series (*Lost* 2004a; Piatt 2006, 81). Another occurs when "Sun wonders if the survivors are being punished for past actions or secrets" (*Lost* 2005a; Porter and Lavery 2006, 100). Yet another happens when

Ana Lucia contemplates killing Sayid in an episode where he has been remembering his past wrongdoings and comments that perhaps she is *meant* to kill him (*Lost* 2005c). Two of the main "spiritual" characters, John Locke and Mr Eko, both at different times believe it to be their *destiny* to press the button in the hatch (and save the world). Hurley, a character more often used for comic relief than deep philosophical ponderings, believes that he might have been destined to end up on the island, but he equates his negative destiny with that of the *curse* he believes accompanied his tainted winning lottery numbers (Porter and Lavery, 2006, 102). And this recurring motif is foregrounded in the first episode of the second season, "Man of Science, Man of Faith," which pits the logical doctor, Jack Shephard, against the spiritual hunter, John Locke (*Lost* 2005b; Porter and Lavery 2006, 103). The conflict between these concepts (and characters) continues throughout the program's duration.

Like *Heroes*, this cycling back to explorations of fate/destiny might be attributed to being a narrative formed post-9/11. In *Living Lost: Why We're All Stuck on the Island*, Wood argues that there are many parallels within the plot that echo "our real concerns since September 11, 2001."

> What *Lost* does so successfully is take these very real concerns straight off the front pages, abstract them into their psychological impression, and then crystallize that sense back into the framework of the narrative. [...] It] involves the psychodynamics of terrorism that the contemporary audience experiences in the everyday world and plays it out on television 24 times a year. As such, *Lost* performs a very necessary function: It gives a narrative (and a safely distant context) to a real-felt sense of trauma. By giving these abstract ideas a tangible narrative with a beginning and ending each week, that sense of terror is contained by the show, and thus becomes something that might actually be manageable. (2007, ix)

In Wood's reading, "the overall narrative of the show abstracts and co-opts our very real concerns over the War on Terror(ism)" and becomes in a sense "a repository for the sense of distress that has been generated, rightly or wrongly, through our media, government, and the collective cultural response to such voices" (ix). In terms of content too, *Lost* fits "the U.S.'s own national narrative since the attacks of September 11, 2001: from plane crashes out of the clear blue to a frightened group under attack to the rallying around a leader figure and the simultaneous distrust of some members within the group" (5). Like the previously mentioned *24*, *Lost* attends to topics fueling national debate, such as torture. This gets touched on in various *Lost* episodes; examples include the episode when Sayid tortures Sawyer for Shannon's asthma medicine, when Sayid himself is tortured once captured by Rousseau, and when Sayid once again turns capturer, holding Ben hostage in the hatch (*Lost* 2004c, 2004d, 2006; Wood 2007, 6–7).

Not quite as obvious is the way the series explores the notion of survival post-trauma. Wood notes that what the fictional survivors on *Lost* "have that most don't is a group that has all survived the same unbelievable trauma to support both the individual and the individual's need to be part of the group … This aspect of the psychology of the show shouldn't look unfamiliar because it's what most people think happened after our own big plane crashes on September 11, 2001. But that kind of response doesn't just automatically 'happen'" (2007, 54). Wood compares the sacrifices made following WWII to 9/11, claiming:

> [the same] things didn't really happen after September 11th, as we were told that our comfy lifestyles would not have to change and no sacrifices beyond simple symbolic gestures were necessary – just think of all the flags posted on gas-guzzling cars in the months after September 11th, while next to nothing was done to lessen U.S. dependence on a fossil fuel economy and its crazy market fluctuations due to events in the places that provide a good deal of those fossil fuels. In its own manner, *Lost* became a model for how we could have responded as a group after a trauma, but weren't able to or chose not to. (54)

Although *Lost* does offer a community united, it does not fail to offer up the us-versus-them binary, sometimes within that united community but also between it and its outside source of conflict: "the others." The inner-group conflict first begins in the second part of the pilot episode when Sawyer accuses Sayid of being a terrorist and having caused the plane to crash, simply because of his Middle Eastern background (*Lost* 2004b). But the mysterious "others" exist as the dangerous "them" that sparks fear in the survivors throughout the first few seasons of the show. The term itself, "other," is packed with cultural baggage, but in a post-9/11 American cultural text, does this necessarily symbolize "terrorist"?

Wood answers this question: "Are the Others terrorists? Not exactly, not in the popular sense: Terrorists need to be dehumanized in the rhetoric used to describe them in order to reinforce their difference from us. This often comes in the form of turning them into animals and monsters. The Others don't use the same tactics we've come to associate with terrorism, like beheadings and suicide bombings" (2007, 107–8). He cautions against reading this too simplistically: "it's not as if *Lost*'s writers and producers actively set out to create some sort of allegory of the times. When you're steeped in the culture (as an artist or consumer), some kind of reaction to events and circumstances will exercise itself through a work, whether directly, obliquely, or actively ignoring those circumstances" (121). *Lost* does not explore our current circumstances as directly as the post-9/11 dramatic "saving" shows previously mentioned, *24*, *Alias*, and *The Unit*. But, in Wood's analysis, this makes sense, especially if we are, as he suggests, "stuck in a state of unconscious distress because we don't have any clear grasp on what it is we're supposed to be afraid of" and therefore "can't really confront that distress directly (because) we just don't know enough about it" (121–2). As a result, the fear citizens feel as a nation post-attack unconsciously resurfaces and seeks resolution in narrative spaces through repetition.

Conclusion: The Continuation of a Televisual Trend

Although *Heroes* and *Lost* serve as great televisual texts housing this cultural baggage, and the 2006–2007 season itself is fascinating for the storylines it offered up to consumers, this sort of narrative "working through" continues at present even past the close of the decade. During the 2008–2009 television, Fox launched another narrative, *Fringe* (which continues to the present), that explores the concerns of a nation (forever) battling an invisible enemy called "terror." Created by J.J. Abrams, Alex Kurtzman, and Roberto Orc, this science fiction program focuses its plot around the FBI "Fringe Division," agents operating under the supervision of Homeland Security. At the heart of this show lies an eclectic team headed by Olivia Dunham (Anna Torv), an FBI agent with enhanced supernatural skills leftover from being part of a childhood experiment; Dr Walter Bishop (John Noble), a mad scientist figure and former government researcher who understands the capabilities existing on the periphery of science; and his son, Peter Bishop (Joshua Jackson), a potential/eventual love interest to Olivia and investigative sidekick. Originally the program was concerned with investigating "the pattern" – a series of unexplainable, and often catastrophic, events caused by fringe science attacks. The perils from which the characters save society hint at mass concerns about the possible use of biological warfare and new technology. Like *Heroes*, this program ended its first season with an obvious moment of wish fulfilment when it presented viewers with a parallel universe in which the Twin Towers had not been destroyed on 9/11 (*Fringe* 2009). This storyline is continued into its later seasons.

Although not as popular, as indicated by their early cancellations, each subsequent year has featured a similar program. In 2009 ABC premiered their new drama *FlashForward* (2009–2010), a program hinted to be the replacement for the soon-to-depart *Lost*. Brannan Braga and David Goya adapted Robert J. Sawyer's 1999 science fiction novel to create this program about a mysterious event that caused a blackout wherein the entire human population lost consciousness for two minutes and seventeen seconds. During this brief time, all unconscious persons had visions of their lives six months later. A team of Los Angeles FBI agents assembled the Mosaic, a database system that compiled the visions of all who volunteered what they saw through an online website. These tentative future visions laid the foundation for their investigation as they attempted to discover not only how this event was possible but how it could be prevented in the future. This program, only airing for one season, both began and finished its run with a catastrophic terrorist attack that was loosely reminiscent of 9/11. The following year NBC tried its own hand at a new post-9/11 drama, promising (even more directly than ABC did with *FlashForward*) that this would be the show to fill the void left by popular culture juggernaut *Lost*. *The Event* (2010–2011) opened with a terrorist attack in which not only was the US government the target (and specifically the president), but the weapon of choice was an airplane. Created by Nick Wauters, the drama is decidedly science fiction, focusing on a group of extraterrestrials who were trapped on earth (some detained by the American government) for sixty-six years. As the one-season program progressed, this group began mounting escalating attacks (first on the United States and then on a wider scale) in an attempt to deplete the human population so that they can occupy Earth. As with the majority of the post-9/11 themed shows, it was up to a small group of people (mostly government officials) to attempt to save the day ... the nation ... the world.

The televisual landscape from 2010 to 2015 further revealed lingering post-9/11 trends. The salvation motif remained in a variety of post-apocalyptic programs, such as NBC's *Revolution* (2012–2014) and AMC's *The Walking Dead* (2010–present). And a proliferation of supernatural/fantasy programs – such as The CW's *The Vampire Diaries*

(2009–present), ABC's *Once Upon a Time* (2011–present), NBC's *Grimm* (2011–present), Fox's *Sleepy Hollow* (2013–present), and ABC's *Agents of S.H.I.E.L.D.* (2013–present) – often found the "good versus evil" theme common to these shows reading as a loose 9/11 allegory. The prevalence of government-focused programs continued, and with subsequent releases the political critique found within such shows escalated: Showtime's *Homeland* (2011–present), ABC's *Scandal* (2012–present), Netflix's *House of Cards* (2013–present), NBC's *The Blacklist* (2013–present), FX's *The Americans* (2013–present), CBS's *Madame Secretary* (2014–present), and NBC's *State of Affairs* (2014–present).

Well over a decade after the terrorist attacks, this type of programming is not ending, and this could be viewed as troubling. After all, as long as viewers continue to buy into the rhetoric that we need to be saved (and consume shows that reinforce this), this cycle could continue indefinitely and we could remain a nation waiting to be saved (from itself) by our protective Big Brother figure, the government, or its right-hand man, the media. However, the more recent addition of shows that provide harsher social commentary and unflinching political critique suggest that perhaps the escapism found in these post-9/11 narratives is not completely problematic. While the catharsis provided by these shows could potentially disarm political engagement and social dissent, in the midst of their hyperbolic plots these shows are providing viewers with an opportunity to grapple with important geopolitical concerns. And therefore, in between their carefully planned cliffhangers and other promotional stunts, perhaps these shows could spark real political action. If so, then maybe fictional television is the unlikely key to saving this nation after all.

NOTES

1 Although there is some scholarly debate concerning the collapsing of the two terms, in this essay I use the terms *affect* and *emotion* interchangeably.
2 I have argued in another work, *Feminism, Postmodernism, and Affect* (2009), that the medium of television can be analysed as a storage house of affects on many different levels. Most obvious would be that television programs store the affects of actors in fictional programming and the (usually) unscripted affect of non-actors in non-fiction programming. These stored programs can then act as an archive of affect in terms of the affect they created in their viewers at that time. Analysing television programs from

the same time period allows one to see trends in collective affect (similar to Raymond Williams' notion of structures of feeling) at that time. However, what makes this notion of television as keeper of affect so interesting is that it gives a technological apparatus a power usually associated with humans alone. Crediting the medium of television (in part) with the stimulation and storage of affects personifies it on some level and simultaneously draws attention to the ways that the human affect system functions similarly to this powerful media tool.

3 As one of the most analysed shows with one of the most active fan bases, *Lost* is the inspiration for many sites full of thematic dissection. One of the most intricate fan sites is *Lostpedia*. The posters on this site have documented the theme of fate/destiny or free will and list it as occurring regularly through seasons 1 through 6 with increased frequency as the series reaches closure. Contributors to this site record references within episodes to the term "destiny," to the concept of having "a purpose," to the word "fate," to the notion of free will, and to incidents highlighting the concepts of serendipity and karma.

REFERENCES

Ames, Melissa. 2009. *Feminism, Postmodernism, and Affect: An Unlikely Love Triangle in Women's Media.* Saarbrücken, Germany: VDM Verlag Dr. Müller Aktiengesellschaft.

– , ed. 2012. *Television and Temporality: Exploring Narrative Time in 21st Century Programming.* Jackson: University Press of Mississippi. http://dx.doi. org/10.14325/mississippi/9781617032936.001.0001.

– 2013. "Engaging 'Apolitical' Adolescents: Analyzing the Popularity & Educational Potential of Dystopian Literature Post-9/11." *High School Journal* 97 (1): 3–20. http://dx.doi.org/10.1353/hsj.2013.0023.

– 2014. "Where Have All the Good Men Gone?: A Psychoanalytic Reading of the Absent Fathers and Damaged Dads on ABC's *Lost*." *Journal of Popular Culture* 47 (3): 430–50. http://dx.doi.org/10.1111/jpcu.12139.

Bader, Michael J. 2006. "The Psychology of Patriotism." *Phi Delta Kappan* 87 (8): 582–4. http://dx.doi.org/10.1177/003172170608700808.

Bolter, Jay David, and Richard Grusin. 2000. *Remediation: Understanding New Media.* Cambridge, MA: MIT Press.

Broe, Dennis. 2004. "Fox and Its Friends: Global Commodification and the New Cold War." *Cinema Journal* 43 (4): 97–102. http://dx.doi.org/10.1353/cj.2004.0027.

Chunovic, Louis. 2001. "Will TV News – or Its Audience – Finally Grow Up?" *Television Week*, 25 September, 15. Quoted in Lynn Spigel. 2004. "Entertainment Wars: Television Culture after 9/11." *American Quarterly* 56 (2): 235–67.

Doane, Mary Ann. 1990. "Information, Crisis, Catastrophe." In *Logics of Television*, ed. Patricia Mellencamp, 222–39. Bloomington: Indiana University Press.

Douglas, Susan J. 2006. "The Turn Within: The Irony of Technology in a Globalized World." *American Quarterly* 58 (3): 619–38. http://dx.doi. org/10.1353/aq.2006.0057.

Fringe. 2009. Episode 1.20, "There's More than One of Everything." First broadcast 12 May 2009 by Fox. Directed by Brad Anderson and written by Jeff Pinkner, J.H. Wyman, Akira Goldsman, and Bryan Burk.

Grusin, Richard. 2004. "Premediation." *Criticism* 46 (1): 17–39. http://dx.doi. org/10.1353/crt.2004.0030.

Heroes. 2006. Episode 1.2, "Don't Look Back." First broadcast 2 October 2006 by NBC. Directed by Allan Arkush and written by Tim Kring.

– 2007a. Episode 1.19, ".07%." First broadcast 23 April 2007 by NBC. Directed by Adam Kane and written by Tim Kring & Chuck Kim.

– 2007b. Episode 1.20, "Five Years Gone." First broadcast 30 April 2007 by NBC. Directed by Paul A. Edwards and written by Tim Kring and Joe Pokaski.

– 2007c. Episode 1.23, "How to Stop an Exploding Man." First broadcast 21 May 2007 by NBC. Directed by Allan Arkush and written by Tim Kring.

– 2004a. Episode 1.1, "Pilot, Part 1." First broadcast 22 September 2004 by ABC. Directed by J.J. Abrams and written by J.J. Abrams, Damon Lindelof, and Jeffrey Lieber.

– 2004b. Episode 1.2, "Pilot, Part 2." First broadcast 29 September 2004 by ABC. Directed by J.J. Abrams and written by J.J. Abrams, Damon Lindelof, and Jeffrey Lieber.

– 2004c. Episode 1.8, "Confidence Man." First broadcast 10 November 2004 by ABC. Directed by Tucker Gates and written by Damon Lindelof.

– 2004d. Episode 1.9, "Solitary." First broadcast 17 November 2004 by ABC. Directed by Greg Yaitanes and written by David Fury.

– 2005a. Episode 1.23. "Exodus." First broadcast 18 May 2005 by ABC. Directed by Jack Bender and written by Jeffrey Lieber.

– 2005b. Episode 2.1, "Man of Science, Man of Faith." First broadcast 21 September 2005 by ABC. Directed by Jack Bender and written by Damon Lindelof.

– 2005c. Episode 2.8. "Collision." First broadcast 23 November 2005 by ABC. Directed by Stephen Williams and written by Jeffrey Lieber.

– 2006. Episode 2.14, "One of Them." First broadcast 15 February 2006 by ABC. Directed by Stephen Williams and written by Damon Lindelof and Carlton Cruse.

Massumi, Brian. 2005. "Fear (The Spectrum Said)." *Multitudes*. http://www.multitudes.net/Fear-The-spectrum-said/ . http://dx.doi.org/10.1215/10679847-13-1-31. Accessed 2 July 2006.

Mellencamp, Patricia. 1990a. *Logics of Television*. Bloomington: Indiana University Press.

– 1990b. "TV Time and Catastrophe, or Beyond the Pleasure Principle of Television." In *Logics of Television*, 240–66. Bloomington: Indiana University Press.

Piatt, Christian. 2006. *Lost: A Search for Meaning*. St. Louis: Chalice.

Porter, Lynette, and David Lavery. 2006. *Unlocking the Meaning of Lost: An Unauthorized Guide*. Naperville: Sourcebooks.

Porter, Lynnette, David Lavery, and Hillary Robson. 2007. *Saving the World: A Guide to Heroes*. Toronto: ECW Press.

Redfield, Marc. 2007. "Virtual Trauma: The Idiom of 9/11." *Diacritics* 37 (1): 55–80. http://dx.doi.org/10.1353/dia.0.0020.

Sedgwick, Eve Kosofsky, and Adam Frank. 1995. *Shame and Its Sisters: A Silvan Tomkins Reader*. Durham: Duke University Press.

Sontag, Susan. 2003. *Regarding the Pain of Others*. New York: Picador.

Spence, Louise. 2004. "Teaching 9/11 and Why I'm Not Doing it Anymore." *Cinema Journal* 43 (2): 100–5. http://dx.doi.org/10.1353/cj.2004.0012.

Spigel, Lynn. 2004. "Entertainment Wars: Television Culture after 9/11." *American Quarterly* 56 (2): 235–70. http://dx.doi.org/10.1353/aq.2004.0026.

Stillwell, Cinnamon. 2007, 31 January. "'24': Television for a Post-9/11 World." *SFGate*. http://www.sfgate.com/politics/article/24-Television-for-a-Post-9-11-World-2652979.php. Accessed 10 April 2008.

Wood, J. 2007. *Living Lost: Why We're All Stuck on the Island*. Garrett County Press.

Žižek, Slavoj. 2002. *Welcome to the Desert of the Real: Five Essays on September 11 and Related Dates*. New York: Verso.

6 Preparation for National Revolution or Acceptance of Inevitable Decay?

DMITRY SHLAPENTOKH

The problem of Russian nationalist extremist and various neo-fascist groups has been a popular subject among those who have watched events in Russia/the USSR for almost a generation. In fact, these quasi-political and intellectual trends in Russian life could well be recorded since the end of Gorbachev's rule, when the authorities ended their control over the country's political and cultural life and thus allowed a variety of political and intellectual groups, including those who professed a number of extremist and nationalist doctrines, to manifest themselves in various ways.

In the very beginning of the post-Soviet era, starting with the dissolution of the USSR and the regime in 1991, the nationalists, usually under the umbrella of what critics called "Red to Brown" opposition (consisting of nationalist-minded "National-Bolshevik" type communists and out-and-out nationalists), were a constant point of reference for those who watched events in Russia unfold. At that time, the notion of "Weimar Russia" was quite popular. This scenario assumed that at that time Russia was quite similar to Weimar Germany and that the humiliation of what the West saw as the USSR/Russian defeat in the Cold War and economic misery would lead to the rise of a regime similar to that of Germany from 1933 to 1945.

Since this scenario did not materialize, interest in Russian nationalists declined along with interest in Russia as a country. In fact, there is not much interest in Russia now except for its connection with gas and oil.

The Russian extremists continue to be noticed and their attacks on non-European-looking people deplored; but not much is done to analyse the context of their activities and even less their ideology. They are usually dubbed "neo-fascists," not to engage in a study of their ideological paradigms but just to provide a sort of moral judgment, in order to emphasize the ugliness of their actions. Still, a close analysis of their views – usually available only on Internet sites and often quickly removed or blocked by the authorities – is quite an important endeavour. It reveals several important social/political and ideological layers. First, it reveals that the conditions leading to outbreaks of violence are implicitly connected with the global demographic and geopolitical shift that is occurring. Russia, in this case, is possibly just one of the proverbial "weakest links." Second, the ideology of the extremists illustrates the peculiarities of the process in Russia. It reveals the idiosyncratic features of present-day Russian capitalism, which is marked not only by increasing social polarization but also by a strong regional polarization, where the social-ethnic animus is directed not just against the elite and the minorities but against the capital, in fact, against the Russian state itself.

An analysis of the views of Russian extremists also points out the peculiarities of the vision of social/ethnic mobilization. On one hand, some of these extremists are full of a twisted form of historical optimism. They believe that Russians will finally rise and smash the regime of the minorities and the rich; for them both groups are actually the same. For others, Russia and Russians have no hope and will disappear, as has happened with other nations.

While Russian extremists are engaged in constant discussions about Russia's present and future, some events stimulate these discussions and prompt a large number of people to exchange their views. One of these events was the ethnic riot in Kondopoga, the small Russian city in the north of European Russia, in Karelia. The event took place in late August/early September 2006 and was the biggest ethnic riot in which ethnic Russians were involved in all of post-Soviet history, or at least in Putin's entire tenure. The riot started as an ordinary brawl but soon evolved into a battle in which hundreds of Russians and Chechens took part. The battle led to pogroms of Chechens in the city and was stopped only by the employment of a considerable force of riot police. The event led to widespread public response and caused extensive discussions concerning the position of ethnic Russians and their relationship with ethnic minorities, mostly those who came from the Northern Caucasus, and in the Russian state.

The Internet discussions, especially those carried on by Russian nationalist youth, provide a good snapshot of their vision of the present and future. Practically all who engaged in these discussions see the present-day regime as being foreign to Russians, the majority. The regime represents the minorities and the rich; for some of those engaged in the discussions, the rich and the minorities were, as noted above, the same. While Jews occasionally emerged as the source of the problems, it is not the Jews – the butt of "Red to Brown" of the Yeltsin era – but the people from the North Caucasus who are the major culprits. At the same time, the Kondopoga conflict was not just a manifestation of ethnic and social tension; it had other dimensions. In the view of the participants in the Kondopoga riot, the exploitive non-Russian nature of the state was manifested in the role of Moscow. The capital's dominant power had made it, in the eyes of Russian nationalists, the very embodiment of the ills of Russian society. Thus, in their view, Russia could not be free unless the power of Moscow was dramatically reduced. Moreover, these Russian nationalists see the entire centralized apparatus of the Russian state as an oppressive machine; and some imply that Russian liberation from Moscow could well lead to the country's disintegration, where a much smaller Russia would be free from what they see as a non-Russian centralized state and, collaterally, the minorities whose interests it represents. At the same time, for some of these Russian nationalists, liberation from Moscow and, implicitly the state should not be a goal in itself but the springboard for national revolution. This revolution should be meticulously prepared through the creation of an underground and legal party or parties and by the most radical changes in the lifestyle and values of Russian youth. This revolution could be successful and, while preserving the Russian state, would make Russia a good place to live for the majority of Russians. However, for other participants in the discussions, regardless of change or the absence of change, Russians are doomed; and here their fate will parallel the fate of other Europeans, and of white people in general. They are all destined to perish or be assimilated by non-Europeans.

Moscow as the Enemy

The riot in Kondopoga and other ethnic riots generated intense Internet discussions about the nature of the problems and how to solve them. One major theme was the regional conflict between the provinces and Moscow. In this case, Moscow's transformation into a non-Russian imperial parasite in what was actually a non-Russian city was seen as the reason for the minorities' domination of ethnic Russians and, consequently, for the ethnic Russians' misery.

The theory that Russia should be divided along regional/ethnic lines where Moscow, and thus the central government, represents the minorities, whereas the poor and oppressed ethnic Russians are residents of the provinces, is not accepted in its totality by all the people of the Russian Federation. Still, even the sceptics accept the idea that regional divisions are important in the Russian Federation, and they are a source of much animosity. This animosity could be seen in the Internet discussions following the events in Kondopoga, centrally in the Internet newspaper *Gazeta.ru*. Some of those who participated in the discussions stated that one should not look at ethnic/regional tensions as the source of the problems that led to outbursts of the Kondopoga type, but instead view the problems from a much broader perspective: one should blame the post-Soviet system.[1]

For instance, a certain "Inkognito" expressed the view that it is naive to see minorities as the source of the problems; rather, it is the social-economic arrangement that fosters corruption and abuses of all sorts and that is responsible for ethnic Russians' misery. Implicit in this is the claim that the post-Soviet regime has brought misery to everyone, Russians and non-Russians, Muscovites and provincials alike.[2] Not only has the post-Soviet system fostered corruption but it has deprived the majority of Russian youth of any prospects for the future. This was the view of "Tataro Bashkir," who stated that the Soviet system of professional education has been destroyed and most Russian youth have no future. It is not coincidental that these young people have become either communists or neo-fascists. Finally, "Vladimir" noted that the rise of ethnic tensions is the result of the twenty-year-old process of destruction of a "great country." And since this process continues, he expected that it would continue in the future.

All of these commentators asserted that the major problems in the system were created by the end of the Soviet system and the USSR as a state. For all of these people, the ethnic/regional problems are either marginal or are derivations from the general problems of post-Soviet society. Still, for other participants in the discussion, regional problems are central, or at least one of the most important consequences of the collapse of the USSR. "Dimonets," expressing the view of such commentators, stated that Russia is divided along regional lines much more than along ethnic lines. There is a sharp division between well-to-do Moscow and most of the country. As a matter of fact, provincials look at Moscow as a "foreign enclave" and hate it deeply.

Gazeta.ru is a mainstream publication; and those who participated in the discussion were usually people who did not want to confront the authorities directly. This was not the case with those who either directly participated in the Kondopoga riot or engaged in similar events that followed. These see Moscow as the enemy of the provincial folk and call for direct action against the imperial capital, without, it seems, concern that the authorities could impose unwelcome consequences. For example, "Comandante," one of the commentators on the *DPNI* site,[3] stated that provincials see Moscow as an "independent state" and hate it. In the case of a mass uprising, the writer continued, Moscow would be cut off from the rest of the country; and masses would destroy any roads that led to Moscow, as well as electricity and gas supply lines. The army would be neutral, and OMON (the riot police) and the militia would not be enough to impose Moscow's power over the entire country.[4]

Separation from Moscow is seen not just as liberation from imperial predators but also as the only way to make Russia free of non-Russians. "Witch Hunter," a Russian who sent his message from Munich, proposed that the residents of various Russian regions separate from corrupted Moscow. After the end of Moscow's rule, the rule that made non-Russian domination possible, Russians in the provinces could create a new society. They should purge all newcomers with the exception of those who have a useful profession.[5] Other radicals who participated in the discussion of Kondopoga and Russia's future and clustered around certain Internet sites share this view. For them, the disintegration of the Russian Federation is seen as an act of both national and social liberation. A certain "Ural" contributor to the Internet discussions on www.apn.ru, most likely from Ural or Siberia, does not regard Russia's disintegration and the creation of an independent Tatarastan, as well as an independent Ural and Siberia, as something horrific. In fact, in his view, it would be just a liberation of Russian land from Moscow's yoke.[6]

Other contributors to the discussions, while generally supporting the idea of Russia partition, assume that this should be done thoughtfully, with due planning. Elaborating on this, a certain "Iaromir" stated that one should not be in a hurry with the partitioning of Russia: Russians were overly hasty in the past when they divided the USSR, and did not benefit from these changes. "Iaromir" believed that Russians could benefit if the changes were made in several steps. First, a truly Russian government should be established in Russia. Second, Russia should evict non-Russians, especially people from the Caucasus. And only then should Russia engage in a division of Russian territory.[7] Although Russians should definitely shed the territories of those minorities who are clearly hostile to Russia, they should not do this with all minorities, especially those who want to live in peace with Russians.

"Iaroslav" stated that there are good Tatars who tried to prove to other Tatars that they are not descendants of a nomadic people but actually of ancient Bulgars, who are close to Russians. This could, he implied, make Russians and Tatars indeed friends.[8]

The assumption that Russians might shed undesirable minorities and maintain their association with others is shared by other parties in the discussion. "Vadim" stated that he would eagerly shed the Northern Caucasus because the people who lived there were "non-human" (*urody*.) At the same time, he is opposed to the view that Russia should shed all ethnic enclaves. He, for example, visited Tuva and found its natives were peaceful and its natural environment impressive. He did not see any Chinese in the area as an indication, he implied, that the region might be absorbed by China in the near future; and he believed that Tuva should be a part of Russia.[9]

There even are those who could be regarded as Russian imperialists and supporters of the unity of the Russian Federation who implied that the dissolution of the Federation could be accepted if this is the only way of liberating Russia from the foreign yoke. "Jckl," one of the participants on apn.ru, serves as an example. "Jckl" stated that present-day Russians are polluted by "Soviet [*sovkovo*]-imperial" ideology. He alluded to the mentality of many ethnic Russians during the Soviet era, when Russians were very proud of being the major group of the mighty Soviet empire, the USSR, and actually dissolved their "Russianness" into "Sovietness," a broad trans-ethnic imperial ideology. This all-embracing, benign imperialism prevented Russians from thinking about their peculiar national interests as ethnic Russians. This sort of mentality has not died out even now that the USSR has fallen apart. Russians continue to see the residents of the former republics of the USSR as a sort of brotherly people, despite the fact, "Jckl" implied, that they are now citizens of independent states; and for this reason Russians let various non-Russians from the former USSR republics enter the country. This dissolving of "Russianness" into "Sovietness," which implies a sort of amalgamation of ethnic Russians with minorities and an erasure of Russians' own identity, is seen as a great asset by some Russian ideologists. Aleksandr Dugin, the leading proponent of Eurasianism in Russia, has regarded this weakness of the ethnic/national identity as a attribute that will help Russians embrace the people of Eurasia and resurrect an empire more grand than the USSR. In this empire Orthodox Russians, while being in the position of leader, would in many ways be blended with other ethnic/religious groups and cultures. Ethnic Russians in such an arrangement would have no special privileges, and in fact would share the onerous burden of maintaining empire, as was the case during the Soviet period. "Jekl" rejects this vision, believing that Russians could build such an empire only if Russians could live well in this empire. A Russian empire, he asserts, should benefit not abstract residents of the empire but ethnic Russians, or at least fully assimilated minorities. He noted that he understands the implications of the ideology that the Russian state should be primarily for ethnic Russians and those who are fully Russified: that this ideology could well lead to the secession of Yakutia, Chukotka, Tatarstan, Bashkiria, and Caucasus, and that Russia, instead of being a grand state, could well be reduced to its small medieval borders. At the same time, he believed that this disintegration is not predestined, and a strong Russian empire with ethnic Russians playing the leading role would culturally assimilate minorities and control them as part of the grand Russian state. But Russians should assert empire only if doing so benefits ethnic Russians. It is not the fate of the Russian empire/state, he implied, but the fate of the Russian people that should be the major concern of the Russian elite and their leaders. And, he insisted, if the Russian empire/state could not guarantee the centrality of the Russian people and their interests, it should be partitioned.

Vodoleev[10] also believed that Russia's territorial integrity should be basically preserved but that some non-Russian land could well be shed. He stated that increasing numbers of Russians understand they are ruled by a government that does not represent them. They also understand that part of Russian territory is not actually in Russian hands and that the wealth of these regions is controlled by a few nouveau riche. Consequently, many of these Russians are ready to shed such regions as the Caucasus, Iakutiia, Chukotka, and Tuva. Vodoleev does not subscribe to such a plan in its totality. He suggests that much of Russia's territory is wrongly viewed as ethnic enclaves of non-Russians. For example, both Iakutiia and Tuva are actually Russian lands. Russians simply allow the natives to live there and could easily, in his view, reinstate their authority. Regions in which they cannot dominate could be shed, such as Caucasian regions. All of this would lead to the loss of not more than one per cent of Russian territory.

The idea that Moscow, a centralized "state" in general, is an oppressive institution and ethnic Russians – in fact all ethnic groups within the Russian population – would be better off if Russia fell apart, or at least shed some of its territories, is shared not just by Russian nationalist-minded separatists but by some leftist radicals. The group "Revolutionary Contact Unity" (Revoliutsionnoe Kontaktnoe Ob'edinenie) is an example. This group is led by Boris Stomakhin, the radical journalist affiliated with the Chechen resistance and recently imprisoned by the authorities. The members of the group regard Russia as an imperial state that started to form as an empire in the fifteenth century, and they believe that only the disintegration of this empire will make Russia free.[11]

From Separatism to National Revolution

According to some participants in the Kondopoga events, ethnic Russians should rise and dismantle the Russian Federation as a way of liberating the Russian majority from the domination of the ethnic minorities supported by Moscow. Other participants, or would-be participants, believe that either the Kondopoga riot or similar events would lead to nationwide revolutions that would replace the anti-Russian regime with one representing the interests of ethnic Russians – the majority of the poor.

The Kondopoga events had an immediate response from a variety of publications, including those that represent opposition to the current regime. One of these was *Zavtra*, a prominent vehicle of so-called Red to Brown folk of "National-Bolshevik-minded Communists" and out-and-out "nationalists." *Zavtra's* relationship with Putin is unstable, and periods when *Zavtra* praised Putin for attempting to undo what they regarded as the disastrous Yeltsin legacy have alternated with periods of strong criticism of Putin's regime. In this interpretation, Putin's regime is not so much an attempt to undo "Yeltsinism" as to perpetuate Yeltsin's regime. Even as *Zavtra* became more pro-Putin, they continued to publish critical articles on the regime; and, of course, during its critical periods the number of these articles increased. Following Kondopoga, *Zavtra* published an article by Ivan Lentsev blaming post-Soviet developments for creating the conditions that made Kondopoga possible.[12]

With all of his criticism of the regime, Lentsev refrained from a direct call to get rid of the regime. Such calls could be dangerous in Putin's Russia. Other commentators were much bolder, taking advantage of the anonymity of the Internet. A certain "Aleksandr," commenting on Lentsev's article, wrote that the events in Kondopoga show that the regime is rotten and needs to be removed. "Amater" supported this view and stated that it was the mansions of the bureaucracy, not the cafes and shops of Chechens, that should be set on fire.

While some readers of *Zavtra* had advocated overthrow of the regime, most did not make such statements. There are a variety of possible reasons for this. To start with, *Zavtra*, still a mainstream publication and legally distributed, discourages such statements, which could lead to trouble with the authorities. Second, the readers of the paper, typically in late middle age or elderly, well remember the repressive power of the state and so avoid making statements that could involve them in difficulties with the authorities. The situation is different for those who participated in the discussions on other, non-mainstream, Internet sites. They represent a younger and bolder segment of the population, who are not afraid to call for direct confrontation with the regime. It is these Internet discussions that are most important in providing a sample of the views of radical-minded Russians who call for overthrow of the regime; and it is not surprising that the discussions were quickly removed and disappeared from cyberspace.

As the events in Kondopoga unfolded, intense Internet discussion sprang up, centring on the websites rusidea.ru, www.apn.ru, and ari.ru. One observer of Kondopoga events and a participant in the discussion on rusidea.ru implied that what he saw in Kondopoga was actually the beginning of a national revolution, which would spell the end of the corrupt and non-Russian regime. He believed that the uprising in Kondopoga would spread to other Russian cities.[13] The people who engaged in the discussion on apn.ru followed suit. "Sergei" sees in the present regime the major enemy of the Russian people and believes this regime should and can be overthrown.[14]

Those who most likely participated in the Kondopoga events and placed their comments on the city of Kondopoga's Internet site (http://www.cityk.onego.ru) stated that Russians should fight against their genocide, it is the Russian government that is responsible for the mistreatment of Russian people,[15] and only by pressure on power could Russians achieve anything.[16]

The Rise of the New Proletariat

Participants in the Internet discussions instinctively followed a revolutionary paradigm in one important respect, without of course understanding this. Most of them were preoccupied with the problem of finding the revolutionary class/group that could engage in revolutionary change. Implicit in this is the assumption that, while revolutionary change would benefit the majority of the people, only a comparatively small subset of the population would be the ringleaders of change. This idea about the importance of revolutionary leaders is especially strong in Marxism, which had been the official ideology in Russia/the USSR for generations. And though Marxism has been removed from public discourse, it still exercises a powerful if unacknowledged influence upon the mentality of quite a few Russians. In the discussions generated during and after Kondopoga, two forces emerged that could engage in national revolution, or at least trigger a mass upheaval and the end of the regime.

It is well known that young people are often the catalysts of change or at least accept new ideas much more readily than older generations. This was the case during the early periods of the Soviet regime, not just because youth were more efficiently brainwashed but also because they saw in the regime prospects for social advancement; this was one of the most important reasons that ambitious youth joined the ruling party. One can see a similar phenomenon in other totalitarian regimes, such as Nazi Germany and fascist Italy.

In the late Soviet era, the situation started to change. There were increasing signs of stagnation and declining chances of social mobility for ambitious youth, and the image of the West as a place of plenty and pleasure increasingly moved Russians towards a sort of spontaneous Westernism. This in a way reflected party policy. In the late Stalinist era (1945–53), the authorities launched a policy against "kowtowing to the West," mostly directed against Russian intellectuals who, in the view of the authorities, paid too much attention to Western cultural and scientific achievements. Russian intellectuals, the authorities insisted, should turn to the great achievements of the Soviet people and especially of the Russian people; and authorities praised the achievements of Russian civilization throughout the centuries. This emphasis on the importance of Russian culture, irrespective of its time of origin, reflected the "National Bolshevistic" evolution of the regime and the corresponding rise of Russian nationalism as the most important aspect of the official ideology. The average Russian youth was not of much concern to the authorities at that time.

By contrast, throughout Nikita Krushchev's regime (1953–64) the authorities increasingly targeted Soviet youth who had become influenced by the West, which they saw as offering a high living standard and a carefree life full of pleasure, with sexual promiscuity as one of the major attractions. By the time of Brezhenev's regime, the fascination with the West, shared by an increasing number of Russian youth, had been politically and ideologically formalized. From this point on, increasing segments of the Russian population, intelligentsia and masses alike, did not just view Western life with fascination; they also viewed the political and social/economic arrangements of the Soviet system as unworkable. It is not surprising that when Gorbachev started his reforms, the majority of Russian youth joined the Westernizers who believed that Russia should be transformed according to Western models. Despite increasing economic problems, the majority of these youth were still on the side of the Yeltsin regime; and this was the apparent reason for such an attitude.

The regime that emerged in the wake of the collapse of the Soviet system and the country provided a spectacular opportunity for some energetic, entrepreneurial, and criminal-minded youth, a few of whom would be the multi-billionaires of the future. Even the spread of general anarchy and the increasing criminalization of society was welcomed by a considerable number of Russian youth: the culture of criminality not only provided them with an opportunity for quick enrichment, but it also led to the end of the controlling, repressive aspect of the state. As a result, promiscuity and alcoholism spread, and this was also welcomed by a considerable number of Russian youth, who equated liberty   in fact, the good life in general – with license. This pro-Western attitude of Russian youth – of course, their image of the West had little in common with the real West – prompted most Western observers to assert that dismantling of the Soviet system and reconstruction following Western models was Russia's future. These Western observers claimed only the older generation, who represented the "Red to Brown" opposition of the Yeltsin regime, were opposed to such reforms, and that the younger generation were firmly behind Yeltsin and his essentially pro-Western policies.

As social and economic development unfolded, the attitude of Russian youth to post-Soviet Russia and the West started to change, as did their approach. On one hand, the educated and successful youth – mostly in a few big Russian cities, especially Moscow – had entered the middle class. While these youth could be quite critical of the West, especially the United States, for pushing Russia around – they blamed the US for the demise of the USSR – they are not much different from the Western middle class in their outlook and behaviour. The story becomes quite different with the increasingly disenfranchised segment of Russian youth who lack the opportunity of educated youth in the big cities and especially the capital. Even in the capital and other large cities – the most prosperous segments of Russian society – not every-body enjoys prosperity, and there is a growing number of underclass youth. For all of these, the present system has become deeply hostile. They can in some ways be compared with the representatives of the "Red to Brown" opposition of the Yeltsin era, but there are substantial differences between the two, particularly in their approach to violence, which is the most important issue here.

"Red to Brown" adherents were not, of course, opposed to violence. In fact, their publications were full of direct calls to get rid of the regime, and they endlessly exhorted Russians to follow the examples of the Russian Revolutions of 1905–20. They also rose up against the regime in the fall of 1993. But despite all their vitriol, they were quite subdued in their actions. Members did not rise up or call for an uprising against the regime even in 1998 when, in the wake of the ruble's sharp devaluation, a considerable segment of the Russian population might well have fol-lowed their call.[17] It is quite a different story with today's disenchanted youth: violence is an integral part of their life, and they are not afraid of direct action.

The second important difference is in the two groups' approach to the West. Certainly, opposition to the Yeltsin regime saw the West as the source of Russia's problems; but they did not ignore Western public opinion and were upset when they were compared with Nazis. The situ-ation is different with Putin-era nationalistic youth. On one hand, many of them are hardly anti-Western. They are, for example, quite fascinated with the European right and neo-Nazis. In fact, they are pretty much fascinated with Hitler; and his birthday (April 20: ironically, almost the same as Lenin's, April 22 – gives them an excuse to harass, beat up, and sometimes kill everyone who does not look European/white. Also in sharp contrast from the "Red to Brown" groups, they are not inter-ested in the Soviet system, plainly because they see in it the lingering problems in present-day Russia. In this, they look similar to Russian Westernized liberals, though in other respects they are very different.

For Westernized liberals, the Soviet regime's problems either were due to artificial unworkable utopian paradigms that Russian Marxists imposed upon the helpless populace, or – in another interpretation – Marxism and the socialist regime just reinforced the negative genetics of Russian historical tradition, such as the Russian autocratic tradition. In the case of Russian nationalist-radical youth, the problem is quite different: it is that the Soviet regime led to the marginalization of ethnic Russians. This group is hardly proponents of Alexandr Dugin and similar thinkers who preach ideas about "Eurasian" symbiosis; and this is a reason why they have marginalized Stalin and are so fond of Hitler as a "truly" European dictator. Their fascination with the European right, including the Nazis, is accompanied with an absolute disregard for Western public opinion. They dismiss as biased the view of Russian liberals. It is these characteristics that make some of the representatives of the new generation of Russian youth a peculiarly revolutionary force.

One contributor to the discussion on rusidea.ru, "Marbett," implied that even if Kondopoga does not unleash a nationwide revolution on its own, it is still a welcome sign of events to come. "Marbett's" point is that events in Kondopoga show that a new generation of Russians is rising. These people have two major characteristics that make them different from the previous generation. First, they are not submissive and are ready to fight for their rights. Second, they are people who do not care what the West thinks about them.[18]

An anonymous contributor to the discussion on ari.ru noted, in this respect, that the mass media, which is in the hands of the Jews, had attributed Kondopoga to Russian extremists and criminals[19] in order to denigrate those who participated in the events and dismiss their rightful grievance. He or she maintains that since the mass media, in both Russia and the West, slander those who fight for their rights, the Russians should in turn ignore what the mass media write about them.

While "Marbett" sees in the new generation of Russian youth a sort of new type of proletariat, one who would liberate itself from oppression, other radicals from apn.ru find in criminals the ringleaders of the future revolt. One writer, using the pen name "Dorogoi Rossianin," sees in criminals the major revolutionary force. "Dorogoi Rossianin" implied that the example of Kondopoga would inspire Russians to act in the same way. He also explained why in his view it was the people of Kondopoga who started to rebel. His point is that there are a lot of ex-convicts among the Karelian population, and this, he believes, is fortunate. He praises ex-criminals as the sort of revolutionary force he actually follows, without realizing this is the paradigm of the European/American left in the 1960s and 1970s, who saw in criminals and similar sectors of the population such as racial minorities a truly revolutionary force. Following the same logic as those earlier radicals, "Dorogoi Rossianin" asserted that not only could ex-convicts not be easily integrated into society, making them, he implied, permanent outcasts ready for revolution, but they were endowed with other great attributes: they are not easily brainwashed and can stand up for themselves.

With restless Russian youth ready to do battle and criminals as a kind of revolutionary vanguard, the Russian revolution has a great chance of victory. Still, those engaged in the Internet discussions believe that Russians should organize themselves before the final onslaught.

Avoiding the Wrong Target

While those who watched Kondopoga and similar events understand the frustration of ethnic Russians that incites them to spontaneous violence against "Caucasians," this does not mean that all of them support these pogrom outbursts. The problem is not one of morality – that pogrom-type violence is not acceptable – but the practical concern of *Realpolitiks* of a sort. And here the participants in the discussion, surprisingly, started to think in Lenin's terms, which denounced Jewish pogroms because they directed the masses' anger in the wrong direction.

Throughout its modern history, Russia has experienced outbreaks of spontaneous violence, including the horrific peasant revolts throughout the seventeenth and eighteenth centuries and the occasional localized peasant uprisings of the nineteenth century. There were no Jewish pogroms between the late eighteenth century, when a large Jewish community became part of the Russian empire after the partition of Poland, and the end of the nineteenth century. The lack of pogroms – as well as of major peasant uprisings throughout most of the nineteenth century – was due to several factors, one of which might be that Russia's arrangements of that time were a sort of replica of the Soviet system. Peasants, predominantly serfs, were under the constant gaze of their immediate masters and the peasant commune. The controlling/repressive aspect of the system constituted a protective safety net of sorts. It was not in the interests of the landlord to let his peasants – his valuable property – starve to death, so he usually provided some assistance if there was a crop failure. In any case, Russia, from the late seventeenth century (the time when serfdom became finally entrenched) to the end of serfdom in 1861, never experienced the catastrophic famines that occurred in Europe at that time.

This combination of control/repression and safety net disappeared by the end of the nineteenth century with the end of serfdom, coinciding with an influx of unemployed and uprooted people in Russian towns and villages. While the authorities kept their eyes on the big cities and especially the capital, this was not the case with the small towns and villages, which by the end of the nineteenth century had been marked by the first wave of Jewish pogroms, after the assassination of Alexander II, the tsar "liberator," by revolutionaries. (The populace attributed the murder to the Jews.) Although those who participated in violence and looting proclaimed their monarchist feelings, the authorities were alarmed. They believed, not without grounds, that violence could get out of control. This anxiety on the part of the authorities was noted by revolutionaries – the Populists, who believed that the peasants were pregnant with revolutionary spirit and could easily rise in revolt. For this reason, Populists occasionally cast a positive light on pogroms in the belief that pogroms would finally explode the entire political and social order. Later, in the beginning of the twentieth century, revolutionaries, and notably Lenin, changed their views on the implications of ethnic violence in general and anti-Jewish pogroms in particular. Lenin proclaimed that anti-Jewish violence is actually fomented by the authorities as a way of diverting the anger of the masses from striking the regime. Some of those who watched Kondopoga followed the same logic. They proclaimed that the Russian masses should not beat up "Caucasians," or at least should not regard them as the major culprits but focus their attention on the real enemies – the regime and ruling elite that in these cases is often identified with Jews.

"Alwyn," a participant in the discussions, warned against pogrom-type activities and, implicitly, called for building an organization to direct Russians' anger against the regime. "Alwyn" supported the view that it was mostly Jews who incited ethnic violence in Russia. This view seems strange at first glance, since the Jews were one of the prime victims of mob-incited violence in Imperial Russia. In the last years of the Soviet regime, the authorities also sponsored official anti-Semitism disguised as anti-Zionism and subtly encouraged the anti-Semitism of the Russian masses; some Russian Jews believed at that time that pogrom-type violence could erupt. But in post-Soviet Russia the situation changed greatly. Not only had official anti-Semitism disappeared, but quite a few Jews had climbed to the top and entered the ranks of the emerging super-rich. This provided the intellectual fodder for "Red to Brown" opposition to the Yeltsin regime – a loose coalition of nationalists and nationalist-minded communists – to see the new regime of the exploitive super-rich as a Jewish regime. In this context, anti-Semitic violence is seen by some Russian nationalists as the way to social liberation. Other Russian nationalists believe, in the present-day context, that the Jews – equated here with the elite and the state itself – are not so fearful of spontaneous pogrom-type violence because they assume it can be controlled and directed against helpless Chechens and other Muslim minorities who can be blamed for the appalling living conditions of the majority of Russians. Muslim intellectuals also spread the idea that it is the Jews who foment hostility against Muslims and divert Russians from fighting their real enemies – the Jewish elite. Thus, the conclusion is simple, at least for "Alwyn" and similar-thinking people: Russians should not engage in senseless pogroms against Chechens or other Muslims but organize and engage in the struggle against their real enemy: the regime.

"Pomor," whose pen name indicates that he most likely is a resident of the northern part of European Russia, proclaimed on apn.ru that in their struggle with the regime, the Russians should not forget about the "Caucasians," who are both the support of the regime, he implied, and a problem in themselves. He stated that Russians should engage in a consistent struggle against these "parasites": they should not buy from shops owned by Caucasians, should not give bribes to them, and should defend Russians against the abuses of the Caucasians. At the same time, the struggle against Caucasians should not divert attention from the most important goal, putting to an end to the rule of "Putin-Yid" – the real puppet-master and source of the problem for Russians. The assumption that, if not a Jew himself, Putin is at least firmly on their side is shared by other participants in Internet discussions.[20] While some believe spontaneous ethnic violence should be avoided, as benefiting the ruling elite, which both foments it and directs it against minorities, other participants maintain that the Kondopoga-type violence was spontaneous and not controlled by anyone, and it is this that could be a real danger: this type of violence could well lead to anarchy from which everyone, including Russians, could suffer.[21] Thus, here the organization became a key to future success. Some discussion participants provided practical advice on how to create an underground organization to fight Russians' enemies.

Organization and Preparation

It seems that at least some of the nationalists who watched or participated in the Kondopoga event understand the importance of organizations, legal, semi-legal, or underground. They grasped that only with
organization could they overthrow Putin's regime and do away with
the rule of the minorities, which these Russian nationalists regard as
the source, or at least a symbol, of their problems. And in understanding the importance of organization, at least within Russia's political
context, these Russian nationalists became, in a way, Leninists. It was
Lenin – and in this he was quite different from Marx – who emphasized
the importance of the organization/party, without which the victory of
revolution would be impossible. One might add that the other forces
that confront Putin's regime – the Muslim jihadists – also started to
emphasize the importance of organization, and even make positive reference to Lenin in this regard.

An understanding of the importance of organization and mass
mobilization of a sort could be seen in the writings of "Dmitrius,"
who stated that he fully supported the people from Kondopoga and
their fight against Chechens. While emotionally he understands the
residents of Kondopoga, he still warned them against spontaneous
outbursts. Although Chechens are supporters of the regime, it is still
the "corrupted power and militia" that is behind Russian problems
in Kondopoga – and, he implied – all over Russia. It is this force that
wants to direct the people's anger in the direction of ethnic violence as
a way of discrediting them and diverting them from the proper target,
the regime. Undermining the foundations of the regime and fighting
Chechens – who (again) are seen as a force behind the regime – requires
a different strategy. He believes that Russians should engage in a long
campaign against those who come from the Northern Caucasus and
who are, he claims, nothing but a bunch of criminals. One way of dealing with these people is a boycott: refusing to buy anything from them.
This is the best way, he suggests, for in such a case people do not violate the law. They could buy goods from anybody else, he continues,
including the Chinese, who are quiet people and for this reason are not
the objects of neo-Nazi hate.

"Dmitrius" recognizes that while a boycott of Chechens and legal
resistance to the authorities and those who support them is essential
for Russia's liberation, it is not enough. Following Lenin's dictum,
without of course acknowledging or understanding that he is doing

so, he pointed to the importance of an organized and, implicitly, underground party.

"Dmitrius" stated that Russians are powerless now because of their lack of solidarity and the absence of an organization that could direct the people's anger. From this perspective, he writes, Russians are quite different from Chechens: "Our main problem is we cannot be united. The majority just wants to live comfortably and do not give a damn for others. And they [Chechens] have a different philosophy. And here they are the good role models. They are stronger than we."[22]

According to him, it is of course not just the Chechens who wish Russians to be weak and disorganized. The authorities also want Russians to remain a disorganized rabble that can be easily brainwashed and subdued. In fact, "Dmitrius" implied, the authorities understand that they themselves are foreign to the majority of Russians and fear that Russians will finally wake up and organize. Thus, "Dmitrius" stated, Russians "should not be afraid of the rulers at any time. They, themselves, are scared of us. They are really scared, especially if you are united, organized, knowledgeable, and wise. But they are not afraid of disorganized hordes."[23] Russians should organize themselves, possibly creating an underground party for future revolt.

"Dmitrius" was hardly alone in seeing in organization the essential path to Russian liberation. For example, "Vic" on apn.ru wrote that Russians need to create underground societies to overthrow Putin's regime. These societies could be presented to the officials as harmless organizations, such as societies of "huntsman and fisherman." In these societies, Russians could acquire the necessary skills to fight, such as markmanship.[24]

Other participants in the Internet discussion agree. Iurii Shliaptsev, discussing an article published by *ARI*,[25] stated that Russians should actively prepare to overthrow the Putin regime. Russians should be cautious, avoiding engaging in unlawful actions that would provide the authorities with an excuse to strike at them. At the same time, they should slowly accumulate the means of ousting the regime, such as creating a "voluntary detachment," supposedly "for supporting the militia." When they have accumulated sufficient force, they should employ that force to topple the regime.[26] S.V. Ivanov (on ari.ru) agreed with this reasoning and added that Russians should acquire ability in martial arts to employ in the brutal struggle and should organize themselves; that Russians should engage in various sports; and that these skills and fighting prowess would be quite helpful in fighting the regime in the future.[27] Another commentator implied that Russians should anticipate an uprising in the near future and stated that Russians need to create "mobile battalions" because only the use of force will liberate Russian land from immigrants.

For some who either looked on or participated in the event, preparation for future struggle should be accompanied by drastic changes in the lifestyle of Russian youth. This was advocated by "Konstantin," for example, on the Kondopoga Internet site; but he went further in suggesting youth also abandon the value system entertained by many Russians since the dawn of Russian history. Russians had an extremely weak middle class even in the late Imperial period, just prior to the 1917 revolutions. Consequently, ideas of self-restraint, so much at the core of Western middle-class values and behaviour, were essentially foreign to them. For many Russian peasants – and they constitute the vast majority of the country's population – the ideal life outside the constraints of the peasant communes and close-knit family was that of "liberty," which was nothing but license, with plenty of drink and sex as the constituents of the good life. The restraints on this "good life" were seen as purely external, as coming from state bureaucracy – from which they felt deeply alienated. The end of bureaucratic restraint usually led to a frenzy of drunkenness and promiscuity, as can be seen after both the collapse of the tsarist regime in 1917 and that of the Communist regime in 1991. This model, "Konstantin" believes, is unacceptable if Russians wish to liberate themselves from the present regime. Consequently, Russian youth should change their behaviour completely. Instead of drinking and chasing girls, they should prepare themselves for struggle with the non-Russian regime: they should study how to throw knives and similar easily accessible weapons, know how to make slingshots and use them efficiently, and should be ready to confront Chechens and, implicitly, the government that is behind them.[28]

"Konstantin" continued that while those who fight for Russia's liberation from a foreign yoke should put their greatest hope in the patriotic Russian youth, criminals, and similar groups ready for revolt, people who serve the regime should not be completely ruled out. Some contributors to the Internet discussion, for instance, said that one should appeal to the army. It is true, Konstantin stated, that many of those in the army are drunkards and are generally passive, but this is not true of all Russian officers, some of whom still have a sense of honour as officers. Such people could rise and defend Russians against Chechens, even against the regime.[29] At the same time, some contributors cautioned that the fight against the regime would not be easy and that one should not entertain the illusion that the army and militia would take the side of the masses.

Confronting the Apparatus of the State

"Sergei" stated that Kondopoga showed one should not believe the militia would take the side of Russians in a conflict, and that Russians should think about how to deal with the militia in case of an uprising.[30] Besides the militia, with its ethnic Russians, the regime would, of course, rely on Chechens and other people from the Northern Caucasus who would play the role of janissaries of a sort. One contributor to the discussion insisted that Ramzan Kadyrov, the official president of Chechnya and Putin's ally, would not necessarily regard the Russians' clashes with Chechens as an excuse for intervention. In fact, Kadyrov's Chechens would not necessarily fly to Kondopoga to fight Russians; they could use Kondopoga as an excuse for intervening anywhere in Russia, where they might engage in murdering Russians[31] and thereby terrorize Russians into submission to Putin's demands.

Other discussion participants, while understanding the difficulties in confronting the Putin regime, which could rely on Chechens, still believed Russians could overcome the obstacles.

One contributor stated that Russians have little chance of winning in a struggle since the minorities have strong support among those who rule in Moscow and offer reciprocal support; but Russians have some chance of prevailing if they unite.[32] Some believed that chances of overpowering the regime are minuscule, while others had a more optimistic, albeit cautious, view. "Vera" (on rusidea.ru), presumably a nationalist-minded female, made the point clearly. She stated that Russians should of course be prepared for a confrontation with non-Russian powers; and the confrontation would not be easy. At the same time, she believed, victory could be achieved and Russians should strike at the appropriate moment, but only when they are sufficiently prepared. Before they are ready, they should not be drawn in by the provocations of authorities. Other participants also believed that despite all the challenges, overthrowing Putin's regime is quite possible in a nation-wide uprising. Resoluteness of purpose was seen as the essential precondition of success. Some participants in the discussion noted that Russians could learn from their enemies, Chechens and Jews. A certain "Viktor" (on ari.ru) stated that Russian nationalists should take Israelis and Chechens as an example, for they deal mercilessly with those who attack them. He took as examples Kadyrov's willingness to send his Chechens to Kondopoga to defend his people, and Israeli strikes against countries that harm Israeli citizens. He contrasted this with the Russian government, which willingly accepted the humiliation of ethnic Russians. Russians, he suggested, should attack their enemies anywhere.[33]

Some thought the very fact that the regime would employ minorities as janissaries might help the rebels. "Khokol" (on ari.ru) stated that if Putin used Chechens and similar people to suppress revolts by the Russian masses, this would be quite beneficial for the national revolution, for it would infuriate Russians and would help them in mobilizing for a confrontation with the regime.. Elaborating on Russia's future, "Khokhol" stated that only a national revolution would put the present regime to an end, and one should understand that this sort of revolution could not be carried out without bloodshed. Indeed, such an act would infuriate Russians. And this certainly would help them to be mobilized for a confrontation with the regime.[34]

Beware of False Friends

While the repressive machinery of the regime and the Chechens – who in this interpretation of events look almost like Cossacks, the quasi-ethnic/social group on which the tsarist regime relied as the major police force in the final decades of imperial rule – is a formidable obstacle, it is not the only one. The problem, discussants believed, is that the Russian people could be deceived by the present-day regime, which would use its political stooges, posing as opposition parties, to lead the Russian people astray. Discussants pointed to a phenomenon that had been recorded by historians of late tsarist Russia. The tsarist regime, alarmed by the prospect of a mass uprising of Russian workers – even before the 1905–1907 revolutions – had before its eyes the example of the European revolutions of 1848 and especially 1871, and therefore decided to take the initiative. Pre-emptive action was launched by Sergei Zubatov (1874–1917), a leading figure in the tsarist police, who planned and created an organization that supposedly catered to the interests of the workers but that would be under the authorities' absolute control (dubbed *Zubatovshchina* by critics), which alarmed Russians. The same suspicion of fake opposition parties or groups could be found in the comments of "Mne bol'she 13," who believed that Vladislav Surkov, one of the leading figures in Putin's entourage, played the role of present-day Sergei Zubatov.

"Mne bol'she 13" (I am older than 13) placed his arguments on the Kondopoga city site together with "Dmitrius." "Mne bolshe 13" stated that Russians should not engage in ethnic violence for a simple reason: pogrom violence is actually incited by "Surkov bitch." This reference to Vladislav Surkov tells us much. Surkov, a member of Putin's inner circle, is not only half-Chechen but has the reputation of being a cunning manipulator, which in the eyes of some Russians makes him a new edition of Boris Berezovsky, the tycoon who made his name as the "gray cardinal" of the Yeltsin era. Surkov, the writer implied, has followed the bidding of his masters, the Russian elite, who enjoy their ill-gotten wealth amidst the misery of the majority of Russians. The elite understands that the Russian populace could rise up and sweep them away, so they try to channel the people's anger towards minorities and incite violence such as in Kondopoga.

"Mne bol'she 13" stated that Russians should organize to deal with the regime that exploits them and should take care not to be misled by organizations that are controlled by the regime. The leaders of these organizations are not formally a part of the establishment, as is the case with Surkov. They could even pretend to oppose the regime. Still, such people are as much puppets of the regime as was Surkov, and they and their organizations tried to deflect Russians from opposing their real enemies: the Kremlin clique. This is the case, he claimed, with DPNI (Movement against Illegal Emigration), which emerged as the leading political force during the Kondopoga events. DPNI, which targeted minorities as the root of all the Russians' problems, shows in its emphasis on minorities rather than the regime that it is a stooge of the regime. The writer also believes that DPNI is a tool in Surkov's hands.[35]

Thus, for quite a few of those engaged in the discussions of Kondopoga events – mostly either young participants or those close enough to watch events unfold – Kondopoga was the beginning of a much-awaited Russian wake-up. There are basically two scenarios of the coming Russian revolution. One would lead to the end of Putin's regime and the creation of a society with Russians at the helm. This national revolution would be at the same time a social revolution: it would replace the corrupt rich – equated with the minorities, their cronies, and the agencies that support them – with the poor who, in this case, are mostly ethnic Russians. The configuration of the future state and the nature of the power structure are not much discussed.

However, dislike of Moscow is very evident: Moscow is equated with the oppression of the rich and thus with the power of the minorities. In this context, Moscow, which since the dawn of Russian history has been a symbol of Russianness, has become a symbol of non-Russianness. This transformation of Moscow from a "Third Rome," the Holy Grail of Russian statehood and the city of countless churches, to the un-Russian Babylon, the proverbial whore, where over-powerful minorities fatten themselves at the expense of the provinces, the real Russia, seals Moscow's fate. Upon the victorious revolt, either the Russian people would drastically reduce Moscow's power, preventing it from being a parasite on the provinces, or it would cease to be the Russian capital.

The second scenario is more radical, albeit it still has an positive outcome for Russians. In this scheme, the Kondopoga events are the beginning of the dismantling of the oppressive Russian state born of the tradition of the Mongol empire. While for Dugin and other Eurasianists the Mongol legacy emerges as a positive phenomenon, the guarantor of Russians' ability to create a great trans-ethnic empire and forsake narrow ethnic interests, most Russian nationalists and leftist radicals who engaged in the discussions of Kondopoga view the Mongol legacy, the Russian state itself, as the great curse. The Russian state is seen as separate from the Russian people, with the interests of the state juxtaposed to the interests of the people. The Russian state's historical foreignness to the people is emphasized by the role of minorities in the creation of the state and its functioning. The end of the Russian state, the shedding of minority-populated enclaves that Russians could not dominate, would not be just a process of ethnic homogenization and Russia's return to itself, but also a process of social liberation, for power and the benefits that power entails would be returned to the majority – ethnic Russians. This scenario – liberation through disintegration – is still optimistic, though it demonstrates both a clear breakdown in the Russian collective conscience and the depth of the crisis. Russians see here the meta-goal of their existence not in Messianic expansion, as was the case throughout most of their history, but in an inverted movement of increasing parochialism and self-centredness. In a way, this scenario is a continuation of the post-Soviet scenario, when most Russians believed that their economic problems were due to the imperial burden – the numerous "friends" and "brothers" such as East Europeans and residents of the USSR republics whom Russians supported – and that shedding this burden would lead to a better life.

This feeling that the empire is the burden is something new in Russian history. For centuries Russians – and they were mostly peasants until the very recent period of rapid Soviet industrial national urbanization – tried to avoid the onerous duties of serving the state and the elite. Yet at the same time as they tried to avoid service to the state, Russian peasants were proud of the glory and might of the tsar – the very symbol of the state and Russia proper. Only quite recently, in the late Soviet era, was the desire to avoid the burdens of service to the empire accompanied by a spreading feeling that empire itself is a burden. And this feeling has continued to increase. In fact, those who adopt this view believe not just that ethnic enclaves should be shed, but that even the Russian heartland needs to be dismembered, "liberated" from what is seen as the Moscow yoke. There is a parallel between this trend of "Russian liberation" from Moscow and the trend that led to the collapse of the USSR; indeed, the thrust of Yeltsin's program was the "liberation" or "secession" of the Russian Federation from the USSR.

At the same time, this feeling of reverse imperialism has a tinge of optimism, a sort of grass-roots Rousseauistic liberation, and echoes some of the theories of the nineteenth-century Populists or those who were close to them, such as Afanasii Shchapov (1830–1876), who saw Moscow as a bureaucratic and oppressive conqueror of free Russian land.

Still, not everyone who engaged in the Kondopoga-related discussions shares this optimistic vision of the future. For some, Kondopoga and similar events are not the beginning of Russian resurgence but the shrieks of a dying nation. These pessimistic or at least mixed views of the Russian future can be seen in discussions centred on the Internet site www.apn.ru.

Kondopoga as a Sign of Russian Demise

To start with, not all Russian residents of Kondopoga were anxious to fight against Chechens or the government. "Potap Potapych," a Kondopoga resident, expressed the feelings of these people. He blamed everything on the nationalists who came from Moscow to stir up things, believing they wanted to foment ethnic violence to satisfy their ambitions and achieve power. According to him, the majority of Kondopoga residents just want to live in peace and hated to see their city devastated, so they asked the Moscow nationalists to leave them alone.[36] While for this participant life is tolerable and so he and many others have no desire to fight, other discussants took a different view. This was the case with many of those who posted on ari.ru.[37] For them, not the country but the Russians themselves had no future. "Sila" stated that the authorities are on the side of the "damn Muslim infidels" (*basurmane*).[38] Not only are Muslims in control of the country, but, he feared, would absorb it completely. He did not believe that Russians could deal with essentially a foreign power, a rising number of non-Russians, and therefore Russians, powerless, would die. Other participants in the discussion on ari. ru had the same gloomy vision in regard to Russians' ability to defend themselves against minorities. On this site "Veleiar" stated that the Russians might be outraged by minorities' attacks against Russians but would never engage in real actions,[39] for they had become too degenerate to offer real resistance to their oppressors.

Other contributors to the discussions, with a sort of pessimistic bend, followed suit in seeing no way that Russia could escape its predicted demise. "Berendei" started his discussion of Russia's future by challenging Russians inborn superiority. He alluded to the belief of Russian neofascists that Russians are Aryans and thus superior to non-Slavic people – implicitly, the people of the Northern Caucasus.[40] "Berendi" stated that Russians could hardly regard themselves as being much different from the minorities, because in fact quite a few Russians have Mongolian blood. These Mongolian, non-Slavic, and therefore non-Aryan ingredients of Russian ethnicity and culture are lauded by Eurasianists, who regard this mixed bloodline as a symbol of the all-embracing character of the Russian culture and as providing one explanation of why Russians created such a great empire. But for "Bernedei" and a score of Russian nationalists, their mixed bloodline was nothing but a sign of degeneration and indicates that Russians cannot stand up for themselves. "Bernedei" related this Asiatic, or at least semi-Asiatic, nature of Russians to Russian political culture: in his view, Russians like other Asiatics can act only if they have a strong leader. And there is currently no such leader, nor does he see any reason to believe one will emerge in the future.

Other participants in the discussion agreed. "Cherchil" pointed out that one should not put much hope in leadership from DPNI, for it is most likely the child of Putin's secret police. It is not just that Russians have no viable political leader or organization to spearhead their opposition to the regime; even those Russians who presently stand against the regime have no support among the army. The problem of the armed forces and their relationship with the Russian populace was raised in other discussions related to Kondopoga. Some participants, as mentioned above, wrote that not all people in uniform are drunkards and unprincipled mercenaries and some could stand behind their fellow Russians, especially in uprisings against non-Russian regimes. But another commentator was sceptical that the Russian army would actually support Russians.[41] While some pessimistic Russian nationalists believe the Russians' doom is predicated on their inability to get rid of the anti-Russian Putin regime, others adopt an even more pessimistic view: Russia is doomed. This is the view of "33-Sergei-1," who argued against those who believed Russians could prosper if Putin's regime was ended. He stated that even if Putin's regime were overthrown the Russia people would not stop declining; they would continue to die out regardless of the nature of the ruler in the Kremlin. "Ch" has the same gloomy vision of the future: that the USSR has disappeared, that Russia would disappear, and that all of this would please the West.

This vision of Russia as a doomed nation is eagerly supported by some participants from the Ukraine; and their gloating over Russia's supposed inevitable doom is a consequence of the dramatic changes in Russian-Ukrainian relations. Since the collapse of the USSR, Ukraine has increasingly drifted apart from Russia, and the drift accelerated during the 2004 "Orange Revolution," which installed a pro-Western regime in Kiev. All of this led to the growing influence of Ukrainian nationalists who, following a tradition that took hold in the nineteenth century, regard Russians not as the inhabitants of a brotherly Slavic nation – the point of both pre-revolutionary and Soviet historiography – but as hostile Asiatics with the negative characteristics attributed to Asiaticism: predisposition to despotism and slavery.[42]

"Witch Hunter 2 Sataneev," most likely a Ukrainian, elaborated on this view of Russians as doomed to be a part of Asia. He was quite sceptical of both DPNI and Russians as a nation, stating that one should not overestimate Russians' hatred of Chechens and their love of freedom. In fact, he claimed, Russians hate Ukrainians much more than Chechens, because Ukrainians are not slaves of despotic rulers, as are Russians. As a country of slaves, Russia has no future: it will gradually fall apart, and part of it will be just a Muslim khalifat. "Pavel," from Kharkov, also believes that Russia has no future. Indeed, in his view, the spread of Nazi views will speed up Russia's disintegration.

Finally, some discussion participants placed their pessimistic views on Russia's future within a more global context. One stated that Russians' disappearance and absorption by Asiatic Muslims is in no way different from the fate of other members of the "white race." Another claimed that white Americans and Europeans are doomed because they follow the rule of "political correctness."[43]

Conclusion

We have considered some aspects of the discussions found on the Internet during and after the Kondopoga riots in late August/early September 2006. Some conclusions are clear and can be placed within the broad context of a process easily seen throughout the West, from the United States to Europe and Russia: the increasing power of non-Europeans, particularly Asians, that heralded the shift of the global centre from the West, broadly defined, to Asia. This is a tectonic shift that the world has not seen since the dawn of the modern era. Moreover, this shift doesn't have just economic and possibly military dimensions. It also has demographic dimensions, with increasing numbers of non-European immigrants entering European and, more generally, Western nations, who have no desire to assimilate and accept the ideologies and cultural paradigms of the East. Islam, for example, has become increasingly popular among Europeans, with number of adherents increased by both immigration and conversion. Nothing of this sort has taken place in the West since the collapse of the Roman Empire. European and American governments try to solve the attendant problems by promoting "multi-culturalism" and attempting to integrate newcomers, but these attempts are not very successful, as testified by the ethnic riots that have erupted in Europe and the United States (in the latter, the problems posed by newcomers reinforce the problems of American blacks). We can place the ethnic tensions in Russia, with Kondopoga as the prime example, in the context of this bigger picture. For a while, the Russian elite entertained the idea of "Eurasianism," which is similar to federalism. Consequently, it is "Rossianes" who are the residents of the Russian Federation. The proponents of this doctrine emphasized that Russia is a unique blend of Orthodox Russians and Muslims of various ethnic origins. The notion of a Eurasian civilization and a sort of "Eurasian" human was related to the notion of "Rossianes," the official name for the residents of Russia. Similar to the term "Eurasian," it could not be translated just as "the residents/citizens of the Russian Federation." The notion implies not just judicial bonds of citizenship and a sense of civil solidarity, but a deeper mutual integration in a quasi-nation/family. And the rise of ethnic/racial tension indicates that this "Eurasian"/"Rossiane" paradigm is as unworkable as the notion of "multiculturalism" in the United States and Europe, where ethnic/racial tensions continued to be strong. Still, with all of their similarities, the events in Russia had unmistakable specifics.

As well as similarities with the situation in Europe and the United States, the events in Russia had strong and unmistakable differences. First, while in Europe and the US it is minorities and immigrants, especially immigrant minorities, who engage in violent riots, in Russia the rioters are ethnic Russians and youth, the rising generations of the future Russia. Second, Western and Russian observers often portray Russian nationalist radicals, especially those who engage in racial/ethnic-motivated violence, as primitive zombies. Certainly, quite a few of those who engaged in the Kondopoga and similar riots behaved in this zombie-type fashion, but this is just one part of the story. Many of those who watched events or possibly participated in them demonstrated political acumen. Some, for example, became spontaneous Leninists, with their emphasis on the importance of organization and the discarding of violence as counter-productive or indirectly promoted by the regime. Third – and this is the most striking difference between Russian nationalist radicals and their Europeans counterparts – is Russians' vision of the state. With all of their disgust with their governments, European nationalists/neofascists never see in their respective capitals, such as Paris or Berlin, the source of their problems. And they would be appalled if the dissolution of their countries was proposed as the solution to a crisis. Yet it was precisely these views that many Russian youth were willing to endorse, revealing their view of Moscow and the Russian state as deeply alienating and hostile entities. The number of disenfranchised and bitter youth in Russia is much greater than in Europe or the United States. The drive to asociality and violence, and deep alienation from society, are not attributes of a comparatively small segment of minorities, as is the case in Europe and the United States, but of the ethnic Russian majority. Nor are acceptance of violence and a complete rejection of the prevailing social-economic order the attributes of the elderly proponents of the "Red to Brown" opposition but of Russian youth, which at the start of the post-Soviet era Western pundits saw as natural supporters of the emerging capitalist order. And there is another notable aspect some have observed of present-day Russia youth: strong anti-Western sentiment. Even members of the prosperous middle class, whose values and lifestyle have become increasingly similar to those of Westerners, are quite critical of the United States or the West in general for not taking Russians as equals and for trying to undermine the country's position. Russians combine this critical assessment of the West with criticism of the present Russian regime, but most are patriotic, believing Russia should expand its influence. By contrast, disenfranchised nationalistic-minded youth – and they are the ones who participated in Kondopoga and similar riots – harbour absolutely no imperial/neo-imperial cravings. They often see the entire Russian state as the enemy of ethnic Russians and view the dissolution of that state as the road to Russian liberation. These nationalists, who are plainly neo-fascists, are not imperialists – as they should be, following the prevailing cliché – but isolationists and even separatists. Their ideology is in one sense structurally similar to that of many Russian Federation residents on the eve of the collapse of the USSR, who believed that Russia's liberation from the USSR and, of course, the East European imperial inheritance, would make the life of Russian residents happier and richer. These Russian nationalistic youth are also quite similar to the majority of European nationalists, who – in sharp contrast to their counterparts of the eighteenth and nineteenth centuries – have no imperialist propensities. Unable to withstand the increasing pressure of the non-European world, they want to cleanse Europe of non-European migrants and isolate it thereafter. What are the implications of these attitudes and actions for the Russian state?

Everything here, as in many other non-European or pre-modern societies, depends on the viability of the state and its repressive apparatus. If this apparatus is strong, the Russian state and society in general could display to the outside world the image of prosperity and stability; it could perplex and even alarm the West in its display of what could be described as neo-imperial impulses. The isolationist fascism of increasing segments of Russian youth could well be ignored, and the occasional outburst of violence could be suppressed comparatively easily. From this perspective the present Russian state might be seen as similar to the tsarist regime in the late nineteenth century when it dealt with many of the problems with the first waves of ethnic violence (Jewish pogroms). It's worth noting that when the tsarist government became weak, mostly due to forces outside Russia's borders – the Russian-Japanese war and WWI – ethnic violence erupted with uncontrollable force, and was interwoven with other manifestations of asocial behaviour and social strife. And all of these forces swept away the Russian monarchs through the 1905–1920 revolutions. The same could happen in Russia if the regime becomes weakened. As with tsarist Russia, the destabilizing force could come from outside Russia (e.g., an economic crisis). But even in the absence of external destabilizing forces, the Russian state may well be in trouble in the long run given, as we have seen, that a significant number of ethnic Russians see Moscow or even the Russian state itself as the source of its problems. These new Russian radicals are quite different from those at the beginning of the twentieth century, though there are parallels: the Bolsheviks, at least before they took power, blasted the Russian empire as the "prison of the nation" and proclaimed the nation's right to self-determination. Still, their emphasis was not on the destruction of the Russian state but on its social-economic transformation. (And the Bolsheviks soon forgot about their promises to the ethnic minorities and, with a speedy "National Bolshevik" transformation of their ideology, reassembled the Russian state/empire.)

Bolshevik ideology and that of present-day Russian nationalists also diverge in other ways. The Bolsheviks offered both political and ethnic programs. They exposed a kind of "Eurasianism" that implied the happy "symbiosis" of Russian toilers and their common work in the destruction of the capitalist West and, of course, the liberation of Western toilers in due time. The situation is very different for present-day Russian nationalists. Quite a few of these ethnic Russians seem to see Russia, both the state and the people, as in danger of being engulfed by the Asian civilization/people, and dread this as a great calamity. This prognosis is shared by quite a few Westerners, who view Western prospects less as a Huntingtonian "clash of civilizations" in which the West would prevail than as calling for Spenglerian pessimism over the "decline of the West." These deep fears and anxieties are well transmitted by popular American serials, like *Life after People*, where Western decline is implicitly presented as the end of humankind.

NOTES

1 The quotations from internet conversations and commentary that follow are culled from the author's direct observation of these websites, all of which were accessed soon after the Kondopoga riot. By the time of observation the regime had passed a law against "extremism" so as to increase control over the internet and create problems for those who control the servers. The state has since been able to remove most of these discussions from cyber space, and so many of the URLs are no longer valid.

2 http://www.gazeta.ru/social/kseno/letter/index.shtml/, 6 June 2007.

3 DPNI, the Movement against Illegal Immigration, is one of the most influential nationalistic movement/quasi-parties in present-day Russia.

4 "Comandante," "Kak Kondopoga sbrosila chechenskyiy 'kryshu,'" http://dpni.rusnabat.org/forum/viewtopic.php?t=58, 14 September 2006.

5 Comments of "Witch Hunter," http://ari.ru/doc/?id=2700.

6 Comments of "Ural," http://www.apn.ru/opinions.comments10319.htm, 21September 2006.

7 Comments of "Ianomir," http://ari.ru/doc/?id=2701, 7 September 2008.

8 Comments of "Iaroslav," http://ari.ru/doc/?id=2701, 7 September 2006.

9 Comments of "Vadim," http://ari.ru/doc/?id=7701, 7 September 2006.

10 Gennadii Vodoleev, "Zivem li nuy v okkupirovannoi strane? Chast' 2, Kak izbavit'sia ot okkupatsii?" ARI, 7 September 2006, http://ari.ru/doc/?id=2701.

11 "My Revolutsionnoe Kontaktnoe Ob'edinenie," http://rko.marsho.net/l.htm, 21 September 2006.

12 Ivan Letsev, "Bumagr terpit-Rossiia-et!" Zavtra, 6 September 2006.

13 "Kondopozhskoe vosstanie perekidyvactsia na drugie goroda," http://www.?rusidea.ru/?part 198&–id=21.41, 5 September 2006.

14 http://www.apn.ru/opinions/commets,10319.htm, 21 September 2006.

15 "Voina poshla po Vsei Rossii," http://www.cityk.onego.ru/forum/viewtopic.php?t=1826& postdays=0&postorder=asc&start, 6 September 2006.

16 "Voina v gorode," http://www.cityk.onego.ru/.forum/viewtopic.php?t=1781, 3 September 2006.

17 Based on personal communications with an anonymous source.

18 http://www.rusidea.ru/?parte=198&ird=2141.

19 Anonymous statement, http://ari.ru/doc/?id=2701, 7 September 2006.

20 See for example "Var'ka Piter" from an ari.ru site discussion.

21 "Voina poshla po User Rossii," http://www.cityj.onego, ru/forum/viewtopic.php?t=1826& postdays=O&postorder=asc&start," 7 September 2006.

22 "Voina v gorode," http://www.cityk.onego.ru/forum/viewtopic.php?t=1781&postdays=O& postorder=usc&start, 6 September 2006.

23 "Voina v gorode," http://www.cityk.onego.ru/forum/viewtopic.php?t=1781&postdays=O& postorder=usc&start, 6 September 2006.

24 "Vic," http://www.apn.ru/opinions.comments.10319.htm, 21September 2006.

25 "Tebia idet ubivat/Kadyrov i Lamadaevy! Na priniatie resheniia ostalos' 2 sekundy," http://ari.ru/doc/?id=2701, 5 September 2006.

26 Comments of "Iurii Shliaptsev." http://ari.ru/doc/?=2697, 6 September 2006.
27 Comments of "S.V. Ivanov," http://ari.ru/doc/?id=2697, 6 September 2006.
28 Comments of "Konstantin," "Voina v gorode," http://www.cityk.onego. ru/forumviewtopic.php?r =1781&postdays= O&postorder=asc&start, 6 September 2006.
29 Tor Vik pisali (9), "Viona v gorode," http://www.cityk.onego.ru./forum/ viewtopic.php?r+ 1781&postdays=0&postorder=asc&start, 6 September 2006.
30 Comments of "Sergei," http://ari.ru./doc./?id=2701.
31 "Tebia idut ubivat' Kadyrovy i lamadaevy! Na priniatie resheniia ostalos' 2 sekundy, ari," http://ari.ru/doc/?id=2697, 5 September 2006.
32 "Voina v gorode," http://www.cityk.onego.ru./forum/viewtopic. php?t=1781&postdays=0& postorder=ascfstart, 6 September 2006.
33 Comments of "Viktor," http://ari-ru/doc/?id=2697, 5 September 2006.
34 Comments of "Khokhol," http://ari/doc/?id=2697, 5 September 2006.
35 "Viona v gorode," http://www.cityk.onego.Ru/forum/viewtopic. php?t=1781asc&start, 6 September 2006.
36 "Viona v gorode," http://www.cityk.onego.ru.forum.viewtopic.php?t=17 81&postdays=0&postorder=asc&start, 6 September 2006.
37 http://ari.ru.doe.?id=2701. [?]
38 The word is a rather archaic definition of Muslims as not Orthodox Christians.
39 Comments of "Veleiar," http://ari.ru/doc/?id=2701, 7 September 2006.
40 One could add here that some Chechen ideologists believe Chechens are included in the very embodiment of Aryanism.
41 IorVik pisal [a], "Voina v gorode," http://www.cityk.onego.ru/forum/ viewtopic.php?t=1781 &postdays=0&postorder=asc&start, 6 September 2006.
42 The assumption that Russians are not freedom-loving Slavs – wholesome European people – can be traced back to the beginning of the nineteenth century. French historian Henri Martin first proclaimed that Russians are actually an Asiatic nation. This idea was later supported by Polish political historian Franciszek Duchinski, and even later by Ukrainian historian Mikhailo Hrushevsky. This vision of Russia is still current among a score of present-day East European intellectuals. See for example Edgar Knobloch, *Russia and Asia: Nomadic and Oriental Traditions in Russian History* (Hong Kong: Odyssey, 2007).
43 "Voina v gorode," http://www.cityk.orego.ru/forum/viewtopic. php?t1781&postdays =09& postorder-asc&start, 6 September 2006.

7 Phobia in an Age of Post-Migrant Rights: The Criminalization of Tamil Refugees

MICHAEL C.K. MA AND DAVINA BHANDAR

This chapter examines the current international migration regime (Coutin 2010; Hindess 2000; Sharma 2008; Walters 2010a) and the manner by which Canada is framing its refugee[1] policy within a specific institutional language of securitization and criminalization. This language emerges from a new style of governance that arises from the development of a discourse framing securitization as part of a "risk" society. The expansion of securitization is founded in the simultaneous production of fear and xenophobic responses to perceived threats to the sovereign authority of the state. In the current management of immigration and refugee policies, we are witnessing an unprecedented assault on the rights of those who seek sanctuary and asylum within the borders of the state. The Canadian response to asylum seekers increasingly follows an international trend that criminalizes refugees through their re-categorization as "irregular" migrants or false refugees. In Canada this has become particularly relevant following the 11 June 2012 passage of Bill C-31, "Protecting Canada's Immigration System Act," whereby the special designate category of the non-determined country of origin or *irregular* migrant has come to have particularly stringent regulations whereby the refugee is subject to detention and deportation rather than sanctuary or resettlement. A refugee who enters the country through the means of an ocean voyage is immediately designated as "irregular" and treated as a special class (Immigration and Refugee Protection Act, Section 20.1 [1], 2012). The new act allows the *irregular migrant* to be disciplined in a number of new ways: automatic detention, lack of review or release for a year, bar on appeal, five-year ban on permanent residence application, bar on family reunification, denial of travel documentation, and deportation to country of origin. We investigate this change in Canadian policy set within an international migration regime shift that is taking place with respect to refugee determination processes, as we see how countries who are signatories to the United Nations High Commissioner for Refugees (UNHCR) Convention on Refugees are working to subvert and challenge previous "best practice" policies. In Canada, a signatory to the UNHCR Convention on Refugees, this new framing of "irregular" arrivals both produces and arises from an irreconcilable and phobic institutional response to Canada's own commitment to acknowledge and accept the rights of refugees. Our research takes as a point of reference the current Canadian and Pacific Rim reaction to the boat arrivals of Tamil refugees.

Tamil refugees have fled civil war and political persecution. Many are now seeking refuge in Pacific Rim countries. But as they land on these shores, instead of meeting with resettlement officials, they face potential deportation, detention, and criminalization. Vic Toews, then Canadian public safety minister, stated that his government will "make this country less welcoming for future shipments of human cargo" (Ibbitson, Chase, and Youssef 2010). In statements such as these, government officials actively dehumanize the refugee, an intrinsic act in the reframing and classifying of this particular group. In the current rhetoric, refugee claimants are seen as "human cargo" and linked to acts of human smuggling that are deemed criminal by institutions responsible for border security, immigration, and refugee resettlement. These institutions are reorganizing their structure and mandate to better enforce restrictive interpretations of lawful/unlawful migration – and in so doing denying unwanted migrants legitimate refugee status. Or, as Walters argues, it is not self-evident that "illegal migration" is a social problem; rather, the problem of illegality has been created by government as a public issue that then naturally becomes the "constitutive force which shapes the social world" (Walters 2010b, 1).

In a post migrant-rights geopolitical world, is it possible, or even rhetorically feasible, to ensure that the rights to safety, mobility, and protection are afforded to refugee claimants? While it is not a new phenomenon to understand the migrant or asylum seeker through the trope of the "dangerous" interloper, we need to question how existing mechanisms and forms of control are being circulated and implemented. In addition, it is no coincidence that Canada's overhauling of its immigration and refugee system has meant that in other categories of migrancy, rights are also becoming much harder to access and guarantee. Through changes that were introduced in 2010 under the

Balanced Refugee Reform Act (BRRA), the government has the authority to "identify designated countries of origin (DCO)." The state understands that these "Designated Countries of Origin are countries that do not normally produce refugees, but do respect human rights and offer state protection" (CIC website, http://www.cic.gc.ca/english/department/media/backgrounders/2010/2010-06-29.asp, accessed 24 November 2012). In establishing this list of designated countries, the minister is able to determine the eligibility of refugee claimants prior to hearing claims, thereby establishing that claimants from these countries "do not normally produce refugees." Since the list of DCOs was established, refugee claimants from these countries have been targeted by the Canadian government: they are no longer eligible for health care provisions while applications are pending, no longer able to access an appeals process regarding their cases, and face immediate deportation if their claims are rejected. While the introduction of the DCO in Canada's refugee system is unique in its impact and criteria, it was preceded by a two-decades-long development at the level of the UNHCR (see UNHCR 1991). As Canada moves to what can only be labelled as a hyper-neoliberal approach in its immigration policy – by increasing the number of temporary foreign workers, placing a moratorium on family class immigrants, and creating a two-tiered system of refugee acceptance – compassion, refuge, and sanctuary are now cast as antiquated and naive notions for managing Canada's border in an age of the *criminal claimant*.

Post-Migrant Rights

A growing network of scholars engaged in contemporary studies of migrant rights, anti-deportation movements, critical security, and citizenship studies have shown how the question of rights embodied in a liberal democratic Western state is limited and non-representative of the political mobilizations in which people, living without status and rights within a nation-state, are formally engaged. Engin Isin, Peter Nyers, and multiple others have argued that the question of rights, rather than being based in the constituent boundedness of formal citizenship, falls away to notions and conditions of being political that exist in a constant state of struggle and political engagement. This line of challenging who is the legitimate bearer of "rights," or the famous question "Who has the right to have rights?" (Arendt 1951; Ranciere 2004), has shaped the political landscape through which the determination of refugee-hood has been established. In the context of post-migrancy those who are deemed out of order and not legitimate migrants or refugees must now act in an extralegal manner to gain legitimacy or legibility in a system that does not acknowledge their universal right to mobility. Legal scholar Audrey Macklin calls this practice a "discursive disappearance of the refugee" (2005, 365). In the context of post-migrant rights and their framing within illegality/deportability, we understand how illegality is shifting as the legal authority engages in a recategorization and remaking of the boundaries of criminality. Nicholas de Genova (2002) illustrates the need for clarity and a specificity of legal authority in determining and demarcating the "illegality" of migration. He shows that "the practice of deportation has emerged as a definite and increasingly pervasive convention of routine statecraft. Deportation seems to have become a virtually global regime" (De Genova 2011, 91). In the context of this examination of the current shift in immigration and refugee determination, the aim of this legislation is to accelerate the process of deportation by criminalizing the very act of mobility for the sake of security.

The terms "mass arrivals" or "irregular arrivals" place the refugee in a quasi "illegal" or "criminal" state of being, a category that is in itself suspect. If the determination of refugee status is predominately based on the ability to prove a "bona fide" claim, the recategorization effectively challenges this ability to claim a legitimacy of refugee subjectivity or the refugee as a non-criminal person. These new terms of reference, which differ from the original terms of "refuge" and "asylum" found in the UN convention, are arrived at through neither parliamentary nor public debate, and they deliberately stray from the language of sanctuary and the legitimacy of asylum. The movement away from the language adopted by the UN convention allows for legitimization of the new language of criminalization. The notion of a right to declare oneself as a "refugee" is no longer understood, nor practised by the state, as a universal right. Only a convention refugee formally selected by an overseas delegation or office can be understood to be a proper refugee. Regardless of the existing international right to make inland claims, all non-government-selected refugees are assumed to be suspect.

Instead of examining the question of rights from a position of struggle and anti-hegemony often found within a politics of anti-deportation and migrant rights, it is productive to examine the claims to a post-rights discourse from within the state. The state lacks interest in protecting the rights of individuals, as citizen and non-citizen alike are watching a slow devolution of a rights-based framework. It is not the case that those with rights are somehow enjoying more freedom, protection, and an expansion of rights at the expense of those without rights. Rather, in this age of austerity measures, the current language of protection and securitization has a disciplining effect upon citizens, while non-citizens, asylum seekers, refugees, and other classes of migrants are further subjugated by a system of reclassification and recategorization. The invention of these new frameworks of security and criminalization has led to unlawful detention, deportation, and extralegal state practices. Thus, the overall landscape of a rights-based discourse in Canada becomes degraded as the right to mobility and asylum are increasingly understood as inconvenient abstract practices from which Canadians must be protected.

The Use of the *MV Sun Sea* as a Catalyst for Criminalization

At the heart of the recent criminalization of migrancy are the events of refugee claimants arriving on the shores of British Columbia. Over the course of two years, the BC coast received two ships carrying refugee claimants whose arrival helped remake the Canadian discourse of migrancy. Their sea-borne arrival became a catalyst for a manipulation of the Canadian population's perception of refugee claimants as out of order and under criminal direction.

On 17 October 2009 the *MV Ocean Lady* arrived on the BC coast bearing 76 passengers who claimed refugee status. On 12 August 2010 the *MV Sun Sea* arrived on the same coast with 492 passengers. The passenger manifest comprised 380 men, 63 women, and 49 minors. By April 2012, only some of these had been processed by the IRB: 6 men remained in detention, 19 were issued deportation orders, 6 were accepted as refugees, 6 were rejected, one family abandoned its claim, 18 more claims were withdrawn, and the rest were still pending (*National Post* 2012). By 31 December 2014, according to an IRB spokesperson, 200 refugee claims had been accepted, 155 had been rejected, and 25 people had been ordered deported (Quan 2015).

In Canada, approximately 25,000 refugee claimants are received each year. Although the recent ocean-voyaged refugee claimants have received the most attention, it is Mexico and Hungary who have been the top nations from which Canada has received claimants in the past few years. For most years, refugee acceptance rates have largely remained consistent at 40 to 45 per cent. Even though Canada's acceptance rates are generally higher than most other countries', Canada's 2010–11 acceptance rate of 38 per cent was a historical low for the Immigration Refugee Board. However, exact comparisons can be difficult, since some European countries offer temporary forms of asylum not covered by the UN convention and not offered in Canada (Human Rights Research and Education Centre 2011).

The arrival of the *MV Sun Sea* and its passengers in August 2010 at the CFB port in Esquimalt, BC, was depicted in all major media outlets as a case of illegals seeking entry to Canada through the means of international trafficking or human smuggling. The media and government of the day were quick to portray the passengers, not as political refugees or asylum seekers, but as potential national threats to Canadian society.

The *MV Sun Sea* was preceded in 2009 by the arrival of seventy-six Tamil refugees from Sri Lanka who were "intercepted by the Royal Canadian Mounted Police (RCMP) off the coast of British Columbia" (Bradimore and Bauder 2012). In their study of media representations and discourses surrounding the arrival of the 2009 Tamil refugees to Canada, Bradimore and Bauder (2012) illustrate the impact that a discourse of "risk" and "securitization" has had on the reception of "boat refugees" in Canada. They note that mainstream print media overwhelmingly represented the Tamil refugee arrivals in the headlines of daily press as "illegal migrants and wanted criminals – migrants risky enough to be tracked and monitored by cooperative efforts of international intelligence agencies" (Bradimore and Bauder 2012, 21). What this and other media studies of boat arrivals (e.g., Greenberg and Hier 2002; Sharma 2005, 2008) illustrate is that an authorizing discourse surrounding the arrival of "boat" refugees has become established. This authorizing discourse present in the Canadian and international media has sedimented a form of xenophobic response to these refugees. It is through this production of a phobia that we can understand how the larger public is disciplined through particular governing logics presented through these state actors.

Indeed, four days before the ship even entered Canadian waters Stephen Rigby, former Canadian Border Services Agency (CBSA) president, reported that the intercepted ship was possibly carrying members of the Liberation Tigers of Tamil Eelam (LTTE), an organization that the Canadian government has labelled a terrorist organization:

As the Canadians assumed control of the ship about 12 nautical miles off Vancouver Island, Canadian sailors were primed for far more than just huddled masses of exhausted migrants. The Harper government was pressing the visitors to verify whether the captain had been a crew member on the last migrant ship to stop in Canada. He was not. Rumours swirled that passengers were members of the LTTE. (Chase 2011)

While the Harper government mobilized a troop of government offi-cials, navy personnel, and other administrative bodies to intercept and receive this group of refugees, the mechanism and forms of govern-mental logic that reinvented the refugee as a criminal or illegal migrant were made very clear. A large group of agencies were recruited into a coordinated task force, including the Canadian Border Services Agency (CBSA), Citizenship and Immigration Canada (CIC), Canadian Secu-rity Intelligence Service (CSIS), Foreign Affairs and International Trade (DFAIT), Department of National Defence (DND), Health Canada, Immigration and Refugee Board (IRB), Public Health Agency (PHAC), RCMP, and Transport Canada. Such a resolute response to this ship and these refugees set the stage for the future development and imple-mentation of a significant policy shift from Canada's historical role in refugee determination processes. Under direction from CBSA and CIC, these agencies worked together to interdict and criminalize the *MV Sun Sea* claimants. The CBSA tightly controlled the media cover-age and provided specific talking points and various scenario-tailored media scripts for each agency (Canadian Border Security Agency 2010). From the government's perspective, it was important that the optics of the seizure of the ship be portrayed as a public safety issue rather than a humanitarian intervention or interdiction. The acts of civilians risk-ing their lives to flee persecution were framed as risky behaviour that brought those individuals in contact with criminal human smugglers. Since talking points and media spin and management were crafted ahead of the actual boarding of the ship and CBSA/IRB processing of passengers, and thus before the merit of each passenger's claim of asylum/persecution and need for sanctuary could be known, it can be assumed that the message of criminalization had little to do with the actual passengers onboard the *MV Sun*, but was constructed as a politi-cal issue.

But why focus on Tamil claimants? Why not on refugee claimants arriving by air, since they are a much larger and more frequent group of claimants? The reason is simple: it is easier to publicly frame a single group of claimants, who arrive by a single ship, as the product of illegal activity and criminal exploitation. The targeting of the Tamil refugee claimants largely occurred because – as an ocean-borne group – they could more easily be perceived as a cohesive group of illegal migrants who arrived through the services of a criminal human-smuggling enterprise. Framing these Tamil claimants as the subjects of human trafficking allowed their status to be more easily invalidated. Framing them as a cohesive group of illegal and potentially criminal migrants (i.e., not convention refugees) –using "criminal-by-association" logic – allowed authorities to subvert or invalidate them as legitimate refugee claimants. In addition, the spectacle of a large ship arriving at the shoreline establishes the penetrability of the border and the justification for a stronger, securitized system of border controls. A recent op-ed commenting on Bill C-31, written by Martin Collacott, former Canadian high commissioner to Sri Lanka and ambassador to Syria, Lebanon, and Cambodia, and current Fraser Institute Fellow, provides insight. He writes:

> The act also would make potential asylum seekers think twice before making a decision to come to Canada with the aid of human smugglers. Such migrants could be subject to detention for up to a year. Even if their refugee claims are successful, they may have to wait five years before being able to apply for permanent residence or sponsor family members. Should asylum seekers return to their country of origin for a visit, they would lose their refugee status and have to leave Canada.
>
> … our laws make it difficult for our officials to remove failed refugee applicants. This explains why we are the target of choice for asylum seekers around the world. If anything, the Preventing Human Smugglers from Abusing Canada's Immigration System Act may prove to be too lax. It is debatable whether it will have much impact on the continued arrival of the tens of thousands of individual asylum seekers who arrive in Canada every year, mainly by air. While most of these refugee applicants also are believed to employ the services of human smugglers, it would be a difficult task to prove this in such scattered instances. (2010)

Collacott's statement illustrates the fact that ocean-voyaged refugee claimants are simply more easily proven to be "smuggled" because of the physical conveyance by which they arrive. As a single boatload of claimants, they can then be more easily criminalized as the cargo of human traffickers/smugglers, as opposed to those who arrive by air as individuals and not as a group. And it can be more easily suggested that as an ocean-voyaged group they are under the direct control of human smugglers.

Ocean-voyaged refugee claimants are being targeted in a manner different than other migrants or refugees. They are singly being targeted and "made to think twice" with the threat of prolonged detention and institutional delay in the processing of their claims. In comments regarding the detention of refugee claimants, UNHRC's high commissioner, Navi Pillay, has criticized Australia for having different standards of processing for air- versus sea-voyaged refugee claimants. She notes that "there was a double standard when it came to European migrants or those arriving by air" (*Bangkok Post* 2012). As Canada harmonizes its method of handling ocean-borne refugees with Australia and New Zealand, Pillay's comments can just as easily be applied to the new Canadian amendments to refugee and migration policy.

Since winning a majority in Parliament, the Harper conservative government has been on a veritable racetrack, speeding through changes to the immigration and refugee determination process in Canada. Indeed, it is the speed and number of these shifts since the arrival of the *MV Sun Sea* that makes it important to examine that case for its importance and effects in the larger political, social and historical context of Canada's refugee determination process and indeed its place in the shifting International Refugee Migration Regime.

The Sri Lankan claimants of the *MV Sun Sea* presented Canada's public safety regime with an opportunity to work in a more coordinated manner with other countries to create a unified front that would quickly criminalize those who might seek sanctuary in Canada or Australia and in Asian countries. According to the *Globe and Mail*, "The RCMP is working actively with Australia – another preferred destination for such vessels – and in Asian countries to identify ships with human cargo" (Ibbitson, Chase, and Youssef 2010).

It not surprising that Canada has attempted to limit and deter refugee claimants. Canadian legal scholar and refugee law expert Sharryn J. Aiken has argued that current policies "contain and manage refugee admission" and "reinforce systemic racism in Canadian law and practice" (Aiken 2010, 145). In the recent past, it was the spectre of terror and threats to security from which Canada must be protected. With the new focus on ocean-voyaged claimants, Canada has moved from a language of national security to that of criminal apprehension and deterrence of human smuggling. In the post-9/11 world, Canadian policy shifted its original focus on human security to state security and the prevention of terror. Now in an age of migration austerity and a "get-tough-on-crime" legislative focus, the border has once again been refashioned to penalize those who seek to make a claim for sanctuary and refuge. In this reframing of the terms regarding freedom of mobility, refuge has been recontextualized as a last and illegal chance for undeserving migrants to exploit. This pervasive logic holds that only criminal claimants would use the "loophole" of refugee status to resettle in Canada. These claimants are simply understood as *queue jumpers* who circumvent the official channels for legal migration. And in this logic, in the eyes of the public, the *refugee* is deliberately equated with an *illegal immigrant*. As the public is disciplined by this new border project, they can no longer conceptually understand either the merits of sanctuary or the legitimacy of those who might claim such status.

As Sri Lankan refugee claimants are unfairly criminalized, they serve the larger function of standing for all refugee claimants. By leveraging their plight as a spectacle of *illegal migration*, the state has been able to make the public case that anyone claiming refugee status can only be acting in a desperate and criminal fashion. The logic used to malign the act of declaring oneself a refugee is circular: ocean-borne refugees come by sea, coming by sea is an act of desperation bringing claimants in contact with criminal elements, therefore ocean-borne refugees are desperate, out of order, and criminal. The reality of the risk and danger of the ocean voyage is supplanted by a spectacle and aura of criminalization that is produced and popularized by the state.

Transnational Criminalization of Ocean-Voyaged Migrants

In Canada's history it has not been uncommon that ocean-voyage refugees and migrants have been viewed with suspicion, as involving danger and risk (see Mann 2009). Prior to the *MV Ocean Lady* and the *MV Sun Sea* we might remember the voyages of the *St. Louis* in 1939 that resulted in its Jewish passengers' return to Germany and their internment in camps, or the *Komagata Maru* incident in 1914 that tested the demand of Canada's "continuous journey" legislation for an unbroken passage from the migrant's country of origin to Canadian waters in order to limit the arrivals of British Indian subjects. More recently, there is the 1999 incident when several hundred refugees arrived to Canada's west coast from the Fujian province of China. While these historical occurrences have variously been used to raise alarm regarding Canada's ability to control its sovereign borders, these scant historical examples still do not explain the level of fear and phobic responses that they have unleashed. This leads us to ask whether there might be an existing transnational trend in which ocean voyages have come under intensified scrutiny, leading to increased international harmonization of border strategies. When one examines the transnational emphasis on nation states protecting waterways from "refugee ships," it becomes clear that global migration and deportation regimes are working in concert. This is nothing less than the practice of a system of "global apartheid" whereby nation-state interests are being strengthened through international bodies such as the UN (Sharma 2005). According to Chris Bowen, Australian minister for immigration and citizenship:

> When you have got a very high number of refugees around the world, 42 million displaced people around the world, they are going to go to the developed countries that are signatories to the refugee convention. They are going to go to Canada, they are going to go to Europe, they are going to go to America and yes, they will seek to come to Australia as well. So of course in that regard we will always be attractive because we are a developed country and signatories to the refugee convention. That is always going to be the case. But what you do need is a regional framework because the trafficking goes through our region, goes through Malaysia, goes through Indonesia and goes through a number of countries on the way to Australia, and dealing with it domestically can only do so much. You need a regional solution to this. It needs to be done in a developed way. (Bowen 2010)

While these comments indicate the position of the Australian government as a nation state under siege by potential boat arrival refugees, and question the motivations of asylum seekers – the desire for a better life in a Western "developed" nation– they are making the case for an extension of border controls to establish a regional answer to a domestic, national, and "internationalized border" issue.

If we consider refugees within a global context, we can see that the problems of displacement and persecution are minor for countries like Australia and Canada. In three geopolitical locations, the Middle East, South Asia, and the Horn of Africa, it is important to note the comparative imbalances that exist in refugee-intensive areas. For example, in the aftermath of the Iraq war many Iraqi nationals fled the country and resettled elsewhere. One such destination of refuge is Jordan. It is speculated that there are 750,000 to 1,000,000 Iraqi refugees currently living in Jordan. This new influx comprises approximately one-sixth of the population of Jordan (5.6 million). Jordan also has absorbed hundreds of thousands of Palestinians over the last fifty years (*Guardian* 2007). In the case of Afghan refugees, according to the Pakistani Ministry of States and Frontier Regions and the UNHCR survey, there are 1.6 million registered Afghan refugees living in Pakistan (*Pakistan Observer* 2012). And according to a July 2012 UNHCR report, over one million Somali refugees have fled the war-torn country and enter neighbouring countries. The number of refugees fleeing Somalia for "developed" countries hit the million mark in the second half of 2011, but the July 2012 figures refer only to Somalia's neighbouring countries of Ethiopia, Kenya, and Djibouti (BBC 2012). In comparison to Western "developed" nations, the example of these three non-Western nations shows a stark imbalance in the area of refugee acceptance. It is in fact neighbouring nations in the Middle East, South Asia, and the Horn of Africa that accept the vast majority of the world's refugees. The perception is that refugees are a burden for developed nations, but statistics reveal that the international refugee system is skewed to protect the interests of developed nations.

It is not just international cooperation but direct emulation of the practices of other nations that is understood by the Canadian state to be a key feature in the war on non-status migrants. In the area of temporary residency, proposed guidelines have been tabled that allow specific residents to be deemed harmful foreign nationals necessitating expulsion. Then minister of immigration Jason Kenney proposed new guidelines giving discretionary powers to the minister regarding the "behaviours and activities" of individuals who are understood as "harmful people." The new guidelines would grant the Office of the Minister discretionary powers of detention and expulsion, which were previously unavailable, aligning Canada with other Pacific Rim nations:

> Unlike many of our key international partners, including the United Kingdom, the United States, New Zealand, and Australia, which already have similar measures in place, Canada currently does not have a mechanism to prevent certain foreign nationals who are otherwise admissible from entering Canada, even though it is in the public interest that they be kept out. (Citizenship and Immigration Canada 2012)

According to this logic, Canada must modernize and harmonize its processes and procedures for dealing with foreign nationals so that it does not inadvertently provide a safe third country for individuals who should be kept out of First World countries. The need to prevent entry of "foreign nationals," who otherwise would qualify to enter the country, suggests that the practice of protecting the borders must extend beyond a notion of rights or law or the conventions governing such individual claimants. The logic suggests that individuals are easily defeating the conventions of law currently in place. Therefore, the battle must be extended to fields of engagement where state policies are altered so as to allow for a denial (or illegalization) of claimants regardless of the conditions or merits of their claim. The status of foreign nationals whose behaviours are deemed harmful to Canadians therefore must be controlled through ministerial discretion and decree. It is presumed that harmful foreign nationals have found ways to circumvent and defeat existing laws and conventions regarding migration and sanctuary. Thus, it is not just a simple war on *illegal migrants*, but rather a *semiotic* war that must redefine such individuals as outside the normative claims of legitimacy. And in the case of "irregular migrants" the loopholes are not just national ones, but international, according to Vic Toews, then minister for Public Safety Canada:

> "To succeed in our fight against human trafficking, we can't act alone. We need strong partnerships," said Minister Toews. "Together, we can and will help address human trafficking both domestically and around the world – we will help the victims of this terrible crime and make sure we punish the offenders." (Public Safety Canada, 30 August 2011)

Minister Toews' comments establish potential refugee claimants as mere victims of criminal human trafficking without allowing for the possibility that they are not victims at all, but legitimate convention refugees. If Toews believed them to be legitimate, then what would be the point of punishing those who allowed them to make claims for sanctuary? The language of victimization, criminalization, and trafficking is intentionally employed in this framework, and the language of fear and exploitation is the expected product of these ministerial pronouncements. Ministers Bowen, Kenney, and Toews are all engaged in a multipronged and inter-ministerial effort to frame ocean-voyaged refugee claimants both as criminal traffickers and as victims of trafficking. None of their statements quoted above show regard for the pressing question of how to extend compassion and sanctuary to those fleeing persecution. Rather, the main focus is on creating a harmonized international barrier and mounting a war against a perceived tide of illegal trafficking occurring under the false flag of the refugee convention.

The international discourse on anti-human trafficking is used to supplant the reality of how refugees and other classes of migrants are able to obtain passage. Sharma illustrates that the collusion between "national and international governance regimes together shape the experiences of migrants exiting, moving in between, and resettling into various nationalized societies, and how increasingly these regimes rely on the trope of 'homeland security' to police the bodies of the majority of the world's migrants" (Sharma 2005, 88). Some bodies cannot achieve legitimate personhood nor the designation of "regular" arrival. The categories of "irregularity" or "mass arrival" are discursively connected to the production of a xenophobic response within the population. The root of the anxiety is connected to governance strategies that have been implemented in the context of changes to the refugee determination process, as outlined by Toews:

> Canada is committed to working with our international partners to target organized criminals that would aim to take advantage of our generous immigration system. Our Government is taking action to prevent the abuse of Canada's immigration system by human smugglers... Human smuggling is a despicable crime. Not only do smugglers take advantage financially of vulnerable people, but they put people's lives at risk. The Harper Government will continue to work with other countries to ensure that migrants are not taken advantage of by human smugglers, while continuing to welcome legitimate refugees and immigrants who are willing to respect Canadian law. (Public Safety Canada, 12 July 2011)

Minister Toews' statement reinforces a system of deportability and illegality firmly situated in an international network of nation-states. Although notions of generosity, despicability, and vulnerability are deployed to frame the Canadian institutions of migration management as both sober and fair in the face of international criminal manipulation, it is not just the transnational *act* of criminal migrancy that is attacked. Rather, this new framing acts in concert with the ontological reframing of the refugee altogether. The refugee must also be invalidated with the creation of new terms of reference existing outside the 1951 convention.

New Categories of Personhood/Refugee

The anticipation and arrival of claimants aboard the *MV Ocean Lady* and the *MV Sun Sea* initiated a series of steps designed to stymie these and future arrivals. One such step was the incorporation of a new language and designation to signify ocean-voyaging refugee claimants. The new terminology creates a new grammar and diction pointing to the alleged illegality of their entry that turns legitimate asylum seekers into irregular or criminal refugees. New categories of naming and personhood being harnessed in this enterprise include "mass arrivals," "irregular arrivals," "designated claimants," and designated foreign nationals." These new terms are deployed to signify the identity of these claimants under new categories of non-refugeehood and illegitimacy of claim. The development of new terminology creates new semiotic and institutional subjecthood. The terms imply that these new subjects are in fact not legitimate refugees under the agreed terms of the convention. Instead, these new terms allow the state to frame these subjects as outside the parameters of refugee law and obligation.

"Designated claimants" is a common legal and actuarial term that has been recently employed to refer to refugee claimants. "Mass arrivals" is a term relating to asylum and extradition that dates back to common parlance in legal scholarship as early as the 1960s; Evans used "mass arrivals" in 1962 to describe the requirements and practice of granting asylum in the United States. However, "irregular arrival" did not appear in official documents and discourse until very recently. In the context of migration studies, the term first appears in Jonas Widgren's 1989 article "Asylum Seekers in Europe in the Context of South-North Movements," used to describe the particular types of movement and resettlement of peoples occurring between Turkey and Iran. And almost a decade later, in 1998, Christopher Hein uses "irregular migration" to frame Albanian migration to Italy (1998, 223). Two years later "irregular migrants" entered into official use in UNHCR documents: its first use was in August 2000 in a UNHRC paper that mentions "irregular migration" and "irregular movers" (UNHCR 2000). These newer, neutralized terms are used to avoid semiotic referencing and framing within the conceptual parameters of asylum and state refuge. It is this "irregular migrancy" that is connected to the sea-voyaged Sri Lankan claimants. The state involves itself in the creation of a new category of reference without invoking or referring to the concept of refuge. The new language helps frame these individuals as criminal or false seekers of refuge who must not be accommodated under existing refugee conventions.

On 11 June 2012, Minister Kenney's Bill C-31, "Protecting Canada's Immigration System Act," received royal assent. The bill formally incorporates the term "irregular arrivals" into policy. In so doing, it shrouds the notions of humanitarian protection, asylum, and sanctuary for displaced persons with a fog of illegitimacy. However, it is important to note that the bill fails to clearly determine a process by which such "irregularity" can be determined, and it fails to provide a clear definition or explanation of what constitutes "irregularity." The bill also adopts the new practice of ministerial discretion allowing for the criminalization and detention of migrants through the political office of the minister.

In the Canadian context, there are two paths by which refugees can seek protection. Refugees can make inland claims by fleeing directly to Canada – as current Tamil refugees have done – or they can be selected overseas by representatives of the government. In both cases, it is the duty of Citizenship and Immigration Canada (CIC) to determine through due diligence whether or not their claims are eligible to be heard by the Immigration and Refugee Board (IRB). If the IRB is a quasi-judicial tribunal functioning independently of CIC, then is it possible for it to conduct its work in an institutional context where "migrancy" and "refugee" status are reframed as states of criminal behaviour? This institutional reframing creates an impossible and potentially schizophrenic position for countries and their agencies who – as signatories of the convention on refugees – must comply with the convention while simultaneously acting as agents of international detention and anti-refuge. With the new designation of "irregular arrival" and the new power of ministerial discretion, it will be difficult for the older system of independent IRB assessment to function as it was originally designed to do.

Instead of broadening the issue of migration and making it more complex, the current doctrine of citizenship and immigration is concerned with reducing its complexity by polarizing the issue through a lens of legality/illegality or legitimacy/criminality. And all the while, the public safety minister is disingenuous in suggesting that the official crackdown on human smugglers is protecting legitimate refugee claimants. At that time, Citizenship, Immigration, and Multiculturalism minister Jason Kenney and Public Safety minister Vic Toews posted a joint news release commending border security for their work on preventing human smuggling:

> Human smuggling is a despicable crime and a deliberate abuse of our immigration system and refugee process. Canada has an internationally recognized fair system for providing refuge for those fleeing persecution

in their home country, and to maintain the integrity of our refugee system, it is important that individuals found guilty of abusing our laws are held responsible for their involvement in these crimes. (Public Safety Canada, 6 July 2012)

The emotional language used in this condemnation deliberately reduces refugee claimants to criminals abusing Canadian law while making no effort to discuss or explain the complex situation of persecution that refugees face and the institutional processes of determination that follow such applications. Further, the statement implies that the government's crackdown on human smugglers serves Canada's commitment to a refugee/sanctuary system. It belies the fact that in the cases of the *MV Ocean Lady* and *MV Sun Sea* the claimants were criminalized and incarcerated as complicit in human smuggling *before* they were accepted as legitimate refugee claimants. The ministers are making two simultaneously contradictory statements: (1) ocean-arriving refugees are presumed criminal before being determined legitimate claimants, and (2) although Canada will uphold its legal obligation to abide by the refugee convention – as long as claimants do not "abuse our laws" – the fact of one's arrival by sea delegitimizes a claimant's legitimacy as a legal seeker of asylum. By invoking the notion that Canada possesses an internationally recognized "fair system," Kenney and Toews were able to suggest that the practice of ocean-voyaged inland claims is actively undermining and radically deforming Canada's existing fair system.

The Inter-Governmental Asia-Pacific Consultations on Refugees, Displaced Persons and Migrants is an ongoing consultative space where state and near-state organizations meet yearly to discuss migration issues. At the 2006 plenary session in Xiamen, China, Irena Vojackova-Sollorano presented the position of the International Organization of Migration (IOM) by stating: "the issues of refugee, migration and displaced persons have blurred as the numbers have grown and the migratory flows have become mixed in their composition" (Intergovernmental Asia Pacific Consultations on Refugees 2006). Her statement illustrates that an ongoing global shift in migrant rights has taken its toll on the valid claims of the identity of the refugee subject. The very nature of claiming the subjecthood of the refugee has become fraught with difficulty; the litmus test for the adjudication of who the refugee is has become overdetermined by a persistent discourse of criminalization and over the question of what determines a legitimate person.

In other words, the determination process of refugees has become less one based on need than one that has reached a legitimation crisis. In the context of this overwhelmingly persistent discourse of equating refugees with "economic migrants" or "smuggled" or "trafficked" illegals, the question has really become "How do you fit within an ever-shrinking and disappearing category"?

The rhetoric of human smuggling is but one device by which the complexity of today's migration is simultaneously simplified and blurred. The claimant's ability to be viewed as a legitimate subject covered by the refugee convention is being slowly eroded by the development of a new language that refers to claimants as "irregular" foreign nationals who conceptually cannot be legitimate displaced persons fleeing persecution.

Manufacturing Crisis: Phobic Language Disarming Discourse

The ubiquitous nature of anxiety and phobia has been linked to the present mode of Western democratic neoliberal political culture (Bhandar 2004; Isin 2004). The xenophobic responses to the ocean-voyage arrivals of refugees can be read as a hyper-alertness or extreme vigilance that has been deployed through the media, government officials, and revised policies. Throughout the deployment of these policies is a perpetual compulsive repetition of the dangerous, suspect, and criminal migrant behavior, a message designed to solicit a reactive anxiety that is completely unintelligible to the very practices of everyday society. Put another way, a politics of fear gives rise to anxieties that are then embedded and exercised in a system of governance of the everyday. Anxiety is not read here simply as a symptom, but as a productive capacity of a neoliberal governance strategy. Thus in a society where we see evidence of the erosion and displacement of the social, there is a simultaneous altering of the subjectivities of those governed through the system. It is difficult to understand how the discourse of the dangerous and suspect immigrant can be perpetuated even in a climate where there has been so much critical dialogue to the contrary. Didier Bigo provides an understanding of the continuation of this discursive construction:

> Securitization of the immigrant as a risk is based on our conception of the state as a body or a container for the policy. It is anchored in the fears of politicians about losing their symbolic control over the territorial

boundaries. It is structured by the *habitus* of the security professionals and their new interests not only in the foreigner but in the "immigrant." These interests are correlated with the globalization of technologies of surveillance and control going beyond the national borders. It is based, finally, on the "unease" that some citizens who feel discarded suffer because they cannot cope with the uncertainty of everyday life. This worry or unease is not psychological. It is a structural unease in a "risk society" framed by neoliberal discourses in which freedom is always associated at its limits with danger and (in)security. (2002, 65)

In Bigo's account, it is the state itself that perpetuates a notion or feeling of unease regarding the migrant subject, in order to bolster the rationale for security and greater systems of control. By the same token, what we have discerned through our research into the shift in contemporary Canadian immigration and refugee policy is a dual system of manufacturing fear based on the immigrant or refugee and simultaneously working to legally redefine those subjects as criminal through the systemic recategorization of classes of migration. What emerges from this systemic reclassification is a union between the discursive organization of "fear" of the immigrant (a long-standing discourse in Canada) and the legal apparatus to legitimate this fear through making the refugee into a criminal.

While we have noted several incidents in the media surrounding the arrival of the *MV Sun Sea* that contributed to the changes embedded in Bill C-31, prior debates in the House of Commons on Bill C-4, "Preventing Human Smugglers from Abusing Canada's Immigration System Act," illustrate the discursive production of criminality and refugees. These debates also show the constructed discourse of xenophobia, whereby the immigration system (read as faulty) and various migrants are placed in the foreground as a potential threat to the security of the state. From the Hansard debates what becomes clear is the state's bewildering shift from a view of immigrants and refugees as seeking safety and security to one that regards their arrival with extreme paranoia, scepticism, and distrust. The nation-state represented in the Hansard debates is symbolic not of a nation comfortable in its legal and political order, but one that must act on extreme suspicion and fear. The phobic response of the government in the debate regarding Bill C-4 is a case study in the actions of a nation-state fearful about its sovereign integrity.

The debate regarding Bill C-4 is interesting because, as MP Jinny Sims pointed out, the legislation itself was being introduced under the auspices of the Public Safety ministry, and not through the Standing Committee of Citizenship and Immigration. Sims states:

> Once again I want to express my concern that this piece of legislation is being presented under public safety when the bill actually deals with immigration and citizenship. This is a real issue. Since when have we as Canadians seen the arrival of immigrants in the country as a public safety issue? I urge the government to send this bill to the Standing Committee on Citizenship and Immigration as it goes through its committee stage. (Hansard 2011)

Sims represents Newton–North Delta, one of the most immigrant-intensive electoral ridings on the west coast of Canada. The riding of Newton-North Delta is also the physical location of the border cities of Delta-Surrey. The discursive framing of this bill is firmly located in a xenophobic structure and acts to produce fear and anxiety not only by appealing to the perceived threat of immigration, but by linking all immigration to potential criminal behaviours. Sims's critique of the government's handling of this issue and its framing of immigration as a public safety concern is highlighted by the response from the government.

In contrast to Sims's position, we can see in the response from Conservative MP Mike Wallace a striking confirmation of a fear of the "other." Speaking in favour of the bill, Wallace drew connections between the infamous lawlessness of the border crossing between Mexico and the United States:

> The smuggling of people is not a new crime. In fact, it has been happening around the world for many decades. I am sure all hon. Members have heard stories of people paying a fee to bypass legal and proper immigration processes to sneak across the Mexico–United States border. My riding of Burlington is not that far from the U.S. border, and on a weekly basis a number of people come to see me regarding the issue of crossing the border illegally. (Hansard 2011)

Wallace, in drawing a parallel between the lawless US-Mexican border and a similar threat of lawlessness along the northern US-Canada border, does nothing but paint a deceptive and mystifying picture regarding the stories often told about the US-Mexican border, and by extension the imagined threat along the Canada-US border. However, the interesting thing to note here is that Bill C-4 is concerned not with land borders but exclusively with migration of peoples by boat. Wallace's constituency is in the geographically challenged (land-locked) Burlington riding, but he outlines how, even though his riding is nowhere near a sea, constituents nonetheless fear boat immigration and its effect on the local community. His explanation collapses the experience of migration with the act of criminality and illegality:

> When I was first elected, I was amazed that individuals in discussing with me how they came to Canada eventually would admit that they got here illegally. They did not follow the legal process. They claimed refugee status when they arrived at the border. Then they would come to my office because they wanted me as their MP to help them continue the illegal process they had started. Out of respect for the office I hold as a Member of Parliament, I told those individuals that I would not interfere in any illegal activity that they had undertaken. I instructed them to follow the legal and appropriate processes to immigrate to Canada, under the refugee system and the immigration system. Often we would call those people back a few weeks later to determine what they had decided to do, but they would be hard to find and in some cases we could not find them at all. It does happen. It happens in Burlington. It happens across this country and has been happening for many years. (Hansard 2011)

In addition to relating his experience of various constituents who admitted to illegal arrival in Canada, Wallace also discusses how his constituents are requesting "a get-tough" approach to the protection of Canadian borders:

> Two events in recent years have served to raise the profile of this issue in the minds of Canadians. One is the ship that recently came to British Columbia aboard the vessel *MV Sun Sea*. This occurred less than one year after the arrival of the *MV Ocean Lady*, which carried 76 Sri Lankan Tamils. These two events are an issue in my riding. Although we are in Burlington, thousands of miles away from where the activities took place, Burlingtonians and all Canadians are concerned about how we could allow those events to happen. (Hansard 2011)

Presumably the so-called bogus refugee claimants that typify his experience with recent immigrants in his riding are not among those who voiced concern over the legality of the passengers on the *MV Sun Sea* or *MV Ocean Lady*.

The other trope that Wallace includes is the often mistaken notion that refugee claimants are *jumping the queue*. He states:

> Further, human smuggling is fundamentally unfair to those who follow the rules and wait their turn to come to Canada, which we all see in our offices. We all sympathize with those who are following the rules and are trying to become Canadian immigrants by following the legal procedure. I am a sixth- or seventh-generation Canadian, but my in-laws came here from Italy. They came through the legal route. They had to wait their turn to come here. They followed the process. They did not come on a boat and claim refugee status after paying a smuggler thousands of dollars to escape from Italy. The followed the rules. They expect everyone to follow the rules. (Hansard 2011)

Wallace employs a well-rehearsed rhetoric framing older waves of migration as more noble and law abiding than current migrants. In fact, the history of Italian immigration to Canada is replete with racism, criminalization, ghettoization, and barriers to social and political integration (Harney 1993; Iacovetta, Perin, and Principe 2000). The question that needs to be raised is why, after so much critique of the securitization and criminalization of migrant/refugee populations, does the image and metaphor of danger, risk, and fear persist? What is the psychological makeup of a society or system of governance that maintains this as an everyday *modus operandi*? Is this the exclusive discourse of a nation-state? Or is it being informed through vectors of international migration regime politics? As borders are hardened, and securitization and surveillance increase, riskier environments are produced. Vulnerable populations are forced into taking extralegal means to access their mobility. For instance, the United Nations Office of Drugs and Crime (UNODC) issue paper "Smuggling of Migrants by Sea" states that:

> According the 2009 UNDP Human Development Report, there are an estimated 50 million irregular international migrants in the world today, a significant number of whom paid for assistance to illegally cross borders. This number is believed to have increased since. While precise numbers of people who are smuggled in the course of irregular migration are not known, it is increasingly assumed that an overwhelming number of irregular migrants use the services of smuggling networks at some stage in their journey. (2011, 11)

The report notes that "smuggling" by sea needs to be put into context, as irregular migrants primarily cross borders via air or land transport. Indeed, Bill C-31's new provisions of detention for all those deemed "irregular arrivals" were first imposed on a group of migrants crossing the land border into Quebec:

> To deal with these land entries, Ottawa is now resorting, for the first time, to new legislative provisions that were largely designed to deal with migrant vessels likes the ones that landed on the B.C. coast in 2009 and 2010. The rules in the Protecting Canada's Immigration System Act, in which the claimants are deemed to be "irregular arrivals," will make it easier for authorities to detain the asylum seekers for at least six months, and to deport them if their refugee claims are rejected. (LeBlanc 2012)

The UNODC report reinforces the use of the new legal apparatus by establishing the fact that arrival by sea is a very limited occurrence in Canada as elsewhere: "Likewise in Canada, the numbers of unfacilitated entries were higher than migrant smuggling interdictions, with most irregular migrants arranging their own journey and border crossings via land. Contrasted to the United States situation however, in recent years Canada has experienced incidents of large non-commercial vessels, of several hundred passengers arranged by smugglers" (UNODC 2011, 11).

Wallace's anti-refugee position well represents Canada's current policy direction within a new internationalization of refugee criminalization. It is a process of criminalization that has led to new powers of government that frame refugees first as criminals and only second as possibly legal seekers of refuge. In the case of the *MV Sun Sea*, prior to any determination of the vessel's passengers as refugee claimants, Minister Toews had already made comments framing the claimants as smuggled migrants. Without confirmation and before any in-land claims were made by the passengers, their criminality was already established (*Toronto Star*, 13 August 2010). It is clear from considering media coverage of the *MV Sun Sea* during the time of the event that the structure of the news story was dependent on the circulation of myths and half-truths that by and large supported the government's agenda. Critical perspectives in the public media did not really surface until after the manufactured crisis had been quelled. Media representation of migrants and asylum seekers and of the question of refugees has been shown to contribute to the public perception of an immigration system that is in desperate need of repair.

Conclusion

The imagination and practice of immigration and refugee determination has radically shifted. The rules governing refugee determination and immigration have become much more restrictive, and the use of deportation has become a major feature of these new systems of sanctuary. In the case of the Tamil refugees, the arrival of the *MV Ocean Lady* and *MV Sun Sea* acted as a catalyst for the Canadian government's reframing of ocean-voyaged refugee claimants as "irregular" and criminally suspect. Their arrival as a single group of claimants solicited a phobic response by the Canadian government. As this chapter illustrates, the growing framing of criminal smuggling and human trafficking that has shaped discourse in the international migration regime was effectively used in this case. The Canadian government, already tightening immigration controls and policies, was able to rely on this discourse of criminality and smuggling to promote a phobic response to the Tamil asylum seekers. Through the example of Sri Lankan refugee claimants, their recategorization as "irregular migrants," and the state's use of a language of criminalization, this chapter has investigated three main issues.

First, we have argued that there is an ongoing regime change in international migration management (Hindess 2000). The new management framework alleges that refugee claimants who arrive by sea are illegal and has led to the denial of people's legitimate claim to refugee status. This change in management is reflected in numerous legal and national contexts –and this chapter has examined the interrelationship and transnational framework that has taken root in the name of securitization and sovereignty. We have traced how Canadian changes in contemporary immigration and refugee policy are heavily influenced by a globalized system of migrant management. We examined how both a rhetoric and coordinated Canadian-Australian policy/practice of criminalization has affected the arrival of the *MV Sun Sea* and the subsequent legislative debates in Canada with regard to Bills C-4 and C-31.

Second, this paper has argued that people who seek asylum, sanctuary, or refuge in Canada via marine voyages are now reframed as illegal actors attempting to exploit Canada's political humanitarian commitment to an antiquated UN convention on refugees. It is an illegality that is aided by the deployment of new terms of reference (e.g., "irregular arrivals," "mass arrivals," "designated foreign nationals"). The statements of Bowen, Kenney, and Toews reflect a concern to secure national borders from human smugglers. They are an expression of a phobic and desperate need to reframe those who seek refuge not as rights claimants but as an entirely new and different type of non-rights claimant or as the unwitting "cargo" of criminal actors. Under this logic, it is the alleged illegality of their entry that turns legitimate asylum seekers into irregular or criminal refugees. In this way, a discourse of security is produced through a xenophobic response to refugees arriving via marine voyages. Individual claimants are erased by the preference for framing these claimants as a criminally smuggled group of "illegal" migrants rather than real or legitimate seekers of sanctuary. The new refugee regime also relies on a semiotic attack on the conventional etymology of asylum. The terms "mass arrivals," "irregular arrivals," "designated claimants," and "designated foreign nationals" are introduced as conceptual disruptions. The marine-voyaged claimant is also made to stand as the example of all refugee claimants. State actors are engaged in the creation of a new category of refugee: a criminal seeker of refuge who must not be accommodated under existing refugee conventions because of the voyage's assumed criminality and the individual claimant's potential harm to Canadian society.

Third, we have examined domestic immigration/refuge reform in Canada in a global context. While at one time immigration refugee policy emphasized solely the domestic sphere – population/demographic issues – today the discourse of the institutional framing (e.g., parliamentary bills) is couched squarely in the language of criminalization/security, sovereignty, and a globalized system of migrant management (Coutin 2010; Hindess 2000). Furthermore, we have argued that Canada's current attack on migrancy is also the product of an attempt to harmonize border policies not only with the United States but also with other sovereign states who believe themselves to be under siege from illegal or fraudulent migrancy claims (e.g., Australia). As Canada institutionally interacts with these international entities – and their institutional agencies and networks – their agencies of citizenship and public safety come together to devise strategies that instantiate this international shared phobia of human movement. A shared phobic response is thus presented as a sober and coordinated approach that closes loopholes established by the original conventions on refugees. Such ministerial practice – driven by an unacknowledged phobia – begins to be increasingly involved with initiatives to manipulate existing conventions and laws in a manner avoiding direct contestation of established and agreed-upon international covenants or conventions. It is not the law such actors want to change; their focus is entirely on creating new protocols that exist alongside older covenants, and that allow for the criminalization and detention of claimants via their framing as foreign and illegal elements harmful to society. The approach is an additive one that attempts to layer on top of existing law the use of discretionary and conjunctural powers that can be effectively used to criminalize or illegalize behaviours of those who choose to come to Canada via ocean voyage. Thus, the deployment of new frameworks of reference (e.g., irregular migrant) allows for a new conception of these claimants as inherently illegitimate and out of order.

We have shown how the state, in the context of migration and refugee affairs, is becoming less transparent and democratic through a shift towards unprecedented forms of ministerial discretion and circumscription of judicial process. Discretion is being enabled through the development of a new language of post-migrant rights whereby the rights of the refugee established in the 1951 convention are circumvented. Sri Lankan refugee claimants are being used to legitimate a new language that establishes a social sphere beyond rights. This development marks a devolution of rights for both citizen and claimant alike. The passing of Bill C-31 marks Canada's full entry into a political period where Canadians no longer have a law of rights. Personhood itself has become expunged from the immigration and refugee act in favour of a post-migrant rights management regime. This shift marks the biopolitical governance of society, whereby the individual rights once held foundational to liberal democratic order are revealed as a system that can no longer presume to guarantee the basic and fundamental right to freedom. In so doing, Canada has moved away from a language of humanitarianism by representing mass arrival asylum seekers as criminals without rights. The language of post-migrancy rights is now devoid of any reference to the rights of specific individuals. The new regime of post-migrant rights acts only to protect the state's power of refugee determination, as it abandons Canada's commitment to an international humanitarianism that once supported the legitimacy of claimants and an acknowledgment of the right of mobility and refuge.

NOTE

1 For our purposes here the term "refugee" is used interchangeably with "refugee claimant" and "refuge" is used interchangeably with "sanctuary" and "asylum." We use "refugee" as it is defined in the 1951 Convention relating to the Status of Refugees and its 1967 Protocol, which removed some temporal and geographic limitations. The convention clearly outlines who is a refugee, what are the rights of refugees, and the state obligations of those who become signatories to this international instrument for sanctuary and protection of refugees. The document defines a refugee as a person with a "well-found fear of being persecuted for reasons of race, religion, nationality, membership of a particular social group or political opinion" (UNHCR 1966, article 1A[2]).

REFERENCES

Aiken, Sharryn J. 2010. "Manufacturing Terrorism." Appendix A in *Our Friendly Local Terrorist*, Mary Jo Leddy. Toronto: Between the Lines.

Arendt, Hanna. 1951. *The Origins of Totalitariansim*. New York: Harcourt Brace.

Bangkok Post. 2012, 14 November. "UN Rights Chief Warns Australia on Refugees." http://www.bangkokpost.com/news/asia/321193/un-rights-chief-warns-australia-on-refugees (accessed 20 November 2012).

BBC. 2012, 17 July. "Somali Refugees Top One Million Mark, Says UN Agency." http://www.bbc.co.uk/news/world-africa-18875139 (accessed 30 November 2012).

Bhandar, Davina. 2004. "Renormalizing Citizenship and Life in Fortress North America." *Citizenship Studies* 8 (3): 261–78. http://dx.doi.org/10.1080/1362 102042000256998.

Bigo, Didier. 2002. "Security and Immigration: Toward a Critique of the Governmentality of Unease." *Alternatives: Global, Local, Political* 27: 63–92.

Boroff, David, and Roque Planas. 2012, 24 January. "Romney Says He Favors 'Self-Deportation.'" *New York Daily News*. http://articles.nydailynews.com/2012-01-24/news/30657385_1_mitt-romney-illegal-immigrants-deportation (accessed 20 November 2012).

Bowen, Chris. 2010. Transcript of interview with Laurie Oakes, Channel Nine's *Today*, 10 October 2010 (regional visit to discuss regional processing centres). http://parlinfo.aph.gov.au/parlInfo/download/media/pressrel/422048/upload_binary/422048.pdf;fileType=application/pdf#search=%22When%20you%20have%20got%20a%20very%20high%20

number%20of%20refugees%20around%20the%20world,%2042%20
million%20displaced%20people%20around%20the%20world%22 (accessed
28 September 2015).

Bradimore, A., and H. Bauder. 2012. "Mystery Ships and Risky Boat People:
Tamil Refugee Migration in the Newsprint Media." *Canadian Journal of
Communication, North America* 36. http://www.cjc-online.ca/index.php/
journal/article/view/2466 (accessed 24 November 2012).

Canadian Border Security Agency. 2010. *Draft: National Communications
Strategy – Arrival of Migrant Vessals.* Accessed through Freedom of
Information Act request, 5 May 2012.

Chase, Steven. 2011, 9 March. "How Canada Laid a Hard Welcome Mat
for the Sun Sea." *Globe and Mail.* http://www.theglobeandmail.com/
news/politics/how-canada-laid-a-hard-welcome-mat-for-the-sun-sea/
article1934720/ (accessed 12 June 2012).

Citizenship and Immigration Canada. 2012. *Faster Removal of Foreign
Criminals Act.* http://www.cic.gc.ca/english/department/media/
releases/2012/2012-10-24.asp (accessed 26 November 2012).

Collacott, Martin. 2010, 25 October. "Martin Collacott: Refugee Act Doesn't
Go Far Enough." *National Post.* http://fullcomment.nationalpost.
com/2010/10/25/martin-collacott-refugee-act-doesnt-go-far-enough/
(accessed 5 April 2011).

Coutin, Susan Bibler. 2010. "Confined Within: National Territories as
Zones of Containment." *Political Geography* 29 (4): 200–8. http://dx.doi.
org/10.1016/j.polgeo.2010.03.005.

De Genova, Nicholas. 2002. "Migrant Illegality and Deportability in Everyday
Life." *Annual Review of Anthropology* 31 (1): 419–47. http://dx.doi.
org/10.1146/annurev.anthro.31.040402.085432.

– 2011. "Alien Powers: Deportable Labour and the Spectacle of Security."
In *The Contested Politics of Mobility,*" ed. Vicki Squire, 91–115. New York:
Routledge.

Greenberg, Josh, and Sean Hier. 2002. "Constructing a Discursive Crisis:
Risk, Problematization and Illegal Chinese in Canada." *Ethnic and Racial
Studies,* 25 (3): 490–513.

Guardian. 2007, 24 January. "Rich or Poor, a Million Iraqi Refugees Strain the
Hospitality of Jordan." http://www.guardian.co.uk/world/2007/jan/24/
iraq.ianblack (accessed 5 November 2012).

Hansard. House of Commons Debates. 2011, 20 September. Volume
146, number 16, 1st Session, 41st Parliament. http://www.parl.gc.ca/
HousePublications/Publication.aspx?DocId=5125112&Language=
E&Mode=1.

Harney, Robert F. 1993. *From the Shores of Hardship: Italians in Canada*. Welland, ON: Éditions Soleil.

Hein, Christopher. 1998. "Migration of Albanians to Italy." In *Regulation of Migration: International Experience*, ed. Anita Böcker, K. Groenendijk, T. Havinga, and P. Minderhoud. Amsterdam: Aksant.

Hindess, Barry.2000. "Citizenship in the International Management of Population." *American Behavioral Scientist* 43 (9): 1486–97. http://dx.doi. org/10.1177/00027640021956008.

Human Rights Research and Education Centre, University of Ottawa. 2011. "By the Numbers: Refugee Statistics." http://www.cdp-hrc.uottawa.ca/projects/refugee-forum/projects/ documents/ REFUGEESTATSCOMPREHENSIVE1999–2011.pdf (accessed 5 April 2011).

Iacovetta, Franca, Roberto Perin, and Angelo Principe, eds. 2000. *Enemies Within: Italian and Other Wartime Internments in Canada and Beyond*. Toronto: University of Toronto Press.

Ibbitson, John, Steven Chase, and Marten Youssef. 2010, 12 August. "Ottawa Plans New Rules for Boat Migrants." *Globe and Mail*. http://www. theglobeandmail.com/news/politics/ottawa-plans-new-rules-for-boat-migrants/article1376987/ (accessed 5 June 2012).

Intergovernmental Asia Pacific Consultations on Refugees, Displaced Persons and Migrants. Chair's Summary. Eleventh Plenary Session, Xiamen China, 23–25 November 2006.

Isin, Engin. 2004. "The Neurotic Citizen." *Citizenship Studies* 8 (3): 217–35. http://dx.doi.org/10.1080/1362102042000256970.

Leblanc, Daniel. 2012, 5 December. "Ottawa Gets Tough with Romanian Asylum Seekers." *Globe and Mail* (Ottawa), http://www.theglobeandmail. com/news/politics/human-smuggling-group-busted-at-quebec-border/ article5992117/ (accessed 20 January 2013).

Macklin, Audrey. 2005. "Disappearing Refugees: Reflections on the Canada-US Safe Third Country Agreement." *Columbia Human Rights Law Review* 36: 365–426.

Mann, Alexandra. 2009. "Refugees Who Arrive by Boat and Canada's Commitment to the Refugee Convention: A Discursive Analysis." *Refuge: Canada's Journal on Refugees* 26 (2).

National Post. 2012, May 16. "MV Sun Sea Owner Charged with Human Smuggling." http://news.nationalpost.com/2012/05/16/mv-sun-sea-owner-charged-with-human-smuggling/ (accessed 4 March 2015).

Pakistan Observer. 2012, 1 December. "0.360m Afghan Refugees Waiting to Return Home." http://pakobserver.net/detailnews.asp?id=184781 (accessed 30 November 2012).

Public Safety Canada. 2011, July 12. "Suspected Human Smuggling Vessel
    Taken into Custody by Indonesian Authorities." Newsrelease. http://
    www.publicsafety.gc.ca/media/ nr/2011/nr20110712-eng.aspx?rss=true
    (accessed 5 April 2012).
– 2011, August 30. "Public Safety Minister Vic Toews Reaffirms the
    Government of Canada's Commitment to the Global Fight against Human
    Trafficking." News release. http://www.publicsafety.gc.ca/media/
    nr/2011/nr20110830-eng.aspx?rss=true (accessed 5 August 2012).
– 2012, July 6. "Ministers Toews and Kenney Commend Canada Border
    Services for Preventing Human Smuggling." News release. http://www.
    publicsafety.gc.ca/media/nr/2012/nr20120706-1-eng.aspx (accessed 5
    August 2012).
Quan, Douglas. 2015, 4 March. "Sun Sea Money Pit: Ottawa Spent $600,000
    on Smuggling Ship before Deciding to Scrap It." *National Post* (accessed 5
    March 2015).
Ranciere, Jacques. 2004. "Who Is the Subject of the Rights of Man?" *South
    Atlantic Quarterly* 103 (2/3): 297–310. http://dx.doi.org/10.1215/00382876-
    103-2-3-297.
Sharma, Nandita. 2005. "Anti-trafficking Rhetoric and the Making of a Global
    Apartheid." *NWSA Journal* 17 (3): 88–111. http://dx.doi.org/10.2979/
    NWS.2005.17.3.88.
– 2008. "Citizenship and the Disciplining of (Im)migrant Workers in the
    United States." In *Refugees, Recent Migrants and Employment: Challenging
    Barriers and Exploring Pathways*, ed. SoniaMcKay. London: Routledge.
Toronto Star. 2010, 13 August. "Police Investigating Refugee Boat to See if
    Human Smuggling Laws Violated: Vic Toews."
UNHCR (United Nations High Commissioner for Refugees). 1966. 1951
    Convention Relating to the Status of Refugees, Convention and Protocol
    Relating to the Status of Refugees, Article 1A(2), UN resolution 2198. XXI.
– 1991, 26 July. "Background Note on the Safe Country Concept and Refugee
    Status." EC/SCP/68. http://www.unhcr.org/refworld/docid/3ae68ccec.
    html (accessed 25 November 2012).
– 2000. "'Three Circles' Consultations: Concept Paper." http://www.icva.ch/
    doc00000184.html (accessed 5 August 2012).
United Nations Office of Drugs and Crime. 2011. "Issue Paper: Smuggling of
    Migrants by Sea." http://www.unodc.org/documents/human-trafficking/
    Migrant-Smuggling/Issue-Papers/Issue_Paper_-_Smuggling_of_Migrants_
    by_Sea.pdf (accessed May 2012)
Walters, William. 2010a. "Deportation, Expulsion, and the International Police
    of Aliens." In *The Deportation Regime: Sovereignty, Space, and the Freedom*

of Movement, ed. N. De Genova and N. Peutz, 69–100. Durham: Duke University Press. http://dx.doi.org/10.1215/9780822391340-003.

– 2010b. "Illegal Immigration."In *The Politics of Migration Management*, ed. M. Geiger and A. Pecoud, 73–95. Houndmills: Palgrave.

Widgren, Jonas. 1989. "Asylum Seekers in Europe in the Context of South-North Movements." *International Migration Review* 23 (3): 599. http://dx.doi.org/10.2307/2546430.

PART 3

Politics by Other Means: Phobias and Political Practice

Part 3 of this volume focuses on the intentional employment of fear to create phobias in political life as tools of social control. The authors discuss three different models that explain why and by what means governments and political entities deliberately capitalize on fear to achieve their goals.

Pautz in chapter 8 notes several tactics politicians use to control public perceptions of right and wrong and to shift blame from the zone of sensible analysis to the zone of defying false norms. These tactics include maintaining a common state of ignorance of the "other," the use of populist rhetoric, the marginalization of opposition, the creation of false "mainstream" movements, and the employment of widely respected and appealing, if vague, notions such as "the will of the people" or "the dictates of history or nature." Any failure of the state, whether social, political, economic, or other, is attributed to the "other's" failure to conform to the political party's self-authenticated moral standards and norms. Thus, a political movement may attempt to convince the entire population that the solution to its problems starts and ends with strict obedience to the political party's self-authenticated standards. The other will be blamed not only for its deviance from those standards but also for the nation's problems.

Following the same line of analysis, Shantz (chapter 9) suggests that governments, as political entities, may employ social phobias to create exclusionary mechanisms that target the "other" to address problems such as terrorism. The common state of fear generated by state-sponsored social phobia is used to justify a gross departure from well-founded and socially rooted principles of justice. Anti-terrorism legislation that represents a wholesale departure from universal human rights potentiates abuse of power in the judicial process and leads to questionable ethical conduct by police, but has been widely accepted by many citizens because of fear of the "other." Terrorism is presented to the population as involving a choice: accept the bad (violations of human rights) or expect the worst (terrorist attacks). The collateral damage, the vulnerable "other" of society, has to comply with phobia-based laws and practices to fall into the category of "worthy citizens."

In chapter 10 Koutrolikou demonstrates one of the governmental tactics employed to control the "other." The government alienates the phobic object from the population via constructed fears of "other" neighbourhoods. Once phobia regarding "other" neighbourhoods has been created through mechanisms such as the media, the prophecy of fear is fulfilled and the "other" neighbourhood becomes in reality a dangerous place. Such tactics, unfortunately, are successful in creating a collective fear that justifies governmental actions against social groups such as immigrants and racial or religious minorities. Nonetheless, controlling fear within the entire population is a difficult task even for the government. Fear may escalate into explosive social situations where various groups of the society actively engage in class war or racial war.

8 Death Panels on the Prison Planet: The New World Order Conspiracy and the Radicalization of American Politics

JOHANN PAUTZ

Obama's world tour provided a foretaste of the reception he can expect to receive. He will probably also stand in some European capital, addressing the people of the world and telling them that he is the one that they have been waiting for. And he can expect as wildly enthusiastic a greeting as Obama got in Berlin. The Bible calls that leader the Antichrist. And it seems apparent that the world is now ready to make his acquaintance.

– Hal Lindsey, American evangelist

The period leading up to and following the United States' 2008 and 2010 elections has seen a tumultuous viciousness in American politics that to outside observers or Americans unfamiliar with the mobilizing passions of the far right must have seemed without precedent and symptomatic of mass insanity. As then senator Barack Obama appeared ready to clinch the Democratic nomination for president, rumours began to swirl through the Internet and talk radio programs that he was not what he seemed: he was actually an Indonesian- or Kenyan-born Muslim. At the same time, town hall–style forums on reforming the United States' broken health care system degenerated into accusations of eugenicist "death panels" while, outside, citizens carrying assault rifles milled around the crowds (Condon 2009). Between these elections, runs on firearms and ammunition exhausted supply; there was unprecedented demand based on animosity towards the new administration and fear of tighter gun regulations (Neary 2009). A new wave of right-wing candidates frequently denounced Democratic incumbents (and occasionally incumbent Republicans) as "domestic enemies of the Constitution" (Corly 2009). Youth service organizations such as AmeriCorps were labelled "political re-education camps," and some conservative politicians and media personalities discouraged participation in the national census, which they portrayed as a prelude to federal government tyranny (Murphy 2011). Most frightening is the well-documented explosion in the number of armed militias and similar far-right groups specifically justifying their existence in opposition to these supposed threats. The rhetoric and ideological assumptions upon which such movements are founded have expanded from the outer fringes to enter the mainstream of politics and political media, exposing mass audiences to their conspiracies.

While the above allegations may seem to be representative of the radical or even lunatic fringes, these claims have significant precedent in American culture, particularly among those prophetic Christian groups generally described as "evangelical" and ultra-conservative nativist and anti-communist groups steeped in Cold War–era fears. Furthermore, within the millenarian and conspiratorial traditions that transcend the American far right's fractured front, the eventual implementation of such tyrannical policies is accepted as inevitable. While there is a significant tradition of grass-roots conspiracism in American culture, the promotion of these conspiracies by official institutions and personalities, as well as the emerging pattern of these frames' activation during periods of Democratic resurgence, suggest elite manufacture of these phobias.

From colonial times into the present, the America cultural discourses of exceptionalism and divine destiny have had their implicit shadow in a deep fear of forces presumed to be in opposition to the supposedly favoured nation's divinely appointed role. During every phase of the United States' history, parallel and indeed intertwined traditions of millennialism and conspiracism have contributed to an ebb and flow in the presumption of evil forces at work, not only in the world but within the nation's political and social institutions. The general schema of American millenarian discourses originates in subaltern religious movements understanding themselves to be engaged in a millenarian struggle against evil, according to varying interpretations of the end times. In its more secular though strongly hybridized counterpart, religious millennialism is complemented by fears of foreign threats, dilution of natives' cultural identity and political agency, and the machinations of treasonous "insiders."

Both of these intertwined millenarian and conspiratorial traditions have been maintained in the form of an adaptive conspiracy theory

positing that the United States, as a result of its singular and exceptional heritage, is the target of an agenda of international subversion.
According to this tradition, the nation state will be dissolved as a result
of incremental moral or cultural changes adulterating the once idyllic
society, taking it from a state of purity into one in which it is absorbed
into a global whole. Paradoxically, the once exceptional and powerful
United States will as a result of its openness, freedom, and tolerance
render itself unto the corrupt world that was its mirror image. It is this
mythos of modern secular values and global unity, juxtaposed to American supremacism, ethnic purity, and national sovereignty, that characterizes the New World Order (NWO) conspiracy theory. This theory,
having common roots with prophecies of a millennial conflict between
Christ and the Antichrist and later becoming synonymous with the
Cold War struggle between the United States and its communist adver-
saries, has moved from the religious and cultural fringes to increasingly
become the dominant cultural lens through which many American conservatives view domestic and international politics and culture. Just as,
similar to most conspiracy theories, some disparate kernels of truth are
here spun into a web-like grand narrative to fit a foreordained conclusion, so an increasingly mainstreamed American far right promotes
a narrative that contextualizes contemporary events within a sinister
simulacrum of the real world.

The NWO conspiracy functions as an expression of perceived relative
deprivation and status anxiety. For several decades, American cultural
conservatives have used slippery slope arguments contextualizing
challenges to traditional race and gender hierarchies and associated
cultural ideologies as a means of juxtaposing national destiny and cultural degradation, all at the hands of a sinister conspiracy. As a result,
Civil Rights–era social changes in the United States have been narrated
as the nexus of the exceptional state and the new face of the global communist conspiracy – a presumed shadow government that has come
to be known as the NWO. This supposed conspiratorial system would
mandate the abolition of patriarchal institutions and demote the United
States from a position of privilege to the status of a global backwater
dominated by foreign forces. NWO conspiracy theories use traditional
anti-Semitic templates to allege a central communist, internationalist,
anti-Christian, and secular humanist agenda, promoted by the United
Nations and similar transnational institutions.

According to the theory, the NWO is a body of elites within and
outside the United States who seek to use the UN and its members'

peacekeeping forces to subjugate the United States and enslave its "traditionalist" (i.e., white, Christian, conservative, gun-owning) population (McAlvany 1999). In anticipation of a UN invasion of the United States, civilian Patriot militias have held drills and stockpiled ammunition and supplies. Similarly, many religious conservatives allege prophetic fulfilment in signs that the nation's population is slowly being conditioned to accept the NWO's communist agenda via the institutions of a secular and humanist state – the purported agenda of the Antichrist (Robertson 1991).

Conspiracy/Theory

The conspiracy theory must be understood as a metaphysical and discursive form that parallels and complements the millennialist tradition that has strongly influenced American culture. The conspiracy theory's utility in reducing complexity into (often Manichean) simplicity and its ability to contextualize otherwise complex systems into familiar though adaptable frames makes it particularly common in "populist" politics (Barkun 2003; Berlet and Lyons 2000). Similarly, the conspiracy theory, through its presumption of hidden (and therefore specifically unidentifiable) evil, uses the visible "other" as a symptom of or proxy for the presumed evil presence. This fungibility, both in the conspiracy theory's specific claims and its identification of the "visible" symptoms of the invisible perpetrators, provides for the theory's adaptability in scapegoating a variety of minorities. Because of its strong association with stresses caused by social or cultural changes, status anxiety, and scapegoating, the conspiratorial form is easily adapted to use by political and economic elites as a means of obfuscating complex issues, deflecting responsibility, or redirecting populist anger (Berlet and Lyons 2000, 11).

Conspiracy and millenarian discourses share many qualities. First, by attempting to unify forces and events that the interpreter considers evil, they both tend to tie disparate incidents and eras together in a narrative that ultimately alleges the existence of a timeless, evil force – a frame that quickly devolves from addressing secular forces to targeting those with otherworldly qualities. The semiotician's search for clues detailing the signs of the apocalypse or the inevitable clinching of the conspiracy's presumed power renders the world as nearly synonymous with the grand realm of the super-conspiracy. The real and the conspiracy become nearly interchangeable; the world is made evil and the ensuing conflict to rectify this wrong is millennial (Barkun 2003). To identify these evil forces the conspiracy theorist, like the millenarian, must become a master semiotician looking for clues to the ultimate truths that lie beneath the surface of the ordinary world. Generally, this is achieved by using unorthodox methods that "map" the world by attributing questionable significance to mundane things and events. The individual conspiracists, millennialists, or their fractious interpretive communities seek hidden significance beneath the surface of the mundane world that they share with the uninitiated. In ways that are not apparent to the lay person, the believer has access to "revealed knowledge" through which nothing is accidental and all things are connected (Barkun 2003).

Hofstadter describes conspiracism as an appealing mechanism for those who feel politically impotent. Their experience is of alienation from the mechanisms of political and economic power, and as a result they see only the outcomes of power instead of its processes (2008, 39–40). In the absence of a popularly accepted explanation for obvious changes in cultural values and social hierarchies, a mythology is developed to explain why formerly empowered social groups have suffered perceived or actual disenfranchisement. In particular, the conspiracist elements of such discourses often serve to rally the culture's standard-bearers against those marginal groups associated with real or imagined threats to their dominance.

As incumbent ideologies become increasingly ineffective in describing the changing world, new discourses emerge to redefine subjectivities and cultural values – particularly the parameters of "good" and "evil." A social group may perceive its "cultural death" as a shift of dominant ideologies and associated social relations that threaten to recontextualize individual and group subjectivities (O'Leary 1998, 32). Such phenomena are often perceived as mobilized and controlled by forces of hidden evil and are therefore associated with apocalyptic and conspiratorial discourse. In this manner, the apocalyptic and conspiratorial forms function as mythologies that describe the liminality of a cultural group's transition from one ideology/subjectivity to another.

"Empty" signifiers of virtue made synonymous with a default group's social identity define that group in opposition to its shadow-self, the "other," which becomes the scapegoat upon which taboo or negative traits are projected. A social group's hardships are rarely attributed to those ideological foundations that are synonymous with its identity. Even problems originating in the cultural or institutional mainstream must be identified and excised, however symbolically, creating a scapegoated minority where one may not have existed previously. The ideologies that enable social reproduction maintain this consistency by mythologizing a correlation between a culture's prosperity and adherence to its traditions and values. In this sense, the identification of evil with a shadowy "other" presents an opportunity for revitalized conservatism and cultural reification, as the default adopts a more rigid and idealized identity constructed in opposition to a scapegoated minority against which it girds itself to fight a perceived agenda of disenfranchisement and persecution.

Conflicts in which a majority population develops a phobia of oppression by minorities in its midst have been described by Arjun Appadurai (2006) as the "fear of small numbers" – an anxiety over an "incomplete" national dominance. In such cases of scapegoating and persecution, the default or majority culture perceives minorities to be a threat to cultural homogeneity and even an agent of cultural decline, characterized by claims of contamination by "outsiders." Such sentiments are associated with the imagining of the romanticized nation or culture and thus the construction of identity. Appadurai refers to Benedict Anderson's concept of the "imagined community": the mediated identity linking vast populations of disparate cultural backgrounds over huge geographic expanses sharing mythologized identification under the banner of the nation state. To the extent that the nation's identity is threatened, so is the identity of its majority. Therefore, a threat to the "imagined" nation – to its hierarchies, privileges, and social relations – is interpreted as an imminent and real threat, nearly always manifested as a reversal of those social relations. Appadurai describes this phenomenon as a "predatory identity" that is "based on claims about and on behalf of a threatened majority ... in many instances, they are claims about cultural majorities that seek to be exclusively or exhaustively linked with the identity of the nation" (2006, 52). Thus the minority, having entered the narrative of the majority's imagined nation, is regarded not as an assimilable group with many similarities but instead is viewed through the lens of difference as a contagion and an affront to the inherent purity of the community.

The default culture's position of threatened perfection requires much fantasy and neglects the fact that "cultural purity" exists only within the imaginings of romantic nationalism and its mythologized histories of national identity. However, the mere possibility that such privileged narratives of purity and destiny can be revised and the default's "divine right" to hegemony can be contested by subaltern groups is a threat to identity politics. The contestation of such narratives need not be limited to the incremental inclusion of subaltern ethnicities, religions, sexualities, or races. The majority's experience of discrepancy between social realities and its ideals demands a category to which the dissonance can be attributed. The dominant cultural narrative of the United States' exceptionalism and millennial destiny originates with the nominally Anglo-Saxon, Protestant cultural mythology established in 1600s New England. The presence of visible minorities poses the question of these populations' roles in "America" and whether the idea of "America" can evolve along with its demographics.

As social phenomena tied to a group's survival, or destiny, millenarian and conspiratorial movements are undeniably political. They seek to solve social problems – not merely individual ones but constellations of problems tethered by a single evil force that has the world poised at the edge of a precipice. Landes states that "millennial thinking, however spiritually put, is political thinking" that has as its goal the transformation of the social and political spheres. He describes the apocalyptic semiotician as navigating a world in which

> everything quickens, everything enlivens, everything coheres. In apocalyptic time, believers become semiotically aroused – everything has meaning, patterns ... Believers commit themselves to this world of transformation, convinced of the superiority of their perceptions, convinced that the uncomprehending masses (including the old elites) will either soon join them or get shredded in the cosmic transformation. (2006, 4–5)

This quality is shared by the conspiracy theory and its extreme dualism and paranoia that separate the theorist from a reality that is, to its core, manipulated by unseen and ill-intentioned forces intent on bringing the world to a sinister point of no return. Hofstadter describes the theorist as "constantly living at the barricades of civilization." Being privy to this dark truth (which most of the human race is either oblivious to or complicit in), the theorist is the messenger entrusted with revealing the hidden and forestalling the inevitable (Hofstadter 2008, 29–30).

Indeed, in conspiracism's contemporary forms, the "other" or minority is increasingly one of political ideology and cultural contestation from within. Thus the communist or terrorist may be anyone – even a neighbour or family member. Such invisible constructions of otherness need not exist as identifiable manifestations signified by ethnicity or race but may be indicated by the challenging of default ideologies such as capitalism, exceptionalism, or various constructions of supremacism.

Because of its use as a pejorative description of subaltern narratives of current and historical events, the conspiratorial label is highly contested and strongly tied to relations of power. These power dynamics are equally likely to be found in the deflection of "conspiratorial" claims alleging wrongdoing by powerful individuals and institutions, as in the promotion of scapegoat conspiracies by elites attempting to deflect populist discontent (Berlet and Lyons 2000, 11). As in Chip Berlet's critique of conspiracy theories, the conspiracy functions as a two-pronged weapon. It deflects blame from powerful individuals or institutions while simultaneously transferring blame to scapegoats who are often disempowered groups (2008).

Conspiracy Tradition in America

While many North American colonies were established for economic reasons, they were nonetheless populated by groups seeking millenarian salvation. Religious refugees fleeing persecution in their homelands expressed their belief in their participation in the divine plan as the concept of manifest destiny. Due to a tradition of searching for prophetic clues in contemporary events, discourses of national mission may at times be indistinguishable from millennial rhetoric. Apocalyptic language, distinguishing religious righteousness from treacherous evil forces, framed the discourses through which many of these communities defined themselves (Weber 2000, 169–70).

American exceptionalism has not only framed the nation's past and present in terms of a millenarian destiny, but has frequently implied the existence of dark forces that stand in opposition to the chosen nation's actualization of that destiny. Early colonists believed that "by mastering prophecy one would be able to understand the course of history and 'cooperate' with it. To be free was precisely to appreciate this destiny and conform to divine will" (Stephanson 1996, 8). Religious New England colonists proclaimed that their newly established settlements would be a moral beacon to Europe and the rest of the corrupt world, a role that would later extend to citizens of the nation. However, the responsibility for actualizing this destiny has been traditionally understood to rest overwhelmingly upon the shoulders of Anglo-Saxon Protestants – the descendants of the original Puritan colonists – though this primary category has been incrementally expanded over generations of immigration. With the "ethnic responsibility" of this burden has come a strong conservative impetus to maintain cultural integrity in the face of immigration, religious pluralism, and similar forms of competition for the label "American." Peter Knight points out that "fears of un-American subversion – no matter how seemingly marginal or fanciful – have played a central role in defining who or what is to count as properly 'American'" (2002, 4).

In nativist discourse, fears of the body politic's contamination by minorities have frequently been expressed as conspiracy theories. During the Seven Year's War the military forces of Catholic France were decried as serving the papist agenda of the Antichrist (Lienesch 1983). Indeed, the fledgling nation's weakness on the world stage, as well as its confrontation with "monolithic Catholicism," would serve as the basis of the NWO conspiracy that characterizes American xenophobia and anti-modernism into the present day. Subaltern religious movements' fears of the Roman papacy, framed within the language of Revelation, would resonate with the predominantly British colonists' cultural history of anti-Catholicism (Bennett 1988, 18).

As the colonies became a nation, the United States' role in world affairs would frequently be described in a language of "political millennialism" (Bennett 1988, 446). Fearing contamination from a world they viewed as evil, Americans generally practised an isolationist foreign policy (albeit in the affairs of the global north) and sought to promote their millenarian agenda by virtuous example. The fear of a monolithic, evil force threatening the American destiny encouraged a catastrophic worldview in which "salvation came only through crisis; required violent conflict, demanded the constant threat of enemies, [and] insisted on readiness" (Bennett 1988, 455). Describing French colonial territories as "North American Babylon" controlled by the "Romish Antichristian power," ministers foretold the woes to be perpetrated by France's demonic forces. Illustrative of standard scapegoating and fear-mongering rhetoric are the comments of John Mellen, who stated, "Our enemies may yet triumph over us, and the gospel taken from us, instead of being by us transmitted to other nations. It is possible, our land may be given to the beast, the inhabitants to the sword, our wives to ravishment and our sons and daughters to death and torture" (Hatch 1974, 418).

While France and Spain, the Catholic superpowers of the day, presented military threats, immigration was decried as both contamination and subversion. During the early 1800s, Irish immigrants were imagined as foot soldiers of an Antichrist conspiracy set to destroy the core of God's chosen nation (Hansen 1972, 374). Whether applied to immigrants or empires, conspiracies painted Catholics as "automatons" likely to serve as an army obedient to the "Romish" agenda of world domination.

Fear of contamination applied equally to race as to religion. Hansen argues that much northern opposition to slavery in the antebellum era was rooted in the fear of racial contamination and thus a dilution of that heritage for which American exceptionalism had been promised (Hansen 1972, 388). Antebellum southern attitudes towards the "peculiar institution" were generally framed in the progressive millenarian belief that slavery was a beneficent and civilizing institution. Following emancipation, however, southerners similarly adopted the belief (easily extended to the eugenicist platform of the second Klan at the turn of the century) that miscegenation risked turning the United States into a "nation of mulatoes," unable to compete with and vulnerable to "the family of white nations" (Trelease 1999, xx).

Complementing supposed threats of infiltration or contamination were fears that less obvious "insiders" might sabotage the exceptional nation's promised trajectory. Representative of these attitudes was Jedidiah Morse, who in 1799 warned about "secret societies under the influence and direction of France, holding principles subversive of our religion and government, [which exist] somewhere in this country" (Morse 1971, 46). Fears of secret societies arose in the aftermath of France's bloody revolution. The revolution's secular and rationalist ideas lead to conspiracy theories of an atheistic agenda of world domination perpetrated by Enlightenment-era organizations such as the Illuminated Seers of Bavaria (though the Freemasons were a frequent substitute). Secrecy, whether as a matter of exclusive association or the isolation of immigrant populations, became the proof that the millenarian destiny that was the birthright of "true Americans" would be snatched from the jaws of victory by subversive and evil forces.

For Morse and later conspiracists such secret societies (including, variously the papacy, immigrants, and secularists) were assaulting the United States through their mechanisms of "unceasing abuse of our rulers, the industrious circulation of baneful and corrupting books, and ... endeavors made to destroy, not only the influence and support, but the official existence of the Clergy." They seek to "subvert and overturn our holy religion and our free and excellent government" (Davis 1971, 47–8). The fear of supposed or actual secret societies (to include unassimilated or ostracized minorities) would become so strong as to lead to the formation of "conspiracies against conspiracies" and "secret societies against secret societies." Exclusive and secretive groups such as the Know Nothings, Ku Klux Klan, and other nativists would mobilize against conspiracies that they associated with immigrants, Catholics, and Freemasons.

By the turn of the twentieth century the fixation with hidden evil had increasingly become associated with nominally economic and political, rather than blatantly cultural, difference. This would continue the conspiracy's adaptive role as ideological mediator of economic reorganization and new waves of immigrants. When industrialization stimulated the growth of workers' unions, labour uprisings prompted overwhelming fear-mongering by journalists, capitalists, and the bourgeoisie (Davis 1971, 150). Key to the promotion of conspiracism as a sinister simulacrum of the real is the belief that "nothing is as it seems." The absence of specific evidence of the conspiracy is projected onto the assumed existence of "invisibles." As Michael Schaack describes labour agitators in his 1889 history of American anarchism,

> their identity they hold sacredly secret. It is only when open revolutionary work has actually begun that they are to come to the front. In the meantime the open workers and agitators report to the individual "invisibles," and act under their advice. The "invisibles" themselves make it a point to practice moderation in their public utterances to divert suspicion. (1971, 228)

Therefore, the presumed but unprovable presence of the "invisibles" within an identifiable community simultaneously justifies the belief in a wide-ranging conspiracy and allows the scapegoating of a larger population, as all are under suspicion.

The United States' traditional isolationism cemented negative associations not only with threats to ethnic homogeneity at home but with integration in the world system. Within this context and following the Bolshevik Revolution, the buzzwords "internationalism" and "communism" would become long-standing epithets in the convergence of American conspiracism and politics. Financial crises, including the Great Depression and earlier panics, repeatedly breathed new life into the oldest of conspiracies. In the modern era, Judaism, understood as a transnational "nation" unto itself, became increasingly associated with "internationalism" and therefore a population whose loyalty, national identity, and patriotism were suspect, if not subversive of the "imagined community." With the romantic ideals of "blood and soil" and the rise of the nation state's mythologized homogeneity as the foundation of modern social organization, the international otherness of the "Jewish" trope facilitated the vocalization of threats to the body politic.

The *Dearborn Independent*, owned by Henry Ford and distributed through Ford automobile dealerships across the country, used content from *The Protocols of the Elders of Zion* to create a hybrid of European anti-Semitism and American nativism, effectively repackaging the forgeries in a populist form (Davis 1971, 228). Under the title "The International Jew," the *Dearborn Independent* printed a serialized essay in effect summarizing, explicating, and advocating the *Protocols'* message to the American public. Ford emphasized "cultural degeneration" as the primary means by which Jews destroyed noble European traditions, subverted Western institutions, and gained control of governments in pursuit of global domination. Mirroring classic conspiracist assertions that evil often lurks beneath benign surface appearance, Ford accused Jews of undermining American society by means ranging from the liquor industry and "immoral films" to jazz music, as well as making more traditional accusations of war-mongering and control of banking (Abanes 1996, 144–5). In Appadurai's terms, the ultimate goal of this presumed conspiracy is for a weak, shadowy group to destroy its more powerful ethnic competitors by causing decay from within, first weakening them culturally and then ruling them politically and economically. Therefore, by extension, the perceived alienation, social discord, and "degenerate" culture associated with modernity are caused by the hidden "Jew."

In the nationalist revitalization that followed the Great War, the Second Klan of the 1920s redefined itself as "pro-American" and populist, speaking out against communist plots while intellectualizing its racism in the language of social Darwinism and nativism. As the archetypal "secret society against secret plots," the Klan positioned itself against hidden bogeymen. The Klan's 1920s documents declare that "Klansmen are not 'against' the Catholics or the Jews, but are 'for' Protestant Christianity, first, last and all the time" while being opposed to "Bolshevism, Sovietism, Anarchism, Communism, and every other 'ism' or cult that has as its objective the overthrow of the United States government" (Exalted Grand Cyclops, n.d.). The Klan promoted itself as the protector of "America" from an onslaught of foreign peoples and ideologies. As always, "American" is narrowly defined as WASP and native born.

Imperial Wizard Rev. Hiram Wesley Evans (1923) describes the Klan's fight for "true Americanism" using millenarian frames to outline the implications of immigration policies as "interwoven with our destiny." Thus the cornerstone of the Klan's nativist and eugenicist mission is the defence of exceptionalism.

While the Klan wielded significant influence in populist politics, Father Charles Coughlin used the radio waves to promote rumours that would seem eerily familiar by the end of the twentieth century. Using Judaism as a trope for internationalism, Coughlin described Jewish plots aimed at subverting the sovereignty of the United States. Decrying internationalism, Coughlin railed against the establishment of the International Criminal Court and the League of Nations (1971, 249). These Depression-era views find their contemporary referents in the American right's disdain for the International Criminal Court, International Court of Justice, and the UN. Similarly, Coughlin kept recent economic conspiracies alive, accusing the "Tory bankers" and Jews of orchestrating the Great Depression and, in a move reminiscent of the late nineteenth-century "Movement for Free Silver," advocating a return to silver currency, which he referred to as the "Gentile metal." With his wide promotion of such internationalist and economic rumours, Coughlin's anti-Semitic populism helped sustain the American conspiratorial tradition and influenced later conspiratorial narratives (Davis 1971).

The New World Order and the Contemporary Radical Right

The roots of the further radicalization of the "New Right" Republican Party via the "astroturf"[1] Tea Party triangulation strategy trace back to the ideological convergence of two Cold War–era far-right fringe groups. The John Birch Society (JBS), while considered an extremist group, has boasted numerous high-profile members with influential roles in religion, industry, government, and the military. Complementing the Birchers' "establishment extremist" niche, a nebulous constellation of white separatist and far-right tax protest groups contest the legitimacy of the federal government and frequently hold it to be an oppressive tool of a "One World Government." The major unifying characteristic of these groups, both radical and establishment, is the belief that the United States government has been infiltrated and subverted, if not replaced by, "invisible" agents of a globalist conspiracy (communist, Zionist, Masonic, etc.). The most essential and virulent expression of the radical right's fractious conspiracism is likely embodied in the localist, anti-government, anti-Semitic, and militant Posse Comitatus and its various Patriot and "sovereign citizen" offshoots.

From the JBS's founding in 1958 by Robert Welch, its members believed the United States to be the default target of the communist agenda because the fate of the world rests upon American destiny. Welch believed that communism and its "disease of collectivism" were the primary threats to the United States, but were not new: they were merely the contemporary incarnation of a centuries-long conspiracy that had previously manifested itself in plots ranging from the French Revolution to Nazism, all of which serve a "globalist" agenda (Levitas 2002). Birchers do not predict eventual communist infiltration but instead continually offer evidence of "insiders" working within the nation's most powerful institutions on behalf of the conspiracy.

For Birchers, international institutions and their supposed secular humanist agendas are the primary vehicles for the communist plot; hence they accuse the UN of subverting the United States' "Christian" and capitalist system. Recalling previous "precious metals conspiracies" associated with gold and silver, Birchers have advocated a return to the gold standard and, along with tax-protest offshoots, consider the Federal Reserve Bank to be the conspiracy's means of subverting the American economy. The JBS equates political democratization with communist influence and thus denounced the civil rights movement and desegregation as conspiracies to weaken the United States. Critiquing the social programs of the New Deal and Great Society along with organized labour, Birchers assumed these phenomena were proof that the United States' battlements had already been breached, that the federal government is a counterfeit substituted by communist agents destroying the nation from within its institutions. Welch's grand conspiracy, in its economic nature combined with its allegations of an ageless plot by an international "other," easily draws comparisons with traditionally anti-Semitic conspiracy theories.

What is undeniable is that the JBS's influence has been far greater than the number of its actual members. Among the JBS's alumni are not just leaders of fringe radical right groups but many architects of the Reagan-era "New Right." Common conspiratorial and anti-communist worldviews attracted these individuals to the JBS and, whether they remained life-long members or left the organization due to divergent views or agendas, their subsequent activities evidence overwhelming ideological resonance. As members of religious, political, or military institutions, these leaders acted as "message multipliers," disseminating the John Birch ideology within their individual professional and community circles. Furthermore, as influential members drifted out of the JBS to pursue their own agendas, they have often functioned as conduits for the JBS's globalist conspiracy template. These leaders brought their various interpretations of the John Birch philosophy across the spectrum of ultraconservative mainstream to white supremacist, militant, millenarian, and anti-government circles that make up the radical right.

While many leaders of the Tea Parties, the Republican Party, and their associates in religious and economic political organizations have backgrounds in the JBS, much of the conspiratorial rhetoric used to mobilize passionate populist support reflects beliefs associated with the more radical fringes of the American far right. For such groups as the Patriot militias and Sovereign Citizens, the New World Order is not merely a narrative of "invisible" actors used to express observed social and political changes. For these groups the stakes are sufficiently high and the consequences sufficiently dire to justify extreme violence against a government that they understand to have been transformed into an instrument of oppression against "true Americans."

The deep anti-government sentiment that forms the basis of these groups' political mobilization is shaped by the conspiratorial fear of their persecution and extermination by the hypothesized "other." So-called sovereign citizen and freemen movements (associated with loose organizations such as Posse Comitatus and radical tax protestors) have developed complex arguments justifying their exemption from federal laws. The sovereign citizenship movement claims that "true Americans" (those who trace their ancestry to pre–Civil War and often explicitly Anglo-Saxon stock) are citizens of their respective states or even counties. Sovereign citizens claim that federal laws apply only to "Fourteenth Amendment" citizens, a second-class citizenship conferred on emancipated slaves (and in some interpretations, their descendants) or naturalized citizens (and their descendants). Thus, individuals who claim their "sovereignty" consider themselves to be exempt from federal laws, often substituting "English common law" as their recognized legal system (Neiwert 1999, 12, 34).

Individuals seeking to become sovereign citizens abandon the legal trappings of citizenship. For this reason, Patriots often have run-ins with law enforcement because they refuse to carry necessary documentation (drivers' licenses and vehicle registration, for example), pay taxes, and comply with firearms laws. These are all supposed benefits enjoyed by Patriots and freemen in emancipating themselves from the federal conspiracy.

In many cases, awakening to sovereignty and theories of the NWO and ZOG (Zionist Occupational Government) comes as a result of legal or financial troubles (seeing a significant appeal during the "farm crisis" and maintaining popularity in the impoverished West) and might be compared to a "born again" experience (Davidson 1996; Stock 1997). In this sense, the armchair study of constitutional law might be considered the secular equivalent of informal biblical prophecy scholarship that has long characterized apocalyptic and millenarian religion in the United States. The conservative evangelical, Patriot, and Tea Party characterizations of the United States Constitution, Declaration of Independence, and Bill of Rights as divinely inspired founding documents solidify the mythology of American exceptionalism and the nation's divine mission (Skousen 2006; Zaitchik 2009). It is in this merging of amateur "constitutional law" and biblical prophecy scholarship that members of the conspiracist and millenarian far right construct an idealized understanding of the United States' founding documents – and seek to defend them and the nation's destiny from the cosmic evil that seeks their destruction.

Revealed to new attendees of tax protest and Patriot seminars, this explication of a vast conspiracy aimed at disenfranchising "true Americans" of their birthright resonates with political and cultural alienation. Particularly in more openly extremist circles, the NWO behind this scheme is referred to as ZOG. The sovereign citizenship theory claims that federal citizenship for otherwise "true Americans" is the product of a mass deception. The advocates of such theories can tie these claims into a host of conspiracies involving the Federal Reserve, the Illuminati, proto-communists, and other bogeymen. If such theories are sufficiently nested within a super-conspiracy, an anti-Semitic theory may well (and often does) emerge, potentially leading to some fringe groups' Anglo-Israelist or Christian Identity roots (Barkun 1994). This anti-Semitic and racist religion is in fact the core history of the purest Posse Comitatus doctrines put forth by the organization's founders (Levitas 2002). However, the average tax protestor, local government/ anti-federalist advocate, or anti-UN conspiracist will focus on his or her specific area of concern, be it a way out of debt, fear of firearm confiscation and disempowerment, or paranoia about a totalitarian, one-world government.

"Globalist" conspiracies of UN treachery, international communism, and the Zionist Occupational Government and other supposed plots circulating in conspiratorial fringes resonate with the pronouncements of political leaders and media personalities, which often serve to confirm them. Particularly apropos here was then president George Bush's labelling, before the United States Congress on 11 September 1990, of the Iraqi invasion of Kuwait as a threat to the "New World Order" (Bush 1990). The emergence of a post–Cold War "Pax Americana" was to be characterized by internationalism, economic stability, and peace, necessitating a stronger leadership role for the United States within the UN as well as diplomatic overtures to the Soviet Union. For many Americans, who had been raised on fear of internationalism in general and the UN and Soviet Union in particular, Bush's speech struck a nerve. Instead of triumphantly marking a new era as it was intended, the speech was seen as evidence that the conspiracy had metastasized. To proclaim a NWO consisting of global integration, cooperation with the Soviet Union, and leadership of the UN and affiliated institutions was for the conspiracy to openly declare its victory.

Some Americans' deeply held belief in an imminent takeover by the NWO has been manifested through their material preparations of stockpiling munitions and foodstuffs in the face of events ranging from the expected Y2K techno-apocalypse to the wild conspiratorial predictions associated with the 2008 election of a Democratic and African American president. In the latter instance, the playbook was quite familiar and echoed some of the accusations leveled at the Clintons. During the early 1990s, ultraconservative talk radio and other media personalities had accused the previous Democratic administration of communist ties, cocaine trafficking, economic improprieties, and the assassination of White House council Vince Foster, all in service of Clinton's purported NWO agenda of persecuting "true Americans" (Neiwert 2009, 40, 50–1). While these are not light accusations, the Obama presidency faced far more heinous charges levelled by far-right media personalities, ranging from claims of Obama's supposedly falsified birth records to charges that his charisma evidenced a key characteristic of the Antichrist as described in biblical prophecy. While such allegations merit little serious attention, they represent a nexus between elite and popular conspiracism. That media personalities and political figures promote or echo the conspiracy theories of far-right fringe groups may complicate the question of whether conspiracist discourse is manipulated by elites or initiated by the grass-roots and then taken up by elites. What cannot be contested is that regardless of origin, not only does promotion of NWO conspiracies by political and media figures give such ideas longevity and credibility, but their repetition from high pulpits assures their mainstream accessibility and adoption as conventional wisdom.

The supposed symptoms of the global conspiracy have become visible as shadows of contemporary policy, with pundits and other leaders proposing sinister motives for ordinary policies ranging from the census to youth volunteer programs. The popular perceptions of many policies are frequently manipulated by interested elites, who frame issues to resonate with NWO conspiracy templates. For example, anti-environmental astroturf political organizations such as "Wise Use" groups have had widespread success using the working poor and social conservatives as a means of promoting their agendas, particularly by framing environmental issues in economic terms. Spurred by the rhetoric of "Wise Use" advocates, many followers of the anti-government far right have latched onto environmentalism and made it part of their anti-UN conspiracy (Hendricks 2005, 33–4). Richard Abanes states that such theories have linked environmentalism to

> the NWO as being part of a plot to steal land away from patriotic Americans. According to this twist on the one world takeover, eco-management is designed to leave citizens homeless and landless, which will in turn make them vulnerable to the enslavement planned by invading UN troops. [Evangelical leader] Don McAlvany says environmental regulations "are to be the vehicle for socialism, and they're a major part of moving us toward world government." (1996, 85)

Similarly, Carolyn Gallaher points out that, as in the case of the earlier farm crisis and in the wake of Western job loss due to putative eco-legislation, far-right and racist groups were quick to step in and offer scapegoats to disenfranchised populations. She writes that

> patriot leaders, and especially those with long-standing far right "credentials," made a conscious effort to tone down racist rhetoric, and to downplay past affiliations with racist groups. Instead they apply their theories of a global conspiracy to domestic issues. They pointed to new environmental restrictions, for example, as evidence the New World Order is chipping away at private property rights. They pointed to government strong-arming as proof that the New World Order poses an imminent threat. (2002, 683–4)

Regulations applied to extractive industries (traditionally staunch financial backers of the political right) are widely trumpeted as communist and are often the object of conspiracies that claim lands are being sequestered as playgrounds and resorts for the global elite or will be used as staging areas for invading NWO troops.

Likewise, NWO frames have been applied to (implicitly Hispanic) immigration, portraying it as a threat to national sovereignty and the longevity of Western civilization itself. Pat Buchanan cites declining white birth rates and secular humanism's destruction of national and racial pride as the basis for his prediction of a soon to be unrecognizable (to him) United States (2002). Ignoring market forces that give capitalist interests a competitive advantage in choosing workers rather than allowing workers to migrate to regions with better wages, nativists portray the increased prominence of Latino/Hispanic populations in the United States as a vengeful plot. Claiming that immigration is in fact a *Reconquista*, far-right pundits and activists describe a Latino/Hispanic conspiracy to reclaim lands lost to the United States' westward expansion (Buchanan 2006). According to this systemic conspiracy, undocumented workers, Latino gangs, drug traffickers, and Chicano movement activists on university campuses seek to establish *Aztlan*, a Latino/Hispanics-only (and supposedly communist) region in what is currently the American Southwest. Expansions of the NAFTA treaty (such as the FTAA) are explained as precursors to a hypothesized hemispheric super-nation: the North American Union. This would be established by (Anglo) population dilution, the adoption of a single currency, and the attendant devaluation of US currency to achieve equilibrium with the peso (explaining contemporary recessions), all on behalf of establishing the globalist NWO (Bennett 2007).

In the face of such dire predictions, far-right commentators and politicians vociferously advocate English-only laws, strict immigration enforcement, and other restrictive policies, promoted as measures necessary to the protection of "freedom." Following the 9/11 attacks, self-described Patriots formed armed vigilante groups and offered their services to Border Patrol agents. Immigration has provided a niche for militiamen whose chosen cause fell out of favour with the general public in the aftermath of the 1995 Oklahoma City bombing. Reminiscent of Bircher allegations that communist-conspiring "insiders" were forcing the United States to lose the Vietnam war, modern-day nativists claim that the United States' inability to stop undocumented immigration is evidence of complicity in the NWO agenda. Not surprisingly, the JBS is a key proponent of this theory (CNN 2007).

The period approaching the millennium and the anticipated technological fallout associated with the Y2K bug linked expectation of social collapse with the period of Tribulation prophesied in the biblical Book of Revelation. By the end of the 1990s, many "rapture-ready" evangelical Christians became increasingly indistinguishable from more secular survivalists (Tapia 2002). Prominent Christian right activists encouraged their followers to hoard food and weapons and avoid cities. This spectre of technological and social collapse, interpreted within a millenarian timeline, led to a convergence of apocalyptic evangelicals and conspiratorial Patriots. In his 1990 book *Toward a New World Order*, New Right and evangelical Christian leader Donald McAlvany trumpeted JBS warnings of the metastasized communist Russia and domestic persecution of Christians and conservatives. According to him, Christians should not only invest in precious metals, acquire firearms, and make provision to store and grow their own food, but must become active in conservative politics (as well as the JBS, Focus on the Family, and Gun Owners of America) (McAlvany 1990, 234–44). Putting fence-sitting conservative Christians on the same page as Patriot groups, he denounces environmentalists as pagans and communists, claims that public schools seek to convert children to homosexuality, and warns that Christians will be persecuted and exterminated when biblical teachings become criminalized by "New Agers" (234–44).

His 1999 book *Storm Warning* further fans the flames of conservative evangelical paranoia. McAlvany predicts the outlawing of Christianity under "hate speech" legislation, the passage of socialized medicine as a population control mechanism, imposition of a national ID card, total gun confiscation, the establishment of a national police force, inoculation of children and implantation of tracking chips, the phasing out of cash, socialism, and the expansion of environmental laws. The remainder of the book describes coming Christian persecution, drawing parallels between exaggerated interpretations of Clinton administration policies and the policies of Nazi Germany. In addition to recommending biblical passages that will provide guidance during this coming period of Tribulation, McAlvany recommends methods for resisting torture and the memorization of scriptures as an effort to preserve Christianity after scriptural materials are banned. These predictions would, at face value, seem to be the rhetoric of marginalized and alienated subculture with little impact on the larger socio-political systems of the United States. However, McAlvany's prominent status in the Republican Party's New Right and his membership in the elite Council for National Policy indicate that the precious metals broker's ideas and rhetoric, however sensational and self-serving, have not alienated him from participation within the power elite.

Conspiratorial Politics

While the rampant conspiracism that mobilizes the recent Tea Party movement reflects inflexible political extremism, the contemporary radicalization of American conservative politics is merely a progression from the New Right's own conspiracist and millenarian ideologies. Through its blending of Bircher conspiracies and Christian prophetic millennialism, the Reagan-era New Right unified religious and economic conservatives. The rhetoric that mobilizes populist participation in New Right politics has constructed a political discourse in which the Republican Party juxtaposes itself to a globalist, communist, and Antichrist conspiracy presumed to be dedicated to the goal of enslaving and persecuting "traditional Americans." The face of the conspiratorial "other" offered to the "traditional conservative" base is one of "cosmopolitan," "elitist," and "anti-American" cultural liberalism.

Since the presidential campaign of 2008 and the subsequent election of the United States' first African American president, the American far right has been increasingly vocal, mobilized, and mainstream. Buttressed and organized by the efforts of interested elites in industry, finance, and media, the far right's populist, xenophobic, and racist rhetoric has become a prominent force in the nation's politics (Zeleny 2009). Though strongly associated with the most ultra-conservative wings of the Republican Party, the contemporary far right has distanced itself even from that constituency, preferring the more fringe ideologies of Constitutionalist, Libertarian, and other "Patriot" political groups, groups whose rhetoric is based not on objective fact and established political philosophies but on fear, conspiracy, and prophecy. In a social dynamic that might well be characterized as resembling key aspects of fascist mobilization, angry and fearful populists have been organized by economic elites, spurred on to wild delusions, conspiracies, and racist scapegoating, distracting from important issues in a time of severe national crisis.

The United States faces numerous crises, including severe economic recession, record unemployment, and multiple wars, none of which evidence significant strategic progress. Environmental catastrophe due to climate change; depleted food, water, and energy sources; and a growing population are significant global crises in progress – and the international community has traditionally expected the United States to lead in addressing these issues. However, in the United States the need to confront these problems has not been met with reasoned and constructive debate. Instead, fringe movements, naively misappropriating the mantle of the United States' founding fathers, have (with the aid of sensationalist media) redirected the discourse from meaningful critiques of establishment institutions and towards imagined scapegoats. The government itself has been put on trial, accused of crypto-communism, persecution, eugenics, and genocide – charges that public officials and even the president himself have been forced to publicly disavow, though significant portions of the public remain unconvinced.

Both astroturf and apparent individual actions were used to spread rumours that candidate Obama was a Muslim, a communist, a non-citizen, or that his administration would enslave whites, confiscate firearms, or otherwise subvert the United States. These rumours, initiated during the run-up to the 2008 presidential election, have become cultural memes, shaping the claims' hybridization with the ambient conspiracism that contributes to the background noise of American politics. Responding to the candidate's large youth following and charismatic public persona, political activists on the right created advertisements portraying Obama as a "rock star" and celebrity – a smooth-talker who would promise his naive followers the nearly impossible. While derisive in its own right, the ad campaign (titled "the One") was intended to resonate with the conservative evangelical Christians who had become the Republican Party's strongest base since the election of Ronald Reagan in 1980. This base understood the ad's subtext: that Obama, promising national renewal, diplomacy, and prosperity in a charismatic persona might, in fact, be the Antichrist – the false prophet who promises peace, leading the masses astray from the true messiah (Sullivan 2008).

Other accusations came in the form of chain e-mails and web videos as right-wing bloggers amplified rumours that the Democratic candidate was in fact a "secret Muslim" (as a child Obama had attended a madrasah in Indonesia), implying that the leading presidential candidate might be in league with Islamic terrorists (Smith and Martin 2007). Accusations that the candidate was not a true citizen of the United States led to a campaign of self-described "Birthers" who demanded the new president's birth certificate, claiming that Obama is in fact a Kenyan citizen and arguing that the copy tendered was a forgery. These claims ignore obvious claims to legitimate citizenship ranging from his mother's being a Kansas native to Obama's own birth in the state of Hawaii.

In the election's aftermath the far right's rumours did not merely follow a natural life cycle but were actively championed by elites in the media and government. This status gave baseless rumours an air of validity among significant sections of the American population. Cable news programs, and particularly Fox News Channel, promoted a variety of conspiracy theories. Similarly, Republican Party supporter Matt Drudge's extremely popular news aggregation site, drudgereport.com, regularly promotes "Birther" and other Tea Party conspiracies while also frequently rewriting headlines to trigger associations with these conspiracies. Furthermore, beginning in the spring of 2010, Drudge began linking to Alex Jones's conspiracy website infowars.com. Jones, whose InfoWars website ("There is a war on for your mind") and associated Prison Planet™ Productions ("Truth will set you free") promotes conspiracies of "false flag" attacks, NWO concentration camps, and Federal Reserve subversion of the United States economy, rests his journalistic credentials on his "infiltration" of a Bohemian Club gathering. Jones's Prison Planet TV produces and promotes conspiracy "documentaries" alleging that terrorist attacks and financial collapses are orchestrated by the NWO with the design of curtailing Americans' civil liberties, imprisoning traditionalists, confiscating firearms, and outlawing Christianity. Several examples of "government overreach" cited by Jones, and indeed his ideological premises, employ the rhetoric of the sovereign citizenship movement (Jones 2002). Indeed, Jones's concern with civil liberties rarely, if ever, strays beyond taxation, the Federal Reserve, surveillance, and "persecution of traditionalists," neglecting the larger spectrum of civil rights infringements in the United States. While Jones is far from mainstream, the increasing frequency of his work's introduction into national political discourse by popular news sites such as drudgereport.com likely signifies that the one-time Austin, Texas, public access host's base of followers will grow.

While a mainstream conservative such as Drudge might introduce fringe ideas to a larger audience by linking to sites such as Jones's, few media personalities have fueled the far right's conspiracy-political nexus more than Glenn Beck. On CNN and later Fox News Channel, Beck frequently promoted conspiracy theories and anti-government rhetoric, including rumours that would later be echoed in the state-ments of Republican politicians, including Senator John McCain's claims that ACORN (the non-profit community development group) had helped Obama steal the 2008 presidential election (Novak 2008). Those deeply dissatisfied with the election's outcome rallied around the host who introduced mass audiences not only to the conspiracies of the JBS but to his own improvisations (Sanchez 2007). Redirecting his viewers' discontent and fear into paranoid political activism, Beck headlined numerous astroturf campaigns ranging from the "9/12 Pro-ject" to the "We Surround Them" campaign, as well as promoting the "Birthers." When the larger Tea Party movement arose, its anti-tax and anti-government agenda, framed by wild conspiracy theories, was fueled by these Beck-centred campaigns. However, the movement's roots were decades older. One of the most celebrated and ideologically pure Tea Party candidates, Texas congressman Ron Paul, has frequently spoken on behalf of the John Birch Society against supposed plots by the Federal Reserve and United Nations to subvert the United States' sovereignty (John Birch Society 2011). However, the "Libertarian Wing" of the Republican Party has been increasingly exposed as an establish-ment instrument.

While highly fractious Tea Party groups claim to be local, independ-ent of the Republican Party, authentically populist, and grassroots, many (assuming earlier authenticity) have been co-opted by the New Right's establishment political action committees (PACs), lobbies, and financiers. The more effective Tea Parties (i.e., those that effec-tively fielded candidates in the 2010 elections) had significant backing from groups such as former congressman Dick Armey's (R-TX) PAC "FreedomWorks" as well as David and Charles Koch's "Americans for Prosperity." The funding of other key Tea Party organizations remains obscure due to tax-code classifications that permit non-disclosure of finances (Jensen 2010).

The Tea Parties have received significant funding and organizational support from the establishment interests of the traditional secular right, including energy and telecom interests. Among these boosters, Charles and David Koch's industry and political foundations have received particular attention; it's worth noting the Koch family's long-time sup-port for the John Birch Society (Mayer 2010; Scaliger 2011). Despite the anti-regulatory agenda of its elite and establishment sponsors, the Tea Parties' momentum is clearly propelled by conspiracist anxieties and its rhetoric amply reflects the influence of the militant Patriot movement's

"sovereign citizen" ideology (Corn 2010). Though many elected officials in the Republican Party have attempted to distance themselves
from a movement that is becoming increasingly volatile, others have
embraced its often-violent rhetoric.

A particularly vile feature of the already extreme political rhetoric
leading to the 2010 mid-term elections was the frequency with which
Tea Party–endorsed candidates pejoratively labelled their opponents
and prominent Democratic leaders as "domestic enemies." The phrase
originates in the United States military's induction oath, which requires
enlistees to swear to "defend the Constitution of the United States
against all enemies, foreign and domestic" (Department of the Army).
Because of the Tea Party's overlap with the JBS, Patriot groups, and their
earlier political incarnation as the libertarian "Constitution Party," this
phrase holds significant and disturbing resonance. The view, popularized by W. Cleon Skousen (2006) and increasingly mainstream among
conservative evangelicals and Mormons, holds that the United States
Constitution is a divinely inspired document from which the United
States' exceptionalism and millenarian destiny stem. However, according to proponents of this view, the United States Constitution has been
misinterpreted and defiled by secular humanists and leftists, especially by expanding the role of the federal government, leading to the
weakening of the United States and its divinely ordained role in guiding world affairs. Thus, not only does the designation as a "domestic
enemy" evoke the invisible "insider" conspiracy trope, but its gravity
and martial association unequivocally sanction eliminationist solutions
to the pronouncement.

The several incidents of this rallying allegation being used by Tea
Party candidates include Rep. Paul Broun (R-GA) claiming that then
House Speaker Nancy Pelosi is a "domestic enemy of the Constitution" (Corly 2009). His earlier pronouncement that Democratic Party
leaders and the president were members of a "socialistic elite" intent
on using disease pandemics as an excuse to declare martial law, along
with an established track record of labelling Barack Obama a "Marxist"
and comparing him to Hitler, further contextualize this rhetoric (Aued
2009). Likewise, the far-right Nevada candidate for the United States
Senate, Sharon Angle, repeatedly used the label "domestic enemy" as
well as her threat that constituents might employ "Second Amendment
remedies" against such office holders (Sargent 2010). Less cryptically,
Indiana Republican (Tea Party–endorsed) candidate for Senate Richard
Behney told an audience of supporters that, should he lose the election,

he was cleaning his guns and "getting ready for the big show" (Barstow 2010). Texas governor Rick Perry has echoed the Tea Party movement's secessionist sentiments, threatening to have his state withdraw from the Union (Hilton 2009).

Tea Partiers have taken obscure policies out of context and inflated them to fit the nefarious NWO templates that shape their expectations. Among these are accusations that some municipalities' participation in environmental impact assessments for urban planning purposes are part of a UN agenda to "resettle" populations and "deindustrialize" the United States (Mencimer 2010). Equally disturbing to Tea Partiers were claims, promoted by Glenn Beck and others, warning that President Obama's exemption of INTERPOL from the Freedom of Information Act would lead to an international police force, responsible to the new president, with the agenda of dismantling the Tea Party movement (Mencimer 2010). Requiring a similar amount of suspension of disbelief was Colorado's Tea Party–endorsed Republican gubernatorial candidate Dan Maes's "exposure" of a UN plot. Maes warned that Denver's membership in the International Council for Local Environmental Initiatives, and especially that city's bike-sharing program, were an attempt by the UN to "reign in" American cities. In classic conspiratorial fashion, Maes advised that this "is bigger than it looks like on the surface and it could threaten our personal freedoms" (Osher 2010). These and other presumed conspiratorial plots have spurred counter-legislation in the United States Congress and Senate. Congressman Mike Rogers (R-MI) introduced a resolution to repeal the Interpol Executive Order. Congresswoman Michelle Bachmann (R-MN) has introduced numerous pieces of anti-conspiracy legislation, including a resolution preventing the nonexistent "Amero" currency from supplanting the dollar as the United States' legal currency (Diaz 2009).

By far the most inflammatory issue arousing the passions of the far right in the aftermath of the 2008 elections was the issue of health care reform. Howls of socialism, communism, and fascism, frequently used interchangeably and applied to the same referents, met the admittedly modest changes to the United States' grossly inefficient health care industry and its powerful insurance and pharmaceutical interests. These reforms, modelled upon those made by presidential candidate Mitt Romney during his time as governor of Massachusetts, were likened to Nazi eugenics and euthanasia policies. In particular, the debate was dominated by accusations that the elderly and infirm would be subjected to "death panels," a term popularized by former vice presidential candidate and Alaska governor Sarah Palin with significant reinforcement by ultra-conservative media personalities Rush Limbaugh and Glenn Beck. Applied to a health care policy first proposed by then president George W. Bush, which would authorize Medicare to fund counselling sessions for the families of patients who might be subject to "do not resuscitate" requests, the resurrected idea was fiercely associated with not only Obama's health reform attempts but the Democrat's pro-abortion stance. With abortion increasingly used as an excuse to characterize Democrats as heirs to the Third Reich's eugenics and euthanasia policies, and NWO templates encouraging the association of a nebulous evil behind such policies, Palin and other far-right personalities claimed that those who opposed the Obama administration would be denied medical care under the proposed system. The implication that "traditional Americans" would face the fate that Donald McAlvany had described a decade earlier – being exterminated by a government bureaucracy via abortion, euthanasia, and imprisonment by foreign police forces for their resistance to the internationalist and secular humanist agenda – resonated with many Americans' millenarian and conspiratorial scripts.

This nightmare scenario was one that many Americans had been primed for and anticipating for decades. The whirlwind of coalescing signs of an imminent revealing of the conspiracy and an approaching point of no return after which resistance would be futile brought out a vicious baring of teeth. Indeed, during the 1990s the JBS and "sovereign citizen"-inspired Patriot militias justified their existences as the nation's last bulwark against the NWO and its legions of UN shock troops. Now, their metastasized political wing, welcomed into the burgeoning far right of a Republican Party that increasingly embraced conspiracy theories, saw the supposed imposter government openly promoting the policies of which they had warned.

The nation was shocked by Tea Partiers carrying assault weapons and loaded side arms to the chaotic town hall–style health-care screaming matches that characterized the 111th Congress's 2009 summer recess. Though such actions might be dismissed as political theatre, the larger picture is one in which the number of hate groups and domestic terrorist organizations has risen sharply in the last decade (Potok 2011). In 2009 President Barack Obama faced an average of thirty death threats per day, according to the Secret Service, an increase of 400 per cent over the previous year (Harnden 2009).

Conclusion

The aftermath of the 2008 presidential election has seen the traditional conservative base of the Republican Party and its astroturf Tea Party offshoots become far more extreme in their rhetoric as well as their actions. Echoing paranoid reactions to the previous Democratic administration, American conservatives experienced successive waves of survivalist panics fueled by both grassroots conspiracy and their reification by elites in politics and the media. The rhetoric of black helicopters, UN invasions, crypto-communist politicians, firearms confiscation, and manufactured crises went mainstream with the aid of conservative media talking heads, calculated political stunts, and elite economic interests, all against a national background of severe and widespread discontent over the economy, unemployment, and losing wars.

Numerous and severe crises threaten the United States and the world at large, though few impending catastrophes other than the possibility of foreign attack and invasion serve to mobilize the American far right. This significant constituency does not anticipate critical economic, ecological, or similar objective crises within the national and world systems. Instead it focuses its resources on a defensive battle – a battle against emerging trends and solutions, whether in social structure, economics, or cultural adaptation.

In their conspiratorial nature, these movements are sometimes reactionary but always oppositional, constructing their agendas as diametrically opposed to the supposed goals of an ill-defined "other." By marginalizing opposition and creating a false mainstream or majority, they use populist rhetoric to create a simulacrum of modern democracy, basing their claims and goals on the demands of unspecified masses, whether a "moral majority" or more volkish masses. In moralizing their own political positions and framing or ascribing unpopular policies as the agenda of a scapegoated "other," the extremist constructs movements by claiming the "will of the people" or "the dictates of 'history' or 'nature'" as demands for a social agenda. Such a monistic political movement's demonization of its opposition plainly makes for millenarian politics aiming to actualize utopian goals via eliminationist policies.

When faced with the wide range of actual and potential problems facing the American and global populations, the rhetoric of the New Right and Tea Party leaders rarely addresses solutions to problems, but instead blames those groups and policies that have challenged

traditional hierarchies. In short, these attitudes underline the significance of scapegoating and conspiracism as the dominant ideological
frame governing conservatism. Therefore, attempts to address national
and global problems are generated through ideological frames that
privilege tradition and see perceived deviances as the causes of these
problems. The remedy prescribed for perceived problems and challenges is thus a return to past values, often represented romantically
but masking implied hierarchies, frequently involving elimination of
the implied invisible "other" that is constructed as an existential threat
to the cultural.

NOTE

1 The term "astroturf" refers to faux-populist movements orchestrated
  by elites. The term derives from "AstroTurf," a synthetic carpet that
  resembles grass, in a play on the words "grass-roots" indicating
  artificiality of origin.

REFERENCES

Abanes, Richard. 1996. *American Militias: Rebellion, Racism, and Religion.*
  Illinois: InterVarsity.
Anderson, Benedict. 1983. *Imagined Communities: Reflections on the Origins and
  Spread of Nationalism.* New York: Verso.
Appadurai, Arjun. 2006. *Fear of Small Numbers: An Essay on the
  Geography of Anger.* Durham,: Duke University Press. http://dx.doi.
  org/10.1215/9780822387541.
Aued, Blake. 2009, 12 August. "Obamacare a 'Rotten Fish' says Broun at Town
  Hall." Athens Banner Herald.
Barkun, Michael. 1994. *Religion and the Racist Right: The Origins of the Christian
  Identity Movement.* Chapel Hill: University of North Carolina Press.
– 2003. *A Culture of Conspiracy: Apocalyptic Visions in Contemporary America.*
  Berkeley: University of California Press.
Barstow, David. 2010, 15 February. "Tea Party Lights a Fuse for Rebellion on
  the Right." *New York Times.*
Bennett, David H. 1988. *The Party of Fear: From Nativist Movements to the New
  Right in American History.* Chapel Hill: University of North Carolina Press.
Bennett, Drake. 2007, 25 November. "The Amero Conspiracy." *Boston Globe.*

Berlet, Chip, and Matthew Lyons. 2000. *Right Wing Populism in America: Too Close for Comfort*. New York: Guilford.

Buchanan, Pat. 2002. *The Death of the West: How Dying Populations and Immigrant Invasions Imperil Our Country and Civilization*. New York: St Martin's.

– 2006. *State of Emergency: The Third World Invasion and Conquest of America*. New York: St Martin's.

Bush, George H.W. 1990, 11 September. Address before a Joint Session of Congress on the Persian Gulf Crisis and the Federal Budget Deficit. http://en.wikisource.org/wiki/Toward_a_New_World_Order (accessed 2 February 2009).

CNN. 2007, 25 July. *Glenn Beck Show*.

Condon, Stephanie. 2009, 10 August. "After Healthcare Distortion, Palin Calls for Restraint." *CBS News*.

Corley, Matt. 2009, 8 October. "Broun Calls Pelosi a 'Domestic Enemy of the Constitution." *ThinkProgress.com*.

Corn, David. 2010, 3 August 2010. "Confessions of a Tea Party Casualty." *Mother Jones*.

Coughlin, Charles. 1971 [1935]. "The Menace of the World Court." In *Fear of Conspiracy: Images of Un-American Subversion from the Revolution to the Present*, ed. David Brion Davis. Ithaca: Cornell University Press.

Davidson, Osha Grey. 1996. *Broken Heartland: Rise of America's Rural Ghetto*. Iowa City: University of Iowa Press.

Davis, David Brion. 1971. *The Fear of Conspiracy: Images of Un-American Subversion from the Revolution to the Present*. Ithaca: Cornell University Press.

Department of the Army. "Oaths of Enlistment." http://www.history.army. mil/html/faq/oaths.html (accessed 20 June 2011).

Diaz, Kevin. 2009, 26 March. "Bachmann: No Foreign Currency." *Star Tribune*.

Evans, Hiram Wesley, Imperial Wizard. 1923, 24 October. "The Menace of Modern Immigration: An Address Delivered on Klan Day at the State Fair of Texas at Dallas."

Exalted Grand Cyclops of Monroe Klan Number 4, Realm of Louisiana. n.d. "Principles and Purposes of the Knights of the Ku Klux Klan." http:// archive.lib.msu.edu/DMC/AmRad/principlespurposesknights.pdf .

Gallaher, Carolyn. 2002. "On the Fault Line: Race, Class, and the US Patriot Movement," *Cultural Studies* 16, no. 5.

Hansen, Klaus. 1972. "The Millennium, the West, and Race in the Antebellum American Mind." *Western Historical Quarterly* 3 (4): 373. http://dx.doi.org/ 10.2307/966863.

Harnden, Toby. 2009, 3 August. "Obama Faces 30 Death Threats a Day, Stretching Secret Service." *Telegraph/UK.*

Hatch, Nathan O. 1974. "The Origins of Civil Millennialism in America: New England Clergymen, War with France, and the Revolution." *William and Mary Quarterly* 3 (3): 418.

Hendricks, Stephanie. 2005. *Divine Destruction: Wise Use, Dominion Theology, and the Making of American Environmental Policy.* Hoboken, NJ: Melville.

Hilton, Hilary. 2009, 18 April. "What's All That Secession Ruckus in Texas?" *Time.*

Hofstadter, Richard. 2008 [1964]. "The Paranoid Style in American Politics." In *The Paranoid Style in American Politics and Other Essays.* New York: Vintage.

Jensen, Kristen. 2010, 21 September. "Tea Party Patriots to Hand Out $1 million for November Election Spending." *Bloomberg.com* (accessed 23 June 2011).

Jones, Alex. 2002. *9/11: Road to Tyranny.* DVD.

Knight, Peter. 2002. "A Nation of Conspiracy Theorists." In *Conspiracy Nation: The Politics of Paranoia in Post-War America,* ed. Peter Knight. New York: NYU Press.

Landes, Richard. 2006. "Millenarianism and the Dynamics of Apocalyptic Time." In *Expecting the End: Millennialism in Social and Historical Context,* ed. Kenneth G.C. Newport and Crawford Gribben, 4–5. Waco, TX: Baylor University Press.

Levitas, Daniel. 2002. *The Terrorist Next Door: The Militia Movement and the Radical Right.* New York: St. Martins.

Lienesch, Michael. 1983. "The Role of Political Millennialism in Early American Nationalism." *Western Political Quarterly* 36 (3): 445. http://dx.doi.org/10.2307/448402.

Mayer, Jane. 2010, 30 August. "Covert Operations: The Billionaire Brothers Who Are Waging a War against Obama." *The New Yorker.*

McAlvany, Donald. 1990. *Towards a New World Order: The Countdown to Armageddon.* Oklahoma City: Hearthstone.

– 1999. *Storm Warning: The Coming Persecution of Christians and Traditionalists.* Oklahoma City: Hearthstone.

Mencimer, Stephanie. 2010, 5 February. "Obama's Secret Police." *Mother Jones.*

Morse, Jedidiah. 1971 [1799]. "The Present Dangers and Consequent Duties of the Citizens." In *The Fear of Conspiracy: Images of Un-American Subversion from the Revolution to the Present,* ed. David Brion Davis. Ithaca: Cornell University Press. 45-48.

Murphy, Tim. 2011, 6 June. "Michele Bachmann Said What!?" *Mother Jones.*

Neary, Ben. 2009, 29 March. "Fear of Regulation Drives Gun, Ammo Shortage." Associated Press.

Neiwert, David. 1999. *In God's Country: The Patriot Movement and the Pacific Northwest*. Pullman, WA: Washington State University Press.

– 2009. *The Eliminationists: How Hate Talk Radicalized the American Right*. Sausolito, CA: PoliPoint.

Novak, Viveca. "The Whoppers of 2008 – The Sequel." http://factcheck. org/2008/10/the-whoppers-of-2008-the-sequel-2/ (accessed 31 October 2008).

O'Leary, Stephen. 1998. *Arguing the Apocalypse: A Theory of Millennial Rhetoric*. NewYork: Oxford University Press.

Osher, Christopher. 2010, 5 August. "Bike Agenda Spins Cities toward U.N. Control, Maes Warns." *Denver Post*.

Potok, Mark. 2011. "The Year in Hate and Extremism, 2010." *Southern Poverty Law Center* Intelligence *Report* 141 (Spring).

Robertson, Pat. 1991. *The New World Order*. Dallas: Word Publishing.

Sanchez, Casey. "Beck Backs Birch: Conspiracy Theory 'Makes Sense.'" *Hatewatch* (blog). http://www.splcenter.org/blog/ 2007/07/31/beck-backs-birch-conspiracy-theory-'makes-sense'/ (accessed 31 July 2007).

Sargent, Greg. 2010, 27 August. "Sharron Angle Twice Refuses to Disavow Claim That There Are "Domestic Enemies" in Congress." *Washington Post*.

Scaliger, Charles. 2011, 10 June. "Fred Koch: Oil Man against Communism." *The New American*.

Schaack, Michael. 1971 [1886]. "The Haymarket Riot." In *The Fear of Conspiracy: Images of Un-American Subversion from the Revolution to the Present*, ed. David Brion Davis, 176–80. Ithaca: Cornell University Press..

Skousen, W. Cleon. 2006 [1981]. *The 5,000 Year Leap: A Miracle That Changed the World*. Malta, ID: National Center for Constitutional Studies.

Smith, Ben, and Jonathon Martin. 2007, 13 October. "Untraceable E-Mails Spread Obama Rumor." http://www.politico.com/news/ stories/1007/6314.html (accessed 13 September 2009).

Stephanson, Anders. 1996. *Manifest Destiny: American Expansionism and the Empire of Right*. New York: Hill and Wang.

Stock, Catherine McNicol. 1997. *Rural Radicals: Righteous Rage in the American Grain*. Ithaca: Cornell University Press.

Sullivan, Amy. 2008. "An Antichrist Obama in McCain Ad?" http://content. time.com/time/politics/article/0,8599,1830590,00.html (accessed 4 June 2011).

Tapia, Andria. 2002. "Techno-Armageddon: The Millennial Christian Response to Y2K." *Review of Religious Research* 43 (March), 266–86.

Trelease, Alan W. 1999. *White Terror: The Ku Klux Klan, Conspiracy, and Southern Reconstruction.* Baton Rouge: Louisiana State University Press.

Weber, Eugen. 2000. *Apocalypses: Prophesies, Cults, and Millennial Beliefs.* Cambridge, MA: Harvard University Press.

Zaitchik, Alexander. 2009, 16 September. "Meet the Man Who Changed Glenn Beck's Life." http://www.salon.com/news/feature/2009/09/16/beck_skousen (accessed 4 June 2011).

Zeleny, Jeff. 2009, 12 September. "Thousands Rally in Capital to Protest Big Government." *New York Times.*

9 Degradation Ceremonies: Fear Discourses, Phobic Production, and the Military Metaphysic in Canada

JEFF SHANTZ

Social phobias, and manufactured fears, play a key part in facilitating policies of social exclusion, which are among the most popular approaches taken by states in addressing terrorism. Practices of social exclusion include tightening borders and making it more difficult for people from specific, targeted areas or backgrounds to migrate. These practices can include denial of entry visas and entry denials as well as detentions and deportations.

The panic set off after the events of 11 September 2001 sparked the introduction of a range of legislative activity and new public policies in countries across the globe, including in the various liberal democracies. The prototypical legislation was the US Patriot Act, which increased and expanded state powers in surveillance, search and seizure, and detention of suspects and strengthened mechanisms of border security.

In the period immediately following 9/11 the Canadian government, along with other liberal democratic governments in the West, rushed to show compliance with the US-initiated "war on terror." While the government jumped at the opportunity to invade and occupy Afghanistan and to support the invasion and occupation of Iraq, much of its energy, under both Liberal Party and Conservative Party leadership, has been directed at the "home front," where broad assaults on civil liberties have been implemented. The central and farthest-reaching legislation has been the Anti-Terror Act (Bill C-36). Under this act people have been detained without charges. Suspicion is based on nothing more than use of any symbol or representation associated with a terrorist group. Conditions of release can be placed on people without charges having been laid. The act also allows for secret trials in which accused are denied access to the evidence against them, of course for "reasons of national security" under so-called security certificates. It is quite telling that these secret trials *already existed*, since 1990 in fact, for immigration cases.

These are processes that have drawn criticism from Amnesty International and Human Rights Watch as well as the United Nations (Behrens 2008). These processes, critics note, bring together in one repressive regime indefinite detention without charge, two-tier justice, racial profiling, and deportation to torture.

The security certificates rely on a troubling type of alleged pre-crime thought formula that claims an individual is possibly a threat because of something they might do or because of associations they might have at some time in the future (Behrens 2008). One of the people held on a security certificate for nearly seven years has only been told that he poses a threat because of certain beliefs he is alleged to hold (Behrens 2008). His inquiry into the government's reasons for believing he holds those views received only the response that that is secret evidence that cannot be revealed for reasons of national security (Behrens 2008). Yet the individual in question has never been associated with the views in question and never been shown to hold those views. Matthew Behrens, one of the community advocates who has done the most to bring details of security certificates to broad public view, sarcastically suggests that the calculation by which the government reaches its determinations on issuing security certificates reads "Arab + Muslim = Possibly Bad at Some Future Date (But We Can't Tell You Why)" (2008, n.p.).

The five men still subject to security certificates have endured a collective thirty-three years of imprisonment in Canada, including years in solitary confinement. For the Canadian government, release will only come with their deportation to countries known to engage in torture, including Egypt, Syria, Algeria, and Morocco (Behrens 2008).

The secret trial process was accompanied by a campaign of character assassination against the men carried out, incredibly, by the Federal Court of Canada itself, prior to any hearings being initiated. The Federal Court used its website to publish unsupported allegations and suspicions about the men, citing only unsubstantiated documents of the Canadian Security and Intelligence Service (CSIS), the federal security agency. The allegations were finally removed after public protest, but only after the one-sided portrait had been allowed to do its damage.

Critics note there is a real risk that governments and civil society groups alike, in claiming concern over terrorism, will overstate fears and threats for political gain. Similarly, law enforcement and security agencies may exaggerate risks in order to gain additional resources or power (Grabosky and Stohl 2010, 88).

This chapter examines mechanisms involved in the production of phobias in relation to fear discourses and repressive practices, in the context of anti-terror mobilization in Canada. The use of terror fears is related to a military metaphysic and the growth of security and intelligence budgets in the Canadian state. As aspects of nation-building in the post-9/11 period, security certificates and unlimited imprisonment as well as public constructions of terrorists, are viewed through their roles in producing "legitimate citizens," culturally and racially codifying non-white subjects within the Canadian multicultural mosaic. These various practices bring together discourses of race, ethnicity, community crime, and citizenship. They also mobilize discourses of assimilation and civic responsibility in ways that maintain racial inequalities and constitute racialized governmentalities.

Military Metaphysics and the Mobilization for War

Anarchist sociologist C. Wright Mills has suggested that the power elite in liberal democracies are bound by certain key shared characteristics. Among these is the guiding framework of a military metaphysic that provides the dominant lens through which they view, understand, act in, and respond to the social world. Through the military metaphysic the power elite view society as being in a state of permanent war. From the framework of this perspective, the response to social problems is a response of war. This is reflected in the prosecution of various "wars" to address what are fundamentally social (rather than military) issues: The War on Poverty, The War on Drugs – The War on Terror.

Part of the mobilization for social war is, of course, broad deployment of propaganda to construct and demonize an externalized enemy against which societal resources and the general civilian population must be mobilized. Part of this mobilization includes the overcoming of concerns about a loss or reduction of civil rights, personal liberties, and social obligations (including a willingness to suppress, to suspend, or to supersede constitutional and other legal protections as well as customary and traditional expectations of freedom or liberty).

Some commentators, most notably Agamben, speak of this as the state of exception – the use of supposed crisis conditions to claim exceptionality requiring the suspension of usual and expected rights and responsibilities. This period of the exception is accompanied by the introduction of new, even draconian forms of social control and regulation such as war measures or martial law. Yet in conditions of permanent war the state of exception is rendered permanent – the always available condition of rule or repression.

Numerous studies, including the vast literature on revolutions and social movements, show that even securely legitimized regimes in liberal democratic polities will readily resort to extreme violence and civil or human rights transgressions when faced with significant challengers and reform movements (Duvall and Stohl 1983; Grabosky and Stohl 2010; Gurr 1986). This may occur out of a sense of hopelessness or perceived inefficacious options in the face of plausible alternatives from challengers (see Shantz 2012). It can include an incapacity of states to deploy positive and negative means available to them (inducements and payoffs or repression) or a lack of receptiveness to these on behalf of opponents (Grabosky and Stohl 2010, 59).

In the Canadian context, alternative globalization movements, building great momentum prior to 9/11, were not susceptible to buy-off or co-optation (though elements within them certainly were). There was enough of a critical mass of militant organizers and proponents of direct action to fend off usual mechanisms of state containment. Even more than this, they were facing growing repression and standing up to it in mass numbers – numbers that were growing and spreading following the demonstrations against the Free Trade Area of the Americas meetings in Quebec City in April 2001.

As many commentators have pointed out, the new legislation, including Bill C-36, the so-called Anti-Terrorism Act, has not been about fighting "terrorism" (which has long been prohibited by the Criminal Code of Canada). The various pieces of recent "anti-terrorist" legislation are really about extending the powers of the state to assist its efforts in quelling dissent and furthering the agenda of capitalist globalization (see Shantz 2012). It might be noted that the phobic response around terrorism extended to the labelling of Native activist groups as terrorist organizations by the military, and of anti-poverty groups by law enforcement officials such as Toronto chief of police Julian Fantino (who later became the federal minister of international cooperation in the Conservative government). Notably, Middle Eastern and Muslim communities have been targeted for public condemnation, surveillance, and punishment by police, government, media, and conservative commentators alike. In 2013 the government of Canada introduced biometric identity screening for people who apply for a temporary resident visa, study permit, or work permit, a policy that affects people from twenty-nine countries and one territory (Government of Canada 2013, n.p.).

As means of expanding the influence of the military metaphysic and securing gains for the power elite, the terror fear discourses have been successful. In the first three years since 9/11, security and intelligence budgets in Canada were increased by over $8 billion. A 2011 study by the Rideau Institute in Ottawa reports that the federal government has spent an additional $92 billion on national security in Canada following the September 11 attacks (Fitzpatrick 2011b). The report identifies a "new national security establishment," built in response to the terrorist attacks over a decade ago, which includes the departments of National Defence, Foreign Affairs, Public Safety, Justice, the RCMP, the Canadian Security Intelligence Service, and the Canada Border Services Agency (Fitzpatrick 2011b). The study reports that since 2000–2001, successive Canadian governments have dedicated $92 billion more to national security spending than they would have if budgets had remained consistent with spending levels prior to the 2001 attacks ($69 billion when adjusted for inflation) (Fitzpatrick 2011b). This is money that could have been directed towards transit programs, a national childcare program, health care, education, or housing but was instead diverted to military and security industries and corporations.

For the fiscal year 2010–2011, Canada spent around $34 billion on national security, or $17 billion more ($13 billion adjusted for inflation) than it would have spent prior to 9/11, according to calculations by the Rideau Institute (Fitzpatrick 2011b). Incredibly, security and public safety program spending grew faster than national defence spending, nearly tripling from $3 billion before 9/11 to almost $9 billion in 2011–2012 (Fitzpatrick 2011b). New agencies were created following 9/11. The Canada Border Services Agency was formed in 2003, and since then its spending has grown by over 177 per cent (Fitzpatrick 2011b). Spending for CSIS grew by 134 per cent (Fitzpatrick 2011b).

In 2005, the Liberal government under Paul Martin announced in its budget that it would provide $13 billion in new funding for the military over the next five years (Schwartz 2012). This was described as "the largest increase in defence spending in the last 20 years" (Schwartz 2012). In 2008, the Harper government released its Canada First defence strategy, in which it detailed plans to spend $490 billion on defence over twenty years (Schwartz 2012). According to a report by the Canadian Centre for Policy Alternatives, military spending by the Canadian government in 2010–2011 reached a level almost 54 per cent greater than it was before the attacks of 11 September 2001. The estimated amount was around $22.8 billion in fiscal year 2010–2011, the last fiscal year reported at time of writing (Schwartz 2012). This figure represents a full 10 per cent of all government program spending (Schwartz 2012). Steven Staples of Global Research reports that "NATO and other international authorities rank Canada as the 13th largest military spender in the world in real dollars, and the 6th largest within the 28-member NATO alliance" (2011, n.p.).

A Department of National Defence report in 2011 suggests that between 2004 and 2010, the number of personnel at DND headquarters rose by 46 per cent (Fitzpatrick 2011a). That number does not include the thousands of contractors and consultants hired by the department. Indeed, spending on consultants and contractors was up $2.7 billion per year (Schwartz 2012). According to the report, between 2004 and 2010 the combined workforce of DND and the Canadian Forces jumped by 18 per cent, representing more than 20,000 people (Fitzpatrick 2011a). By March 2010 the various departments employed 144,744 people, including 67,857 in the regular forces, 35,665 reservists, and 29,348 civilians (Fitzpatrick 2011a). In another report of 2009, DND reported to NATO that it intended to devote 17.5 per cent of its spending to equipment expenditures in 2010, representing a 38 per cent increase from the previous year (Staples 2011).

Producing Phobias: Conservative Terror Discourses

Wartime mobilization is typically accompanied by calls for material sacrifice and austerity as well as a push to sacrifice values dearly held among the working classes and oppressed, such as freedom of assembly, freedom of movement, or freedom of expression. If one need not give up butter to afford guns (as in the popular call of World War Two), one might still give up civil liberties to "stop the terrorists" (see Grabosky and Stohl 2010, 88). Speaking of state terrorism campaigns, Grabosky and Stohl note that "almost all cases of state terror are preceded by campaigns which seek to marginalize and dehumanize the potential victims and are further justified in the name of national security" (2010, 59). The manipulation of a climate of fear prepares ground for the advance of repressive policies and the restriction or erosion of civil liberties.

In mobilizations for social war, the corporate mass media (Canwest Global or National Broadcasting Corporation [NBC]) as well as state media institutions (such as the Canadian Broadcasting Corporation [CBC], or Public Broadcasting System [PBS]) play, as always in times of war, a central and even pivotal role. In particular, the mass media play a major part in the manufacture of moral panics and the construction of fear.

Media coverage in the West tends to be characterized by what Bennett, Lawrence, and Livingston (2007) call a built-in authority bias that privileges official commentary in framing events. Grabosky and Stohl argue that

> to some extent, contemporary news media perform the function of medieval morality plays, allowing the public to identify with the "good guys" and to distance themselves from the "forces of evil." A public seeking simplicity and certainty is often uncomfortable with moral ambiguity. This is somewhat problematic in a world where there are many gray areas. (2010, 107)

Moral panic in these cases centres upon the externalization of threats (in the form of the social "other," including the invasive other) and the construction of social phobias in response to this external or invasive other and the threat it poses as a potential contaminant or source of social infection. Even those liberal democracies, like Canada, that picture themselves as peacemakers and immerse themselves in discourses of inclusion, openness, multiculturalism, or plurality exhibit social phobic responses in a framework of permanent war and the military metaphysic.

The deployment of the external and/or invasive threat as a means of hegemonic constructions of panic has particular usefulness in times of permanent war. As Grabosky and Stohl suggest, "First, by invoking the spectre of an evil threat, a state may attempt to engender social solidarity among its own citizens. Second, the image of evil may be used to justify extraordinary action against 'the other' and to help reduce inhibitions on the part of those who might be called up to take such action" (2010, 108). The Canadian state has a deplorable history from which to draw in this regard. It, like the US, deployed extraordinary measures to demonize Japanese, Italian, and German civilians in Canada during World War Two.

The audience may be as important a target as the victims of anti-terror mobilizations (Grabosky and Stohl 2010, 59). The aim is often to create general fear within the audience groups.

In addition to the mass media, conservative commentators in Canada and the United States work hard to prepare the ground for an increasing securitization of Canadian and American society – with their ideal goal the achievement of a fully integrated security apparatus in what they term "Fortress North America." Canadians have supposedly developed a false sense of security, and it is the role of conservatives to shatter this. This terror concern is always associated with Muslims or people from the Middle East. It is not portrayed in association with, say, Irish or Italian or Spanish groups.

For conservatives, the RCMP and CSIS are highly effective agencies in dealing with the monitoring of terrorist groups in Canada (which are proposed but not proven to exist). The problem for conservatives is that these agencies are undermined by social and political institutions and practices (especially civil liberties and constitutional rights) that Canadians are far too fond of. As Stewart Bell puts it, the RCMP and CSIS have not been able to put terrorist groups out of business because governments, mindful of public concerns about civil freedoms, "have not given them the tools they need to do so" (2004, 210).

Bell claims that "Canada nurtures and exports terrorism around the world" (which is the subtitle of one of his books) and suggests that it will continue to do so in the absence of extreme legislative and social measures – including pre-emptive arrests and indeterminate detentions. For conservatives like Bell, "The security culture that will be required in the coming decades does not exist in Canadian society or in its political institutions, and it will not exist without fundamental changes in both public attitudes and government policies" (210). Conservatives have tasked themselves with seeing that these fundamental changes are effected, and the main measure they have taken is to prepare an environment of fear and phobia. According to conservative fear discourses:

> The list of specific government failures is extensive, from an immigration system seemingly incapable of deporting even known terrorists, to laws that have proven ineffective at shutting down charities and ethnic associations fronting for terror. But it all stems from a political leadership unwilling to take a stand and secure Canadians and their allies from the violent whims of the world's assorted radicals, fundamentalists and extremists. (Bell 2004, 209)

A veritable who's who of arch-conservatives in Canada, including David Frum and George Jonas, replay the myth of Canada as a terror haven in stark terms designed to frighten the public. In the promotional commentary for Bell's book, Lee Lamothe refers to Canada as a "Club Med of terrorism." The emphasis on threat and the basis for fear – and the insistence that Canadians should be terrified – is consistently replayed in these blurbs, along with the appeal to extreme measures. For Frum, former speech writer for G.W. Bush, the story is truly terrifying and Canadians have cowardly politicians (of the left and liberal centre) to blame. For Martin Rudner of the Norman Paterson School of International Affairs at Carleton University in Ottawa, Canadians must become alert to "the threat and dangers in our very midst." For Lee Lamothe, tales of terrorists in Canada should serve to "bring a chill to any Canadian." And that is why the tales are told.

The claim is made that Canada is a major base for international terrorism. The conservative Bell describes Canada in panicked tones as "a country that was harboring every major international terrorist organization on the planet, a country where terrorists were building bombs; raising money for weapons; plotting; recruiting; and then going out into the world to spread terror. That country is Canada" (2004, xii). It is even suggested that there is a vast "terrorist underworld in Canada" (xviii).

The terrorist organizations said to be operating in Canada extend to Al Qaeda, the fear manufacturers claim. According to Bell, "Since its inception, Al Qaeda has used Canada as an offshore base" (xv). An internal CSIS document written in the period following 9/11 asserts: "Al Qaeda has operatives and intelligence gatherers in Canada" (CSIS 2002).

More outrageously, conservatives suggest that "Canada is the land of opportunity for terrorist groups" (Bell 2004, xxiii). Conservatives even go so far as to suggest publicly that Canada is an untrustworthy ally in the war on terror. Or worse, it is no ally at all. Canada, they contend, "has become known as a nation that is not fully committed to the war on terrorism" (xvi). For conservatives, "Canada risks being isolated and perhaps even punished for its inaction on terrorism" (xxvi). All of this despite the fact that the Canadian state has provided massive material and ideological support to the invasions and occupations of Iraq and Afghanistan, increased militarization of society, tighter border controls, and so on.

If the terrorist threat in Canada is not stopped, according to conservatives, Canadian citizens will be looked upon with suspicion in the rest of the world. This puts them in grave danger. Conservatives provide this, incredibly, as the explanation of the torture of Maher Arar, a Canadian citizen who was deported by US authorities to Syria where he was tortured (the torture is always only alleged for conservatives) while the Canadian government did nothing.

Even worse, "terrorists themselves have taken note of Canada's posture" (Bell 2004, xvi). Canada is a place where violent radicals run rampant (but out of plain sight). And regular Canadians should be afraid, very afraid. In his endorsement of Bell's book, David B. Harris, director of INSIGNIS's International and Terrorist Intelligence Program, goes further. In frantic language he asks: "Will Canada be the next Bosnia, the next Lebanon? Most intelligence officers think so." For Harris, quoted in the promotional material at the front of Bell's book, Canadians are facing a "catastrophic slide." In his view "it is much, much, later than we think."

Yet the terror-in-Canada story is Bell's discovery and his alone. It is neither corroborated nor confirmed. Still, supporters, including Harris, claim Bell is "now at risk in his own country." The murderous terrorist legions are after him, and you. Be afraid.

The supposed terrorists are described in a manner that has clear undertones of other phobias on the right (such as homophobia); they are painted as weak, scared, effeminate – as a woman – though elsewhere terrorists are depicted as bombastic and sinister. These are "not ordinary people" (Bell 2004, xii).

As with other manufactured threats, the enemies are mysterious. They move in the shadows to which they return when spotted. They could be anywhere or everywhere. They are all around us: "some terrorists are arrested, released on bail by immigration judges, and then just disappeared" (Bell 2004, xv). Of great cause for fear is the unpredictability of the anonymous enemy. According to an internal CSIS report, "Al Qaeda's global links, including to residents of Canada, and its use of sleeper agents make its activities unpredictable and a threat to the security of Canada" (2002). For the phobia producers, these phantom Al Qaeda links cannot be emphasized enough. This must be replayed for people: "We must not forget that in the eyes of Al Qaeda, Canada is the enemy" (Bell 2004, xxvi).

Terror identities within the phobia discourses are always presented as Muslim, Palestinian, Sikh, Tamil, or Arab (rather than Irish, German, or Italian, for example). These groups are somehow different in their sameness with other terrorists. For Bell, "Propaganda is especially critical to Islamic terrorism" (xxv). As it is in fact for, say, any terrorist? Or for any state? Or political party? Or corporation (ads, anyone?)? Similarly, "in Islam violence in the name of self-defence is permissible" (xxv). As it is in, say, Canada or the US? The Muslim groups are said to be extreme even for terrorists. Indeed, "The world has seen its share of terrorists over the past half-century, but radical Islamic fundamentalists are by far the most dangerous" (210).

Islamic terrorism has two defining and horrifying characteristics, Bell explains:

> First, it preaches violence without limits. To those indoctrinated into this way of thinking, terrorism serves not only a strategic purpose, but fulfills the will of God, and so the bigger, the better. Imagine if people with this mindset were to get their hands on chemical, nuclear or biological weapons. The second concern is that Islamic extremists are patient. Their hatred arises from centuries-old grievances and their aim is long-term: a world under the rule of Islam, the one true faith. (211)

For conservatives like Bell, even the suggestion that "freedom is never given; it has to be fought for and won" (a basic truism of all social history and movements for justice) is viewed as some awful insight into the terrorist mindset and unceasing glorification of violence (xviii). For conservatives, there are no freedom fighters – other than, ironically, state security agents (who may in fact condone, support, or participate in torture and other acts of illegality). For conservatives, liberation is always to be put in quote marks.

Coddling the Terrorists: Rights as Wrongs in Phobic Productions

The construction of terror fear in Canada is part of a narrative of history. Conservatives devise what might be called a terrorography (rather than a historiography). For some conservatives the threat of terrorism is even rooted in Canadian history: indigenous groups and organizers are branded as terrorists (see Shantz 2012). Iconic figure Louis Riel, a hero of struggles for indigenous rights and founding member of Canadian confederation, is reconstructed as a terrorist and traitor rather than a "Father of Confederation" or a resistance fighter or opponent of genocide. The October Crisis of 1970 in which members of the Front de libération du Québec (FLQ), a movement for Québécois liberation and autonomy, kidnapped political figures, killing one, is another national precursor for conservatives. Of course union movements and strikes, such as the Winnipeg General Strike, also provide source materials for conservative terrorography.

The central part of the problem for conservatives is the social democratic heritage in Canada. Conservative anti-terror discourses are directed at dismantling that heritage. In Bell's view, Canada is currently *the* land of opportunity for terrorists because "welfare is generous" (2004, xxiii) – despite the fact that social assistance rates have been massively cut in provinces like Ontario and British Columbia and frozen for years elsewhere. Harris, in his promotional blurb on Bell's book, suggests that the Canadian social system, and especially social democratic policies, are to blame and assails "the political collusion and betrayal, the corruption of immigration and ethnocultural lobbying systems, that justify fears that 'the peaceable kingdom' is on its way out." Notably, the key target in this phobia is the immigrant other as represented in migration and "ethnocultural" (suggesting a racialized other) lobbying.

A May 2003 report from the Washington, DC–based Center for Immigration Studies (a right-wing think tank) was circulated to support the claims and stoke the fear. It exclaims: "To many Americans the longest undefended border in the world now looks like a 4,000-mile-long portal for terrorists." Canadians certainly do not want to appear complicit in allowing this or in appearing untrustworthy to Americans, so something must be done. They must act. Once again, though, the real focus is on migration and the desire for restricted borders.

Formal procedures towards the construction of a "Fortress North America" continue apace. Under a bilateral treaty signed with little notice or public discussion at the end of 2012, almost all applicants seeking a visa to enter Canada will be subjected to an identity check against American immigration databases. Cross-checking against US immigration data began immediately with the treaty signing, and the United States will now do the same with Canadian immigration databases. In addition, all visa applicants from a highly racialized list of thirty countries will now be fingerprinted with biometric data retention and further cross-checking with US immigration databases and Canadian police records (Koring 2013, n.p.).

The rhetorical underpinning for this database integration is the claim that migrant purveyors of terror are bringing their local grievances into Canada. They are even importing their wars. The claims are quite bold: "Canada has provided a haven, money, propaganda, weapons and foot soldiers to the globe's deadliest religious, ethnic and political extremist movements, murderous organizations that have brought their wars with them, turning this country into a base for international terror" (Bell 2004, xiii).

This is a replay of standard anti-immigrant rhetoric. Refugees from specific communities keep fighting the wars "back home in Sri Lanka or India or the Middle East" (Bell 2004, xxv). The backgrounds are identified with a purpose: this is not a random draw. In these refugee communities "extremists have seized control of community institutions" (xxv). All associations within these communities are suspect, including charities or social service providers.

The other aspect is that migrants, despite working long hours at jobs for which they are overqualified, are abusers of the "generous welfare" system. Thus in conservative anti-terror discourse, the dual spectres of migrants and welfare cheats, images that haunt conservative fantasies, are deployed simultaneously. Charities too are suspect, particularly those that are associated with specific communities (ethnic blocs) or are attuned to human rights issues. This is a world in which benevolence and compassion are mere shields for terror.

Part of the mobilization of fear is telling the story that national security agencies are not equipped (legislatively, materially, socially) to deal with the mounting threat. This relates especially to the characteristics of migrant terrorists and the unstable conditions of the countries from which they migrate. According to Bell:

> The government agencies charged with national security have been unable to stop the parade of terrorist organizations into Canada. Security background checks are routine, but it is no easy task to investigate someone whose home is halfway around the world, especially if there is war and upheaval in the country, and if migrants are not forthright about their past or even their true identity. The regions from which they come are not the kind of places that keep accurate records, and so Canadian authorities are unable to properly screen for terrorists. (2004, xiv)

Again the story is one of outsiders who, coming from questionable background contexts, are able to deceive hard-working security agents.

Even worse, the mechanisms for dealing with terrorists who have been identified are less effective. Bell writes:

> Even when everything works as it should and terrorists are caught in Canada's security screening system, the worst fate they suffer is usually deportation. And even then, many of those ordered out of the country never leave. Under the Canadian system, they are allowed to launch appeal after appeal after appeal. Government counterterrorism agencies

can spend years building a case against a terrorist, at a cost of over $1 million per investigation. Canada's immigration system, however, is so cumbersome that few of those arrested ever get deported. (2004, xv)

The point is driven home over and over again that Canada's "liberal" social policies coddle terrorists (or criminals in other contexts, for conservatives). And respecting human rights or paying attention to humanitarian and compassionate considerations is not only foolhardy, it is costly. Thus if the fear of terror is not convincing, conservatives can fall back on another favoured threat – the fear of public spending, budget expenses, and, underlying it, the implied threat of tax increases.

What is more, the government, far from being incompetent, is actually abetting the terrorists. Liberal democratic government is complicit in terror in Canada. The conservative phobia producers claim that there are dual epidemics of terror and denial in Canada against which they need to intervene to inoculate the public against the complacency that has put them to sleep, rendering them terror zombies.

Canadian politicians, despite their regimes of invasion, war, and occupation, are not resistant to the plague. Supposedly they are, in the terror myths, routinely "skillfully manipulated and coopted by radicals until eventually they give more credence to the exaggerations and propaganda of front groups than they do to their own intelligence professionals" (Bell 2004, xix). Politicians receive intelligence reports but refuse to read them, even when the reports are made easier to read. The reason for political corruption in this regard, according to conservatives, is that politicians do not want to alienate key voter blocs, which are always posed as specific "ethnic blocs." Even more important, members of terrorist groups are said to have a special influence on or sway over the ethnic voting blocs and "interest groups." Notably, these groups are always "othered" along racialized lines. For the conservative fear producers, politicians, of the left especially, are a virtual fifth column for terrorists. So too are civil libertarians and human rights activists.

The conservative fear discourses mirror standard media discourses of moral panics and crime. As in the usual crime panic script, the heroic police (in this case security agents) are undermined by uncaring, inept, or bleeding-heart politicians and legal advocates who care more about the terrorists (criminals) than they do about public safety or "the victims." The security forces are portrayed as being caught in the middle, the only honest players in a corrupt game. In this frame, "Canadian counter-terrorism officials have been forced to fight two wars – one against terrorists and the other against the Canadian politicians who pretend that terrorists either do not exist or are not a threat to Canada" (Bell 2004, xx–xxi). This coincides with a similar story of tireless immigration agents sold out by lax policies and sleepy politicians. The occasional anecdote featuring an unnamed agent rounds this story out. Bell relates: "An immigration official told me how he works all day at trying to get terrorists out of the country, and then watches as politicians court these same violent organizations for votes. When he gets home, his wife sometimes asks him why he even bothers. 'I honestly don't know what to tell her,' he said" (xx). Once again the trouble stems from ethnic voting blocs who harbour terrorists and terrorize politicians into acquiescence.

Notably, criticisms of racism or Islamophobia are merely part of the terrorist plot. Lobby groups turn potential successes into failure by crying racism or prejudice. Indeed, Canada's concerns about intolerance play into the lobbyists' hands as accusations of intolerance simply shelter the terrorists. Within the conservative logic, the harassment of racialized minorities is simply proof that terrorism is real and that minorities are actually *not* harassed. In Bell's formulation: "It would be easy to get the impression from some of Canada's media outlets that intelligence agents are renegades who enjoy harassing minorities" (2004, xxi). We have this from the same media that have played such a prominent role in stoking the terror fear in the first place.

With reference to Mohamed Harkat, one of the men held under security certificates, Bell implies with some certainty, despite having no access to the case against him, which even Harkat and his lawyers have been denied, that because he has been accused he must be guilty. All who support him – including his French Canadian wife Sophie – are supporters of terrorism, the mythical Canadian dupes. Bell even condemns Sophie Harkat and her mother for a photo in which they are hugging their husband and son-in-law: "The symbolism is striking, though unintended: Canadians embracing a suspected terrorist" (xxii). Striking indeed: loved ones hugging one another – social democracy run amok. Harkat's efforts to defend himself and clear his name, a basic right of all accused, are demeaned. His supporters, and those merely concerned about due process, are sneered at as enablers of terror.

The Standing Senate Committee on National Security and Defence declared in 2003: "Never has a combined physical and economic threat to the Canadian homeland been more palpable, but rarely have

Canadians been more sanguine about their well-being" (n.p.). Clearly, for conservative commentators, the public cannot turn to the institutions of liberal democratic government, which are untrustworthy. For Bell, "The government has not only failed to stop terrorists, it has actively aided them" (xv).

The reasons for fear are deeply rooted in political traditions of liberal democracy. According to former CSIS director Ward Elcock, "As with other democracies, our openness and respect for rights and freedoms limit the ability of the state to suppress terrorism in a ruthless, repressive fashion" (see Bell 2004, xvi). This is, fundamentally, what the conservative phobia producers desire: conservatives regret, or resent, the openness and respect for rights and long for a time of unimpeded repression and state violence – deployed against specific individuals and groups. They busily work to lay the groundwork for that day to come. Part of that work is constructing fear and social phobias against targeted and associated groups, especially the foreign "other." At least there is some recognition that Canadian terror strategy is about managing appearances "to prevent the Americans from imposing border security measures that would slow North-South trade" (Bell 2004, 210).

The terror fear is potentially particularly effective as a mobilizer of public phobia and related policy shifts. And the terror fear is a permanent one; it must never be allowed to weaken. The phobia against Muslims can have no end point because Islamic terrorists are unique, according to the conservative constructions: "Radical Islamists are willing to wait it out until things die down, until the inconveniences imposed since 9/11 in the name of national security no longer seem necessary, and public pressure builds to rescind antiterror laws. Then the extremists will be able to start plotting freely again. They know it will happen, and they are probably right" (Bell 2004, 211). Thus, state and public vigilance can never waver. Restrictions on rights and freedoms must never be let up. Remember, the problem is rooted in the fact that some Muslims believe (unlike Christians) that theirs is the one true faith.

Even appeals to end repressive policies are really appeals to assist the terrorists. There are no options aside from the repressive one. The imposition of punishment and the militarization of society are required developments according to conservative fear manufacturers. This, then, expresses in clear terms the military metaphysic in action. In the end it is nothing less than social war mobilization with campaigns at home and abroad. Social priorities must be shifted and social relations reorganized. Martial resources must be deployed and social perceptions brought in line with the military metaphysic that must frame social development at all levels.

> These people are not looking for foreign-aid money, or changes to U.S. foreign policy, or greater tolerance of their beliefs. They are irrational religious zealots. What is needed to combat such fanaticism is a forceful security and intelligence response that seeks to dismantle the terror networks within Canada, coupled with an overseas military strategy that attacks the dens of terror. That cannot happen as long as the government is in denial and fails to recognize that terrorists have declared war on our values, our way of life and our society. (Bell 2004, 212)

Here the Western-centrism is laid bare. The fear is posed as a fear of those who would destroy Western capitalist culture and values (whatever these might be).

The fight cannot end. And it must be carried out in Canada. According to the story: "Terrorists can now recruit, train and conspire within the comfort of the West simply by exploiting the liberal democracies of the world. And those nations that are most open and least attuned to the terrorist threat will become the most likely havens" (Bell 2004, 212–13). Never mind that until now those countries that have provided the real havens have been ones that are least open and most attuned. They are not liberal democracies but rather include authoritarian governments like those of Pakistan, Indonesia, or Afghanistan and highly attuned polities as in India.

The real target remains migrant communities within Canada (or North America or the West). In honest moments the conservatives make this clear:

> Altruistic Canada, after all, takes in immigrants and refugees from all over the world, many of them from zones of conflict. What makes Canada a refuge for some makes it a haven for others. An RCMP intelligence report that deals partly with the recruitment of terrorists from within Canadian ethnic communities notes that 17 percent of Canada's population is foreign born, as opposed to 9 percent in the United States, "making Canada more vulnerable to these tendencies than are other developed nations." (Bell 2004, 213)

The proper response for conservatives involves at its heart the securitization of migration: the military metaphysic trained on a border war.

In this view, "A country such as Canada, a top destination for global migration, should logically have the toughest antiterrorism policies and the lowest tolerance for terrorists, if only to protect the vast majority of Canadians who want to live in peace" (Bell 2004, 213). If policies are distasteful and violate basic human or civil rights, well, "so be it" (213).

Facilitating this, and preparing the public for the social changes to come, requires the playing out of degradation ceremonies. These public shows allow for the terror labels to be applied. They also get the public accustomed to the outlandish claims and repressive practices of the incoming terror regimes.

Up to now, "Canada has tried to smother terrorism with kindness" (Bell 2004, 214). Try telling that to all of those detained for years or returned to torture and/or death. Tell it to their families.

Labelling and Degradation Ceremonies:
The Toronto 18 Media Trial

Labelling theories emerged and became prominent within sociology and criminology during the period of mass social and cultural struggles during the 1960s and 1970s. This was a period in which the hegemonic social consensus of the 1950s was shown to be a social myth as various groups, particularly of those excluded from or unhappy with their role and place in the 1950s "consensus," organized to challenge and openly confront the assumptions of social agreement around issues of gender, race, sexuality, and culture more broadly. Movements, and the collective direct actions, of women, racialized minorities, indigenous people, gays and lesbians, and the poor called into question the basis of perceived consensus of privileged wealthy, white males and offered alternative perspectives on society, history, and politics. The social movements of the excluded and exploited, and the struggles that they waged, revealed the post-war dream of capitalist progress to be a fiction for much of the population and showed that there was, in fact, no social consensus. Social reality was very much a matter of social conflict, disagreement, and challenge.

The formal beginnings of labelling theory date to the early works of Franklin Tannenbaum in the 1930s, particularly *Crime and Community* (1938). Tannenbaum points out that the intervention by authorities into social contests begins a process of change in the manner in which the targeted individuals or groups and their activities are perceived and treated. There is a gradual shift from the definition of specific acts as evil to the redefining of the individual him or herself as evil. Everything about the individual or group – friends, clothing, speech, music, and so on – is turned into an object of scrutiny and into evidence for a delinquent or threatening nature. This process Tannenbaum refers to as the "dramatization of evil," as the individual is separated out of its context and subjected to negative treatment. Not only criminals are made deviant in this manner, but others who simply violate norms or conventions rather than laws, particularly members of subcultures or minority groups. Tannenbaum noted that the poor are more likely than the wealthy to get caught up in this process.

Building upon these insights, labelling theory attempts to examine the social and interpersonal processes through which acts, attributes, and beliefs are constructed as deviant. It seeks to explain how cultural and individual perceptions create and sustain deviant identities – even in the absence of evidence for actual deviance. For labelling theories, deviance results from the enforcement of rules rather than specific acts. The deviant person is simply someone to whom the label "deviant" has been successfully applied, not someone who is fundamentally different. What is more, they are people who have come to believe the label as it applies to them.

The processes of identification, arrest, and hearings or trial, and perhaps being detained or incarcerated, represent what labelling theorists call a "degradation ceremony" in which the person or group subjected to it is initiated into a deviant role and assigned a deviant label. These are public shamings and the public construction of threat. In this way criminal justice systems, and the media that report and promote them, are massive deviance-producing machines. Within their operations people, who may not be engaging in harmful activities, are taken into the system and converted into deviants – they are given new deviant identities that they did not previously bear. This is the identity they carry with them publicly.

This process typically alters a person's self-concept as well as disrupting personal relationships and changing life chances and opportunities, including negatively affecting employment, housing, and education. To be publicly defined as deviant is to carry the expectation that you will behave in certain, deviant or threatening, ways. By assigning negative identities, conforming members of society and those with the power to assign labels strongly influence the future behaviour of targeted individuals or groups.

On 2 June 2006 a series of police raids around the city of Toronto resulted in what would become the most dramatic post-9/11 terror allegations in Canada. The arrests of fourteen adults and four youths made international news and brought widespread praise for the efforts of the federal police, the RCMP, and CSIS. Of great significance for the governing Conservative Party of Canada, concerned with proving its worth as a credible security partner in Fortress North America, the police actions won strong praise from US Homeland Security officials and from the White House. To reinforce the point, Prime Minister Stephen Harper even phoned President George Bush to show his appreciation for US assistance in foiling the plot. Harper took the opportunity to stress that this action showed that, contrary to the claims of some American conservatives, Canada was not a safe haven for terrorists.

The young men, collectively labelled "The Toronto 18" by the media, were presented as being a homegrown terror cell inspired by Al Qaeda. The activities they were purported to be planning were stunning: beheading the prime minister, blowing up the headquarters of the RCMP and their security arm CSIS, capturing Parliament Hill and holding representatives hostage. The arrests were accompanied by a blizzard of dramatic media reports, distributed internationally, that presented the Canadian state's version of events.

The day after the arrests, the police held a press conference at which they revealed evidence designed to show the public the extent of the supposed cell's intentions: two-way radios, a handgun, a cellphone detonator, and quantities of ammonium nitrate supposedly acquired for use in truck bombs. The public perception of the threat posed by the would-be cell became even more pronounced days later when it was revealed that one of the accused, Steven Chand, intended to behead the prime minister. Later it was suggested that the group planned to blow up the CN Tower, Toronto's most famous landmark and the tallest free-standing structure on the planet.

As Kutty (2006) notes, the police claimed the citywide raids foiled a major terrorist plot, and the media followed in step, uncritically replaying the police account of the situation. According to Kutty, the media suspended their critical and investigative role and instead "proceeded to try and convict the suspects before even a single one of them appeared for a bail hearing. In fact, some members of the press went further and, reverting to guilt by association, convicted their families and the Muslim community as a whole" (44). Almost every aspect of the Toronto 18 case – notably the defence arguments and much of the actual evidence – remained shrouded in secrecy.

Once the unofficial story had been circulated far and wide, the court issued a sweeping media ban that prevented the public from gaining access to any evidence presented against the Toronto 18, as contained within court documents or submitted at bail and preliminary hearings. At the same time, however, the public had been treated to much of the state's accusations against the 18, some of which is incredible. A total publication ban, as enforced in the case of the Toronto 18, contributes to a social context of fear, especially in cases involving supposed terrorism in which the state and media have already conditioned a climate of fear and anxiety as part of everyday discourses of security and preparedness.

Much of the state's case rested on the evidence provided by two informants. The first, whose name cannot be published, was reported to have been paid four million dollars by the government for his contributions (Walkom 2007). He was identified as a participant in the plot to build a fertilizer bomb. The second informant, Mubin Shaikh, went public, turning himself into a media star and unofficial spokesperson for the case despite the publication ban. Shaikh, a former army cadet, claimed to be the person who organized a terror training camp for the 18 in northern Ontario. In addition to offering disparaging opinions about the psychological state of various plotters, Shaikh suggested that they were planning to organize a "Chechen-style" Muslim resistance movement in northern Ontario, a vast region with very few Muslim residents. He was paid at least five hundred thousand dollars by the government (Freeze and El Akkad 2007).

Shaikh was in the middle of giving his testimony on the case when the prosecution abruptly ended the preliminary hearing and announced its intention to move directly to trial. The preliminary hearing is intended as a means for determining whether there is enough evidence to justify a trial. It also offers the defence an opportunity to hear the prosecution's case and to cross-examine witnesses such as Shaikh. Critics have been left to ask why the prosecution made the unexpected decision to move to trial. Some wonder whether something was about to be revealed in court that the government did not want disclosed. Others suggest the prosecution was feeling nervous about its informants, especially following Shaikh's arrest on charges of assault against two twelve-year-old girls (Pazzano 2008).

Less than a year later, by March 2007, the largest case of supposed homegrown terrorism in Canada was beginning to appear as some-. thing much less threatening. A member of the federal government's

Advisory Council on National Security, David Charters, concluded that the cell posed little real danger, representing nothing more than the boisterous posturing of young men looking for recognition from each other. Charges were stayed against three of the four youth and the case against the others started to unravel.

In a keynote address to the Canadian Aviation Security Conference, Charters concluded: "I will be surprised if more than two or three are ever convicted of serious crimes. To anyone the least bit familiar with security, their so-called 'plans' were scarcely credible. While not calling into question their desire to do something dramatic, it is clear their reach exceeded their grasp." Charters went on to note that most of what the cell actually engaged in was talk. "And it was big, loose talk – violating the most fundamental security principles of terrorist groups – that did them in" (quoted in MacLeod 2008, n.p.).

These developments have led some critics to look more closely at the case. They have questioned the state's motives in breaking the case when they did and in the manner they did. It was not lost on some that the case was broken weeks before the government's anti-terror laws were set to undergo parliamentary review. The arrests also came only two weeks before the appeals of three cases involving security certificates and the use of secret evidence (Kutty 2006). And they came during a period in which the Canadian government had been subjected to sharp criticism from US officials, including the ambassador to Canada, that Canada was not doing enough to address possible domestic terror threats. These questions became even more pressing when the police revealed that not only did they control the delivery of nitrate supposedly intended for bomb-making, but they had been investigating the cell for around two years.

Despite this, the case is still being used, including by David Charters himself, to suggest that there remain concerns over terrorism within Muslim communities in Canada. Charters uses the incredible term "complicit communities" to suggest that fears of specific groups' supposed support for or endorsement of terrorism in Canada are real. According to him, the Toronto 18 case shows that radicalization "is happening at a much younger age; there are 'talent spotters' who are willing to exploit the idealism, rage or lack of maturity of youngsters and to give them a target, an outlet and a justification for violence; and finally they don't have to travel to be trained" (here and below, quoted in MacLeod 2008, n.p.). He went on to suggest: "From a security agency's perspective, this is the stuff of nightmares; it really could be 'the kid next door.'" Yet the Toronto 18, by Charter's own admission, posed little threat.

Still Charters felt compelled to reassure his audience: "And while there might exist in Canada small pockets of 'complicit communities' prepared – willing or otherwise – to tolerate terrorism, the country as a whole does not. In fact our history suggests just the opposite – that we are more likely to come down hard on it. These factors may explain, at least in part, why, compared to the rest of the world, Canada has experienced so little terrorism." The contrasting of small pockets of "complicit communities" that support terrorism with the country as a whole, with its history of opposition to terrorism, serves once again to imply that there are those within Canada that might undermine Canadian values and even Canadian history.

Really, this is the main emphasis of media events like the spectacular Toronto 18 busts. It keeps the focus on so-called complicit communities, which are always racialized or rendered "ethnic" as Muslim, which require surveillance, and which might be subjected to the loss of rights necessary under conditions of emergency. As Kutty notes, the arrests of the Toronto 18 served to place the growing Muslim communities in Canada "under a microscope" (2006, 44). The arrests also placed pressure on Muslim communities to constitute themselves as "mainstream" and willing to work with government agencies to address the issues of "extremism," whether extremism existed within their specific communities or not. They were compelled to show publicly, in something akin to a "degradation ceremony," that they were, or were willing to become, "worthy citizens." Kutty suggests: "Clearly, if mainstream Muslims are not seen to be (and actually are not) part of the team working on a solution, then their alienation will only add to the problem" (2006, 44). This responsibility to perform worthy citizenship has led some "moderate" Muslims to make accusations of extremism against specific communities or mosques or to exaggerate the degree of extremism within Muslim communities.

The one-sided media reporting of the state narrative, which offered variations of police accounts seasoned with innuendo and stereotypes, served to raise the spectre of homegrown terrorism and Muslim "extremism." While carried out largely on the terrain of myth and rumour, it had very real effects on Muslim communities:

> Agenda-driven armchair pundits and self-proclaimed "moderate" Muslims quickly joined the fray, blaming Canadian immigration policies

and multiculturalism for incubating this "homegrown" threat. Some have taken it even further by reinforcing baseless assertions such as the claim that extremism is rampant in the Muslim community. Those raising alarms about extremism have failed to define it, however. Instead they have effectively pinned the blame on the Muslim leadership and mainstream Muslim community – apparently forgetting that rebels are not known for following mainstream views or leaders. (Kutty 2006, 44)

Extremism is not a crime in Canada, yet the diverse Muslim communities of Canada, numbering some 750,000, are placed in the position of being made responsible for the activities of anyone who might be associated with "the Muslim community," written in the singular. This requirement of collective responsibility is not placed on any other community in Canada and is certainly not placed on the state when it comes to national histories of racism, colonialism, and genocide. As Kutty notes, "Muslims cannot and do not ask mainstream Canadian society to take responsibility for the actions of the criminals who vandalize mosques, threatened an imam with a knife or for the dozens of companies that are alleged to have discriminated against Muslim employees in the wake of the Toronto arrests" (2006, 44). Of course there is still an important distinction between holding extreme views on social issues and engaging in acts of violence.

Despite the absence of real evidence to suggest that Canadian Muslims, and particularly Muslim youth, are given to extremism or support the use of political violence, or that institutions within Muslim communities are propagating hatred against non-Muslims, several national Muslim organizations have felt compelled to do something to show their concern over extremism within their communities. In one display of worthy citizenship, the Islamic Society of North America, the Islamic Circle of North America, the Muslim Association of Canada, and the Muslim Students' Association (National) came forward to call for a national summit to examine extremism and support for terrorism among Muslim youth.

It is to state the obvious that Canadian Muslims are concerned about the country's national security. Major Muslim organizations came out after the arrests and commended law enforcement for breaking up an alleged plot. Even CAIR-CAN [Canadian Council on American-Islamic Relations], which has been highly critical of law enforcement and intelligence strategies and tactics, called on Muslims to cooperate with authorities as their civic and religious duty. This despite the fact that the relationship between such agencies and the Muslim/Arab community has been strained over the years. (Kutty 2006, 44)

At the same time, however, and showing the power of worthy citizenship discourses to construct state subjects, Kutty himself feels compelled to concede that "as members of a civil society the Muslim community does owe the mainstream a duty to address the perception – whether real or imagined – that extremism is a major issue in the community" (2006, 45). He even goes so far as to identify those within Muslim communities who are neither secular nor ultra-orthodox as potential star players in state agencies' "war" against terrorism. The pressure to display one's worthiness is felt even among sharp critics in this context.

Following the Toronto 18 arrests, a panel discussion titled "Terrorism in Toronto: What Does It Mean for Canadian Multiculturalism?" was convened at the University of Toronto to discuss the implications of the various anti-terror arrests for the Canadian cultural mosaic. The panel included a number of high-profile and respected academics and community activists, including Tarek Fateh of the Muslim Canadian Congress; Alia Hogden of the Canadian Council of Muslim Women; Jeffrey Reitz, professor of ethics, immigration, and pluralism studies at the University of Toronto; and Randall Hansen, Canada Research Chair in Immigration and Governance at the University of Toronto. The panellists addressed the role of Canadian multicultural policy in fostering cultural extremism, a claim that has been raised by conservative commentators. The panel agreed that multiculturalism was not at the root of extremism within Muslim communities in Canada (Dellandrea 2006, n.p.). Participant Melissa Williams, director of the university's Centre for Ethics, noted that there "is no evidence ... that there is any logical, causal relationship between policies of multiculturalism and the formation of such (radical) groups" (quoted in Patrick 2006, n.p.). Yet none of the panellists questioned the relationship between extremism and the Muslim community in Canada. This critical gap prompted one audience member, Rinaldo Walcott, the University of Toronto Canada Research Chair of Social Justice and Cultural Studies, to accuse the panellists of racism before abandoning the talk.

Again, however, the point had already been made. The very fact that busy community organizers and prominent academics had been put through the public ceremony of defending multiculturalism and cultural autonomy, against assimilationism, showed clearly the powerful effects of recent legislation, secret trials, and incarceration in framing the context of national discourse.

Conclusion

In a sense the whole anti-terror mobilization emphasizes the aspects of the state as what some critics term "a protection racket." As Tilly has suggested, "If protection rackets represent organized crime at its smoothest, then war making and state making – quintessential protection rackets with the advantage of legitimacy – qualify as our largest examples of organized crime" (1985, 161). The pattern undertaken by various Canadian governments is a troubling one. It suggests the possibilities for further and more expansive regimes of repression targeting vulnerable groups, which is precisely what conservative commentators, and many members of the Conservative Party, have been calling for.

On the five-step political terror scale devised by Stohl, Carleton, and Johnson (1984), recent practices would place Canada at level three out of five (two steps up the scale). The scale describes activities at level three as follows: "There is extensive political imprisonment, or a recent history of such imprisonment. Execution or other political murders and brutality may be common. Unlimited detention, with or without trial, for political views is accepted."

The general consensus, outside of conservative circles, is that the various pieces of legislation enacted against terrorism are a massive overreaction and misplacement of priorities (Grabosky and Stohl 2010, 104). Yet the pitched rhetoric surrounding the introduction of the legislation and the breadth of the powers assigned to state authorities serve to heighten the sense of fear and crisis.

The Toronto 18 arrests and trials represent a classic case of state disruption through the use of paid informants and provocateurs. The participants seem to have been incited largely by a member who was, in fact, working for and on the payroll of police authorities.

As all of the people incarcerated in Canada under anti-terror laws have involved Muslim men, it is important to pay attention to the impact on Muslim communities in Canada in terms of degradation ceremonies aimed at the constitution of "worthy citizens." Compelling community leaders to publicly proclaim themselves as moderates and willing partners with state agencies further reinforces this process.

The carceral practices deployed under anti-terror legislation in Canada are the state of exception in response to crisis that proves the rule of state control. The anti-terror practices make clear the state's role as the arbiter of citizenship. Because security certificates, for example, have no discernible basis for application other than a vague suspicion of a possible relationship to possible terrorist groups at some point in the future, they hold out the permanent possibility of applicability. That they have only been applied to people of Muslim background makes the unspoken basis for application clear. Security certificates, secret trials, and unlimited incarceration are aspects of coercion of specific racialized groups, through the embodiment and performance of abject individuals.

REFERENCES

Behrens, Matthew. 2008, 11 March. "Secrecy Piled on Secrecy: Democracy Day in Secret Trials Land." http://justiceforharkat.com/news. php?extend.2698.66

Bell, Stewart. 2004. *Cold Terror: How Canada Nurtures and Exports Terrorism around the World*. Toronto: Wiley.

Bennett, W. Lance, Regina G. Lawrence, and Steven Livington. 2007. *When the Press Fails: Political Power and the News Media from Iraq to Katrina*. Chicago: University of Chicago Press.

CSIS. 2002, 22 November. "Counter Terrorism Presentation to Solicitor General Wayne Easter."

Fitzpatrick, Meagan. 2011a, 19 August. "DND Report Lays Out Plan to Save $1B." *CBC News*. http://www.cbc.ca/news/politics/story/2011/08/19/pol-dnd-report-cuts.htmlhttp://www.cbc.ca/news/politics/dnd-report-lays-out-plan-to-save-1b-1.992916.

– 2011b, 7 September. "Security Spending after 9/11 Tops $92B." *CBC News*. http://www.cbc.ca/news/canada/story/2011/09/07/pol-911-security-spending.htmlhttp://www.cbc.ca/news/politics/security-spending-after-9-11-tops-92b-1.1043068.

Freeze, Colin, and Omar El Akkad. 2007, February 2 (updated 31 March 2009). "Terror Informant Wanted $14-Million." *Globe and Mail*. http://www.theglobeandmail.com/news/national/terror-informant-wanted-14-million/article1070245/.

Government of Canada. 2013. "Countries and Territories Whose Citizens Will Soon Need to Provide Biometric Information to Enter Canada as Visitors." http://www.cic.gc.ca/http://www.cic.gc.ca/english/visit/biometrics. aspenglish/visit/biometrics.asp.

Grabosky, Peter, and Michael Stohl. 2010. *Crime and Terrorism*. Los Angeles: Sage.

Koring, Paul. 2013, January 4. "Applicants for Canadian Visas Will Be Checked against U.S. Databases." *Globe and Mail*. http://www.theglobeandmail.com/news/politics/applicants-for-canadian-visas-will-be-checked-against-us-databases/article6934557/.

Kutty, Faisal. 2006. "Canada Calling: Toronto Arrests Spark Debate about Muslim Extremism." http://faisalkutty.com/publications/washington-report/canada-calling-toronto-arrests-spark-debate-about-muslim-extremism/https://archive.is/20130122165158/http://faisalkutty.com/publications/washington-report/canada-calling-toronto-arrests-spark-debate-about-muslim-extremism/.

Macleod, Ian. 2007, 6 March. "Terror Analyst Says 'Toronto 18' Suspects Posed Small Threat." *National Post*. http://www.nationalpost.com/news/canada/Terror+analyst+says+Toronto+suspects+posed+small+threat/357602/story.htmlhttp://www.nationalpost.com/news/canada/Terror+analyst+says+Toronto+suspects+posed+small+threat/357602/story.html.

Patrick, Kelly. 2006, June 13. "Panelists Agree Multiculturalism Not Linked to Terror." *National Post*. http://www.canada.com/topics/news/politics/story.html?id=8f6e1469-996a-4bca-9213-eaebf7754ca5&k=68496.

Pazzano, Sam. 2008, July 4. "Students' Insults Upset Spy." *Sun Media*. http://cnews.canoe.com/CNEWS/Crime/2008/07/04/6064211-sun.html.

Schwartz, Daniel. 2012, 12 November. "What Kind of Military Can Canada Afford?" *CBC News*. http://www.cbc.ca/news/politics/story/2012/11/09/f-military-policy.htmlhttp://www.cbc.ca/news/politics/what-kind-of-military-can-canada-afford-1.1230004.

Staples, Steven. 2011, 2 June. "Military Spending in Canada." *Global Research*. http://www.globalresearch.ca/military-spending-in-canada/25091.

Walkom, Thomas. 2007, September 25. "Terror Trial Proceedings Troubling." *Toronto Star*. http://www.thestar.com/opinion/columnists/2007/09/25/terror_trial_proceedings_troubling.html.

10 Manufacturing the *avaton* and the Ghetto: Places of Fear in the Centre of Athens

PENNY (PANAGIOTA) KOUTROLIKOU

In everyday life, phobias and fears are considered influential on ways of perceiving, behaving, and treating others, particularly those who happen to be the "other." In politics, phobias also play significant roles as governance tactics by invoking popular sentiments and (re)actions; this is employed by both governments and oppositions. Discourses about the state of exception (Agamben), the politics of fear (Furedi), the shock doctrine (Klein), and about safety and security (Foucault, Deleuze, Marcuse) and biopower (Foucault, Rose) have all discussed the use of fears and phobias in the terrain of governance.

These cultural, psychological, and political aspects of phobias often entail spatial associations or manifestations. From Simmel's description of anxieties of metropolitan life to Vidler's "warped spaces" and to "designing-out crime" policies, urban space frequently embodies real or constructed phobias. Moreover, contemporary discussions about security and resilience in cities reflect phobias of "emergencies" – be that terrorism, attacks, or disease – which besides their significant political dimensions, also shape cities and urban life.

Yet there are points where the political, cultural, and spatial dimensions of phobias and their use become intertwined. One of these points is the construction of the ghetto. The ghetto – culturally, psychologically, and spatially – simultaneously embodies phobias of crime and insecurity, of "others," of social and personal decline, as well as governance tactics related to control and real estate.

This essay explores the processes of manufacturing ghettoes and the possible uses of such construction. It does so by analysing the construction of the ghetto and the *avaton* in two inner-city neighbourhoods of Athens, Greece: Exarcheia, the *avaton* (a "no-go area"), which in popular perceptions is mainly associated with anarchists and riots, and Agios Panteleimonas, which was increasingly tagged with the "ghetto" stigma by media and policy makers from 2008 until 2012. Through these two cases we can explore how phobias concerning these neighbour-hoods are manufactured, mobilized, and manipulated by the media, governments, political groups, and real estate interests.

Introduction

Fear: such a frequently used word, yet such a difficult word to ana-lyse and explain. Fear, and particularly what is feared and what causes fear, entails numerous elements and interpretations and often changes over time. In their analysis Gold and Revill (2003, 31) identified eight elements to which fear is predominantly linked: anxiety, awe, phobia, insecurity and uncertainty, threat, hate, loathing, and trauma. Some of these have a stronger relevance to individual fears, while others reflect socio-political constructs that are reproduced or embodied by the indi-vidual. Medicine, psychology, and psychoanalysis also offer their own analyses and judgments about what fear is, what causes it, and whether it is rational or irrational. Here, I will explore place-related fears and how these fears are constructed, discussing what has been termed the "politics of fear" in relation to places.

If we accept Massumi's (1993) argument that "fear is everywhere," then in our primarily urbanized world fear and the urban become inter-twined in many ways. However, cities have for decades been a privi-leged terrain for discussing fear and the politics of fear. It has been more than a century since Simmel wrote his seminal work on the "metropolis and mental life," describing how metropolitan life of the early twenti-eth century affects residents' anxieties and mental life. Since then, the "geography of fear" has become a popular topic in many disciplines.

The 1980s, through structuralist, feminist, and everyday life approaches, brought about a change in the study of fear by focusing on its socio-political context rather than seeing it as an individual issue or problem (Pain 2009). By the 1990s, these approaches incorporated critiques about the relations of fear and governance and fear's use as a political tool (Beck; Garland 1996). In the twenty-first century, as Pain (2009) writes, "fear is back in fashion," combining fears emerging from our "risk society" with fears mobilized by the "war on terror" and its consequences.

On the local level, fear becomes a measurable feature in city statis-tics, with crime and fear of crime shaping dominant representations of neighbourhoods and being integrated within urban renewal agendas. Yet the existence of both criminality data (albeit contested) and perceptions of fear illustrates both their significance and the differences (or even divergences) between perception and data (or experience).

But what are these geographies of fear? Predominantly, they tended to refer to places (or the neighbourhoods) of crime, vice, and immorality, places of the working classes, of the marginalized (such as the ghettos of the US), or of the "different." At times they even entail public places, since being in public involves boundary crossing and occasionally increased anxieties (Sibley 1995), while encounters in public involve (or used to involve) encounters with strangers (Sennett 1977; Wilson 1990). Fear of crime and violence is commonly the root cause of these geographies of fear, yet this often obscures negative stereotypes and fear of the "other." However, more often than not, this fear does not correlated with crime statistics and has greater relevance to what or who is associated with crime and violence. This is where the politics of fear in relation to place become crucial.

Politics of Fear

The phrase "politics of fear" implies that fear becomes a governance tactic of political power or, as Furedi (2006) writes, that "politicians self-consciously manipulate people's anxieties in order to realize their objectives," which can be control, influence, remaining in power, or personal or collective gains. As a means of manipulation, the politics of fear provide a tool for controlling public discourses (Shirlow and Pain 2003) and for influencing public agendas and policies.

In our highly media-based world, the dominant media become the main means of politics of fear, influencing public discourses, perceptions, and language. As a significant feature of the mass media, Altheide (2003) argues, the politics of fear enter into news, popular culture, and entertainment, influencing our everyday lives and often "enabl[ing] simple lies to explain complex events." Accepting the "reality" of fear legitimizes the taking of action to deal with whatever is portrayed as the cause of fear.

In order to fully employ politics of fear, it is not enough to play on and strengthen people's fears; the problem, the cause of these fears, must be named. Thus, "as a tactic of power, the politics of fear not only construct, reproduce, or magnify fears, but also point to and construct the threat" (Koutrolikou 2015a). Similar to the self/other dipole, the "othering" entailed in politics of fear constructs the "others" that are to be feared (the dangerous, the violent, the criminal) (Altheide 2003; Ramoneda 2011; Shirlow and Pain 2003), defines those whose fears are heard and justified (often as deserving citizens or "normal" individuals), and constructs the boundary that distinguishes the rightful from the "others." As Shirlow and Pain argue:

> Like any word with such powerful connotations, fear is a term that is controlled via processes of legitimisation, exclusion and prescribed interpretation. It is a word which in wider political terms is licensed to those whose fears are "legitimised" by dominant political and media structures. At the same time its use is denied to those in the ranks of the "deviant" or "transgressive." (2003,15)

Politics of fear legitimize certain claims, fears, and people, while whichever "other" is perceived as a threat is targeted and excluded from public discourse, from voicing their claims, and often from spaces. Furthermore, processes of interpretation influence or construct realities, name the particular threats, and prescribe the resolution of problems.

However, as much as the politics of fear have to do with manipulating public opinion into a preferred path, this is not their only use. They may also facilitate the construction of moral orders and panics (Altheide 2003; Shirlow and Pain 2003), hinder public reactions (Furedi 2006), and facilitate the implementation of exceptional measures through evocations of a crisis (Ramoneda 2011).

The politics of fear have a double effect: they concern the everyday, the mundane, as much as they concern the exceptional. Altheide (2003) writes that the constant use of fear becomes the "normality" of everyday life. Yet the politics of fear become critical in the constructions or enhancement of crisis, in "exceptional periods." Fear magnifies the possible consequences of any crisis – which in turns magnifies fear – and thus justifies any measures that aim to resolve or avert that crisis – "exceptional measures," in Agamben's (2007) words.

The politics of fear wouldn't be so widespread if it was not a powerful political tool. It can touch upon a number of issues of global, national, or local appeal.

As Shirlow and Pain (2003) observe, the media's spread of a politics of fear influences the decisions of government and policy makers, who often fail to address the problems causing these fears. From another perspective, by targeting the "other" as the cause of fear governments and policy makers can divert attention from more difficult problems. This approach has often led to criminalization of the "other" (as has been the case with immigrants, youth, or political activists) and increased control (Garland 1996). Fears of the vulnerable, often accompanied with calls for greater security, are dealt with via policies of control and security – increased policing, surveillance, "proactive" searches – while private and state agents of control become some of the key stakeholders in the security business (Altheide 2003).

There is yet another consequence of the politics of fear. The increased security and control regime that often accompanies it may or does legitimize structural violations and injustices in the name of greater safety (Marcuse 2006; Ramoneda 2011): violations of political rights (such as to demonstrate), restrictions of freedoms (through surveillance technologies), or even acceptance of "legal" violence (as in the case of police brutality).

This safety and security apparatus becomes highly visible not only in borderlands (airports, etc.) but mostly in everyday life in cities. The urban holds a prominent position in the geographies of fear, and "defensive architecture" and "designing-out crime" programs are common practices, as is the expansive use of CCTV (England and Simon 2010; Fyfe and Bannister 1996). These architectures and practices have a strong exclusionary character, since the protection or defence they provide is structured around exclusion of whomever is deemed dangerous or undesirable (Davis 1992; Deutsche 1998; Mitchell 1995; Raco, 2003). This is the case for public spaces, the territory *par excellence* of urban fears, but it is also true of whole neighbourhoods that are characterized as "places of fear." "No-go areas," "ghettoes," "banlieues," and "critical neighbourhoods" are some of the labels often given to "neighbourhoods of fear," evoking symbolism and images from films, literature, and myths. In such neighbourhoods fear of crime (actual or perceived) is commonly intermingled with fear of the "other" (the minority, the immigrant, the poor, the different). Here, the politics of fear play an additional role: the processes of "naming" and "othering" result in stigmatization of both neighbourhoods and people (Tissot 2008; Wacquant 2008). As with other issues where a politics of fear is involved, the stigmatization of these neighbourhoods of fear leads to the exclusion of their residents and avoidance of the particular neighbourhoods, thus increasing their isolation. Again, measures proposed to deal with these places of fear focus on increased security through control and criminalization of "others," while often failing to resolve the actual problems of people and places (Tissot 2008; Wacquant 2008). And if any of these places happens to be located at a privileged position, initiatives for redevelopment accompany the measures for control, frequently resulting to gentrification or displacements (Banister et al. 2006; Smith 1996).

Ramoneda (2011) argues that "the discourse of fear breeds fear" and Ferraro that "that fear reproduces itself, or becomes a self-fulfilling prophecy (quoted in Altheide 2003). As well as the measures the state adopts to deal with fears, one may observe an increase of community initiatives of rather aggressive rationale (such as vigilante groups) whose "proactive" approach of "protecting themselves" frequently results in new fears and violence and harsher exclusionary practices. For example, after more than a decade of a politics of fear that targeted migrants and Muslims, the rise of xenophobia and far-right groups and parties in Europe especially comes as no great surprise (Azmanova 2011; Fekete 2005; Schuermans and De Maesschalck 2010).

This account of the politics of fear doesn't diminish the importance of people's fears and uncertainties, nor the impact of crime and violence on people's lives. On the contrary, it argues that the politics of fear allow governments to avoid addressing some of the key causes of these fears. There is a need to politicize fear and its politics, as Shirlow and Pain (2003) claim, in order to unveil the consequences of such politics for people and places, consequences that may lead to increased problems and more extreme situations (as recent events relating to the rise of the far right hint).

Manufacturing the *avaton*: Exarcheia, Athens

Exarcheia, a central neighbourhood of Athens, is a much loved or much hated place, depending on one's point of view. It holds a special place in the social and political history of Athens, since several significant moments in the city's history took place in or were associated with it.

As is often mentioned, Exarcheia is and feels like a neighbourhood although it's in the centre of Athens. It is a neighbourhood where many people enjoy living and spending time, and is located among several university departments, so students form a significant part of its population. Walking there, one encounters numerous small bookshops, printing houses, art shops, and some theatres, reflecting that the neighbourhood was and is a favoured area of intellectuals and artists. It is also an entertainment area, full of cafes, bars, and restaurants that appeal to the broader population of Athens. Even more so, it is and has been a political area: it has an active residents' group; many left-ist, radical, and anarchist organizations, centres, and squats; centres for migrants and several alternative initiatives; and its walls resemble a street newspaper where one can find out what is happening and what the calls for action are.

Yet the neighbourhood's political character and its association with anarchist groups and riots is a feature that causes some people to fear it and others – the police and the governments – to target it for imposing "social order." Due to its proximity to universities, Exarcheia was asso-ciated with struggles against the dictatorship in the 1970s and before (Urban Anarchy 2010). Its rise to infamy came in the early 1980s, when the flight from the centre to the suburbs was accompanied by the attrac-tion of non-mainstream lifestyles and an increasing appeal to leftist and radical political groups along with a rise in drug use (mainly heroin). The area acquired a reputation as "the centre" for heroin dealing and as a hotbed of political violence and riots, while harsh police operations (named "Virtue," 1984) targeted the "different" (eagainst.com 2013; Ios 2007). The 1990s brought more people to the area, which became the place to be for the alternative music scene in Athens, while drug use and dealing as well as political actions continued. Riot police running up and down the central part of the neighbourhood and clashes with the police became familiar sights – and still are. However, the increase in the neighbourhood's popularity was accompanied by rising house prices and increased commercialization. So while the "legend" of Exarcheia continued to be woven around political action, violence, and drug use, the area simultaneously moved into the mainstream, becom-ing a major entertainment destination. Of course, political groups, ini-tiatives, and actions continued to be strongly rooted in the area, while drug use decreased (actually, it moved further down the road).

On numerous occasions Exarcheia has been depicted as "a ghetto" (in the past) or as an *avaton* (a no-go area, more recently) in public dis-course and in the media, transforming it into a place of fear – both in terms of riots, political actions, or drug-dealing or in terms of police violence and brutality – where violence was the everyday reality of the neighbourhood. Some people accordingly avoid visiting the area (particularly on specific dates), though many others don't, as is evident from its thriving cultural, political, and night life.

In the recent history of the neighbourhood, one of the seminal moments in the construction of Exarcheia as a feared *avaton*, and one that had a significant impact on several political agendas as well as neighbourhood realities, began on 6 December 2008 when a sixteen-year-old boy was shot dead by a policeman in Exarcheia – an event that marked the following months and political mobilizations in Greece in general.[1] Within a context of generalized discontent with the government and an array of instances of police brutality (often murderous) that were rarely punished, this event triggered immediate reaction: people took to the streets almost instantly. For several weeks there were demonstrations, occupations of universities and public buildings, political discussions, acts of civil disobedience, violent clashes with the police, and a destructive urge predominantly directed – beyond the police – at state buildings and banks, large department stores, and chain stores (Koutrolikou 2015a). The centre of Athens was the main site of these actions, and Exarcheia one of the main points within that centre.

The government's initial response was to try to excuse the murder by claiming that the teenager was part of a group that attacked the police and that the policeman feared for his safety and therefore shot the boy. By projecting the neighbourhood's "image" on the boy, many media were quick to portray and condemn him as an anarchist. In terms of riot control, the state's response was increased police presence at every demonstration and in Exarcheia as well as heavy usage of tear gas and stun grenades. Needless to say, these measures triggered more violent reactions. Other violent events that took place around that time (such as acid thrown on a migrant woman syndicalist and a hand grenade thrown at a political centre in Exarcheia) further strengthened the demonstrations and political actions.

Any analysis of the events of December 2008 must grapple with the considerable complexity of these events. What is significant is that these new urban movements in Athens went beyond simple rejection and confrontation in order to enter into the collective creation and radical changes of space and of everyday life in the city (Petropoulou 2010). What also became important was the way that the state dealt with the events and how the public discourse was shaped, particularly in relation to fear and Exarcheia.

One governmental tactic was to try to distinguish the "good" protestors from the "hooded rioters" who were destroying people's property. Images of destroyed shopfronts and distraught shop owners dominated the media, as the government held forth about "citizens' property rights," about their right to their "consumer citizenship" (Bannister et al. 2006) since people wanted to go Christmas shopping, and about the internal enemy that was damaging the country's main industry, tourism. Only a couple of years later, these same arguments would be used again, against other political actions.

Another element, which would be critical for the coming months, was the legitimization of what the media termed "indignant citizens," who wanted, in common parlance, "to defend their and others' properties from the thugs who only wanted to loot and destroy." In this light, the "disobedients," the rioters, were transformed into thugs who only wanted to violate the property rights of "deserving" people – they had no respect for hard work or for people's properties and living, and "active frustrated citizens" needed to take the law into their own hands (since police were not present) to protect themselves and their fellow citizens from the thugs (Koutrolikou 2015a). Of course, what was not written in the media was that these "frustrated citizens" were often harassing and attacking random demonstrators (Bithoulkas and Xekimoglou 2008; Ios 2009), often with the protection of the local mayor or the police. What was equally omitted was the fact that many of these "frustrated citizens" were members of parastatal/fascist groups and were often tolerated by (if not, one might argue, in cooperation with) the police and certain political authorities.

The situation was soon described as an "emergency," and thus as one that would require exceptional measures in order to be resolved, even if that meant violating or jeopardizing political rights. The politics of fear have been crucial in manipulating public opinion and shaping the public discourse of the time; they strengthened the representations of "exceptional" crisis and the necessary measures. They also supported voices demanding increased control and security and a restoration of social order.

The dominant media, especially TV, were happy to continuously broadcast images of burned cars and buildings and of clashes with the police. They overplayed both the violent acts of (some of) the demonstrators and the violence of the police (the state), presenting the centre of Athens as a zone of riots and destruction. Fear was a crucial element in these representations and in political tactics employed by the state. The representations played on people's fear of encountering violence and of disruption of their daily routines. They also played on the fears of those wishing to participate in the demonstrations, since one could expect violence if one participated, from demonstrators and from the police.

The distinction between "deserving citizens" who might go to demonstrations and "hooded rioters" constructs an "other," a feared "other" that is only violent, loots and destroys, and is a threat to the state as much as to "normal citizens" and their lives. Furthermore, central areas of Athens were presented as places of fear, where violence dominated and danger was around every corner: places to be avoided. Exarcheia, of course, had a prominent part as a place of fear. As the place where the boy was murdered, as a reference point for the demonstrations, and as already associated with anarchists and other political groups and with clashes with the police, Exarcheia became the exemplar of violence and danger in the public discourse. The image of Exarcheia as *avaton* was transformed into Exarcheia as an "anarchist's ghetto," a place of fear and a threat to the normality of the city and its citizens. And as such, action needed to be taken so that "normal citizens" could reclaim these central neighbourhoods of Athens. Hence police presence in the neighbourhood increased substantially, with riot police continuously patrolling the main roads. As might be expected, this resulted in more clashes with the police in the neighbourhood and more use of tear gas in this residential area (to the point that residents were collecting signatures against the police)

In the middle of this governmental discourse of "deserving" citizens, rioters, anarchists, and neighbourhoods, another issue was brought to the forefront: that of university asylum[2] and the existence of university buildings in the centre of Athens (in particular, the architecture department of National Technical University of Athens in Exarcheia). The occupation of university buildings during December 2008 to January 2009 and the – actual or exaggerated – damages they suffered offered an "exceptional" excuse to bring this issue back on grounds that the asylum legislation was exploited by the "rioters" and the academic body could not defend its "proper" use. Questions were raised about the "usefulness" of relocating the remaining NTUA departments out of the centre, and especially out of Exarcheia, since the architecture department's location there posed a threat to both it and the area (primarily the businesses) due to the links between the academic body and leftist and radical political groups.

In essence, then, the "other" found its territory – and that territory was Exarcheia, a ghetto not in the ethnic/racial sense but as a threatening, political forbidden area, a political *avaton*. To be fair, there were some newspaper articles that wrote about the "neighbourliness" of the area as well as its "disobedients." But what was rarely presented was the intensity of the use of chemicals by the police in the area, which was something that affected residents, demonstrators, "disobedients," and shopkeepers alike.

However, in the case of Exarcheia, the dominant discourses and representations were counterbalanced, at least locally (see also Eptakoili and Maglinis 2009; Kakissis 2010; Kathimerini 2008; Xourmouzi 2009). The residents' association as well as other locals pointed out the benefits of their area and the problems caused by state and police actions, while various others wrote in defence of the area and its youth. Nevertheless, the popular consciousness – as well as the political debate – was primarily dominated by the image of Exarcheia as a place of fear.

Until recently, Exarcheia has been a heavily policed neighbourhood – and most probably it will become so again. It frequently comes up in the news or in police reports as associated with the appearance of small-scale political groups and anti-terrorist operations. However, the aftermath of the December 2008 events and the attack on Exarcheia and those associated with it seem to have had the opposite of the expected effect. The area was not discredited, and its "stigma" strengthened its symbolic political capital. Several political actions have taken place there since then, some of which became reference points in their own right (such as Navarinou Park; see Dimitriou and Koutrolikou 2011). People came together and solidarities were strengthened or even created, some lasting until now and others dissolving shortly after. Of course, everyday life and local politics are not all rosy; they include internal conflicts and struggles, disappointments, and actions that not all parties agree on. However, once again in its history, Exarcheia has become a territory of grassroots mobilizations that don't just react against violence, oppression, or fears but create something (Petropoulou 2010).

Manufacturing the "Ghetto": Agios Panteleimonas, Athens

The Context: Immigration and Integration in Athens

Before we consider the case of Agios Panteleimonas, it is useful to examine how migration affected Athens and how the state responded to migration and migrant groups. In the 1990s the majority of the migrants coming to Athens were from Balkan or Eastern European countries; other migrant ethnic groups included people from the Middle East, South East Asia (mainly Bangladeshi, Pakistani, and Phillipinese), and specific African countries (mainly Ethiopia and Nigeria). Some migrant groups have lived in Athens for a long time while others migrated to Athens after the political transformations of East and Southeast Europe

(Triandafyllidou and Maroufof 2008). Greece's shift from being a country of emigration to being one of immigration was accompanied in the 1990s by rising xenophobia that mainly targeted Southeastern and Eastern European people, particularly Albanians, who were the most numerous migrant group in Greece (reflected in the name given to this targeted xenophobia, "Albanophobia"). At the same time this xenophobia distinguished among "problematic" migrant groups (such as Albanians, Romanians, and Russians) and "good," "cultured," or "peaceful" groups (such as Filipinos, Polish, and Bangladashi).

Due to either lack of experience (as some argued and many would like to believe) or opportunism, Greece developed a policy of "non-policy" regarding immigration (Alexander 2003) and migrant integration (Baldwin-Edwards 2005). One result was that the new migrant residents of Greece were left without a safety net of social welfare (apart from the minimum) or rights and in extremely vulnerable positions of exploitation and discrimination. At the same time, the public discourse – shaped mainly by the mainstream media, particularly TV – strengthened xenophobic views and assumptions concerning migrants' responsibility for rising crime rates. However, on the everyday level, due to a pattern of "vertical differentiation"[3] (Maloutas and Karadimitriou 2001), most inner-city neighbourhoods remained quite mixed while everyday interactions were facilitated by proximity of residence and migrants' use of local services such as schools (Vaiou et al. 2007). Yet this "conviviality" didn't mean actual integration of migrants, since several of the legal, social, and cultural aspects of integration (Penninx 2004) were missing.

As is often the case, the global and the local become intertwined in many urban issues, and migration is one of them. The implementation of the EU Dublin II agreement significantly affected the number and the country of origin of migrants to Greece after 2000. It meant that a number of migrants – if they were not forcibly deported – remained trapped in transit countries (such as South European ones) (Amnesty International 2010). Around 2005, with the economy showing the first signs of post-Olympic crisis, newer migrants found themselves in substantially worse off than before, with fewer job opportunities, deteriorating living conditions, and no legal framework operating for their protection (even for asylum seekers). The two biggest Greek cities and the major ports received the majority of the newer migrants, who were forced to live in squalid conditions (in rooms/beds rented per head) or on the street and had limited chances of leaving Greece for Europe.

The "crisis of the centre of Athens," as it was presented in most accounts, occurred because of the number of migrants there; because of drugs, prostitution, and criminality; and because of the inertia of the authorities. Others, though, saw this situation as a "humanitarian crisis" (Médecins du Monde 2010) related as much to social changes as to poverty and to the reduction or lack of welfare and supportive measures (Maloutas 2011).

The Case of Agios Panteleimonas

Until recently (2005–7) Agios Panteleimonas was an ordinary neighbourhood of the Municipality of Athens named after the church located in its main square. As with many inner-city neighbourhoods, it faced the flight of a number of residents to the suburbs, following which the flats were rented (or occasionally owned) by migrant residents that arrived in Greece in the 1990s. Like several other inner-city neighbourhoods of Athens, Agios Panteleimonas has a significant percentage of migrant residents (with or without papers) who are accommodated via the vertical social differentiation pattern that characterizes most of Athens' neighbourhoods. At the same time, for the last ten or fifteen years it has been considered a deprived area facing a number of problems, such as increased illegal sex work (it borders one of the informally established prostitution areas in Athens), organized criminal activity often expressed through fights between rival groups, and petty crime.

Agios Panteleimonas was affected by the Dublin II agreement and the post-Olympic economic downturn. An increased number of newer migrants and refugees (mainly from Afganistan, but also from some Arab countries) moved into the area, some living in rooms of flats rented per head, others homeless and occasionally finding shelter around the homonymous church in the middle of the square. While undoubtedly the area was facing problems, not until 2006 or 2007 did it, and other inner-city areas, begin to enter public discourse.

While the term "ghetto" was rarely associated with inner-city neighbourhoods of Athens (apart from occasionally for Exarcheia), and when it was applied it was usually to warn of a future possibility, from 2007 the term began to be frequently used to describe a particular neighbourhood of the commercial centre, Gerani. This characterization was not based solely on the presence of migrants or minorities; it was more broadly based, incorporating the presence also of homeless people, drug-addicts, and sex workers in the area (Haris 2008; Trivoli 2007). The dominant public discourse was quick to pick up on the "ghetto" of Athens, which term had by 2008 come to be applied to several inner-city neighbourhoods, with Gerani being the focus of the ghetto discourse in Athens.[4]

At the same time, in 2008 Agios Panteleimonas came strongly into the media spotlight, with the dominant TV channels devotedly presenting disenchanted residents complaining about their area. The main complaints were the rise of criminality (which they associated with migrants), cleanliness (associated with the number of migrants living in the flats or on the streets), and becoming "foreigners in our neighbourhood" – obviously referring to the migrants residing in the area. Thus this story of Agios Panteleimonas became a popular feature of newspaper stories and was given a substantial portion of precious TV airtime. It wasn't long before the aired views as well as the public discourse included Agios Panteleimonas in the ghettoes of Athens, giving further support to the publicized views. Simultaneously, through the ghetto discourse and its symbolic associations,[5] the area was presented as a highly dangerous one with flourishing street and house crime, where residents were quickly selling their flats and moving away – an area where fear ruled. Moreover, the discourse named *the* problem of this and other areas as the migrants, who were represented as "the root of all evils" and as "too numerous" in these areas.

However, there is another side to this story. Undoubtedly, the neighbourhood was (and is) facing several problems, and some of the complaints came from residents unhappy with what was going on in the neighbourhood. Yet several of the broadcasted voices – most notably the members of the "Residents' Committee of Agios Panteleimonas and Plateia Attikis" – belonged to people (residents or not) strongly associated with the far right (especially with the fascist political party Golden Dawn). Yet, this aspect of the story, and the role Golden Dawn played in mobilizing residents and others, was strongly denied until some years later, when the web of such associations became evident (see Infowar 2013; JungleReport 2010; Kandylis and Kavoulakos 2011).

As mentioned above, the events of December 2008 partly legitimized in public discourse the "right" of residents to defend their areas against perceived threats (anarchists, migrants, "others"). Thus mobilizations of "indignant citizens" in the area (influenced or organized by the far right) were seen as defending "their" area from threats. One such mobilization resulted in the closure of playground in the square so that migrant children wouldn't play there, reportedly because the residents involved in the mobilization were afraid of diseases that migrant children allegedly were carrying (Dama 2009). Their rationale was that since migrant children were too numerous and as a result overcrowded the playground, leaving no room for other children (and, as it was presented, since their – mainly Muslim – mothers were also occupying the space and were "dirty"), then neither should migrant children be able to play there. In this case, there were counter-mobilizations trying to open the playground as well as clashes with the police and with the far-right, but in the end the playground remained closed for a long time.

The domination in the media of the ghetto discourse regarding inner-city neighbourhoods, together with the publicity given to particular views from Agios Panteleimonas and the privileged media presence of populist-right (and anti-migrant) party representatives, resulted in the legitimization of a far-right anti-migrant discourse and its proposed measures and in defining migrants as *the* problem of inner-city "ghetto" neighbourhoods.

The legitimization of this racist and far-right discourse also partly legitimized far-right practices – which often involved violence against migrants. The police, the media, and the broader rise of the far right further supported the (alleged) "residents' groups" and this legitimization. And the success and legitimization of "residents' groups" emboldened them to take further actions against migrants. "The far right saw the square of Agio Panteleimonas as a clear victory and, encouraged by the relatively friendly dominant discourse, often used the square for rallies and speeches and tried to expand its "reclaimed territory" to nearby squares ("Battle of Attica Square" 2010)" (Koutrolikou 2015b; see also the documentary "Battle of Attica Square" 2010). Its darker side involved harassment and violence against (mainly visible) migrants and those that "looked different," while those who disagreed with its position were harassed out of the square. Its power in the area was further reflected in the votes it received in the local election (when the ultra-far-right party elected a representative in the Council of Athens), which further enhanced its perception of victory.[6] Leftist and anarchist groups attempted to counter-mobilize and challenge the unfolding situation, albeit initially with limited success.

Beginning in 2010, yet another aspect of the story (until then circulating as a rumour) began to emerge: the role of real estate and the fear that motivated a change of neighbourhood. A TV documentary (Vax-evanis 2010) and some articles picked up this aspect of the story, and soon it was repeated on far-right blogs, viewed as another displacement of the "rightful" residents.

At this point the tide shifted slightly: the rise of the far right and of Golden Dawn in mainstream politics started to create frictions in the political arena, and the dominant discourse began to present more negative aspects of the far right (albeit without reversing the anti-migrant discourse). International criticism was influential here, but another turning point was a pogrom against (racialized) migrants that took place in May 2011 as an act of revenge for the murder of a Greek man in a nearby area; this resulted in the death of a Bangladeshi man and injuries to hundreds of others.

This account of the Agio Panteleimonas neighbourhood, which is by no means a detailed one, reveals certain aspects of the interplay among fear and places. The point is not to examine whether a neighbourhood is technically a ghetto or not, but to note that its construction as a ghetto, as a place of fear, is substantially influenced by discourses and the politics of fear. These discourses named *the* problem – the migrant "other" – legitimized far-right views and voices, stigmatized the area further, and facilitated the violence of local vigilantism while pushing for zero-tolerance policies of greater securitization. This account does not argue that Agios Panteleimonas has no problems; it has quite a few, and significant ones, such as poverty, lack of services, and organized crime. However, the adopted politics and discourses of fear – which resulted in multilayered geographies of fear – seem to have had the adverse effect of increasing violence without doing anything for the area's problems.

Conclusion

The characterization of neighbourhoods and areas as "places of fear" resonates with a discussion about the politics of fear, its influence on public discourse, and its intentional or unintentional consequences. Despite their differences, the two cases presented in this paper reflect how fear and its politics were spatially manifested and how the adoption of a discourse and a politics of fear by the dominant media affected the two areas. A discourse and politics of fear constructed realities about these neighbourhoods in the public mind and targeted the particular "others" that were deemed threatening.

As some scholars argued, the politics of fear affect people's everyday lives and often become a mundane everyday feature (Altheide 2003). This is one dimension, especially regarding the case of Agios Pante-leimonas. However, what becomes more evident through both cases is the relation of the politics of fear to crises and the legitimization of "exceptional circumstances" that tend to become the norm rather than the exception (Agamben 2007). In the name of such "exceptional circumstances" an array of measures and responses become justified, measures that, as Ramoneda (2011) noted, tend to target or exclude people, limit certain rights (especially civil ones), and fast-track rede-velopment initiatives.

Moreover, diverting attention to issues of fear and security that are associated with the "places of fear" and their stigmatization obscures the need for greater transformations or reforms, such as dealing with poverty, with rights violations, with issues of justice – matters that demand different approaches than simply securitization (Minton 2008). This view echoes Minton's (2008, 2) observations in research about the "spiralling of fear and distrust in 21st century Britain," where she found that "increasing levels of fear are the consequence of growing visible physical inequality and segregation in the environ-ment," that societies with greater wealth disparities present greater levels of fear, and that policies and initiatives that address the symp-toms through increased security in fact fail "to lower crime and … to reassure people, actually making them more scared and fuelling the cycle of fear further."

As mentioned before, fear breeds fear and can become a self-fulfilling prophecy. The discourses and politics of fear, together with the local and broader context, in the case of Agios Panteleimonas facilitated the development of a fertile ground for the rise of far-right groups and their anti-migrant violence. Yet on certain occasions the same authorities that "play" with politics of fear seemed to have become uncomfortable or even frightened by its unexpected consequences and the explosive-ness of the associated political-social situations.

Pain (2009) argues that the politics as well as the geographies of fear should not only focus on the discursive or top-down aspects of it, but also account for the agency and resistance that fear might initiate. The two cases discussed in this chapter illustrate two different instances where local agency developed and acted, or as some might argue, behaved as some form of social movement (Kandylis and Kavoulakos 2011). However, as with any community mobilization, the actions of resistance, especially those influenced by fear, do not necessarily comply with the dictates of social justice.

I want to reiterate that this discussion of the politics of fear and its spatialization in no way diminishes the very real issues of crime or violence that afflict people and areas, nor does it claim that the neighbourhoods discussed here are problem-free and that people's fears about them are irrational. Rather, I have explored how politics of fear are incorporated into governance tactics and how they affect people and places. This politicization of the discourses and politics of fear might reveal hidden factors about decisions taken as well as the – intentionally or not – obscured issues that should be addressed but that require an approach beyond enhancing security.

NOTES

1 For accounts of the events of December 2008 see Urban Anarchy 2010, Economides and Monastiriotis 2009, Bratsis 2010, Mentinis 2010, and Memos 2010.

2 The university "asylum" legislation was put in place in order to safeguard freedom of speech and meant that the police or military could not enter the university unless the Council gave its permission to do so (in exceptional circumstances). This legislation was recently amended and significantly weakened.

3 Vertical differentiation, briefly, means that socio-economic differences are reflected in living space that is vertically stratified: the richest live in flats at the top of building and the poorer (commonly newer migrants) occupy the lower floors or basements. This contrasts with horizontal spatial segregation as a marker of socio-economic differentiation.

4 See also (in Greek) Kampilis 2009, Ismailidou 2010, Katsounaki 2010, Karanikas et al. 2010, and Karanatsi 2010.

5 These symbolic associations with the ghetto are often shaped by (mainly American) films and literature and some research about black urban ghettos, which are represented as having high rates of violent and other crime, of dereliction, of social problems, and of immorality. While several scholarly works have challenged such representations and beliefs, images and words greatly influence people's views – especially since few (if any) have been there.

6 Rumours and comments on far-right blogs occasionally compared Agio Panteleimonas with Exarcheia, characterizing the "victorious reclaiming" of Agio Panteleimonas as "their own Exarcheia."

REFERENCES

Agamben, Giorgio. 2007 [2003]. *State of Exception*. Trans. M. Oikonomidou. Athens: Patakis.

Alexander, M. 2003. "Local Policies toward Migrants as an Expression of Host-Stranger Relations: A Proposed Typology." *Journal of Ethnic and Migration Studies* 29 (3): 411–30. http://dx.doi.org/10.1080/13691830305610.

Altheide, David. 2003. "Notes towards a Politics of Fear." *Journal for Crime, Conflict and the Media* 1 (1): 37–54.

Amnesty International. 2010, March. *The Dublin II Trap: Transfers of Asylum Seekers to Greece*. London: Amnesty International.

Atkinson, Rowland. 2003. "Domestication by Cappuccino or a Revenge on Urban Space? Control and Empowerment in the Management of Public Spaces." *Urban Studies (Edinburgh, Scotland)* 40 (9): 1829–43. http://dx.doi.org/10.1080/0042098032000106627.

Azmanova, A. 2011. "Crisis – What Crisis?" *OpenDemocracy*, 9 May.

Baldwin-Edward, Martin. 2005. *The Integration of Immigrants in Athens: Developing Indicators and Statistical Measures* (Pre-final version). Athens: Mediterranean Migration Observatory, Panteion University Athens.

Bannister, Jon, Nicholas Fyfe, and Ade Kearns. 2006. "Respectable or Respectful? (In)civility and the City." *Urban Studies (Edinburgh, Scotland)* 43 (5–6): 919–37. http://dx.doi.org/10.1080/00420980600676337.

Bratsis, Peter. 2010. "Legitimation Crisis and the Greek Explosion." *International Journal of Urban and Regional Research* 34 (1): 190–6. http://dx.doi.org/10.1111/j.1468-2427.2010.00947.x.

Bythoulkas, D., and Hekimoglou, A. 2008. "Hood-Wearers, Golden Dawners and Indignant Citizens." *Vima*, December 14. http://www.tovima.gr/politics/article/?aid=246573.

Dama, Georgia. 2009. "Agios Panteleimonas Acharnon: The Corner of Terror and Racism." *Eleutherotypia*, 27 May (in Greek). http://www.enet.gr/?i=news.el.article&id=48314.

Davis, Mike. 1992. *City of Quartz: Excavating the Future in Los Angeles*. New York: Vintage.

Deutsche, Rosalyn. 1998. *Evictions: Art and Spatial Politics*. Cambridge, MA: MIT Press.

eagainst.com. 2013. "35 Years Siege, 'Virtue' and Police Violence." http://eagainst.com/articles/eksarxeia/.

Economides, Stavros, and Vassilis Monastiriotis, eds. 2009. *The Return of Street Politics? Essays on the December Riots in Greece*. The Hellenic Observatory. London: London School of Economics and Political Sciences.

England, Marcia R., and Simon Stephanie. 2010. "Scary Cities: Urban Geographies of Fear, Difference and Belonging." Editorial. *Social & Cultural Geography* 11 (3): 201–7. http://dx.doi.org/10.1080/14649361003650722.

Fekete, Liz. 2005. "Immigration, Integration and the Politics of Fear." *IRR European Race Bulletin* 52 (Summer): 1–14.

Furedi, Frank. 2004. "The Politics of Fear." *Spiked*, 28 October.

– 2006. "Living in Fear, Lost for Words." *Age* 23 (January).

Fyfe, Nicholas, and Jon Bannister. 1996. "City Watching: Closed Circuit Television Surveillance in Public Spaces." *Area* 28: 37–46.

Garland, D. 1996. "The Limits of the Sovereign State: Strategies of Crime Control in Contemporary Society." *British Journal of Criminology* 36 (4): 445–71. http://dx.doi.org/10.1093/oxfordjournals.bjc.a014105.

Eptakoili G. and Maglinis E.. 2009. "Exarcheia Are Still Alive," *Kathimerini*, 15 February (in Greek).

Gold, J.R., and G. Revill. 2003. "Exploring Landscapes of Fear: Marginality, Spectacle and Surveillance." *Capital and Class* 27 (2): 27–50. http://dx.doi.org/10.1177/030981680308000104.

Haris, Giannis. 2008. "Our Own Ghettoisation." *Ta Nea*, 26 July (in Greek). http://yannisharis.blogspot.com/2008/07/blog-post_27.html).

Herbert, Steve, and Elisabeth Brown. 2006. "Conceptions of Space and Crime in the Punitive Neoliberal City." *Antipode* 38 (4): 755–77. http://dx.doi.org/10.1111/j.1467-8330.2006.00475.x.

Infowar. 2013. "When the Channels Were Orchestrating the Phenomenon Agios Panteleimonas" (in Greek). http://info-war.gr/όταν-τα-κανάλια-έστηναν-το-φαινόμενο-α/.

Ioanna, Kakissis. 2010, 19 May. Rebels Hope New Austerity Rekindles Spirit of Greece's Activist Heart. *New York Times*.

Ios. 2007. "Exarcheia 1984–2007: The Story of a Pseudo State" (in Greek). http://archive.enet.gr/ online/online_print?id=42797740.

Ismailidou, Elli. 2010. "They Push Us towards Civil War." *To Vima*, 24 October (in Greek). http://www.tovima.gr/politics/article/?aid=362720.

Kampilis, Takis. 2009. "Does Athens Have Its Won Ghetto?" *Kathimerini*, 31 January (in Greek). http://news.kathimerini.gr/4dcgi/_w_articles_columns_2_31/01/2009_301591.

Karanatsi, Elena. 2010. "The Mapping of Deprivation." *Kathimerini*, 9 February (in Greek). http://www.kathimerini.gr/4dcgi/_w_articles_ell_1_09/02/2010_390099.

Karanikas, Xaris, Giannis Papadopoulos, and Katerina Voutsina. 2010. "Athens Zero Time." *Ta Nea*, 25 October (in Greek). http://www.tanea.gr/ellada/article/?aid=4600773.

Kathimerini. 2008. "Exarcheia: The Neighbourhood behind the Myth." 28 December (in Greek).

Katsounaki, Maria. 2010. "Dangerous Signs of Ghettoisation in Athens." *Kathimerini*, 5 September (in Greek). http://www.kathimerini.gr/4dcgi/_w_articles_ell_2_05/09/2010_413678.

Koutrolikou, P. 2015a. "Governmentalities of Urban Crises in Inner-City Athens, Greece." *Antipode*. http://onlinelibrary.wiley.com/doi/10.1111/anti.12163/abstract.

– 2015b. "Socio-spatial Stigmatization and Its 'Incorporation' in the Centre of Athens, Greece." *CITY* 19 (4): 510–21.

Xourmouzi, Lena. 2009. "Exarcheia: The Neighbourhood That Talks." *Athens Voice* 284: 15.

Maloutas, Thomas, George Kandylis, and Michalis Petrou, eds. 2011. *The Centre of Athens as (New) Political Stake*. Athens: EKKE.

Maloutas, Thomas, and Nikos Karadimitriou. 2001. "Vertical Social Differentiation in Athens: Alternative or Complement to Community Segregation?" *International Journal of Urban and Regional Research* 25 (4): 699–716. http://dx.doi.org/10.1111/1468-2427.00340.

Marcuse, Peter. 2006. "Security or Safety in Cities? The Threat of Terrorism after 9/11." *International Journal of Urban and Regional Research* 30 (4): 919–29. http://dx.doi.org/10.1111/j.1468-2427.2006.00700.x.

Massumi, Brian, ed. 1993. *Politics of Everyday Fear*. Minneapolis: University of Minnesota Press.

Médecins du Monde. 2010. "Athens, a City in a Humanitarian Crisis." Press release.

Memos, Christos. 2010. "Neoliberalism, Identification Process and the Dialectics of Crisis." *International Journal of Urban and Regional Research* 34 (1): 210–6. http://dx.doi.org/10.1111/j.1468-2427.2010.00950.x.

Mentinis, Mihalis. 2010. "Remember Remember the 6th of December ... A Rebellion or the Constituting Moment of a Radical Morphoma?" *International Journal of Urban and Regional Research* 34 (1): 197–202. http://dx.doi.org/10.1111/j.1468-2427.2010.00948.x.

Minton, Anna. 2008. "Why Are Fear and Distrust Spiralling in Twenty-First Century Britain?" *Viewpoint (The Social Evils Series)*. Joseph Rowntree Foundation. http://www.jrf.org.uk/publications/why-are-fear-and-distrust-spiralling-twenty-first-century-britain.

Mitchell, Don. 1995. "The End of Public Space? People's Park, Definitions of the Public, and Democracy." *Annals of the Association of American Geographers* 85: 108–33.

Pain, Rachel. 2009. "Globalized Fear? Towards an Emotional
   Geopolitics." *Progress in Human Geography* 33 (4): 466–86. http://dx.doi.
   org/10.1177/0309132508104994.

Penninx, Rinus. 2004 "Integration of Migrants: Economic, Social, Cultural
   and Political Dimensions." Background paper for the European Population
   Forum, Geneva.

Petropoulou, Chryssanthi. 2010. "From the December Youth Uprising to the
   Rebirth of Urban Social Movements: A Space-Time Approach." *International
   Journal of Urban and Regional Research* 34 (1): 217–24. http://dx.doi.
   org/10.1111/j.1468-2427.2010.00951.x.

Raco, Mike. 2003. "Remaking Place and Securitising Space: Urban
   Regeneration and the Strategies, Tactics and Practices of Policing in the
   UK." *Urban Studies (Edinburgh, Scotland)* 40 (9): 1869–87. http://dx.doi.org/
   10.1080/0042098032000106645.

Ramoneda, Josep. 2011. "Politics of Fear: A Frightened Left." *Open Democracy*,
   11th May. http://www.opendemocracy.net/josep-ramoneda/politics-of-
   fear-frightened-left (accessed 31 July 2011).

JungleReport, 2010. "Οι χρυσαυγανακτισμένοι πολίτες του Αγίου
   Παντελεήμονα και οι εισθέσεις στους Συριζαίους." http://jungle-report.
   blogspot.com/2010/10/blog-post_27.html.

Schuermans, Nick, and Filip De Maesschalck. 2010. "Fear of Crime as a
   Political Weapon: Explaining the Rise of Extreme-Right Politics in the
   Flemish Countryside." *Social & Cultural Geography* 11 (3): 247–62. http://
   dx.doi.org/10.1080/14649361003637190.

Sennett, R. 1977. *The Fall of Public Man*. Cambridge: Cambridge University Press.

Shirlow, P., and Rachel Pain. 2003. "The Geographies and Politics of
   Fear." Special issue. *Capital and Class* 27 (2): 15–26. http://dx.doi.
   org/10.1177/030981680308000103.

Sibley, David. 1995. *Geographies of Exclusion*. London: Routledge. http://
   dx.doi.org/10.4324/9780203430545.

Simmel, Georg. 1980. "The Metropolis and Mental Life." In *Urban Place and
   Process*, ed. I. Press and M.E. Smith, 19–30. New York: Macmillan.

Smith, Neil. 1996. *The New Urban Frontier: Gentrification and the Revanchist City*.
   New York: Routledge.

Stelios, Elliniadis. 2009. "Exarcheia of Music Schools and Ideas."
   Eleutherotypia, 15 November (in Greek).

"The Battle of Attika Square." 2010. Documentary. TV 2 Norway. http://
   www.youtube.com/watch?v=gPl9PW7ONIQ.

Tissot, Sylvie. 2008. "French Suburbs: A New Problem or a New Approach to
   Social Exclusion?" Center for European Studies Working Paper Series no. 160.

Triandafyllidou, Anna, and Michaela Maroufof. 2008. Immigration towards Greece at the Eve of the 21st Century: A Critical Assessment. Unpublished project report. Athens: Hellenic Foundation for European and Foreign Policy.

Trivoli, Despoina. 2007. "Euripidou and Around: The New Ghetto of Athens." *LIFO*, 4 October (in Greek). http://www.lifo.gr/mag/features/241.

Urban Anarchy. 2010. "Athens, Unfortified City: Spatial Analysis of December's 2008 Insurgence" (in Greek). www.urbananarchy.gr.

Vaiou, Dina (scientific coordinator) et al. 2007. *Intersecting Everyday Lives and Space-Time Transformations in the City: Migrant and Local Women in the Neighbourhoods of Athens*. Final report (in Greek). Athens: National Technical University of Athens

Vaxevanis, Kostas. 2010, November. "Businesses Cries and Whispers in Agio Panteleimona." Documentary. NET Channel 8 (in Greek). http://www.koutipandoras.gr/?p=1554.

Vaiou, Dina (scientific coordinator). 2007. "Intersecting Everyday Lives and Space-Time Transformations in the City: Migrant and Local Women in the Neighbourhoods of Athens." Final report (in Greek), PYTHAGORAS II, 2005–7.

Wacquant, Loic. 2008. *Urban Outcasts: A Comparative Sociology of Advanced Marginality*. Cambridge: Polity Press.

Wilson, E. 1990. *The Sphinx in the City*. Berkeley: University of California Press.

Afterword:
Opposing Phobias Going Forward

HISHAM M. RAMADAN AND JEFF SHANTZ

Phobic productions have become more pervasive in modern societies, notably the United States and Canada in the present period. Fear
has been detached from specific events or occurrences, the domain of
most moral panics for example, to become a generalized sentiment.
The phobias take on a life of their own, characterizing social contexts
more broadly. The expressions of fear outlive and outdistance the
events around which they were constructed. While fear of the objects
of moral panics, the so-called folk devils (such as hippies, homeless
youth, punks, or ravers), tends to subside with the passing of legislation targeting these groups, within phobic mobilizations the fear only
increases, and suspicion of the targeted group is inflamed, with the
passage of laws and policies.

Phobia comes to play a central part in social framing processes. As
media sociologist Graham Knight suggests, generalized fear becomes
"a dominant resource in the construction of frames for public discourse
and, by implication, private life" (2003, n.p). For Knight, fear can be
universalized effectively as an axis of identification. It "cuts across different objects and fields, and provides a convenient way to articulate
a common experience and identity at a time when conventional forms
of social commonality seem to be in retreat" (2003, n.p.). Phobic constructions step in to fill the gaps in the anonymous, detached conditions of what might be called *Gesellschaft* societies. Where communal,
face-to-face, intimate, and familiar relations have receded or disappeared and common ideas have been eclipsed, phobic discourses, particularly given broad circulation through media and political venues
and fora, provide a means of connection, of identity. The phobic other
can provide a powerful focus of opposition, and thus generates social

cohesion. This gives phobic constructions their power and makes them particularly dangerous.

The deployment of phobias must, at the same time, be situated within the context of specific political frameworks in the contemporary period. In particular, the connection of phobic productions to the New Right or neoliberal ideologies is relevant and is identified in each of the previous chapters in various ways. The period of economic crisis and political austerity has been suited to the circulation of phobic productions. It is perhaps particularly relevant when analysing social life in the North American political context. As Knight suggests:

> The neo-liberal aspect of this ideology has actively promoted the weakening of the state's willingness and capacity to meet social demands at the same time that it has strengthened the power of market forces over people's lives. Neo-liberalism has generated new forms of insecurity, marginality and precariousness that reinforce an individualized, privatized sense of responsibility for the management of risk, and undermine the micro-solidarities that tied people to family, community, and work. At the same time, the neo-conservative side of New Right ideology has capitalized on these fears and uncertainties to promote more coercive forms of social control as the panacea for solving a whole range of social problems. (2003, n.p.)

Here the sense of anxiety, disconnection, and fear associated with isolation in the modern context is heightened or reinforced through phobic productions (that reflect social uncertainty and anxiety in the first place). At the same time the phobic productions provide the justification for a range of punitive and repressive social responses (particularly via mechanisms of the state).

Here also the dual thrusts of neoliberal politics articulate through phobic productions. As Furedi (1997) has suggested, cultures of fear are often associated with a morality of lowered expectations. This is precisely the morality of neoliberal austerity and the assertion by political and economic elites that we all must sacrifice and be satisfied with less.

Reflections

Whether phobias, as social phenomena, are generated purposefully or inadvertently, numerous factors contribute to their creation and to public responses. These factors include media practices, racism, the state's official polices, social stratification, and various class struggles for domination.

The accounts in this collection highlight the role of media in phobic constructions. Corporate mass media's focus on the drama and turmoil of current affairs, as narrative hook, is a typically effective means of audience capture and profit maximization. The villain/victim narrative allows for an individualization of blame and sets up punitive law–and-order approaches to "stop the bad guys." Hisham Ramadan discusses the negative impact of media on various groups throughout history, particularly Muslims, which intensified after the 9/11 tragedy, and Melissa Ames points out that post 9/11 media created inadvertent censorship by banning all negative portrayals of the tragedy and simultaneously attempting to remedy the negative effect of tragedy. Indeed, media in contemporary societies have become malleable tools, lending themselves to construction or distraction as the occasion warrants.

This point applies not only to corporate mass media, which has received most of the attention, but to the alternative media of political actors as well. As Jeff Shantz outlines, conservative phobia producers deploy their own media to stir popular fears related to specific groups, ideologies, or identities. At the same time social movements wield their own media sources to defend targeted groups and contest phobic productions.

Similarly, the writings in this collection show that it is not solely political decision makers within accepted positions of authority who drive phobic agendas. In various cases phobic entrepreneurs within the general public (though often tied to public institutions as advisors, commentators, pundits, think tank leaders, or writers, for example) are the most active in mobilizing phobic productions. Future research might do well to examine the actions of these phobic entrepreneurs, including those in the psy disciplines, who generate and disseminate phobic constructs, often for personal gain.

In the present context, states routinely employ media to control and direct the collective moral consciousness of a society. Amir Mirfakhraie explains that states, in order to promote their sponsored ideology, may intentionally create phobias towards the "other." Here, phobia is a tool used to maintain the desired identity of the state. To achieve this objective, the state employs traditional instruments as well as the educational system to demonize the "other," praise the dominate group of the society, and direct the public to accept the state-sponsored ideologies as the norm. Race, religion, and ethnicity might be used to differentiate and to claim superiority of the dominant group. The "other" – that is, the feared or distrusted – is portrayed as in dreadful need of help and leadership.

As Heidi Rimke points out, this construction of a need for help is typically expressed in discourses of pathology and medicalization. Commonly psy discourses, and associated practices of therapy, are deployed against members of targeted groups. This corresponds with the construction of social phobia, as the psychologized are viewed as not only different but requiring treatment (detainment, restraint, conditioning, or pharmacology) in order to overcome their malady – which may simply be political or social opposition to specific instituted authorities.

Although Mirfakhraie's research addresses only the Iranian case, the similarities to the international community are unmistakable. Numerous Western democracies, driven by fear of a competing culture, social class, or religion – an "other" – directly or indirectly attempt to eliminate such competition. Ramadan outlines how in European states, through the European Court of Human Rights, legislation, and governmental policies, state-defined identity is officially endorsed. Similarly in Canada, as Shantz illustrates, the government has enacted anti-terrorism legislation that is targeted against some of the most vulnerable; to this it has added a questionable protection of the public against crimes already prohibited, for terrorism was a criminal offence in Canadian criminal law prior to enactment of the Anti-Terrorism Act. Consider the law of conspiracy, which predated that act: it claims global jurisdiction to Canada by prohibiting conspiracy regardless of location of the crime, that is, whether the conspirators commit the crime in or outside Canada. Thus if two or more individuals conspire to kill a Canadian while they are in Afghanistan, China, Africa, or anywhere else, they are liable and can be prosecuted before the Canadian courts notwithstanding the existence of the new anti-terrorism law. Therefore no new law was necessary to combat acts of terrorism, and the newly revised anti-terror laws were clearly oriented towards something other than the prevention of terrorism.

Moreover, phobia towards the "other" reaches far beyond mere stigmatization of the "other." Michael Ma and Davina Bhandar clarify the point that phobia regarding the "other" has driven Canada to pass legislation, such as the recently enacted refugee law, that encroaches upon the right to life and equal dignity, rendering these dependent on the acceptance of asylum seekers' applications.

Johann Pautz further discusses how in the United States phobia can be used as a majority tool to maintain dominance and is a defensive mechanism against the cultural competition of the minority, which is perceived to be "a threat to cultural homogeneity and even an agent of cultural decline." Accordingly, political forces create phobia, based on the questionable "moral majority" or moral norm, to achieve their political agenda. To vindicate their actions morally, they paint their social agenda with glossy socially appealing notions such as "the will of the people" or "the dictates of 'history' or 'nature.'" The aim of this process is not simply to force-feed the entire population certain values, but also to eliminate and demonize the opposition.

In the case of non-government-sponsored phobia, as Penny Koutrolikou points out, the infusion of fear into the public consciousness prompts decision makers to address the causes of phobia. The response varies from criminalization of the "other" to attempts to contain the threat of the "other." In Greece, phobia creators succeeded in manipulating public opinion, resulting in acceptance of the exceptional measures taken by the government. The "other," immigrants, were subject to stigmatization that led to the creation of immigrants' neighbourhoods of fear, no-go areas. This is an obvious example of clashes between social classes, the dominant and the "other." In this case the clash was not only ideological but took on physical form, played out in clashes between anti-riot police and the "other" when that "other" protested criminalization of their status in society.

Alternatively, as Dmitry Shlapentokh suggests, some states have adopted non-confrontational approaches to containing the "other," including assimilation, "multiculturalism," and fostering of nationalism. These approaches are, however, neither universally successful nor fair. In Russia, they have led to disenfranchisement of a large sector of the population and radicalization of opinion against the "other." And they are not fair because they ignore the "other's" right to maintain his or her identity with respect and dignity. Assimilationism and nationalism – melting pot notions – are at best an attempt to erase the identity of the other and replace it with the dominant group's identity. And although multiculturalism seems satisfactory in theory, its results, at least in Canada, have not been unproblematic. Both Ramadan and Ma and Bhandar have shown that politicians demonstrated intolerance towards Muslims in Ontario and racism in Quebec; in addition, they created refugee legislation that aimed to penalize illegal entry of asylum seekers. While this seems natural and straightforward at face value, in reality it affects mostly Asians. These are only a few examples of the many intolerances shown the "other." Multiculturalism should not be the rug under which we hide our intolerance.

Finally, the economic impact of phobia should not be underestimated. As Shantz points out, the increase in government spending on phobia-related issues, such as on the war on terror, necessarily involves serious cuts to social services. Koutrolikou documents how phobia leads to the neighbourhoods of the "others" becoming less desirable, resulting in a major economic burden to residents and creating an area of fear. These facts are sufficient to trigger rigorous academic examination of phobia's economic impact on the society in which it is deployed. Truly, phobia hurts everyone, not only the "other."

Thinking Forward

Until recently, sociologists have paid relatively little attention to the place of emotions in social life. This has changed in the last decade, but there is much work to do in examining contemporary processes by which emotions are constructed and deployed. Emotional emphases are key features of phobic mobilizations.

While fear as a social impulse may have positive outcomes, such as ensuring the survival of individuals, groups, or communities, the social phobia phenomena is mostly harmful. More studies are needed to examine the impact of phobia on the fundamental human and political rights of the "other," including phobia-driven policies, legislation, executive actions, and court decisions. As a start, it is time to rethink the Anti-Terrorism Act and refugee law from a public policy point of view. The Supreme Court of Canada's decisions should not be assumed to reflect the collective moral conscious of Canadian society at large. For instance, the Supreme Court, in *R. v. Khawaja*, recently endorsed the Anti-Terrorism Act notwithstanding its violations to the Canadian Charter of Rights and Freedoms. The federal legislature has in the past had to intervene to reinstate socially sanctioned moral judgments when Supreme Court decisions seemed unsatisfactory to it, as in the recent revision of sex work laws by the Conservative government to reimpose punitive policies where the Supreme Court had called for less punitive laws.

Media as a major player in creating or enhancing phobias should also be subject to extensive academic examination. Further studies are required to investigate the media's positive and negative effects on public and government actions. This necessarily raises the question: What limits, if any, should be imposed on freedom of speech, especially when such freedom is used/abused to promote phobia, which in turn harms the vulnerable "other"? We have seen the law prohibit hate speech but tolerate phobic creations although the negative outcomes are the same. What public and moral policies, if any, justify such a distinction?

Gary Kinsman (2010) has suggested that there is a need to further examine the social processes of phobic productions in shifting formations of racialization and class. While his focus has been local, within a Canadian context, the current collection helps to move this conversation forward, incorporating global processes and concerns. Further studies might pursue specifically settlerist forms of phobic construction within settler societies like Canada and the United States. This research could take a historical approach to transformations of phobic discourses as part of white settler colonialism.

Future research should also develop the critique of phobias from within the various psy disciplines. It has been suggested that the conversion of fear into phobia or social anxiety has been effected through the so-called therapeutic revolution, including the spread of popular psychology and self-help programming (Bourke 2005). Much work still needs to be done to challenge both the validity of phobic assessments or diagnoses within psy disciplines and the claims to scientific veracity of what are largely political assertions. Even more must there be challenges to the deployment of psy, or biological, discourses to explain what are socially constructed phenomena. Recommendations must shift from the individual pathologization within phobic expressions to address social causes and consequences. Rimke's work in this volume provides a good framework for such critical efforts.

Future work should also focus extensively on the various emerging community mobilizations against phobic constructions in specific contexts. These efforts might further examine the critical responses to phobic discourses and practices, and the ways in which community advocacy groups challenge notions of contamination or epidemic in relation to specific populations as well as the explicit use of phobia-producing expressions of power. Often movements are too caught up in the day-to-day concerns of advocacy work or community defence to analyse properly the role of discursive practices, such as phobic discourses, in constructing the political frames they confront, though some have begun to (e.g., the No One Is Illegal networks, the Ontario Coalition Against Poverty, Anti-Racist Action). Similar work has been done by immigrant defence coalitions in Arizona before and since the SB 1070 legislation that targets people simply believed to be migrants without status. Movement participants will hopefully find some of the analyses presented here instructive.

Conclusion

Through phobias, people define their social situations and structure their interactions with the world around them. They also shape their own identities. Phobia has come to have an independent existence, and in itself, as opposed to the specific phobic object, poses a distinct contemporary problem. Increasingly, issues are dealt with through narratives of phobia. Specific fear objects have been cultivated as touchstones for social, political, economic, and cultural anxieties. Often the phobic objects bring all of these anxieties together in the form of one figure (see Furedi 2007).

In terms of national security, alternative, innovative approaches might produce better results, such as inclusion of the "other" to make them the front line of defence for countries like Canada rather than the aggravating policies mandated by legislation such as the Anti-Terrorism Act. This proposed approach must include listening, without biases, to the "other's" observations and then assessing whether such observations can be rendered in a humane, universally morally accepted, economic and legal manner. Even more, as academic activists like Gary Kinsman suggest, this may mean an empathic process of becoming other as an antidote to phobic constructions.

The role of phobia is neglected in the social sciences outside of psychology and psychiatry (Hankiss 2001). While it has attracted some attention in theology and philosophy, it has been addressed minimally in sociology (Furedi 2007) and, even worse, virtually ignored in criminology. There is a real need for this situation to change and for greater sociological and criminological assessment of phobic productions and the social role of phobias as potent manifestations of collective life in the contemporary period. The current work offers some corrective to this.

The best war on the "other" is the war that was never fought.

REFERENCES

Bourke, J. 2005. *Fear: A Cultural History*. London: Virago.

Furedi, Frank. 1997. *The Culture of Fear: Risk Taking and the Morality of Low Expectations*. London: Cassell.

– Furedi 2007. "The Only Thing We Have to Fear is the 'Culture of Fear' Itself." *Spiked*,4 April. http://www.spiked-online.com/index.php?/site/article/3053/.

Hankiss, E. 2001. *Fears and Symbols: An Introduction to the Study of Western Civilization*. Budapest: Central European Press.

Kinsman, Gary. 2010. "Against National Security: From the Canadian War on Queers to the 'War on Terror.'" In *Locating Global Order: American Power and Canadian Security after 9/11*, ed. Bruno Charbonneau and Wayne S. Cox, 149–66. Vancouver: UBC Press.

Knight, Graham. 2003. "Review of *Creating Fear: News and the Construction of Crisis* by David L. Altheide." *Canadian Journal of Sociology*, January–February. http://www.cjsonline.ca/pdf/fear.pdf.

Contributors

Melissa Ames is associate professor at Eastern Illinois University, specializing in media studies, television scholarship, popular culture, feminist theory, and pedagogy. Her work has been published in a variety of anthologies and journals, ranging in topic from television study, new media, and fandom to American literature and feminist art. Her most recent and forthcoming publications include her books *Women and Language: Gendered Communication Across Media* (McFarland, 2011), *Time in Television Narrative: Exploring Temporality in 21st Century Programming* (University of Mississippi Press, 2012), and *How Pop Culture Shapes the Stages of a Woman's Life: From Toddlers-in-Tiaras to Cougars-on-the-Prowl* (Palgrave, 2016); chapters in *Grace Under Pressure: Grey's Anatomy Uncovered* (2008), *Writing the Digital Generation* (2010), and *Bitten by Twilight: Youth Culture, Media, and the Twilight Saga* (2010); and articles in *The Journal of Dracula Studies* (2011), *The Women and Popular Culture Encyclopedia* (2012), *The High School Journal* (2013), *The Journal of Popular Culture* (2014), and *Pedagogy* (2017).

Davina Bhandar is associate professor in Canadian Studies at Trent University and adjunct at the Faculty of Communication, Arts and Technology, Simon Fraser University, and the Department of Political Science, Kwantlen Polytechnic University. She has published in the journal of *Citizenship Studies and Resources for Feminist Research* and also co-edited the collection *"Too Asian?": Racism, Privilege, and Post-Secondary Education* (with R.J. Gilmour, Jeet Heer, and Michael Ma; Between the Lines Press, 2012) and is contributing editor to two forthcoming collections: *Charting Imperial Itineraries: Unmooring the Komagata Maru* (with Rita Dhamoon, Renisa Mawani, and Satwinder Bains;

UBC Press) and *Reflections on Dispossession: Critical Feminisms* (with Brenna Bhandar). Her current monograph, provisionally titled *Unsettling Migrations: Examining the Practices of Citizen Making, Emplacement, and Belonging,* is in process with Routledge Press.

Penny (Panagiota) Koutrolikou teaches urban planning at the University of Thessaly, Greece, and urban sociology at National Technical University of Athens, Greece. She is an architect (DipArch) with an MA in urban sociology (Goldsmith College, UK) and a PhD in Planning Studies (University College London, UK). Her research interests include intergroup relations in deprived or divided urban areas, multicultural societies, urban politics and governance tactics, public(s), and in-between spheres and spaces.

Michael C.K. Ma is a faculty member in the Department of Criminology at Kwantlen Polytechnic University, Vancouver. He works in the areas of social justice, community advocacy, anti-racism, and human rights. Previously, he was a community anti-racism coordinator and a co-founder of the Peterborough Partnership Council on Immigrant Integration. He was also actively involved with the Metro Network for Social Justice, Toronto; Alternative Planning Group, Toronto; and the Chinese-Canadian National Council, Toronto Chapter.

Amir Mirfakhraie is a member of the Sociology Faculty at Kwantlen Polytechnic University, Vancouver. He received his PhD in educational studies from the University of British Columbia, specializing in the sociology and anthropology of education with a focus on Iranian textbooks and multicultural, anti-racist, and global education. Amir's research interests include anti-oppression and anti-racism education, curriculum studies, critical pedagogy, citizenship education, and Canadian and Iranian diaspora studies. His research focus is on the immigration of Iranians to Canada and British Columbia, ethnic and racialized diversity in Canada, anti-racist/anti-oppression pedagogies; and the construction of national identity, the family, the state, the economy, "race," ethnicity, and gender in Iranian school textbooks. He is currently working on two manuscript projects, entitled "Transmigration, Multiplicity, Neo-Orientalism, and Racialized Identity Construction: The Case of Iranians in Canada, 1900–2012" and "Iranian School Textbooks and Representations of Ethnic, Racialized, Gendered, and Religious Diversity: Situating the 'Ideal Iranian Citizen' in Local and Global Contexts."

Johann Pautz is professor of humanities at Florida State College at Jacksonville, where he teaches cultural studies courses, the topics of which include American conspiracy and millenarian traditions as well as courses in media and culture. Johann holds an MA in literature from the University of Louisiana-Lafayette and a PhD in interdisciplinary humanities from Florida State University. His research interests focus on millennial and conspiratorial rhetoric in American culture, particularly the post-apocalyptic fiction of the Patriot Militia movement and Christian far right as expressions of those groups' political ideologies, and their influence on the larger political climate in the United States.

Hisham Ramadan received his Doctor of Juridical Science (SJD) from the University of Wisconsin, specializing in Islamic law, criminal law, comparative law, and human rights. He has taught at the University of Queensland, Australia; Michigan State University; and Loyola University, Chicago, and is currently teaching at Kwantlen Polytechnic University, Vancouver. He previously served as legal protection officer, United Nations High Commissioner for Refugees, and has authored numerous books and articles, including *Reconstructing Jury Instructions in Homicide Offenses: Rethinking Homicide Law; Understanding Islamic Law: From Classical to Contemporary;* and *Contemporary Ijtihad: Limits and Controversies.*

Heidi Rimke, PhD, studies and teaches criminology and sociology at the University of Winnipeg. She is currently associate professor and offers courses in classical and contemporary social and political theory and philosophy, deviance and social regulation, historical and political sociology, critical studies in medicine and psychiatry, and the sociology of law and criminology. Her work examines police deviance, cannibalism, and the pathological sciences of crime and criminality; the politics of in/security; and 'psy' discourses/practices. Most of her research is concerned with the social production of suffering, the rise of psychocentrism, the invention of "normal," the failures of government, and the pathologies of capitalism/patriarchy/colonialism.

Jeff Shantz (PhD, York University, Toronto) is a full-time faculty member in the Department of Criminology at Kwantlen Polytechnic University, Vancouver, lecturing on community advocacy, human rights, elite deviance, contemporary sociological approaches, and critical theory.

He is the author of numerous books, including *Commonist Tendencies: Mutual Aid beyond Communism* (Punctum, 2013) and *Green Syndicalism: An Alternative Red/Green Vision* (Syracuse University Press, 2012). He is the editor of *Beyond Capitalism: Building Democratic Alternatives for Today and the Future* (Bloomsbury, 2013, with José Brendan Mcdonald); *Racism and Borders: Representation, Repression, Resistance* (Algora, 2010); and *Protest and Punishment: The Repression of Resistance in the Era of Neoliberal Globalization* (Carolina Academic Press, 2012). Shantz is the co-founder of the Critical Criminology Working Group (http://www.radicalcriminology.org/) and the founding editor of the journal *Radical Criminology* (http://journal.radicalcriminology.org/). Scholarly interests include critical theories, migration, critical surveillance studies, corporate crime, transnational crime, and social movements. Samples of his writing may be found at jeffshantz.ca.

Dmitry Shlapentokh is associate professor in the Department of History, Indiana University-South Bend. He is the author of several books, most recently *Global Russia: Eurasianism, Putin and the New Right* (Tauris, 2013) and over one hundred articles. Dr Shlapentokh holds master's degrees from Moscow State University and Michigan State University as well as a PhD in Russian/European history from the University of Chicago. He has taught and held research appointments at Harvard University's Russian Research Center and Stanford University's Hoover Institution.

Index

abortion, 235
activism/activists: US state repression of, 19–20
affect theory, 122–3, 122–4
Agamben, Giorgio, 244, 273
Agios Panteleimonas, 271, 282–3, 285, 286
Albanians, 281
Alias (ABC TV show), 127, 128
Al Qaeda: in Canadian phobic constructions, 250–1, 251, 261; US misrepresentation of Muslims as, 41
Althusser, Louis, 62
America. *See* United States
Ames, Melissa, 8–9, 58, 67–8, 116, 295, 303
anarchism, 219
anarchists, 244, 276, 277, 279
anonymity, 55, 293; as reinforcing a framework of suspicion, 55; of the Iranian self, 109
antebellum era, southern US, 218
anthropophobia, 17
anti-capitalism: criminalizing and pathologizing activists of, 17, 24
anti-Catholicism, 217

Antichrist conspiracy, 209, 211–12, 217–18, 225, 229
anti-God phobia, 76–77, 80–1, 84, 103. *See also* Antichrist conspiracy; secularism, fear of
anti-"other" propaganda, 27. *See also* "others"; "othering"
anti-Semitism, 157–8, 211, 220–1; Russian nationalists', 158
Anti-Terror Act (Bill C-36, Canada), 242–3, 296, 298, 300
anti-terror legislation, 267–8
anxiety, 52, 55, 58, 95, 192, 194, 271, 294, 299; constant, as television's affect, 122–4, 126; societal, risk avoidance, 3
apocalyptic conspiracy tropes, 10
Appadurai, Arjun, 214, 220
Arab(s), racist/stereotypic depictions: in Iranian textbooks, 96, 101–2; in Canadian discourse, 243, 251, 265
articulation (creation of meaning), 62
Aryan, Persian Iranian history as, 93–5, 102
Aryan-Pars: Aryan-Pars-Shi'as "race," 97, 102; chauvinism, 76, 86, 93–6;